The Encyclopedia of

WORLD COOKERY

The Encyclopedia of

WORLD
COOKERY

ELIZABETH CAMPBELL

SPRING BOOKS · LONDON

Published by

SPRING BOOKS

SPRING HOUSE · SPRING PLACE · LONDON NW5

Printed in Czechoslovakia

The Encyclopedia of

WORLD
COOKERY

———

ELIZABETH CAMPBELL

———

SPRING BOOKS · LONDON

Published by

SPRING BOOKS

SPRING HOUSE · SPRING PLACE · LONDON NW5

Printed in Czechoslovakia

Contents

Introduction

For years I have collected foreign recipes, some from my own travels, some drawing on the experience of friends. The simplicity and variety of foreign cooking, as well as its excellence, seemed something I would like to share with a wider audience than my own circle of friends, and consequently I thought of enlarging my collection sufficiently to justify a new book of international recipes. It wasn't hard to do this — the difficulty, where so much is good, is deciding what to leave out.

The thing about good cooking is that it is creative and imaginative, but not difficult technically — so that with a little guidance and encouragement any ordinary person with a liking for food can become an excellent, instead of an ordinary, cook. I haven't included chefs' recipes, triumphs of decoration and elaboration which would be out of place in an ordinary home. They are a different kind of thing altogether, requiring years of training and practice. I have concentrated on dishes which can be made by anyone with a minimum knowledge of the basic techniques of the kitchen. And I have included a few hints about these techniques which I have gained by experience, and which do not always appear in the books.

The meals I have eaten abroad and which have left the most abiding memory fall into this same category. They are not the grand hotel meals which are much the same the world over, but the meals served deliciously in station buffets or unexpectedly in student restaurants. Coming back from the Engadine once, where we had been staying in a hotel which was a gastronome's paradise of *truite au bleu* and *profiterolles* in creamy chocolate sauce, we stopped in Zurich before catching the night train for England. One of our party had been a student there and remembered a students' restaurant in a back street which he thought had been good. He suggested that we should try to find it. After a search we reached the place, in the corner of a tiny square, up a steep hill. We had an excellent soup and then *Wiener Schnitzel* fried to such a nicety and with such a perfectly right coating of egg and breadcrumbs that it fulfilled the demands of the exacting Viennese in this matter. A *Schnitzel* to be satisfactory, they say, should be so dry that you could sit on it and rise without a grease stain on your trousers. With the *Schnitzel* we had a green salad with French dressing. Doubtless we had cheese afterwards, but the perfection of the *Schnitzel* effaced the memory of the rest of the meal. The best meals are often the simplest: good ingredients perfectly cooked and perfectly accompanied can more than hold their own with all the pink sauces coating indifferent fillets of sole and hiding under a fancy foreign name.

I once ate a dinner at a friend's flat in Paris of similar simple excellence — this time it was a *tournedos*, grilled, and topped with a pat of very fresh butter. The trick that transformed this from any ordinary steak, my friend told me, was that it was rubbed with butter not only before it was cooked, but once during its grilling as well. A lemon cream of the most melting kind ended this meal — a lemon cream made with whipped cream, lemon juice, sugar and egg yolks, ingredients not difficult to come by, but exquisitely blended on this occasion.

One of the most vivid food memories of my life comes from a holiday spent when I was ten with friends in Normandy. We were camping and usually we ate miraculously well considering the torrential downpour that memory tells me prevailed throughout my stay. We had a potato soup, the taste of which I can still recall with pleasure. But the vivid memory is not of the good soup, but of the apprehensive excitement with which we all got ready to dine with the owner of the farm, whose wife was going to give us octopus for supper. Alas the apprehension was justified, octopus on this occasion turned out to be just the hard rubbery lumps of flesh we had expected. But the tables were turned twenty years later when spending another holiday with the same hosts, but this time in the South of France. Cooking facilities were primitive in the tiny peasant's cottage near Marseilles which we shared, but the food was uniformly excellent and particularly memorable were the baby octopus or *poulpes* cooked with rice which we had one day for lunch.

Similar memories come flooding back from Greece where the food is not uniformly good — the Western stomach finds some difficulty in accommodating itself to an endless diet of warm fat mutton (the Greeks, being often too poor to own ovens of their own, have their food cooked in the baker's oven, and this accounts for their food never being really hot). But sometimes the staple *mousaka* becomes more than minced mutton with tomato sauce. And in Greece, as indeed in all Mediterranean countries, all the fruit is of a quality unknown in harsher northern climates. I have eaten melons, from which the inside has been scooped and which have been stuffed with any other fruit in season, which seemed the most exquisite food man could expect to eat.

Food, as everything else, depends so much not only on being perfect of its kind, but also on being of a kind suitable to the time and place. I remember reading a description in a book of two bachelors meeting in the war and sharing a meal of fresh boiled eggs, fresh bread with farmhouse butter and strawberry jam. There was no doubt in their minds that, eaten in those circumstances, this simple meal was better than a banquet. Much of the food in this book has been devised for other climates than our own. Provided, however, that one does not make the mistake of eating the rather heavy kind of food devised by the Dutch and Germans for their cold winters, during a heat wave, or a light and appetising Mediterranean salad meal on a cold winter's night, other people's food is surprisingly adaptable.

Most of the ingredients mentioned are easily available in England. The interest awakened in England in foreign food has encouraged more and more imports of exotic materials: aubergines, chicory, endive, passion fruit are all obtainable at the proper times of year. More and more delicatessen stores are to be found selling unexpected spices, sausages and foreign cheese. I have made a list of the best-known London stores selling things that may be difficult to obtain; these shops will accept orders by post for the benefit of readers living in the country.

I do not want to give the impression that English food is in any way to be despised. It is excellent, though very many things are in danger of being forgotten. For this reason I have included about a hundred recipes from England, Scotland, Ireland and Wales. I have, however, concentrated on foreign recipes because I feel there is so much we can learn from other people. We can learn to use their seasonings — herbs and spices — as well as our own. The clove favoured by the English and the German caraway and anise seed are equally excellent, but nothing is less appetising than the regular use of one or the other. How stimulating to find apples flavoured with cinnamon or nutmeg instead of the familiar clove. The French in Provence, and indeed many of the Mediterranean peoples, put a sliver of lemon or orange peel into stews which is a simple enough thing to do, but provides a piquancy a sometimes lacking in our own meat dishes. The Hungarian use of paprika, the Russian custom of cooking in sour cream, the American flair for mingling sweet and savoury, all can enrich our own meals.

We can also learn to make the best use of the cheap staple foods of other lands. Italian *pasta* — spaghetti, ravioli, tagliatelli — with suitable sauces provide splendid, satisfying and most inexpensive meals. Similarly Italian *risotto*, rice cooked with fish, meat or vegetables, if properly cooked is simple and delicious. French *cassoulet* — haricot beans, cooked with boiling sausage, onion and tomato — is most nourishing and very tasty. I could elaborate the list considerably, but I hope readers will experiment at my suggestion and find out for themselves.

The space given to each country represented has been allotted according to two principles. I have considered firstly the availability of the necessary ingredients and suitability to English tastes. These two necessarily very often coincide; we cannot easily get whale blubber and undoubtedly would not like it if we could. Secondly I have been influenced by the variety and genius in the culinary arts of each country. For various historical reasons the Austrians outclass the Germans in this field despite similar geographical and climatic conditions, and therefore I have included more recipes from Austria. For similar reasons I have included twice as many recipes from France as from any other single country. There can be no question that French cooking is the subtlest, the most imaginative and the most varied in the world, and consequently it is from the French that we can learn most.

There is a widely held popular view that French cooking is elaborate and difficult. This is a misconception arising partly from a confusion between *haute cuisine* and the cooking of the ordinary French housewife. 'French cooking' is restaurant cooking, showy and sometimes grandiose. The cooking of the French housewife is like that of the housewife anywhere else, except that she is more attentive and imaginative, so that what might be a commonplace dish in other lands is transformed by the loving care with which it is seasoned and flavoured. There is no difficulty about making a sauce flavoured with cider, capers, and rosemary to serve with pork chops, but it lifts the dish from the realms of ordinary food to something worthy of our guests. This raises the question of time and trouble. There is no doubt that good cooking demands both, but since even an indifferent meal cannot be achieved without spending a certain amount of time and energy — even a tin opener has to be washed up — one might as well spend a little bit more to achieve really good results. Very often, however, the demands made are on imagination and thought rather than on time. It takes no longer to make the kind of pastry needed for French apple tart than English; it takes only the imagination and energy to try a new recipe rather than use one already well known.

Many, probably most, of the recipes in this book do not require any ingredients other than those generally at hand in every kitchen supplemented by a few less usual spices. The most frequent exception to this rule is wine. Almost all foreign cookery demands the use of wine with many meat dishes, even such comparatively simple ones as *spaghetti bolognaise*. This is not really a great difficulty: cooking wine is quite inexpensive and a little goes a long way. If you keep two bottles of cheap wine, one white and one red, and cork them carefully after use, they will last a long time as the amount used in each dish is very little. And you will be amply rewarded by the results.

Olive oil is another regular ingredient of the food of many European countries which may not be in the usual English store cupboard. Olive oil is one of the things which it pays to buy in large quantities — a gallon at a time is ideal. It does not deteriorate in any way and the financial saving compared with buying small quantities at a time is enormous.

Cooking with cream presents rather greater difficulties, and I think can only be seriously considered for special occasions. Some dishes can be made with the top of the milk instead, but there is no substitute for the real thing. Evaporated milk and synthetic creams are worse than useless: the first has a strong taste of its own which is discernible through the strongest flavourings, and the second has a texture quite different from natural cream. The only exception to this rule is where a recipe calls for sour cream. Here I have used yoghourt and smetana with a fair degree of success, but again they have perceptible individual flavours. Apart from cream, however, none of the ingredients is prohibitively expensive. Wine, olive oil, nuts, olives, spices can all be added to a dish for a fraction of the cost of the basic meat or fish, and make all the difference to the quality of the dish.

If, for any reason, you are forced to use substitutes for the original ingredients, do not use the classic name for the dish. An approximation to *bœuf stroganoff* can be made with yoghourt, but it must be recognised that it is not the real thing. Failure to accept this rule leads to the debasement of such great classic dishes as *sole véronique* or *crêpes suzette* and a consequent diminution of standards.

10

It always pays to buy the best possible basic ingredients you can afford and to use them suitably. However good the sauce, nothing will disguise poor meat or fish. If, as so often happens nowadays, one cannot afford fillet steak, it is best to abandon the idea of fried meat and make a dish of braised meat or a risotto.

In planning a meal for guests there are two things to be borne in mind. The first, and I think the more difficult to observe, is not to allow yourself to become overenthusiastic and ambitious. Never try out more than one new dish in one meal. Never have more than one dish which needs last minute preparation. No one can enjoy a meal at which the hostess appears hot and exhausted from the efforts of creation. Secondly, make sure that the meal is properly balanced. If the sweet is to be rich let the main course be simple. If your main dish is ambitious let it be preceded by grapefruit or a simple hors d'œuvre and followed by fruit and cheese. But if there is no sweet, serve plain chocolate with the coffee, so as to round off the meal properly.

Almost all the recipes give quantities for four people. Obviously the amounts will vary a bit according to the size of the appetites and what other dishes are to make part of the meal.

The essential quality in a good cook is a taste for good food. If you like good food, and are prepared to take a little trouble in preparing it, you will be sure of an appreciative audience for these recipes when you try them out.

The Tools of the Trade

Knives: Good, very sharp knives are essential and save both time and temper. The size and type of these is largely a matter of personal choice, but it is a good idea to keep one special one for vegetable peeling and one for cutting up meat. If you have a dual-purpose knife for these, it has to be constantly washed between operations. It is also as well to keep a separate knife for cutting garlic, so that there is no danger of inadvertently cutting butter with the same knife. A palette knife is also essential.

Spoons: A large number of wooden spoons of different shapes and sizes must be kept for different purposes. Small ones with one flattened edge are invaluable for sauces as they can get into the edges of the pan. A perforated metal draining spoon is useful for poaching eggs, removing dumplings when cooked, etc.

Boards: Pastry-board, bread-board, chopping-board are all essential. It is most unwise to try to make one do the work of another.

Mechanical Aids: I have found the Mouli range of food mills invaluable. The *passevite,* provided with three different sized sieves, saves endless time in serving soups, etc. The mouli-grater, a small and most inexpensive tool, saves hours when grating cheese and the *parsmint* halves the time taken chopping parsley, lemon-peel and so on. A mincer and an egg whisk are the only other mechanical aids which I regard as essential, but I have no doubt that the electric mixer with its infinite variety of attachments will within measurable time come to be regarded as equally essential. It can save both time and trouble and bring certain dishes which are arduous to prepare within the range of the shorthanded housewife.

Storage Jars: Get small glass jars with screw tops in which to keep spices and dried herbs, and bigger ones for fresh herbs. Fresh herbs, like fresh salad, will keep very well for some time in an airtight jar.

Cooking Vessels: At least one heavy saucepan, which can be quite small, is essential for sauces, otherwise they stick to the pan. A fairly small pan with rounded sides kept specially for omelettes and pancakes is a great help.

Invest in an enamelled cast-iron cooking pot with a lid. This makes it possible to fry onions and meat for stews in a pan which can be transferred to the oven and saves dirtying two receptacles. The English firm, Izons, make excellent ones at half the price of those imported from Sweden. These are obtainable at John Lewis's of Oxford Street and some of their branches.

Kitchen Scales: I find the Tala measuring cup, which is very inexpensive and universally obtainable, far more convenient than scales for all but large-scale jam making operations.

A Few Hints

Cream: can be soured by the addition of a few drops of lemon juice. Leaving it to turn sour is not satisfactory if the cream has been pasteurised.

Pastry: any pastry shell which is to be filled with a wet mixture should be brushed with melted butter to prevent sogginess.

Tomatoes: English tomatoes are often slightly under-ripe and should therefore be slightly sweetened. They are improved by a little sugar, and so are new carrots.

Sauces: are less likely to lump if the liquid being added is hot. This is particularly important with milk sauces.

Mayonnaise: must be made in a cool place or it will curdle; if it curdles it can sometimes be restored to the proper consistency by the addition of another egg yolk.

Icing: sugar and baked breadcrumbs: if these are put into paper bags before being rolled out they cannot fly all over the place and can easily be poured into a bowl.

Flouring meat, fish, etc.: do this on a sheet of clean paper which can be thrown away. It saves a lot of messy washing up.

Pancakes: keep a small bowl of melted butter beside the stove and brush the pan with it between each pancake.

Deep fat frying: olive oil is the most satisfactory for this as it boils at a higher temperature than animal fat. A pint of olive oil kept especially for the purpose lasts a long time.

Potatoes: ideally potatoes should always be washed and then cooked in their skins. This takes slightly longer than peeling them but is rewarding. Potatoes should be mashed with butter, *not* milk.

Lettuce: never cut lettuce leaves; if they *must* be reduced in size, tear them.

Vinegar: always use wine or tarragon vinegar. Malt vinegar is only suitable for pickling.

Butter: use real butter whenever possible, though the margarines containing ten per cent butter make a good substitute. Margarine, however, is not good for frying.

Stock: keep meat trimmings, vegetable water, etc. for the stock pot if you have one.

Concentrated *bouillon* cubes are very good (particularly the ones made by the Swiss firm, Knorr) but do not provide the variety of the home-made kind.

Vanilla: vanilla pods have a flavour different from, and far nicer than, vanilla essence. They keep indefinitely in airtight jars. Keep one in a jar of sugar reserved for cooking cakes, pastries, etc., which demand vanilla flavouring.

Cinnamon: cinnamon, too, is much better bought in the piece than in powder form.

Wine: cooking wine costs about 6s. a bottle. It takes at most one glass to enrich a soup or stew: not a very great additional cost. To be satisfactory the wine must actually be cooked, it must bubble and reduce in quantity. It must therefore be added before the dish is taken from the stove. Do not worry unduly about having exactly the wine specified. White wines for sweet dishes and fish, and red wines for meat, is the general rule to keep to if the particular kind is not available.

Where to get special ingredients: many of the unusual ingredients mentioned are obtainable at *Delicatessen Shops*.

Most can be bought from Harrods, Knightsbridge, London, S. W. 1.; Fortnum & Mason, London, W. 1., or Selfridges, London, W. 1. Eastern foods can be obtained from the Bombay Emporium, 70 Grafton Way, W. 1., and Veerasawmy, 15 Clarendon Road, N. 8. specialise in Indian curry powders.

Africa

SOUTH AFRICAN ESCALLOPED MEALIES OR SWEET CORN

4 ozs. cooked mealies, cut from
 the cob
2 eggs
2 ozs. melted butter
1 tsp. sugar
¼ tsp. nutmeg
¼ pint milk
salt, pepper

Mince or pound the mealies, add the beaten eggs, butter, sugar, salt, pepper, nutmeg and the milk. Mix well together. Butter a shallow fireproof dish and bake in a moderate oven for 20 minutes.

SOUTH AFRICAN MEALIES (Corn on the Cob)

8 mealies (for 4 people or as many
 as liked)
2 tsp. salt
2 tsp. sugar
butter to serve

The mealies must be young and the husks green. They must be thrown into enough boiling water to cover, salt and sugar added, brought to the boil and simmered for 20 minutes. The husks and 'silk' may be removed before boiling, or only the 'silk' or both. They are of course served free of husks and 'silk' and eaten with plenty of butter and salt, held in the hand and picked clean with the teeth, as a separate course, generally to start the meal.

SOUTH AFRICAN PICKLED FISH

2½ lbs. cod
3 ozs. flour
1 tsp. salt
¼ tsp. pepper
fat for frying
1½ pints vinegar
2 bay leaves
2 large onions, sliced
1 tsp. peppercorns
1 oz. flour
1 oz. curry powder
1 tbsp. vinegar

Cut the fish in slices 1½ inches thick. Roll in the 3 ozs. flour, salt and pepper. Fry in hot fat till done. Heat the 1½ pints vinegar in a saucepan, add peppercorns, bay leaves, onion slices, bring to the boil and cook until the onions are soft. Mix the 1 oz. flour, curry powder with the 1 tbsp. vinegar to a paste, add to the boiling vinegar and cook all together for 2 minutes. Arrange the cooked fish in a shallow dish and pour over the vinegar sauce. Keep in a cold place and eat after 48 hours. If kept cold this dish will keep for weeks.

FRICADELS (Mutton Rissoles)

2 lbs. minced raw mutton
1 large finely chopped onion
2 slices white bread soaked in milk
2 tbsp. tomato purée
1 beaten egg
¼ tsp. grated nutmeg
salt, pepper
breadcrumbs

Squeeze the bread dry and mash with a fork. Add the mutton, onion, tomato purée, egg, nutmeg and salt and pepper. Mix all well together, roll into balls the size of an egg, roll in the breadcrumbs, and fry in hot fat till brown.

BOBOTIE

2 lbs. raw minced mutton
1 thick slice white bread soaked in
  milk
2 medium sliced onions
1 apple sliced
2 beaten eggs
2 ozs. curry powder
½ oz. sugar
2 ozs. butter
12 blanched chopped almonds
2 ozs. currants or sultanas
½ tsp. salt, pepper

Squeeze the bread and mash with a fork. Melt the butter in a stewpan, add the onions and apple, stir, fry for 4 minutes. Add the curry powder, sugar, salt, almonds, currants or sultanas and the minced mutton. Stir well together and cook gently for 3 minutes. Grease a deep fireproof dish and put in this mixture. Mix the eggs well into the milk, season with salt and pepper, pour over the meat mixture and cook in a very slow oven for 1 hour till the custard is set.

SASSATIES

3 lbs. raw mutton
2 ozs. dried apricots, soaked
  overnight
3 large onions, sliced
2 cloves of garlic, chopped
2 ozs. dripping
a pinch of cayenne pepper
6 lemon or orange leaves
1 oz. curry powder
1 oz. sugar
½ tsp. salt
3 tbsp. wine vinegar

Cut the mutton in small pieces, 1½ inches square. Remove any fat and cut in ½ inch squares. Place on wooden skewers, meat then fat, till each skewer is full.

Cover the apricots with water and boil till soft. Press through a sieve.

Heat the dripping in a saucepan and cook the onions and garlic for 5 minutes till transparent and soft. Add the apricot pulp, leaves, curry powder, sugar, pepper and salt and the vinegar. Stir well, bring to the boil and boil this sauce for 1 minute. Place the skewered meat in a shallow enamel or china dish, not a metal one, cool the sauce, and pour over the meat. Leave to soak overnight, or longer, up to 20 hours, turning the 'sassaties' occasionally. Drain them and grill them under a hot grill on all sides till nicely brown. Heat the sauce, pick out the leaves and pour over the grilled 'sassaties'.

SOUTH AFRICAN BROWN RAISIN RICE

8 ozs. rice
¾ pint water
grated rind of ¼ lemon
½ tsp. cinnamon
½ tsp. turmeric
½ tsp. salt
3 ozs. raisins, seedless
2 ozs. butter
2 ozs. sugar

Wash the rice thoroughly, add lemon rind, cinnamon, turmeric, salt and water. Bring to the boil, cover the pan and simmer for 20 minutes, stirring once or twice, add the raisins and simmer for 20 minutes longer, or until the rice is soft, but not pulpy. Melt the butter, add the sugar and mix lightly into the mixture. This can be eaten with roast mutton or pork, or as a supper sweet dish, with sweetened cream.

SOUTH AFRICAN CHICKEN PIE

1 3½-lb. chicken
2 medium onions, each cut in
   8 pieces
1½ pints water
4 allspice
¼ pint white wine
¼ tsp. nutmeg ⎫
1 bay leaf   ⎬ in a muslin bag
12 peppercorns ⎭
1 tsp. salt
2 ozs. butter
1 oz. tapioca
3 tbsp. lemon juice
1 egg yolk, beaten
2 hard boiled eggs, sliced

4 ozs. cooked ham, sliced
short crust pastry
milk and egg

Cut the chicken in joints. Put these with the water, wine, onion and the bag of spices in a covered stewpan. Bring to the boil and simmer for 30 minutes. Add the salt, butter and tapioca, re-cover and simmer for 20 minutes more or until the chicken is tender. Add lemon juice, egg yolk, hard boiled eggs and ham. Cool. Put in a pie dish, cover with the pastry, brush the top with a little milk and egg mixed together, and bake in a moderate oven for 45 minutes.

ROAST QUAILS

8 quails
8 green chillies
8 rashers fat bacon
8 fresh vine leaves
4 ozs. dripping
pepper

Quails should not be 'hung', as they decompose very quickly.

Pluck, clean and draw the birds. Put a chilli inside each, wrap a rasher of bacon round each bird, dust with pepper, then wrap the whole in a vine leaf, secure with small wooden skewer. Melt the dripping in a roasting pan, put in the pan and roast in a moderate oven for 30 minutes, basting frequently.

TOMATO BREDIE

4 large or 8 small mutton chops
2 ozs. dripping
3 lbs. ripe tomatoes
2 large sliced onions
1 tsp. cinnamon powder
1 bay leaf
1 tsp. salt
¼ tsp. pepper
2 ozs. brown sugar

Trim surplus fat off the chops. Skin the tomatoes, and chop in quarters. Heat the dripping and fry the chops for 3 minutes each side, remove and put in a large stew pan. Fry the onions till golden brown; add to the chops. Now add the tomatoes, cinnamon, bay leaf, salt and pepper. Turn up the heat and stir gently till the tomatoes dissolve. Taste and if necessary add the sugar. This largely depends on how much sun has ripened the tomatoes, English greenhouse ones are generally not sweet enough. Cook the chops very gently in the tomato purée for 1 hour or until the meat is quite tender and the purée thick and sweet.

SOUTH AFRICAN BANANA FOOL

8 or 10 bananas
3 eggs
2 tbsp. brandy or rum
¼ pint cream, whipped
2 ozs. caster sugar
a pinch of nutmeg

Crush the bananas and whip the pulp. Separate the eggs, beat the whites till stiff and the yolks well. Add the yolks to the pulp and half the stiff whites plus the brandy or rum and 1½ ozs. sugar. Mix all well together. Mix ½ oz. sugar with the remaining egg whites. Serve, very cold in glasses, with cream on top and the sweetened egg whites on top of the cream. Sprinkle with nutmeg.

GRANADILLA OR PASSION FRUIT FOOL

12 granadillas
3 ozs. sugar
½ pint whipped cream

Cut the tops off the granadillas and scoop out the fruit. Mix well with the sugar, add the cream and serve cold in separate glasses.

PAWPAW

pawpaw
sugar
lemon juice

Cut the pawpaw in half. Scoop out all the seeds. Cut in wedges and serve cold with sugar and cut lemons separately as a dessert.

PEACH ISLAND

6 South African canned peach
halves
2 eggs
2 tbsp. caster sugar
⅛ tsp. salt
½ pint hot milk
¼ tsp. vanilla essence
2 tbsp. grated coconut

Separate the eggs. Whip the whites till stiff. Beat the yolks with the sugar and salt. Put in a double boiler and slowly pour on the hot milk, stirring all the time till the mixture thickens to a custard. Cool, then fold in the egg whites. Arrange the peaches in the serving dish, pour on the custard, and sprinkle with the coconut.

PEACH WHIP

4 ripe peaches, fresh or stewed
2 stiffly beaten egg whites
3 ozs. caster sugar
4 ozs. cream
glacé cherries

If fresh peaches are used, peel and stone them. Sieve the fruit. Add half the sugar to the beaten whites, beat again, add the rest of the sugar and the peach pulp. Continue beating till soft and fluffy. Whip the cream, pile on top and decorate with the cherries.

PINEAPPLE FRITTERS

1 pineapple
2 ozs. sugar
4 ozs. flour
½ tsp. salt
1 egg
¼ pint milk

Make the batter by mixing the flour and salt together. Add the beaten egg and one third of the milk, mix thoroughly and smooth, add the rest of the milk, leave for 1 hour. Peel the pineapple, cut in ½ inch rings, sprinkle with sugar. Have a pan of smoking fat, dip each sugared piece in the batter and fry till golden brown outside and soft inside. Dust with sugar and serve.

SOUTH AFRICAN PUMPKIN FRITTERS

8 ozs. cooked pumpkin
4 ozs. flour
1 tsp. baking powder
2 eggs
¼ tsp. salt
2 ozs. caster sugar
1 tsp. cinnamon
1 lemon
fat for frying

Mix the pumpkin, flour, baking powder and salt thoroughly, add the beaten eggs. Form into flat rounds 3 inches across, 1 inch deep, and fry till brown in deep smoking lard or butter. Mix the cinnamon well with the sugar, sprinkle over the cooked fritters and serve with cut lemon, as a sweet course.

SHREDDED PINEAPPLE

1 pineapple
4 ozs. caster sugar
½ pint cream

Peel and grate the pineapple. Stir in the sugar, mix till dissolved, add the cream, whipped till fairly thick, and serve very cold.

STUFFED MONKEY

8 ozs. flour
6 ozs. butter
6 ozs. brown sugar
1 whole egg, 1 egg white
½ tsp. cinnamon
¼ tsp. salt

STUFFING:

2 ozs. chopped lemon peel
4 ozs. ground almonds
1½ ozs. melted butter
1 egg yolk

Sift the flour, cinnamon and salt, rub in the butter, add the sugar, mix well, add the beaten whole egg and mix to a soft dough. Divide in two pieces and roll ⅛ inch thick. Mix all the ingredients of the stuffing well together. Pile on one piece of dough, damp the edges, put the other piece of dough on top and seal the edges. Brush with the egg white and cook in a moderate oven for 30 minutes. Cut in squares and serve.

MAAS BOLETJIES

½ pint hot milk
4 ozs. butter
4 ozs. sugar
2 tsp. salt
1 yeast cake
6 tbsp. warm water
2 tbsp. caraway seeds
1 lb. flour

Melt the yeast and sugar in the warm water. Sieve the flour and the salt, add the seeds, and the butter, mix lightly with the fingers till the mixture looks like breadcrumbs. Gradually add the milk and yeast water. Knead very thoroughly for 20 minutes. Cover and put in a warm place for 1½ hours. Shape into pieces the size of an egg and pack tightly into a greased straight-sided tin. Brush the top with milk and sugar and bake in a moderate-to-hot oven for 25 minutes.

MEALIE MEAL PORRIDGE

4 ozs. mealie meal
2½ pints water
1½ tsp. salt

Boil the water in a thick pot, add the salt, sprinkle in the meal, stirring all the time, cook briskly for 5 minutes, stirring all the time, lower the heat and continue cooking very gently for 1 hour, stirring from time to time to prevent burning and 'lumping'. A milk and water mixture may be used instead of plain water.

WEST AFRICAN SPICED TURKEY

1 10-lb. turkey
1 oz. flour
1 tsp. sugar
1 tsp. salt
1 tsp. pepper
1 tsp. cinnamon
½ tsp. ground ginger
½ clove of garlic, crushed
2 ozs. butter
2 large onions, chopped
warm water
roast potatoes

Mix the flour, sugar, salt, pepper, garlic and spices together. Rub the turkey well inside and out with this mixture and leave for 12 hours.

Put the bird in a large saucepan, add the onions and cover with warm water. Bring to the boil slowly and simmer for 2½ hours or until tender, but not falling apart. Drain. Put in roasting pan, dot with butter and bake in a hot oven till brown, basting with the stock from time to time. Serve with roast potatoes.

WEST AFRICAN GROUNDNUT CHOP

boiled rice
2 lbs. cooked chicken or lamb cut
  in ½ inch squares
2 tbsp. olive oil
4 tbsp. peanut butter or *6 ozs.*
  ground peanuts
1½ pints water
2 tsp. salt
¼ tsp. black pepper

mango chutney, fresh grated coco-
  nut, grated green or red peppers
  may be served as accompanying
  dishes.

Take a large saucepan and melt the oil in it. Add the peanut butter or peanuts, stir well, add the water, salt and pepper. Cook for 2 minutes. Add the meat, stir into the sauce, cover the pan and simmer gently for 7 minutes. Serve with hot rice and all or any of the accompanying dishes.

Austria

CABBAGE SOUP

1 large cabbage
1 oz. flour
1 oz. dripping
2 pints stock
salt
pepper
8 small frankfurters

Remove the hard stalks from the cabbage and shred it. Brown it and the flour in the dripping, pour in the stock, season with salt and pepper. Simmer for 1 hour. Boil the sausages separately, cut them into slices and add to the soup just before serving.

BEEF BROTH

2 lbs. topside
1 lb. beef bones or chicken bones and giblets
4 onions
2 leeks
4 celery stalks, inc. the leaves
1 turnip
1 cauliflower broken into flowerets
3 tomatoes, peeled & quartered
2 ozs. dripping
8 peppercorns
salt
pepper
parsley

Cut the onions, leeks, celery and turnip into large pieces. Brown them in the dripping, sear the meat in the fat. Add the cauliflower, the tomatoes and the bones. Pour in enough water to cover the contents of the pan. Add salt, peppercorns and parsley. Put a lid on the pan and simmer until the meat is tender (about 3 hours). Remove the meat and the bones, pass the vegetables through a fine sieve. The meat can be served as a separate dish accompanied by freshly cooked vegetables and horseradish sauce.

GOULASH SOUP

½ lb. shin of beef, cut up very small
3 cooked potatoes, diced small
3 or 4 onions, sliced
2 tbsp. tomato purée
1½ oz. dripping
1 tbsp. paprika
½ tsp. caraway seeds
salt
2 cloves garlic, well crushed

Brown the onion in the dripping, add the meat and brown it. Add all the other ingredients except the potato. Stir, cover with water and bring to the boil. Simmer the meat until it is tender. Five minutes before serving add the potatoes.

KALTSCHALE (Fruit soup)

1 lb. berries (raspberries, straw-berries or red or black currants)
4—6 ozs. sugar
1½ pints scalded and chilled milk

Cook the berries until they are just tender. Pass them through a sieve. Whisk up this fruit purée with the sugar until it is frothy and light. Mix into it the milk. Put it into the refrigerator and serve it very cold.

BREAD SOUP

4 slices or crusts of stale bread
2 pints veal stock
2 smoked sausages or large frankfurters
1 egg yolk
salt
black pepper
2 tbsp. parsley fried in butter
2 hardboiled eggs for garnishing
2 ozs. butter

Bake the bread crisp. Break it up and put it into a saucepan with the warm stock. Leave it to steep for 15 minutes, season with salt and pepper and simmer for 1 hour. Then sieve it. Beat the egg yolk and mix it quickly with 2 or 3 tablespoons of the hot soup. Add it to the soup, taking care not to let the mixture boil again. Five minutes before serving add the chopped sausages, and add the parsley when serving.

BATTER DROPS

1 egg
2—3 tbsp. milk
2 ozs. flour
salt
deep fat for frying

Stir the egg, milk and salt carefully into the flour, keeping the mixture smooth. Beat thoroughly. Adjust milk and flour to make a thick batter. Drip the batter into smoking fat through a coarse grater or perforated spoon. Cook till golden, drain and serve as a garnish for clear soup.

NOODLES

6 ozs. flour
1 egg
1—2 tbsp. water
salt

Put the flour and salt in a bowl. Make a well in the centre, break in the egg and mix with a knife, adding the water as required so as to make a stiff dough.
  The resulting dough can be treated in two ways:
1. Press the dough through a coarse sieve or perforated spoon into boiling soup and simmer for
   5 minutes.
2. Roll out very thinly, leave it to dry for 30 minutes.
   Cut it into narrow strips or squares, leave it to
   dry again for 30 minutes and simmer for 10 or
   15 minutes in soup as required.

LIVER DUMPLINGS

½ lb. liver, coarsely minced or
  chopped
4 ozs. stale bread, soaked and
  squeezed
2 ozs. butter
1 small onion, sliced
salt
black pepper
1 tsp. chopped marjoram
1 tbsp. chopped parsley

Gently fry the onions and parsley in the butter. Add the other ingredients and beat well. Leave the mixture to cool. Shape into small round dumplings, adding more breadcrumbs if the mixture is too wet. Drop these into boiling soup and simmer for about 20 minutes.
  These dumplings may be varied by pressing the mixture through a very coarse sieve or perforated spoon into the boiling soup and cooking for 3 or 4 minutes.

EEL

1 medium sized eel
½ pint white wine or cider
2 ozs. parsley
salt
pepper

SAUCE:
1 oz. butter
2 mashed hard-boiled egg yolks
¼ pint stock
1 tbsp. vinegar
2 tbsp. chopped parsley

1 tbsp. made mustard
salt
1 tsp. sugar
black pepper

Cut the eel into pieces, salt them well, and stand them in a cold place for 4 hours. Drain off the water, then pack them tightly in a saucepan and add the wine or cider, parsley and the seasoning. Simmer for about 45 minutes or until tender. For the sauce: Melt the butter and mix with the other ingredients. Season with salt and pepper. Serve the fish accompanied by the sauce and slices of lemon.

PAPRIKA FISH

2 lbs. fish, preferably carp, but fresh haddock, bass and mackerel are also suitable
1 lb. onions, sliced
4 ozs. butter
salt
pepper

¾ pint cream
2 tsp. paprika

Fry the onions lightly in the butter. Put the fish on the onions and add the cream mixed with the paprika, salt and pepper. Bake till tender. Strain the sauce over the fish.

FISH STEW

2 lbs. fish, fresh water if possible
light stock or water
6 onions
2 tsp. paprika
salt
black pepper

2 ozs. butter
¾ pint sour cream

Brown the onions in the butter. Add the fish cut into pieces and the seasoning. Just cover with stock or water and simmer for 1½ hours, stirring carefully to keep the fish pieces whole. Just before serving add the sour cream.

AUSTRIAN CABBAGE

1 small head of cabbage
butter or bacon fat
½ tsp. salt
1 tsp. paprika
1 tbsp. minced onion or crushed clove garlic
½ pint sour or sweet cream

Shred and wash the cabbage. Sauté it lightly in the butter or bacon fat. Add the salt, paprika and onion or garlic. Put it into a baking dish and pour the cream over. Bake in a moderate oven for about 20 minutes.

SAUERKRAUT (How to make it)

12 firm cabbages
2 lbs. salt
peppercorns
juniper berries

Remove all the discoloured outer leaves from hard white cabbages. Quarter them, take out the hard centre stalks and shred. Press a layer of shredded cabbage into a crock and sprinkle with salt, a few juniper berries and peppercorns. Continue filling the crock with alternate layers of cabbage and salt, peppercorns and juniper berries until it is three-quarters full. Press the cabbage down but take care not to break it. Cover it with several thicknesses of butter muslin. Place a lid or plate over it and put a heavy weight on this. After a while fermentation will start and the weighted lid will sink under the salt water. Remove some of the brine but leave enough to cover the lid. The sauerkraut will be ready for use after a month.

When sauerkraut is taken out of the crock, wash the lid and the cloth before replacing them and pour a little fresh water on the cover. Wash the sauerkraut before cooking it so as to get rid of the smell of the fermentation.

SAUERKRAUT (How to cook it)

1 quart sauerkraut
1 oz. butter or bacon fat
2 small or 1 large onion, sliced
1 medium sized potato or 1 large tart apple
enough stock to cover the sauerkraut
1—2 tbsp. brown sugar (optional)
1 tsp. caraway seed (optional)

Melt the butter in a large frying pan and sauté the sliced onion in it until transparent. Rinse the sauerkraut and drain it. Add it to the onion and butter and sauté it for 5 minutes. Peel and grate the potato or apple and add it to the sauerkraut. Cover it with the stock. Cook it without a lid for 30 minutes, then cover it and cook it in a moderate oven for a further 30 minutes. Season it with the brown sugar and caraway seeds if desired.

POTATO SALAD

2 lbs. waxy potatoes boiled in their jackets
1 tbsp. finely chopped onion
1 clove crushed garlic
2 tbsp. olive oil
3 tbsp. wine vinegar
salt
pepper

¾ tsp. French mustard
1 tbsp. parsley to garnish

Peel and slice the potatoes while still warm. Put them in a salad bowl with the onions, garlic and seasoning. Bring the oil, vinegar and mustard slowly to the boil, pour over the potatoes. Mix carefully. Serve cold, garnished with parsley.

CUCUMBER SALAD

1 large cucumber
salt
black pepper
2 tbsp. chopped parsley
French dressing (see p. 159)

Peel and slice the cucumber thinly. Sprinkle with salt and leave for 30 minutes. Squeeze gently in a clean cloth to remove the moisture. 15 minutes before serving pour French dressing over it and sprinkle with chopped parsley and black pepper.

LENTIL SALAD

½ pint stock
½ pint lentils
2 tbsp. chopped parsley
1 tbsp. chopped onions or chives
French or sour cream dressing
   (see pp. 34, 159)

Soak the lentils for 2 hours. Cook them gently in the stock until tender. Mix them with the parsley, onions and dressing. Serve cold or warm with sour cream dressing.

RAVIOLI FILLING (1) (Cheese)

3 large floury cooked potatoes
4 ozs. chopped ham
6 ozs. cream cheese or equal quan-
   tities of cream cheese and thick
   cream
1 egg yolk
salt

black pepper
1 tbsp. chopped chives
1 tbsp. chopped parsley
1 tsp. marjoram

Sieve the potatoes and blend thoroughly with the other ingredients to make a smooth mixture.

RAVIOLI FILLING (2) (Meat)

8 ozs. finely minced lean pork
8 ozs. finely minced lean veal
8 ozs. finely minced lean ham
1 egg
2 minced carrots
2 ozs. butter
salt
black pepper

3 tbsp. stock
breadcrumbs

Fry the meat, carrot and seasoning gently in the butter for 5 minutes. Add the stock and continue cooking until the meat is done (about 20—30 minutes). Re-mince the mixture, add the beaten egg and parsley and leave to cool before shaping. If it is too moist to shape when cool, add breadcrumbs as necessary.

RAVIOLI FILLING (3) (Meat)

1½ lbs. finely minced cooked meat
1 egg
1 small onion, finely chopped
salt
black pepper

2 tbsp. chopped parsley
gravy

Blend the egg, parsley and seasoning with the onions and meat. Moisten with gravy if very dry. Shape into balls.

CABBAGE SALAD

DRESSING:
1½ tbsp. wine vinegar
salt
black pepper
1 dsp. sugar
few caraway seeds
¾ lb. chopped fried bacon

1 medium cabbage, raw, cooked
   or blanched

Shred the cabbage finely and pour it over the well mixed dressing ingredients. Garnish with the bacon.

DUMPLINGS (Nockerl)

8 ozs. flour
2 eggs
3 ozs. melted butter
salt
water to mix to a stiff dough
   (about ⅛ pint)

Put the flour and salt into a bowl, make a well in the centre, break in the eggs, stir carefully so as to draw the flour gradually into the eggs, add the melted butter and the water as required. Leave the dough in a cold place for 30 minutes before use. Cut out teaspoonfuls of the mixture with a hot spoon. Cook these for 2 or 3 minutes in boiling water. Rinse them under the cold water tap. Heat them without browning them in butter or dripping. Serve with Goulash, etc.

CHICKEN STUFFING

8 ozs. cooked chopped chicken
   meat
2 ozs. butter
1½ ozs. flour
¾ pint white stock or milk
2 ozs. mushrooms
salt
pepper

Sauté the mushrooms and chicken gently for 5 minutes in the butter. Remove them from the butter and keep them hot. Make a roux with the butter and flour, add the heated stock gradually to make a very thick sauce. Blend the sauce with the chicken and mushrooms.

FORCEMEAT FILLING

4 ozs. breadcrumbs
2 ozs. fine suet
2 ozs. ham, minced
2 ozs. cooked chicken, veal or
    pork, minced
1 small egg

2 tbsp. parsley
1 tbsp. sage and thyme chopped
1 tbsp. paprika
salt

Mix all the dry ingredients together, using enough beaten egg to moisten the stuffing.

CHEESE PASTRIES

8 ozs. flour
4 ozs. butter
4 ozs. soft cream cheese
¼ tsp. salt (optional)

Sift the flour and resift it with the salt. With a knife, cut the butter and cream cheese into it. When the dough is well blended wrap it in greaseproof paper and put it in the refrigerator for 12 hours. Roll it out on greaseproof paper until it is only ⅛ inch thick. Cut the dough into rounds with a biscuit cutter. Place the rounds on an ungreased baking sheet and cook them in a hot oven (450°) for about 12 minutes. Serve them hot.

MEAT OMELETTE

4 eggs
4 ozs. flour
¼ pint milk
4 ozs. chopped ham or leftovers,
    squares of bacon, etc.
salt, black pepper
chopped parsley to garnish
2 ozs. butter for frying

Mix the flour, seasoning and meat together in a bowl, make a well in the centre and add the egg yolks and milk gradually to make a smooth batter. Leave to stand for 30 minutes. Fold the stiffly beaten egg whites into the mixture. Melt the butter in a heavy frying pan and pour in the egg mixture when it is just turning colour. Fry gently till brown, turn to brown the other side. Tear the mixture into pieces with two forks and continue frying until evenly coloured on all sides.

STUFFED SAVOURY PANCAKES

3 large eggs
3 ozs. flour
¼ pint milk
¼ pint cream
2 ozs. butter
salt
black pepper
butter for frying

Warm the milk, cream and butter together just sufficiently to melt the butter. Beat the eggs into this mixture. Put the flour into a bowl, make a well in the centre, gradually sift in the egg mixture to make a perfectly smooth batter. Leave it to stand for 30 minutes. Fry as usual for pancakes. Stuff with any of the fillings given for Ravioli (see pp. 31, 32).

RAVIOLI

8 ozs. flour
2 eggs
1 oz. melted butter
salt
water to mix to a stiff dough
  (about ⅛ pint)

Put the flour and salt into a bowl, make a well in the centre, break in the eggs, stir carefully so as to draw the flour gradually into the eggs, add the melted butter and the water as required. Knead the dough thoroughly with the hands. Leave the dough in a cold place for about 30 minutes before use.

Roll out the dough very thinly. Cut it in half. Roll one of the ravioli fillings (see pp. 31, 32) into small balls and place these balls on one sheet of the rolled out dough about 2 inches apart from one another. Cover this with the other sheet of dough. Press it down carefully between the balls of filling. Stamp out the ravioli with a biscuit cutter of suitable size. Crimp the edges to make them stick firmly together. Cook them in fast-boiling salted water for 15—20 minutes, according to size. Serve in hot sauce or gravy, with browned butter or with melted butter and cheese.

HAM AND NOODLES

1 lb. pasta of the flat ribbon type,
  cooked
2 ozs. butter
4 ozs. chopped ham
3 eggs
⅓ pint sour cream
salt
pepper
breadcrumbs

Cook the noodles and chopped ham gently in the butter for 5 minutes, season with salt and pepper. Blend the egg yolks with the cream, add the ham and noodles. Fold the stiffly beaten egg whites into the mixture. Pour it into a buttered fireproof dish, previously sprinkled with breadcrumbs. Bake in a moderate oven for 45 minutes. Serve with sauerkraut or green salad.

SOUR CREAM DRESSING

1 beaten egg yolk
2 tbsp. wine vinegar
½ pint sour cream
1 tbsp. chopped chives or onion
black pepper

Mix the vinegar into the egg yolk, blend in the slightly beaten cream and the onion, season with freshly ground black pepper.

SCHNITZEL SAUCE (1)

4 ozs. butter
12 anchovy fillets, pounded
1 tbsp. paprika

Blend and heat the ingredients and pour them over the hot cooked schnitzel.

SCHNITZEL SAUCE (2)

¼ pint cream
¼ pint water
1 tbsp. chopped capers
1 tbsp. paprika
salt

pepper
juice of 1 lemon

Blend the cream and water. Add the capers and the seasoning. Heat in the pan in which the schnitzel was cooked. Pour over the schnitzel.

KREN (Austrian horseradish sauce)

beetroot
horseradish
cream
very little vinegar
pepper

salt
sugar

Grate the horseradish and beetroot finely. Add enough cream to bring it to the consistency of horseradish sauce. Mix well and add the seasonings to taste.

CHOCOLATE SAUCE

¼ lb. plain chocolate
2 ozs. caster sugar
¼ pint water
½ vanilla pod

Melt the ingredients in a double saucepan until hot and well blended. Remove the vanilla pod before serving.

BACKHANDEL (Spring chicken)

1 spring chicken
4 ozs. flour
1 beaten egg
breadcrumbs

Clean a young chicken and cut it up into joints. Remove the meat from the bones of the carcass. Remove the skin from all the pieces of chicken. Dip them into flour and then into the beaten egg and finally into the breadcrumbs. Fry the pieces in deep fat and drain them on soft paper. Serve very hot with a green salad and new potatoes.

ROAST GOOSE

1 young goose
4 eating apples
4 lumps of sugar
2 tbsp. chopped marjoram
salt
black pepper

dripping for roasting
red currant jelly

Rub the goose inside and out with salt and pepper and chopped marjoram. Peel and core the apples. Put a sugar lump into each and stuff the goose with them. Baste frequently while roasting. Serve with red currant jelly.

CHICKEN PAPRIKA

1 young chicken
1 oz. butter
1 oz. lard
3 onions, chopped
2 tsp. paprika
1 pint vegetable or light stock or
    water
1 tsp. flour
salt
½ pint sour cream

Cut the chicken into joints and sprinkle it with salt. Melt the butter and lard in a heavy pan, add the chopped onions and simmer them until they are browned. Add the paprika and the stock. Bring these ingredients to the boil and then add the chicken. Cover the pan and simmer the chicken until it is tender (about 1½ hours). Stir the flour into the sour cream and pour it slowly into the pan. Cook, without boiling, for a further 5 minutes.

ROAST PIGEON

4 young pigeons

STUFFING:
4 ozs. calves' liver
1 dsp. chopped thyme
2 ozs. butter
4 anchovy fillets
4 juniper berries (optional)
salt
black pepper
1 large onion

butter for roasting
breadcrumbs fried in butter
¼ pint sour cream
apple or red currant jelly

Chop all the stuffing ingredients finely and fry them in the butter until tender. Stuff the pigeons and roast them in butter, baste well. When they are cooked, pour a little sour cream over each of them and serve with the fried breadcrumbs and apple or red currant jelly.

HARE OR RABBIT GOULASH WITH WINE

2 lbs. hare or rabbit, boned and
    cut in cubes
4 ozs. bacon, chopped
1 large onion, chopped
1 oz. dripping
2 ozs. flour
1 pint dry red wine or cider
¼ pint stock
1 tbsp. paprika
salt

2 cloves garlic (optional)
¼ pint sour cream

Fry the bacon and onions gently in the dripping for 10 minutes. Brown the meat on all sides. Sauté the meat, onions and bacon over a low heat for 10 minutes. Sprinkle in the flour, paprika, salt and pepper and the garlic. Stir and blend thoroughly. Add the wine and enough stock to cover the meat well. Cook in a slow oven for 2 hours or till tender. Five minutes before serving stir in the sour cream. Reheat without boiling. Serve with rice or nockerl (see p. 32).

HARE

1 young hare
3 carrots
3 small turnips
3 onions
2 cloves garlic, crushed
parsley
1 sprig each of rosemary and
   thyme
1 bay leaf
peel of ½ lemon
12 peppercorns
red wine
¼ pint sour cream

salt
black pepper
stewed currants or red currant
   jelly

Rub the hare with salt and pepper. Simmer the sliced vegetables and herbs for ½ hour in equal quantities of wine and water. Add the hare and enough extra wine and water to cover. Simmer in a covered pan until tender. Remove the hare. Joint it ready to serve. Strain the sauce, blend with the cream and pour over the hare. Serve it with stewed currants or red currant jelly.

GOULASH

1 lb. lean stewing beef cut into
   cubes
1 lb. onions, sliced
1 lb. potatoes
2 ozs. dripping
stock
1 tbsp. paprika
salt
½ tsp. caraway seeds

pinch of marjoram
2 cloves garlic

Fry the onions and the garlic for a few minutes in the dripping. Add the paprika, salt, marjoram and caraway seeds. Just cover the meat with the stock and cook in a covered pan in a slow oven for 3 hours or until perfectly tender. Half an hour before serving add the potatoes. Long and very slow cooking improves this dish. Serve with nockerl (see p. 32).

CARAWAY SEED ROAST

2 lbs. sirloin or rib of beef, rolled
   and boned
2 lbs. beef bones
2 ozs. bacon fat or dripping
2 large onions, finely chopped
salt
black pepper
2 tbsp. caraway seeds
2 tbsp. vinegar
2 tbsp. flour (for roux)
2 ozs. dripping or butter (for
   roux)

Mix 2 tablespoons of chopped onion with 1 tablespoon of caraway seeds and a good pinch of salt. Unroll the meat, spread with this mixture, re-roll and tie. Put the rest of the onion and the bacon fat into a roasting tin and sauté in the oven for five minutes. Then put in the meat and sprinkle it with the remaining caraway seeds and the vinegar, salt and freshly ground black pepper. Arrange the bones round the meat and pour in enough water to come a quarter of the way up the meat. Roast in a moderate oven for about an hour. Baste frequently. Make a brown roux with 2 ozs. flour, 2 ozs. dripping or butter and seasoning, and mix this gradually with the strained juice from the roasting pan. Season. Serve with nockerl (see p. 32).

MINCE ROAST

½ lb. beef
½ lb. pork
1 small onion
1 egg
2 Vienna rolls
salt, pepper, parsley
fat
flour

GRAVY:

1 oz. butter or dripping
1 oz. flour
2 ozs. fat bacon
salt
pepper
1 dsp. chopped capers
2 tbsp. sour cream
¼ pint stock, hot

Remove crust from rolls and soak in milk or water. Mince meat finely. Squeeze out moisture from rolls and add to meat, together with salt, pepper, egg, chopped parsley and finely chopped onion previously fried in a little fat. Knead well and shape into a roll. Dust with flour.

Heat the dripping in a pan with a lid. Put in the meat roll covered with the fat bacon. Baste the roll with the melted dripping, put the lid on and roast in a moderate oven for 45 to 60 minutes according to the thickness of the roll. Fifteen minutes before the roll is cooked remove the lid and the fat bacon to allow the meat to brown. When it is cooked, remove the roll to a hot dish. Drain the surplus fat from the pan, stir in the flour, cook for a few minutes and then gradually add the stock and the sour cream, seasoning and capers. Do not boil the sauce after adding the cream. Serve the roll and the sauce separately.

TYROLEAN LIVER

1 lb. calves' liver, sliced thin
1 onion, sliced thin
2 ozs. dripping
black pepper
1 tsp. marjoram, chopped
¼ pint stock (optional)
1 oz. flour (optional)

Fry the onions in the dripping until they are just turning colour. Increase the heat, move the onions to one side of the pan, put in the liver, marjoram and pepper and fry fast for about 4 minutes, turning the liver frequently. Add the salt just before serving to avoid toughening the meat. If gravy is required, remove the cooked onions and liver to a hot dish, stir the flour into the fat in the pan, cook for 3 or 4 minutes, add the stock gradually and season to taste. Serve with rice or nockerl (see p. 32).

WIENER SCHNITZEL

1 large escallop per head, cut ⅛ inch to ½ inch thick, either fillet or cut slantwise from the leg
1 egg, beaten
6 ozs. fine breadcrumbs
3 ozs. flour
4 ozs. melted butter
salt
black pepper
2 lemons

Beat the escallops gently to half their original thickness. Pour the juice of one of the lemons over the meat. Leave it for 1 hour, turning several times.

Mix the flour with the seasoning. Dip the marinated veal first into the flour and then into the beaten egg. Last of all, dip it into the breadcrumbs. Fry the schnitzel in the butter for about 1½ minutes on each side. Drain the schnitzel on soft paper, keeping it hot. Serve with quarters of lemon.

VEAL ESCALLOP

1 lb. veal cut in slices from the
   fillet
6 ozs. butter
1 or 2 quartered lemons to garnish
juice of 1 lemon

Marinate the escallop in the lemon juice for 1 hour, turning frequently. Fry it in the butter, allowing 1 minute for each side. Serve with quartered lemons and the frying butter.

PAPRIKA BEEF

1 lb. fillet of beef cut in ½ inch
   thick slices
2 ozs. dripping or butter
1 oz. flour
3 onions, chopped
2 lbs. sliced potatoes
½ pint sour cream
2 tbsp. tomato purée
salt
pepper
2 tsp. paprika
½ pint water

Beat the slices of beef to half their original thickness and rub them with salt and pepper. Sear the beef quickly on both sides in the dripping. Remove the beef from the pan and put it into a fireproof casserole with lid. Fry the onions golden, add and stir in the water. Pour this sauce over the meat, cover the casserole and cook in a slow oven for 3 hours. Add the potatoes 45 minutes before serving and the cream 5 minutes before serving. After adding the cream, heat but be careful not to boil. Serve with quarters of lemon or with kren (see p. 35).

SAUTÉED KIDNEYS

1 lb. ox kidney
1 large onion, sliced thinly
2 ozs. dripping or lard
salt
black pepper
½ teaspoon marjoram

Skin the kidneys and slice them thinly, removing all the core. Steep the slices in cold water for 30 minutes. Change the water, rinse and repeat. Rinse thoroughly, drain and dry carefully with a clean cloth. Sauté the onions until just turning colour, draw them to the side of the pan and raise the heat. Add the kidney slices, the marjoram and the pepper, and sauté quickly for 5 minutes, turning frequently. Add salt just before serving. Serve with green salad.

PORK AND SAUERKRAUT

1 lb. pork, cut into cubes
¾ lb. sauerkraut, fresh or tinned
1 onion, thinly sliced into rings
salt
pepper
1 tbsp. paprika

1 clove garlic, crushed
water

Fry the onion rings in the butter until just turning colour. Add the seasoning, sauerkraut and meat and stir to mix thoroughly. Just cover the meat with water and simmer gently with the lid on for about 1 hour. Serve with dumplings.

BEEF AND SAUSAGE ROAST

2 lbs. lean roasting joint
4 long frankfurters
1 large onion, finely chopped
2 ozs. dripping
1 oz. flour
salt
black pepper
paprika
1 pint water approx.

Cut 8 holes through the meat with an apple corer. Thread half a sausage through each hole, trimming the sausages to the thickness of the meat. Rub the meat with salt, black pepper and paprika. Simmer the meat trimmings with the water, and some salt and pepper. Melt the onion in the dripping in a metal casserole. Add the meat and sear quickly on both sides. Sprinkle in the flour and blend it with the onions. Just cover the meat with the stock made from the meat trimmings. Cook it in a slow oven for about an hour and a half until tender. Serve the meat sliced so that rounds of sausages appear in each slice. Strain the gravy over it.

STUFFED SADDLE OF LAMB

saddle of lamb
6 shallots
4 ozs. ham
2 ozs. suet
4 slices of bread (soaked and
    squeezed out)
2 tbsp. parsley
3 eggs
salt

pepper
1 oz. butter

Remove the bones from the lamb, rub it thoroughly with the cut sides of a shallot and with salt and pepper. Leave it in a cool place for 8 hours. Chop the shallots, ham and parsley and fry them lightly in the butter. Add the 2 beaten eggs and seasoning. Cook gently till set. When the lamb is ready stuff it with this mixture. Tie the joint and roast it in the usual way, basting frequently.

LEG OF PORK

leg of pork
2 large onions
2 carrots
bouquet garni
2 sticks celery
salt
pepper

SAUCE:

2 lbs. tomatoes
½ pint white wine or cider
salt
black pepper
1 tbsp. brown sugar

Put the leg of pork, vegetables, herbs and seasoning in a pan with enough water to cover them and cook gently until the meat is tender. Allow roughly 25 minutes per lb. When it is cooked cut a suitable number of slices and serve it with the sauce given below.

Stew the tomatoes in the wine with the seasoning and sugar. Reduce to a thick pulp and strain.
Serve with dumplings or nockerl (see p. 32).

ESTERHAZY BEEF STEAK

2 lbs. rump or chuck steak cut into
   small neat steaks and flattened
4 ozs. good dripping or bacon fat
3 carrots, coarsely chopped
2 onions, coarsely chopped
2 stalks celery, coarsely chopped
½ green pepper, coarsely chopped
salt
black pepper
2 tsp. capers
2 tsp. paprika
1 oz. flour
½ pint good stock
3 tbsp. sour cream
3 tbsp. Madeira

Melt half the dripping in a metal casserole, add the seasoning and vegetables, cover and sauté gently without stirring for 10 minutes. Remove the lid and raise the heat. Still without stirring, but shaking the pan, brown the vegetables, adding a little of the stock as necessary. Sprinkle in the flour. Stir gently. When blended, stir in the remaining stock and the sour cream. Heat the other half of the dripping in another pan. Sear the steaks quickly on both sides. Add the steak to the vegetables and gravy. Cover with a tightly fitting lid and cook in a moderate oven for about 30—45 minutes depending on the thickness and quality of the meat. Add the wine 5 minutes before serving.

CALVES' TONGUE

8 slices calves' tongue
4 fillets of anchovy, crushed
4 ozs. butter
juice of 2 lemons
salt
black pepper
6 ozs. breadcrumbs
dripping for frying

Melt the butter and add the lemon juice, seasoning and crushed anchovies. Simmer for 5 mins. When the sauce is cold, dip the tongue slices first in this and then in breadcrumbs. Fry them till golden. Serve with the sauce heated and poured over the tongue.

APPLE FLAN

short crust paste (see p. 205)
¼ lb. lump sugar
1 oz. ground almonds
1½ lbs. cooking apples, peeled
   and sliced
¼ pint water
½ pint whipped cream

FOR THE MERINGUE:

4 ozs. caster sugar
2 egg whites

Leave the paste to rest for half an hour. Line a buttered, floured flan tin with the paste and bake blind. Boil the sugar and water together for 10 minutes, add the other ingredients and simmer gently until the apples are tender. Meanwhile beat the egg whites stiff and fold the sugar in gradually. When the pastry is cooked fill the shell with the apple mixture, cover this with the meringue and bake for ½ hour in a slow oven.

COFFEE CREAM

½ pint strong black coffee
½ oz. powdered gelatine
2 ozs. caster sugar
2 ozs. vanilla sugar
½ pint whipped cream

Dissolve the gelatine with the plain sugar in a little of the coffee. Bring the rest of the coffee up to the boil and pour over the mixture. Stir to dissolve the gelatine completely. Leave in a cold place to set. When almost set, beat until frothy, add the cream and vanilla sugar, pour into a wetted mould and leave for at least 4 hours.

LOCKSMITHS' APPRENTICES, BAKED

12 large prunes
12 blanched almonds
½ lb. flour
white wine or cider to mix
1 oz. sugar
salt
1 egg yolk

FOR THE GARNISH:
2 ozs. caster sugar
2 ozs. plain chocolate, grated

Soak the prunes overnight. Stew until tender. Replace each prune stone with an almond. Make a paste with the flour, salt, and egg yolk and wine. Roll out thin, cut into 12 rounds and wrap one prune in each. Bake on a very well buttered baking sheet in a moderate oven for 30 minutes, turning at half-time to brown both sides. Serve hot rolled in sugar and chocolate.

LOCKSMITHS' APPRENTICES, FRIED

12 large prunes
12 blanched almonds
¼ lb. flour
salt
¼ pint water or cider

TO GARNISH:
2 ozs. caster sugar
2 ozs. plain chocolate

Soak the prunes overnight. Stew until soft. Replace the prune stones with blanched almonds. Prepare a batter by beating the wine into the flour and salt. The batter should be runny. Dip the prunes into the batter and fry in deep hot fat until golden. Drain on soft paper. Roll in grated chocolate and sugar. Serve hot.

CANARY MILK

½ pint milk
1 egg yolk
2 ozs. caster sugar
1 vanilla pod

Cut the vanilla pod into 5 or 6 pieces and bring to the boil with the milk and sugar. Mix the egg yolk with 3 tablespoons of the hot milk while stirring briskly. Pour the remaining milk over this mixture, return to the pan and cook gently until it thickens. Serve hot or cold.

APPLE PUDDING

1½ lbs. cooking apples
3 eggs, separated
4 ozs. vanilla sugar
3 ozs. cake crumbs

Peel, slice and core the apples, stew them gently in the butter until tender but not brown. Sieve the cake crumbs. Beat the egg yolks and sugar until pale, stir in the cake crumbs and apple. Whisk the egg whites stiffly and fold them into the mixture. Steam for 1 hour in a well buttered basin covered with greased paper. Serve hot with Canary milk (see p. 42).

APPLE SNOW

1½ lbs. cooking apples
¼ lb. vanilla sugar
3 egg whites stiffly beaten
juice of 1 lemon

OPTIONAL SAUCE:
½ pint white wine or cider
½ lb. caster sugar
3 egg yolks

Chop the apples with the skins on, stew in very little water until tender. Sieve the apple, add the sugar and lemon juice and whisk over warm water until thick. Remove from the heat, whisk until cool, fold in the egg whites. Serve as cold as possible.

FOR THE SAUCE:
Whisk all the ingredients over hot water until thick. Serve hot.

COLD RICE PUDDING

¼ lb. Carolina rice
½ pint milk
½ pint double cream
2 ozs. sugar
1 vanilla pod
¼ oz. gelatine

Boil the rice, sugar and vanilla pod in the milk until soft, stir frequently. Soften the gelatine in a tablespoonful of milk then stir it into the cooked rice. Stir in the cream, remove the vanilla pod and pour into a cold wetted mould. Serve plain or with fruit syrup (see below).

FRUIT SYRUP WITH CREAM

½ pint any fruit juice
sugar to taste
¼ pint double cream whipped
½ tbsp. powdered gelatine

Blend the gelatine with ½ of the fruit juice. Bring the remaining ¼ pint of juice to the boil, add the mixed gelatine and juice and stir over the heat until the gelatine is dissolved. Remove from the heat. When cool beat until thick and light; keep very cold while whipping. Fold in the whipped cream.

CANARY PUDDING WITH CHOCOLATE SAUCE

3 ozs. butter
3 ozs. sugar
3 ozs. flour
3 eggs separated
grated rind of ½ lemon

Cream the butter and sugar and beat until light. Add the beaten egg yolks gradually. Fold in the sifted flour and stiffly beaten egg whites alternately, add the lemon rind, and steam in a buttered basin for 1 hour.

For the sauce for Canary pudding see p. 35.

FRUIT JELLY

¼ lb. fresh red currants
topped and tailed
¼ lb. fresh black currants
topped and tailed
¼ lb. strawberries, hulled
¼ lb. black cherries, stoned
¼ pint white wine or cider
¼ pint water

½ oz. gelatine
¼-½ lb. caster sugar to taste

Lightly stew the currants with the sugar and water and then sieve them. Mix the gelatine with a little of the wine then pour the hot purée over it. Add the rest of the fruit and the wine and pour into a mould to set. Serve with whipped cream or Canary milk (see p. 42).

CANTALOUPE WITH BRANDY

1 cantaloupe melon
1 small glass brandy
¼ lb. icing sugar
juice of 1 lemon

Peel the melon finely, remove the seeds and cut the flesh into neat cubes. Mix the other ingredients together and pour over the melon pieces. Cover tightly and stand in a cool place for at least 2 hours. Mix gently and serve with whipped cream.

COMPOTE OF APPLES OR PEARS

1½ lbs. cooking apples or pears
¾ pint water
¾ lb. sugar
juice and peel of 1 orange
½ lb. cherry jam

Boil the sugar and water together fast without a lid for about 15 minutes until it thickens. Peel, halve and core the apples or pears. Cook these halves in the syrup a few at a time, being careful to keep them whole. When cooked remove from the syrup, arrange on a dish and fill the core hollow with jam. When all the halves are cooked, reboil the syrup with the orange peel and juice and half the apple cores and peel for 15 minutes or until it will set on a cold plate. Strain the syrup over the fruit. Serve cold with whipped cream or Canary milk (see p. 42).

MAGDA (Coffee and chocolate jelly)

½ pint strong clear coffee
1 level tsp. granulated gelatine
4 tsp. chocolate powder
sugar to taste
little vanilla
pinch of salt
whipped cream to garnish

Heat the coffee and the salt. Dissolve the gelatine in it. Add the chocolate powder, sugar and vanilla. Cook for a few minutes, until it is smooth and the chocolate is completely melted. Cool it, stirring from time to time. Pour into glasses when it is on the point of setting. Chill thoroughly. Top with whipped cream just before serving. Serve with sweet biscuits or sponge fingers.

LITTLE APPLE TURNOVERS

short crust pastry
  (see p. 49)
4 cooking apples peeled and
  quartered
4 ozs. caster sugar
1 tbsp. rum
1 egg yolk
1 tbsp. milk

Leave the pastry dough to rest for half an hour after mixing. Mix the rum with the sugar, pour over the apple. Leave to stand for half an hour. Roll out the dough and cut into 16 squares. Put one apple quarter on each square, draw up the corners and press the edges together but leave the tips open. Arrange on a buttered floured baking sheet. Brush with egg and milk and bake in a hot oven for 20 to 30 minutes. Dust with vanilla sugar and serve hot or cold.

APPLE STRUDEL

strudel dough (see p. 49)
1½ lbs. cooking apples
2 ozs. currants
2 ozs. stoned raisins
2 ozs. dry breadcrumbs fried in
  butter
4 ozs. caster sugar
½ tsp. ground cinnamon
grated peel of ½ lemon
4 ozs. melted butter

While the strudel dough is resting before being pulled out, prepare the filling. Peel, core and slice the apples thinly then mix them without breaking them, with the rest of the ingredients. When the dough is ready, trim off the thick edges and spread with the apple mixture, leaving an inch uncovered all round the edges. Roll the dough very gently and pinch the edges together and place on a buttered baking sheet. Brush with melted butter and bake in a hot oven for 20 minutes, lower the temperature to moderate and bake for a further 30 minutes. Brush with the melted butter 2 or 3 times during baking. Serve sliced hot or cold.

LEMON SOUFFLÉ

4 eggs separated
2 ozs. icing sugar
juice and rind of 1 lemon

Line a soufflé mould with buttered paper and sprinkle with icing sugar. Beat the egg yolks with the sugar, lemon juice and rind until thick. Fold in the stiffly beaten egg whites, turn into the prepared mould and bake in a hot oven for 15 to 20 minutes.

CREAM CHEESE STRUDEL

strudel dough (see p. 49)
¼ lb. sieved cream cheese
4 ozs. caster sugar
4 ozs. butter
⅛ pint sour cream
1 egg, beaten

While the strudel dough is resting before being rolled out, beat all the other ingredients together to blend thoroughly. Then proceed as for apple strudel (see p. 45).

VANILLA CREAM

½ pint milk
1 large egg
2 ozs. caster sugar
1 oz. cornflour
1 vanilla pod cut into 4 or
 5 pieces

Mix the cornflour, sugar and egg yolk to a paste with a little of the milk. Heat the remainder of the milk with the vanilla pod in a double saucepan. Pour the hot milk over the other ingredients, stirring all the time. When blended, return to the double saucepan, cook and stir until thick.

FRIED YEAST CAKES (Gebackene Mäuse)

½ lb. flour
2 ozs. butter
⅛ pint milk (approx.)
1 egg beaten
½ oz. yeast
½ oz. sugar
2 ozs. sultanas
½ tsp. salt
1 tbsp. rum
frying fat

Scald the milk with the butter and cool to lukewarm. Cream the yeast with the sugar and stand in a warm place for 5 minutes. Warm the flour in a large mixing bowl. Make a well in the flour and, using the hand, gradually beat in the egg, yeast mixture, milk mixture, salt and sultanas. Knead thoroughly. Cover the bowl with a cloth and stand in a warm place to rise. When the dough has doubled its bulk, in about an hour and a half, knock down lightly. Scoop out teaspoonfuls of the dough and fry in deep hot fat. Turn the 'buns' to brown on both sides evenly. Drain on soft paper, serve hot with fruit syrup or vanilla cream (see p. 43 and above).

CHERRY STRUDEL

strudel dough (see p. 49)
1½ lbs. black cherries
4 ozs. breadcrumbs fried in butter
2 ozs. currants
4 ozs. caster sugar

½ tsp. ground cinnamon
grated peel of ½ lemon
4 ozs. melted butter

Proceed exactly as in the recipe for Apple Strudel (see p. 45) but use black cherries instead of apples.

EMPEROR'S SCHMARREN

¼ lb. flour
¼ pint cream
2 eggs separated
1 oz. caster sugar
salt
1 oz. raisins stoned
1 oz. butter

Beat together the egg yolks and cream, stir these into the flour, raisins, salt and sugar. Fold in the stiffly, beaten egg whites. Melt the butter in a shallow baking pan, pour in the batter and bake in a hot oven for 10 minutes or until brown underneath. Turn the batter over and brown the other side, then tear into small pieces with two forks, return to the oven for a further 3 or 4 minutes. Serve hot with vanilla sauce (see p. 46).

BREAD OMELETTE

4 thick slices stale bread or 4 rolls
  or brioches
½ pint milk
2 ozs. sultanas
1 apple peeled, chopped
1 egg
1 oz. sugar
salt
4 ozs. butter for frying

Cut the bread into cubes. Mix all the other ingredients together and pour them over the bread. Leave to stand for 15 minutes. Heat the butter in a frying pan, pour in the batter, fry until brown, turn and brown the other side. Tear the omelette into small pieces with two forks, continue frying for a few minutes, shaking the pan. Serve with hot vanilla sugar.

CREAM CHEESE AND JAM PUFFS

¼ lb. flour
¼ lb. butter
¼ lb. cream cheese
¼ lb. approx. jam, jelly or strained
  stewed fruit

Sift flour on to pastry board. Cut butter into small pieces, crumble cream cheese and butter into flour, handling dough very lightly.

Roll out the dough to ¼ inch thickness, and cut into squares. Put a dab of jam or fruit on each square, gather up the corners and press them firmly together. Bake in a hot oven for about 15 minutes. Serve hot sprinkled with icing sugar.

APPLE SLICES

short crust paste (see p. 49)
1½ lbs. cooking apples peeled and
  thickly sliced
4 ozs. sugar
3 ozs. cocoa or 2 ozs. stoned
  raisins
1 egg white
salt

Divide the pastry in half. Roll each half out to a square, spread one square with apple slices, sugar and cocoa or raisins. Bake for 15 minutes in a moderate oven. Cover with the other half of the pastry, brush with beaten egg white and bake in a hot oven for about 30 minutes. Serve cold, sliced and dusted with icing sugar.

BUCHTELN

6 ozs. butter for glaze
dough as for rich streusel cake
  (see p. 55)
½ lb. jam

Melt the butter in a roasting tin. When the dough has doubled its size, knock down and roll out to ¼ inch thick. Cut into 2½ inch squares. Put a good teaspoonful of jam on each. Draw up the corners to enclose the jam, put them gathered side down on the prepared roasting dish, brush all over thoroughly with the melted butter in the tin. Pack the buns closely together, stand in a warm place for half an hour. Bake in a moderate oven for 45 to 50 minutes. Remove from the tin, separate, dust with icing sugar. Serve hot or cold.

DALKEN (1)

rich streusel cake dough (see p. 55)
4 ozs. melted butter
½ lb. apricot jam (approx.)
1 oz. melted lard (approx.)

When the dough has doubled its bulk, knock it down and roll out to ¼ inch thick. Cut into 2 or 3 inch rounds and leave on a floured board in a warm place for 30 minutes. Brush a griddle or heavy frying pan with lard and lightly fry the Dalken on both sides. Keep hot until all are done, brush quickly with melted butter, spread with apricot jam and serve very hot.

DALKEN (2)

4 ozs. flour
3 eggs
½ pint milk
2 ozs. caster sugar
pinch salt
2 ozs. melted butter
½ lb. apricot jam
¼ pint whipped cream

Make a smooth batter with the flour, eggs, milk, sugar and salt. Leave it to stand for 30 minutes. Brush large shallow bun moulds with melted butter. Half fill the moulds with the batter and bake for 10 to 15 minutes in a hot oven, turn them over and return to the oven for a further 5 minutes. Keep the Dalken hot until all are done, then spread with apricot jam and cream, serve at once.

TO WASH BUTTER

Fill a large bowl with very cold water, preferably with ice cubes added. Stand this bowl with the butter in it under a running cold tap. Squeeze the butter between the fingers for 5 minutes. Squeeze in a floured cloth to remove surplus moisture. Keep in a cold place (not a refrigerator) until needed.

PUFF PASTE WITH YEAST

½ *lb. flour*
6 *ozs. butter*
1 *egg*
⅛ *pint milk approx.*
½ *oz. yeast*
½ *oz. sugar*
salt

Mix the yeast with the sugar. Scald the milk, add the salt, 2 ozs. butter, cool to lukewarm, add the yeast mixture. Meanwhile warm the flour in a large mixing bowl. Make a well in the flour and beat in the beaten egg and the milk and yeast mixture. Mix with the hand to form a smooth elastic dough adding milk or flour as necessary. Stand in a warm place, covered with a cloth until the dough has doubled its bulk (1½ hrs. approx.). Turn the dough onto a floured board and knead a little, roll out into a long strip 3 times as long as its width. Wash the remaining butter (see p. 48). Spread a third of the butter over the middle third of the dough, fold the ends to form a three tiered square, give a quarter turn and repeat this process twice more so that the dough has had three rollings and all the butter is used. If possible stand the dough in a cold place for 30 minutes, between rollings and again before use.

SHORT PASTE

8 *ozs. flour*
6 *ozs. butter*
1 *egg yolk*
salt
3 *tbsp. sour thin cream (approx.)*

2 *ozs. caster sugar*
½ *tsp. lemon juice*

Sift the flour with the salt and sugar. Rub or cut the butter into it. Mix with the egg yolk, cream and lemon juice to form a rather dry dough. Cover and stand in a cool place for 1 hour before use.

STRUDEL DOUGH

8 *ozs. flour*
1 *egg yolk, beaten*
salt
¼ *pint warm water (approx.)*
1 *tbsp. melted butter*

Put the flour and salt into a warmed basin. Make a well in the centre and with the hand stir in the beaten egg yolk, butter and enough warm water to make a soft dough, knead thoroughly on a warmed, well floured board. When smooth, cover with a warm bowl and a cloth. Cover a table with a clean cloth. Sprinkle the cloth with flour, place the dough in the middle and roll it out as thin as possible with a warmed floured rolling pin. Slip your hands palm down under the dough and gently pull it out thinner from the middle, using mainly the balls of the thumbs. Ideally it should be pulled out thin enough to read through but this takes much patience and practice.

CROISSANTS

8 ozs. flour
8 ozs. butter, washed (see p. 48)
½ pint milk
1 oz. butter to mix with milk
1 egg beaten
1 oz. yeast
½ oz. sugar
½ to 1 tsp. salt
1 egg yolk ⎫
2 tbsp. milk ⎭ for glaze

Cream the yeast with the sugar. Scald the milk, add 1 oz. butter and the salt, cool to lukewarm, add the yeast mixture. Meanwhile warm the flour in a large mixing bowl. Make a well in the flour and beat in the beaten egg and the warm milk mixture. Mix with the hand to form a smooth elastic dough adding milk or flour as necessary. Stand in a warm place covered with a cloth until the dough has doubled its bulk, about 1½ hours. Put the dough, covered with a cloth, in the refrigerator or as cold a place as possible for 3 or 4 hours. Knock the dough down, roll it out into a strip three times as long as it is wide. Spread a third of the butter over the middle third of the dough, fold the ends over to form a three-tiered square, give the dough a quarter turn and repeat this process twice more so that the dough has had three rollings and all the butter is used. Stand the dough in a cold place between rollings and again before shaping. Roll the dough out to ¼ inch thickness and cut it into 4 inch squares, then into triangles. Roll each triangle up starting at the wide base so that the point is in the centre, curve the ends round to form a crescent. Arrange on a buttered floured baking sheet, brush with egg and milk and bake in a hot oven for about 20 minutes. Cool on a wire rack.

GUGELHUPF

12 ozs. flour sifted with ½ tsp. salt
6 ozs. butter
3 eggs
½ pint warm milk (approx.)
1 oz. yeast
½ oz. sugar
1 10-inch diameter centre tube
    mould
2 ozs. raisins, stoned
2 ozs. currants
grated rind and juice of 1 orange
2 ozs. blanched sliced almonds

Blend the yeast with the sugar, stir in the warm milk. Stand in a warm place for 5 minutes. Rub the butter into the warm flour and salt in a large warm mixing bowl. Make a well in the centre and add the beaten eggs, warm milk, raisins, currants, orange rind and juice and yeast mixture. Stir to mix thoroughly. Prepare the mould by buttering it and dusting it with cornflour and strewing it with the almonds. Fill the mould half full and stand it in a warm place to prove. When the dough reaches the top of the mould it is ready to bake in a moderate oven for ¾ hour to 1 hour. Turn out on a rack to cool.

RICH GUGELHUPF

½ lb. flour
10 egg yolks
8 ozs. butter
4 ozs. sugar
⅛ pint warm milk (approx.)
10-inch centre tube mould
salt
1 oz. yeast
4 ozs. stoned raisins
4 ozs. blanched chopped almonds
cornflour or breadcrumbs to line
tin

Cream the yeast with a tsp. of the sugar, add the warm milk and stand in a warm place. Cream the butter, add the eggs gradually, alternately with the flour, add the sugar, salt and raisins and beat thoroughly. Stir in the milk and yeast mixture gently until thoroughly blended. Butter the mould, dust with cornflour or dry breadcrumbs and strew with chopped almonds. Fill the mould not more than ¾ full, stand in a warm place to rise. When the mixture is just above the top of the tin, bake in a moderate oven for 45 minutes to 1 hour. Turn out and cool on a cake rack.

CAKES (General)

1. Austrian sponge cake mixtures should be beaten by hand for 30 minutes. If an electric mixer is used it must be set at a very low speed, otherwise the air bubbles are too large and the mixture too light and frothy. Fatless sponge cakes are best beaten by placing the bowl in which they are mixed in a larger bowl of very hot water.
2. The tins in which they are baked are greased and dusted first with flour and then caster sugar.
3. The secret of the celebrated Sacher Torte was very carefully guarded and there are therefore various different recipes for it. I have included two of these.

CLASSIC AUSTRIAN SPONGE CAKE

3 eggs
5 ozs. caster sugar
3 ozs. flour

Beat the eggs with the sugar until white. Fold in the sifted flour very gently. Bake in tin prepared according to general directions above in a moderately slow oven for 1 hour. Turn out when cold.

VARIATIONS:
1. Use vanilla sugar instead of caster sugar, ice with chocolate frosting and fill with the filling for Sacher Torte.
2. Add melted cooking chocolate to the mixture after the flour. Cover with white icing and fill with thick vanilla cream (see p. 46).

DOUGHNUTS

½ lb. flour
2 eggs
⅛ pint warm milk
½ oz. yeast
1 oz. sugar
1½ oz. melted butter
salt
½ lb. jam (approx.)
deep fat for frying

Mix the yeast with a teaspoonful of the sugar and half the warm milk. Warm the flour in a large mixing bowl. Make a well in the centre and pour in the yeast mixture. Sprinkle with flour and stand in a warm place for half an hour. Then add the rest of the warm milk, the butter, melted, one whole egg and the egg yolk beaten, the salt and the remaining sugar. Mix well and beat until smooth and the dough leaves the sides of the bowl clean. Add more milk and flour as necessary. Cover the bowl and stand in warm place to double its bulk, about 1½ hours. Turn onto a floured board and knead lightly, roll out to a quarter of an inch thick. Cut into rounds, arrange the rounds in pairs. Put half a teaspoonful of jam in the middle of one round, brush round the edges with beaten egg white and cover with the other round, press the edges together firmly. Leave the doughnuts to rise in a warm place until well risen and light. Fry a few at a time in deep hot fat. Brown the first side with a lid on the pan, turn and brown the other side without the lid. Drain on soft paper and roll in caster sugar.

SACHER TORTE (1)

8 ozs. cooking chocolate
8 ozs. butter
8 ozs. ground almonds
8 eggs
6 ozs. caster sugar
1 tbs. cornflour

FILLING:

apricot jam or sauce (see p. 54)
4 egg yolks
2 ozs. sugar
2 ozs. cocoa
¼ pint double cream
1 oz. vanilla sugar (see p. 55)

Melt the chocolate with a little water. Cream the butter, add the chocolate, beaten egg yolks, ground almonds and sugar. Beat all ingredients together until very light and creamy. Add the cornflour and beat again. Fold in the stiffly beaten egg whites. Transfer gently into a prepared cake tin (see p. 51) and bake in a moderately slow oven (300°) for 1 hour. Leave in the tin to cool thoroughly before turning out.
FILLING: Cook the beaten egg yolks, sugar and cocoa in the top of a double saucepan, stirring all the time, until the mixture thickens. Whip the cream, add the vanilla sugar and fold into the cocoa mixture when it cools.

Cut the cake in half and spread the lower half with the filling. Replace top half and spread with sieved apricot jam or apricot sauce. Ice with chocolate frosting (see p. 54).

Serve with whipped cream.

SACHER TORTE (2)

8 ozs. cooking chocolate melted in
   a little coffee
8 ozs. butter
8 ozs. sugar
6 ozs. s. r. flour
5 eggs
apricot jam or sauce
filling and icing as in (1)

Cream the butter and sugar until white, beat in the egg yolks one at a time. Beat the egg whites until stiff, add them alternately with the sifted flour, keeping the mixture as light as possible. Fold in the chocolate. Transfer to a tin prepared according to the instructions above. Bake in a moderately slow oven (300°) for 1 hour. Leave to cool in the tin, turn out. Fill and ice the cake in the same way as for Sacher Torte 1.

ALMOND CAKE

10½ ozs. ground almonds
5 large or 6 small eggs
9 ozs. caster sugar
grated rind of 1 lemon

Beat the sugar and egg yolk together for half an hour. Whip the egg white stiff and add it to the yolks and sugar. Stir in the ground almonds. Bake in a well buttered and floured tin for 45 minutes in a moderate oven. Cool on a rack. When cold, top with whipped cream and chopped mixed nuts if liked.

CHOCOLATE CAKE

6 ozs. butter
9 ozs. caster sugar
6 eggs, separated
3 ozs. breadcrumbs
4 ozs. milk chocolate
5 ozs. bitter chocolate
5½ ozs. ground almonds
2 tbsp. water

Beat the butter and sugar until very light, about half an hour. Add the egg yolks and stir for a further half an hour. Add the breadcrumbs. Melt the chocolate in the water and add the mixture with the ground almonds. Beat the egg whites stiff and beat them into the mixture. Turn into a well buttered and floured cake tin and bake for 1 hour in a moderate oven. Cool on a cake rack, when cold spread with apricot jam and chocolate frosting (see p. 54).

SPITZBUBEN (Nut Biscuits)

8 ozs. butter
8 ozs. sugar
8 ozs. flour
4 ozs. ground almonds
1 tsp. vanilla
red currant jelly

Cream the butter and add the other ingredients. Mix thoroughly. Pat out with the hands onto a floured board. Cover the dough with greaseproof paper and roll it out until it is only ⅛ inch thick. Cut out biscuits with a small size biscuit cutter. Put them on a greased baking sheet and bake them for 35 minutes in a slow oven. Allow them to cool. Stick them together with a little red currant jelly.

LINZER TORTE

6 ozs. flour
½ teaspoon cinnamon
4 ozs. sugar
2 ozs. ground almonds
2 ozs. butter
2 egg yolks
juice and grated rind of 1 lemon
raspberry jam

Sift the flour, sugar and cinnamon. Cut in the butter, add the almonds, egg yolks and lemon peel. Work to a smooth paste with a little lemon juice. Roll on a floured board, leave in a cool place for an hour. Roll again and line a greased tart tin with pastry, fill with raspberry jam, cover with criss-cross strips of pastry. Sprinkle with sugar and bake in a moderately hot oven for 30 minutes.

APRICOT SAUCE

½ lb. apricots or 4 ozs. dried
   apricots
sugar to taste

Cook the apricots with the sugar and a little water until tender. Pass through a sieve.

CHOCOLATE FROSTING

1 egg yolk
1 lb. icing sugar
⅛ pint hot strong black coffee
3 ozs. butter

Cream the butter and egg yolk, add the sugar and cocoa gradually, alternately with the hot coffee, adding just enough of the coffee to make a spreading consistency.

PLAIN STREUSEL CAKE

FOR THE DOUGH:
¼ lb. flour
1 oz. fat
½ oz. yeast
¼ oz. sugar
¼ pint milk
¼ tsp. salt

FOR THE STREUSEL:
8 ozs. butter
8 ozs. sugar
4 ozs. flour
1½ tbsp. cinnamon

FOR THE GLAZE:
2 ozs. melted butter

Proceed exactly as in the recipe for yeast puff paste (see p. 49). When the dough has doubled its bulk, knock down lightly and pat into a round cake about ¼ inch high. Put this cake on a well buttered and floured roasting tin. Put in a warm place until the dough has nearly doubled its bulk. Brush the top with melted butter and cover evenly with the following streusel:

Cut these ingredients together until crumbly and well mixed. Bake in a moderate oven for 30 minutes to 45 minutes.

RICH STREUSEL CAKE

½ lb. flour
1 large egg beaten
5 ozs. butter
¼ pint milk
½ oz. yeast

¼ oz. sugar
salt

FILLING:
as for plain streusel cake

Follow the method for plain streusel cake.

RUM DOUGHNUTS

4 ozs. flour
2 ozs. butter
½ pint water
3 eggs
salt
2 tbsp. rum
1 tsp. powdered cinnamon
2 ozs. caster sugar
deep fat for frying

Boil water and butter, add flour and salt and beat over low heat until it forms a smooth ball of paste which will leave the sides of the pan clean. Chill slightly, add slightly beaten eggs. Beat these in gradually, making mixture smooth after each addition. When cool stir in the rum. Using an icing bag with a half-inch nozzle, force 3-inch strips of the paste into the hot fat. Fry golden on both sides keeping the lid on the pan during the cooking of the first side. Drain on soft paper, serve hot, dusted with sugar and cinnamon.

MOCHA COFFEE

1 pint strong coffee
1½ pints milk
4 ozs. cooking chocolate
4 ozs. sugar

Strain the coffee, mix it with 1 pint hot milk. Dissolve the chocolate and the sugar in ½ pint milk. Stir the chocolate mixture into the coffee. This can be beaten until frothy and served hot with whipped cream or used for flavouring.

VANILLA SUGAR

1 vanilla pod
2 lbs. caster sugar

Cut the vanilla pod into 4 or 5 pieces. Put it with the sugar into an airtight jar. Screw the lid down firmly. The same pod can be used for about 2 months, the jar being refilled with sugar as required.

ASPIC

1 pig's trotter, chopped to fit into
   a saucepan
1 knuckle of veal, chopped to fit
   into a saucepan
½ lb. ham or bacon rind
1 onion
3 carrots
3 stalks celery
bouquet garni (bunch of parsley,
   ½ bay leaf, sprig of thyme)
1 clove
8 peppercorns
salt
strip of lemon rind
5 pints water
2 egg whites and crushed eggshells

juice of 1 lemon
2 small glasses of white wine or
   cider

Wash and blanch the trotter and knuckle and add all the other ingredients except the egg whites, shells, lemon and 1 glass of the wine. Bring to the boil and simmer for 4—5 hours. Strain and leave it to set. Remove *all* the fat. Whisk up the egg whites and shells, the lemon juice and remaining glass of wine, together with some of the warm stock. Add this to the contents of the pan, bring to the boil. Cover and simmer for 20 minutes. Strain the stock through a damp cloth.

Aspic can be poured into jars and stored in the refrigerator; but it will need boiling every 2—3 days.

The Balkans

AUBERGINE SALAD (Greek)

4 large aubergines
2 cloves of garlic
2 tbsp. olive oil
½ lemon
3 tsp. chopped parsley
salt, pepper

Boil enough water to cover the aubergines and simmer till tender, about 15 minutes. Peel them and pound in a mortar with the garlic, salt and pepper. Add the oil drop by drop, stirring with a wooden spoon, then the lemon juice and parsley. Spread on bread or toast, or, as in Greece, serve in a bowl and each guest dips his bread in the purée.

ISTANBUL EGGS

olive oil
Turkish coffee
outside skins of onions
eggs

Take as many eggs as are required, cover with an equal quantity of olive oil, Turkish coffee and the brown skins of 2 large onions. Cover the pan and simmer very gently for 12 hours. The egg whites will be coffee coloured when done and the yolks brilliant saffron yellow and the eggs will taste like chestnuts.

COLD LEEK SALAD (Greek)

8 leeks
boiling water
1 tbsp. cornflour
1 tbsp. olive oil
juice of 1 lemon
salt, pepper

Wash the leeks thoroughly. Cut off the green part. Cover with salted boiling water, boil for 20 to 30 minutes till soft. Drain, keeping ½ pint of the liquid. Cool the liquid and mix with the cornflour. Pour over the leeks in the pan and cook gently till the sauce has thickened, stirring all the time. Add the lemon juice and oil, stir for another 3 minutes. Season with salt and pepper. Chill and serve very cold.

TARAMÁ (Dried Grey Mullet Eggs)

¼ lb. Taramá or
½ lb. smoked cods' roe
the juice of 1 or 2 lemons
¼ pint olive oil
black pepper

If smoked cods' roe is being used, scoop the roe out of skin. Put this or the mullet eggs into a mortar, pound it very slowly with the lemon juice and pepper, add the olive oil very slowly and pound till it forms a thick smooth paste. Serve very cold on bread and butter or hot toast.

AVGOLEMONO (Chicken, Egg and Lemon Soup)

2 pints chicken stock
2 ozs. rice
2 eggs
juice of 1 lemon
salt, pepper

Bring the stock to the boil, throw in the rice, simmer for 20 minutes. Beat the eggs with the lemon juice. Add 4 tbsp. of the very hot stock to the eggs and lemon, stirring all the time. Remove the chicken and rice soup from the heat, pour in the egg lemon mixture, season with salt and pepper. Serve at once.

Never boil again once the eggs have been added.

EGG AND CHEESE SOUP (Greek)

2 pints chicken stock
4 egg yolks
4 ozs. grated cheese

Heat the stock. Beat the eggs, add the cheese, stir over a very low heat in the soup pan until the cheese has melted. Slowly pour in the hot chicken stock, stirring all the time, heat again and serve.

GREEK FISH SOUP

2 lbs. any firm white fish
1 cod's head
1 onion chopped
1 leek chopped
4 sticks celery chopped
1 clove of garlic
1 sherry glass white wine
3 tbsp. tomato purée
2 ozs. flour
½ pint milk
2 tbsp. chopped parsley
1 tsp. chopped fennel
1 strip chopped lemon peel
salt, pepper

Put the fish, cod's head, onion, leek, garlic and celery in a large pan, season with salt and pepper, cover with cold water, bring to the boil and simmer until the fish is soft. Time cannot be accurately given as it depends on the size or sort of fish. When cooked lift the fish out carefully. Cool, remove any bones, and break into large pieces. Simmer the stock for 20 minutes longer, strain and return to the pan. Mix the flour with the milk to a smooth paste, add the tomato juice and white wine, mix well. Add this to the fish stock, simmer and stir till it thickens. Now carefully put the cooked fish back in the soup, add the herbs. Serve with toast, one large piece of fish in each plate.

OKROCHKA (Iced Fish, Meat and Cucumber Soup)

4 ozs. diced fresh cucumber
1 oz. diced pickled cucumber
3 ozs. diced cold cooked chicken
   or cold meat
4 ozs. cooked shrimps or crab
   or lobster
1 oz. chopped leek
1 tbsp. chopped fennel
2 tbsp. chopped parsley

1 bottle yoghourt
½ pint milk
2 hard boiled eggs, sliced
salt, pepper

Mix the yoghourt with the milk, add all the ingredients except the eggs. Chill for 3 hours. Serve very cold with an ice cube in each serving and slices of hard boiled egg floating on top. Sprinkle with more parsley if wished.

BOILED CHICKEN WITH LEMON

1 chicken
1 lemon
½ lb. carrots, chopped
½ lb. onions, chopped
3 sticks celery, chopped
½ lb. mushrooms, sliced
2 ozs. butter
¼ lb. blanched almonds
½ glass sherry
1 egg
½ pint chicken stock
4 tbsp. cream

Squeeze the lemon. Rub the bird with lemon juice and plenty of salt and pepper. Put ½ the lemon in the bird. Boil enough water to cover the bird, put it in with the vegetables. Simmer till tender. An old bird will take about 3 hours. When done put the chicken on the serving dish and keep warm. Now cook the mushrooms in butter till soft. Pour the chicken stock into a saucepan, add the cooked mushrooms, sherry, almonds, heat slowly. Beat the eggs and cream together in a basin, pour the very hot stock on gradually, stirring all the time till it thickens. Pour over the chicken and serve.

CHICKEN PILAF

8 ozs. cooked chicken
8 ozs. rice
1 medium chopped onion
2 ozs. butter
2 pints chicken stock
2 large peeled chopped tomatoes
2 ozs. chopped walnuts
salt, pepper
¼ tsp. chopped thyme

Cut the chicken meat into strips. Fry these with the onion in the butter, in a large pot until brown. Add salt, pepper, thyme. Add the rice, stir well for 5 minutes to prevent sticking. Pour in the stock, tomatoes and walnuts. Cover the pot with a clean cloth and simmer gently till all the liquid has been absorbed and the rice is soft. With a fork stir all together. Leave covered in a warm place for 20 minutes and serve.

ARMENIAN AUBERGINES

10 small aubergines
½ lb. lean minced lamb
2 medium finely chopped onions
2 green or red pimentos, seeded
    and finely chopped
3 chopped garlic cloves
2 tbsp. chopped parsley
2 ozs. pine kernels
2 ozs. white fresh breadcrumbs
salt, pepper
¼ pint olive oil

Do not peel the aubergines, cut off the stalks. Heat the oil in a large frying pan, cook the aubergines gently for 10 minutes. Lift them one by one out of the oil. Put the chopped onion and pimentos into the oil and cook very gently for 10 minutes. Meanwhile cut the aubergines in half, longways, and scoop out the flesh without breaking the skins. Add the onions, pimentos, garlic, parsley, pine kernels, breadcrumbs and the minced lamb to the aubergine flesh, season with salt and pepper and mix well. Fill the aubergine skins with the mixture, arrange in a shallow fireproof dish, pour over them the remaining oil in the frying pan and cook in a slow oven for 15 minutes.

SHERKASIYA (Boiled Chicken with Nuts)

1 chicken
8 ozs. rice
½ pint chicken stock
2 medium chopped onions
2 ozs. butter
1 red pepper or pimento, seeded
   and chopped
3 ozs. walnuts chopped
3 ozs. almonds chopped
   and blanched

3 ozs. hazel nuts chopped
salt

Boil the chicken and rice in the usual way. Carve the chicken in 4 pieces, arrange on the rice and keep warm. Fry the onions in butter till transparent. Pound to a paste, in a mortar, the nuts, red pepper and salt. Add these to the onions in the frying pan, mix well. Pour the chicken stock over; stir over a low heat. Pour this sauce over the chicken and rice.

AUBERGINES WITH PEPPERS AND TOMATOES

4 aubergines
4 peppers (pimentos)
2 bottles yoghourt
2 large peeled sliced tomatoes
6 tbsp. olive oil
salt, pepper

Cut the aubergines in slices, salt and pepper them. Take out the core and seeds of the pimentos, slice them, add salt and pepper. Salt and pepper the tomatoes.

Heat the oil, first fry the aubergines till soft, remove and drain and put on the warm serving dish. Now do the same to the peppers and put on top of the aubergines. Add the yoghourt. Fry the tomatoes in the oil and put on top. Serve hot.

AUBERGINES WITH YOGHOURT

2 aubergines
4 tbsp. olive oil
2 crushed cloves of garlic
2 bottles yoghourt
salt

Cut the unpeeled aubergines in ¼ inch thick slices, sprinkle the rounds well with salt, leave for 30 minutes. Wash and dry. Heat the oil and fry till soft. Remove and keep warm on the serving dish. Crush the garlic, stir into the yoghourt and pour over the aubergines. Serve hot.

BALKAN PASTRY TART WITH SPINACH FILLING

1 lb. chopped spinach
1 large chopped onion
2 ozs. butter or dripping
1 tbsp. boiling water
salt, pepper

Wash and chop the spinach finely. Heat the butter in a stewpan, add the finely chopped onion and cook till transparent, then add the spinach, boiling water, salt and pepper. Stir well, cover and cook quickly, stirring from time to time, for about 20 minutes. Drain well and fill a pastry case — as for Cheese and Mincemeat Tart.

DOLMAS (Stuffed Vine Leaves)

3 dozen vine leaves
2 cups cooked rice (2 ozs.
uncooked)
1 medium finely chopped onion
1½ tbsp. olive oil
juice of 3 lemons
salt, pepper
½ pint tomato juice

Throw the leaves into boiling salted water and boil for 3 minutes. Drain. Heat the oil and fry the onions till golden brown. Remove from heat. Mix the onions and the oil with the cooked rice, add salt and pepper. Put 1 tsp. of this mixture on the smooth side of each leaf, fold up into a little parcel, squeeze in the palm of the hand. Pack tightly the stuffed leaves in a shallow fireproof dish, sprinkle with the lemon juice, pour in the tomato juice. Put a plate on top to prevent them moving about and simmer for 30 minutes. Eat cold.

BALKAN STUFFED PIMENTOS

4 large pimentos
2 cups cooked rice
2 small finely chopped onions
1 clove of finely chopped garlic
2 tbsp. currants
4 ozs. finely chopped cooked beef,
lamb, etc.
salt, pepper

4 tbsp. olive oil
2 tbsp. tomato purée

Remove the stalks and slit the pimentos down one side, cut out the core and seeds. Wash thoroughly under the tap to remove every fiery seed. Mix all the ingredients except the oil and tomato purée and stuff the pimentos. Arrange them in a fireproof dish, pour over the oil and tomato purée, cover and bake in a moderate oven for 30 minutes.

SAVOURY RICE

8 ozs. rice
2 pints boiling meat stock
or water
½ lb. liver
4 ozs. dripping
3 medium finely chopped onions
1 large peeled chopped tomato
1 oz. sugar
1 tsp. black pepper
2 tsp. salt
2 ozs. currants
2 ozs. pine nuts

1 tsp. chopped parsley
1 tsp. chopped sage
½ tsp. mixed spice

Melt the fat in a large pot, chop the liver in ½ inch pieces, and fry for 3 minutes. Take out the liver, keep warm. Now cook the onion for 4 minutes till soft. Add the nuts and rice and fry for 5 minutes, stirring all the time. Add salt, pepper, currants, tomato, and pour on the boiling stock. Cook as for Plain Pilaf (see p. 64). Add the liver, sage and parsley. Cover and stand, warm, for 20 minutes.

PLAIN TURKISH OR GREEK PILAF

8 ozs. rice
2 pints meat stock
3 ozs. dripping or butter
1 tsp. salt
1 tsp. black pepper
2 ozs. melted butter

In a large pot melt the fat, add the rice and fry for 5 minutes. Boil the stock and when boiling pour onto the frying rice, add salt and pepper. Cover the pot with a clean cloth and then clamp on the lid. Cook on a very low heat until there is no liquid left, about 50 minutes. Remove from heat, still covered, and stand for 20 minutes. Pour the melted butter over and mix well before eating.

RISSOLES

1 lb. minced meat, mutton or beef
1 large chopped onion
2 ozs. grated cheese
1 tbsp. chopped dill
1 chopped clove of garlic
3 eggs
salt, pepper

3 ozs. flour
4 ozs. cooked rice

Mix the mince, onion, cheese, garlic, dill, salt and pepper well to make a stiff paste. Add two eggs, mix thoroughly for 2 minutes. Form into small cakes, about 2½ inches across. Dip in 1 beaten egg, roll in flour. Fry in deep fat till brown.

Serve hot with Lemon and Egg Sauce (see p. 69).

PINE NUT AND MEAT RISSOLES

1 lb. mince meat
3 medium boiled potatoes
1 egg
1 oz. pine nuts
1 oz. currants
½ tsp. chopped thyme
½ tsp. chopped dill
½ tsp. chopped parsley

salt, pepper
tomato sauce

Mash the potatoes with a fork, add the mince, stir in the beaten egg. Add the nuts, currants, herbs, salt and pepper. Mix together and form into little round flat cakes about 2 inches across. Fry in deep fat till brown. Serve with tomato sauce.

SPAGHETTI WITH YOGHOURT AND TOMATO PASTE

8 ozs. spaghetti
2½ pints boiling water
3 ozs. butter
2 bottles yoghourt
1 chopped clove of garlic
2 tbsp. tomato paste
salt, pepper

Throw the spaghetti into the boiling salted water, boil till soft, about 20 minutes. Drain and put under the hot tap. Melt the butter in the pan, add the garlic, tomato paste, and pepper, stir and cook gently for 3 minutes. Add the cooked spaghetti, pour over the yoghourt, stir well and serve.

SPAGHETTI WITH YOGHOURT

½ lb. spaghetti
4 pints boiling water
2 tsp. salt
4 ozs. butter
2 bottles yoghourt
2 tsp. paprika pepper
1 crushed clove of garlic

Put the salt into the water and bring to the boil. Throw in the spaghetti. Boil for 20 minutes. Strain and run under the hot tap for 2 minutes. Melt 2 ozs. butter, add the garlic and the cooked spaghetti, stir gently and cook for 3 minutes. Add the yoghourt. Melt 2 ozs. butter, add the paprika and pour over.

BALKAN STUFFED TOMATOES

12 large tomatoes
4 ozs. cooked rice
2 finely chopped medium onions
2 ozs. currants
2 chopped cloves of garlic
¼ pint olive oil
4 ozs. cold mutton or beef,
    chopped finely
salt, pepper

Cut the tops off the tomatoes, scoop out the flesh. Mix this flesh with the other ingredients, season with salt and pepper, and stuff the tomatoes. Pour the oil into a shallow fireproof dish or roasting pan and heat for 10 minutes in a moderate oven, arrange the tomatoes, cover the dish (greaseproof paper, if no lid available) and bake for a further 20 minutes.

TRAY BOREK (Flaky Pastry with Cheese and Minced Meat)

PASTRY:
8 ozs. plain flour
3 ozs. melted butter
2 eggs
2 tbsp. cold water

FILLING:
2 ozs. cream cheese
3 ozs. cooked minced meat
salt

Make a dough with the flour, a third of the butter, 1 egg and the water. Roll into 2 balls and leave for 15 minutes in a cold place.

Roll each piece very thinly, spread with melted butter. Do this again and again until all the butter is used up. Roll into 2 rounds as thinly as possible—paper thin is perfect. Grease a round shallow baking tin and spread one round on the bottom. Pinch it with the finger tips to crumple it. Mix the cheese, minced meat and salt well together, place on the pastry, put the other round on top, damp and seal the edges.

Beat the third egg, brush the top and bake in a moderate oven for 35 minutes.

LAMB PILAF

8 ozs. cooked lamb

Proceed as for Savoury Rice (see p. 63), but use cooked lamb cut in strips instead of liver.

BRAISED CALVES' BRAINS

2 calves' brains
4 ozs. butter
1 cup cooked pearl barley
4 ozs. cream cheese
½ tsp. chopped sweet basil
salt, pepper
blanched vine or cabbage leaves

Soak the brains in cold salted water for 1 hour. Clean and dry thoroughly. Melt the butter in a saucepan, add the brains, cook gently for 15 minutes. Chop in ½ inch squares, mix with the barley, cream cheese, basil, salt and pepper. Put a little of the mixture on each blanched leaf, roll up and peg with a matchstick or tie with cotton. Arrange in a shallow fireproof dish, pour over the butter in which the brains have been cooked and bake in a moderate oven for 20 minutes, with the dish covered. Remove pegs or threads and serve hot.

BOILED LAMB

2½ lbs. lamb
1½ pints cold water
½ lb. carrots, chopped
3 sticks of celery chopped
2 medium onions, chopped
2 ozs. dripping
2 ozs. flour
4 egg yolks
1 dsp. cold water
juice of two lemons
salt, pepper

Cut the meat in 1½ inch squares, add the carrots, celery, onions, salt, pepper and the water. Bring to the boil, remove the scum, and simmer for 1½ hours. Strain the dish. Put the meat and vegetables on the serving dish and keep warm. Melt the dripping, add the flour, stir for 2 minutes, pour over the hot meat liquid gradually, stir and cook for 5 minutes till it thickens. Mix the egg yolks, lemon juice and water, pour into the hot thick sauce, stir well, do *NOT* boil. Pour over the serving dish.

MOUSAKA

1 lb. minced beef or lamb or
  mutton
10 small onions, finely chopped
2 tbsp. olive oil
4 sliced unpeeled aubergines
¼ pint olive oil
1 bay leaf
salt, pepper
½ pint meat stock
1½ pints tomato sauce
¼ pint cream or milk
1 egg

Fry the sliced aubergines till soft in hot olive oil for 3 or 4 minutes. Fry the onions in butter till transparent. Take a medium roasting dish, pour a tbsp. of oil on the bottom. Arrange a layer of aubergines, then a layer of mince, sprinkle with salt and pepper and add the bay leaf, then a layer of onions. Fill the dish with layers like this. Pour over the stock and tomato sauce. Cover the dish and cook in a slow to moderate oven for 45 minutes, or until the liquid has reduced considerably. Beat the egg in the cream or milk, season with salt and pepper and pour over the dish. Cook for 30 minutes or so more in a very slow oven, to form a custard on top of the dish.

TURKISH LAMB STEW

2 lbs. lamb, cut in 3 inch pieces
1 lb. potatoes, peeled and
  quartered
3 large tomatoes, peeled and
  sliced
3 large onions sliced
1 tsp. chopped sage
1 tsp. chopped fennel

1 tsp. dill
2 bay leaves
1 green pimento seeded and sliced
2 cloves of garlic, chopped
salt, pepper
1½ pints meat stock

Put all the ingredients in a large pot. Simmer for 2½ hours.

PICTI (Pig's head brawn)

1 pig's head
4 bay leaves
20 peppercorns
the juice of 4 lemons
salt, pepper

Cover the pig's head with warm water, add the bay leaves, peppercorns, salt and pepper, bring to the boil and simmer for 5 hours. Let it cool in the water, skin and pick off all the good meat. Cut into 1 inch squares. Reduce the stock by half. Strain and add the lemon juice. Arrange the meat in a basin and pour over the stock. Leave it to set.

SKEWERED LAMB (Sis Kebabs)

2 lbs. leg of lamb
1 large onion, grated
2 large onions sliced
4 tbsp. olive oil
1 tsp. salt
¼ tsp. black pepper
1 bay leaf

Beat the lamb, rub with the salt, pepper and grated onion. Cut into 1½ inch squares. Put into a bowl and pour on the olive oil and the bay leaf, leave for 2 hours, turning occasionally. Slice the onions thinly and cut the bay leaf into pieces. Impale the meat on skewers with a slice of onion and bay leaf between each piece. Grill under a fierce heat, watch carefully and turn till all sides are cooked.

STIPHADO (Greek Beef Stew)

2 lbs. steak
6 tbsp. olive oil
3 lbs. small onions
4 cloves of garlic, chopped
½ pint thick tomato paste
¼ pint red wine
salt, pepper

Cut the steak in pieces, 3×2 inches. Rub well with salt and pepper. Heat the oil in a stew pan, fry the meat, onions and garlic till brown. Add the tomato purée, and the wine. Cover very tightly and simmer very slowly for 5 hours, till the sauce is thick, like jam.

YOGHOURT AND TOMATO STEW

2 lbs. leg of lamb
2 medium sliced carrots
cold water
salt, pepper
2 large peeled chopped tomatoes
1 pimento, chopped and seeded

2 bottles yoghourt
2 tsp. chopped mint

Cut the meat in 1½ inch squares. Add the carrots, salt and pepper, cover with ¾ pint cold water and stew very gently for 1 hour. Add the tomatoes and pimento and simmer for 1 hour. Stir in the yoghourt, add the mint and serve.

BROAD BEANS AND JERUSALEM ARTICHOKES

8 artichoke 'hearts'
2 lbs. broad beans
2 tbsp. olive oil
1 level tsp. cornflour
¼ pint bean stock
1 lemon
2 tsp. chopped parsley

Cook the beans and artichokes separately. Remove the hearts from the artichokes. Strain these, keeping ¼ pint of the bean water. Melt the oil in a thick saucepan large enough to hold the vegetables, stir in the cornflour, add the bean water, the juice of the lemon and the parsley. Add the vegetables and stir gently till they are coated with the oily sauce.

FRIED HARICOT BEANS

4 ozs. haricot beans
2 tsp. chopped parsley
1 medium onion
1 clove of garlic
1 level tsp. bicarbonate of soda
2 ozs. white bread
½ tsp. salt
dripping for frying

Soak the beans overnight. Put the soaked beans, onion, garlic, through the mincer. Soak the bread in water and squeeze dry. Pound the minced mixture, bread, parsley, salt and bicarbonate in a mortar till soft and well mixed. Leave for 2 hours. Flatten on a floured board, cut in 1 inch squares and fry till golden brown in deep fat.

POTATO KEPHTIDÉS

1 lb. cold boiled potatoes
½ oz. melted butter
2 finely chopped spring onions
2 large tomatoes, chopped and
  peeled
2 ozs. flour
salt, pepper
olive oil or dripping for frying

Sieve the potatoes and mix with all the ingredients. Knead slightly and roll ¾ inch thick and cut in rounds about 2½ inches across. Heat the oil or dripping till smoking hot, and fry quickly.

These potato rounds can be baked on a greased oven sheet in a hot oven till golden brown. They should be crisp outside but very soft inside.

BALKAN AUBERGINE PURÉE

2 aubergines
1 medium onion, finely chopped
1 tbsp. chopped parsley
2 tsp. salt
¼ tsp. black pepper
3 tbsp. olive oil
2 tsp. lemon juice

Take off the stems of the aubergines. Grill the aubergines just as they are under a moderate heat till the skins brown and split. Poke a skewer in to see if they are soft; when they are, remove and peel. Slice and pound in a mortar, with the onion, salt, pepper and parsley, till smooth. Add the oil drop by drop, stirring all the time with a wooden spoon. Add the lemon juice and mix well. Serve on brown bread or toast.

LEMON AND EGG SAUCE

2 eggs
2 tbsp. lemon juice
¼ pint vegetable stock
salt, pepper

Beat the eggs, add the lemon juice drop by drop, stirring all the time. Pour over the stock, cook in a double saucepan for 5 minutes, stirring continually, add salt and pepper.

LEMON AND MUSTARD SAUCE

2 tbsp. lemon juice
4 tbsp. olive oil
2 cloves of garlic crushed
1 tsp. dry mustard
½ tsp. salt
¼ tsp. black pepper
1 tsp. chopped parsley

Mix the lemon juice and oil together, add the garlic, mustard, salt and pepper. Stir thoroughly, sieve and add the parsley. Good with grilled fish.

THICK TOMATO PASTE

tomatoes
salt
olive oil

Take ½ tsp. salt for every lb. of tomatoes. Chop the tomatoes, add the salt, cook slowly till all reduced to a pulp. Sieve, then return to the pan and cook slowly to reduce the juice and make the pulp thick and fairly stiff. Spoon into bowls and put in the sun to dry out, or failing this a warm place or cool oven will do. Pour oil over each bowl to seal and store.

This paste is used in stews, rice and macaroni dishes in Greece.

AVGOLEMONO SAUCE

½ *pint chicken or meat stock*
3 *egg yolks*
juice of one lemon

Heat the stock. Beat the egg yolks with the lemon juice, pour on the very hot stock, stir till thick. You may make this in a double boiler, if preferred, taking care not to boil, or the eggs will curdle.

Serve with practically any meat dish, especially rissoles and boiled rice.

TOMATO SAUCE OR PURÉE (Greek)

2 *lbs. large ripe tomatoes, peeled*
  and chopped
4 *lumps sugar*
1 *chopped garlic clove*
1 *medium chopped onion*
2 *ozs. minced beef*
salt, pepper

½ *tsp. chopped basil or*
½ *tsp. chopped fennel*

Put all the ingredients in a large stew pan. Cover and simmer very slowly, stirring from time to time for 30 minutes. Sieve this pulp. If the sauce is too liquid, return to the pan and reduce till thick enough.

SKORDALIÁ (Greek Garlic Mayonnaise Sauce)

2 *egg yolks*
4 *ozs. ground almonds*
2 *ozs. white breadcrumbs*
6 *cloves of garlic*
1 *pint olive oil*
1 *tbsp. lemon juice*
2 *tsp. chopped parsley*
¼ *tsp. salt*
¼ *tsp. pepper*

Pound the garlic in a mortar, add the egg yolks, almonds, breadcrumbs, stir with a wooden spoon, add salt and pepper and the oil drop by drop as for mayonnaise sauce, stirring all the time, last stir in the lemon juice and parsley.

Serve with cold fish, cold meats, cooked cold vegetables, potatoes boiled in their skins; in fact, with what you fancy.

SEMOLINA MOULD

4 *ozs. semolina*
2 *ozs. butter*
4 *ozs. caster sugar*
¾ *pint water*
¾ *pint milk*
¼ *lb. blanched chopped almonds*

Heat the butter in a saucepan and add the semolina and almonds. Stir with a wooden spoon till brown. In another pan add the sugar to the milk and water and very slowly bring to the boil. Pour this slowly over the browned semolina and nuts, stirring all the time over a low heat. When thick, cover with a clean cloth, then put the lid on, keeping on the gentlest heat till all liquid has been absorbed. Pour into a wetted mould. Turn out when cold and set.

HONEY SOUFFLÉ

6 tbsp. honey
4 eggs
¼ pint cream

Separate the eggs, whip whites till stiff. Whip cream till thick.

Beat the egg yolks and honey. Put in double saucepan, stir until the mixture thickens: do *NOT* boil. Cool. Fold in the whites and the cream.

Serve very cold.

MAHALLEHI OR MILK PUDDING

1½ pints milk
¼ pint water
4 ozs. sugar
2 ozs. rice
1 oz. ground rice

Bring the milk and water to the boil, throw in the rice, simmer for 10 minutes. Mix the ground rice to a paste with enough milk from the pan. Add to the cooked rice and simmer for 10 minutes more. Eat cold, sprinkled with cinnamon or coarsely ground mixed nuts.

SIPHANIC HONEY TART

½ lb. milk cheese
2 tbsp. honey
1½ ozs. sugar
4 ozs. plain flour
4 ozs. butter
cold water
2 eggs
1 tsp. cinnamon

Make the pastry of the flour, sugar, butter and water. Roll out and cover a plate or shallow dish. Mix the cheese and honey together, add the beaten eggs and half the cinnamon. Spread on the pastry, sprinkle the rest of the cinnamon on top. Bake in a moderate oven for 35 minutes.

YOGHOURT

Serve as a sweet course with dried apricot, blackcurrant purée, or orange marmalade. Brown sugar is best with it. Any stewed fruit is good hot or cold.

PALACE BREAD (Esh es Seraya)

8 ozs. honey
1 lb. crustless stale bread
¼ lb. sugar
¼ lb. butter
Devonshire cream

Dice the bread. Mix with the honey, sugar and butter in a saucepan over a low heat, stirring into a moist paste. Press into a shallow round dish. When cold cut like a cake. Serve with the cream.

TURKISH COFFEE

coffee
sugar
water

Turkish coffee should be made in a Turkish coffee pot, one to each person. However, it can be made for 4 people in a lipped saucepan. The secret is that it must be strong, sweet and frothy.

For 4 people, take 4 tsp. coffee, 4 tsp. sugar and 4 coffee cups cold water. Bring to the boil, remove from the heat and stir. Bring to the boil, remove and stir. Repeat once more, three times in all. Serve immediately while still frothy. If more cups are wanted, boil a fresh brew.

TURKISH DELIGHT

2½ lbs. sugar
1¼ pints water
4 ozs. cornflour
   mixed to a paste in cold water
½ tsp. tartaric acid
1 tbsp. rose water
icing sugar
2 ozs. chopped pistachio nuts

Mix the tartaric acid, rose water and cornflour paste together. Boil the sugar and water together to a thick syrup. Stir the cornflour mixture into the syrup, add the nuts. Pour into a shallow tin, greased with almond oil. Cool, dust well with icing sugar. Ease from the tin, dust with more icing sugar, cut into squares. Roll each piece in icing sugar.

Belgium

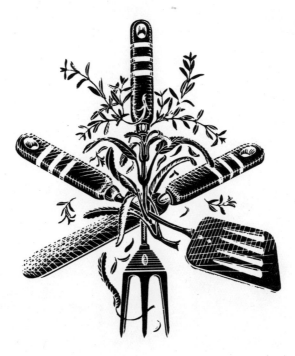

CHICKEN PÂTÉ

1 small roasting chicken
1 lb. bacon fat
½ lb. lean pork
2 glasses brandy
½ lb. streaky bacon rashers
1 bay leaf
thyme
salt
pepper

Carve the breast of an uncooked chicken into thin slices. Remove the rest of the meat from the bones and first mince it and then pound it until very smooth, with the bacon fat and the pork. Season with salt and pepper. Add the brandy. Line a shallow earthenware dish with bacon rashers, lay a bay-leaf and a sprig of thyme on them. Put half the minced meats into the dish, cover with the sliced breast, fill the dish with the rest of the minced meats. Arrange bacon rashers on the top. Cook very slowly in a *bain-marie* (see p. 425) for 2 hours. Put weights on top of the dish and leave to cool.

BRUSSELS SPROUT SOUP

2 lbs. Brussels sprouts
2 pints chicken stock
2 egg yolks
½ pint cream
1 oz. butter
½ oz. flour
salt
pepper
nutmeg

Cook the sprouts in boiling salted water. Drain. Toss them in the butter, stir the flour into the fat, gradually add the hot stock. Cook until sprouts are very soft. Pass through a sieve. Beat the eggs with the cream. Stir the soup into the egg mixture gradually. Season with salt, pepper and nutmeg. Reheat, but do not boil. Serve in warmed plates.

FRICADELLES (Minced Meat Balls)

2 lbs. minced pork
2 small onions, sliced
2 slices bread
1 gill milk
1 glass white wine
2 eggs
2 ozs. lard
1 pint stock
bouquet garni
4 medium potatoes

salt
pepper

Fry the onions lightly in 1 oz. lard. Mix with the meat. Add the bread, previously soaked in a little milk, the wine and the egg yolks. Season with salt and pepper. Beat well together and fold in the stiffly beaten egg whites. Shape into balls, roll in flour and fry in the lard until brown. Poach the meat balls in the stock with the *bouquet garni* and quartered potatoes for 30 minutes. Remove the bouquet. Serve the balls in their sauce, sprinkled with parsley.

EEL, STEWED WITH FRESH HERBS

2 lbs. eel
2 ozs. butter
2 glasses white wine
2 egg yolks
mint
salt
chervil
parsley
sorrel

juice of 2 lemons
pepper

Cut the eel into 2-inch lengths. Stew in the butter with the chopped herbs for 15 minutes. Add the wine and enough water to cover the fish. Simmer for 10 minutes. Put the fish in a shallow earthenware dish. Mix the egg yolks and lemon juice together, add gradually to the stock, season with salt and pepper. Pour over the fish. Leave to cool.

BRAISED CHICORY

8 heads chicory
8 slices cooked ham
2 ozs. grated Gruyère cheese
½ pint white sauce (see p. 205)
1 oz. butter
nutmeg
lemon juice

Simmer the chicory in salted water with a few drops of lemon juice for 25 minutes. Drain. Add half the grated cheese and a little nutmeg to the sauce. Wrap a slice of ham round each head of chicory. Lay them in a shallow fireproof dish. Pour the sauce over them. Sprinkle with the rest of the grated cheese. Dot with butter. Bake in a moderate oven for 20 minutes.

KIDNEYS WITH JUNIPER BERRIES

4 veal kidneys
4 ozs. butter
½ glass white wine
12 juniper berries
salt
pepper

Sprinkle the kidneys with salt and pepper. Brown on both sides in half the butter. Cover the pan and cook slowly for 2 minutes. Add the wine, the crushed juniper berries and the rest of the butter cut into small pieces. Continue to cook slowly until the kidneys are tender.

CHICKEN WATERZOIE

1 boiling fowl
2 onions stuck with cloves
3 sticks celery chopped
3 leeks sliced
1 carrot sliced
bouquet garni
1 lemon
½ bottle white wine
salt

pepper
parsley

Rub the chicken with lemon. Simmer with the vegetables in just enough water to cover. When the water boils add the *bouquet garni* and the white wine. Season with salt and pepper. Continue simmering for 1½ hours. Cut the chicken into pieces, remove the *bouquet garni*, serve the chicken in the stock with the vegetables, garnished with chopped parsley.

CELERIAC WITH CHEESE SAUCE

1 lb. celeriac, sliced
4 ozs. grated Parmesan cheese
2 ozs. butter
¼ pint stock
salt
pepper

Butter a shallow fireproof dish. Fill it with alternate layers of celeriac and grated cheese, and pour the stock over it. Season with salt and pepper. Dot with butter. Bake in a moderate oven for 45 minutes.

RABBIT WITH PRUNES

1 rabbit, jointed
½ bottle red wine
2 tbsp. vinegar
4 peppercorns
2 bay leaves
thyme
2 ozs. butter
2 ozs. flour
salt
pepper

1 lb. prunes
1 tbsp. red currant jelly

Marinate the rabbit in the wine and vinegar with the peppercorns and herbs for 24 hours. Drain and fry lightly on all sides in the butter. Stir in the flour. Add enough water to cover. Season with salt and pepper. Add the prunes, soaked if necessary, cover the pan and simmer for 1 hour or until tender. Stir in the red currant jelly before serving.

CARBONNADE OF BEEF

1½ lbs. stewing steak
4 onions sliced
2 ozs. dripping
½ pint beer
2 tbsp. concentrated tomato purée
½ pint stock
bouquet garni
flour
nutmeg
pepper
salt

Fry the onions lightly in the dripping. Cut the meat into pieces, dredge with seasoned flour. Transfer the onions to a casserole. Seal the meat on all sides in the dripping. Put it with the onions. Pour the beer into the frying pan, simmer uncovered until the beer is reduced by half. Add the stock and the tomato purée, mix well together and simmer for 1 minute. Pour the sauce over the meat, add a *bouquet garni* and a pinch of nutmeg. Cook, covered, in a moderate oven for 2 hours.

CHICORY SALAD

4 heads chicory
2 tbsp. olive oil
1 tbsp. lemon juice
½ tsp. sugar

½ tsp. salt
pepper

Shred the chicory. Mix the olive oil and lemon juice thoroughly. Stir in the sugar, salt and pepper. Pour over the chicory.

MEAT ROLLS

8 thin slices rump steak
8 rashers streaky bacon
1 oz. lard
1 large onion
½ pint stock
1 glass red wine
chopped parsley
salt
pepper

Lay a rasher of bacon on each slice of beef. Season with salt, pepper and chopped parsley. Roll and secure with cocktail sticks. Fry in the lard until all sides are lightly browned. Transfer to a shallow fireproof dish. Fry the chopped onion until golden. Add it to the meat. Add the stock and the wine, cover the dish and cook in a moderate oven for 1 hour. Season the sauce with salt and pepper and reduce it if necessary.

Canada

TOMATO SOUP WITH MACARONI

1 oz. butter
1 oz. flour
1 tbsp. chopped onion
1 tbsp. chopped green pepper
1 pint brown stock or consommé
4 medium tomatoes
2 tbsp. macaroni rings
salt
pepper
cayenne pepper
½ tsp. vinegar

1 tbsp. grated horseradish or
2 tbsp. horseradish sauce

Cook the chopped onion and pepper in the butter for 5 minutes. Add the flour and blend. Add the stock and tomatoes and simmer for 15 minutes. Pass through a sieve. Season highly with salt, pepper and cayenne pepper. Cook the macaroni separately. Just before serving add the horseradish, vinegar and cooked macaroni. If horseradish sauce is used instead of fresh horseradish, less vinegar will be necessary.

KIDNEY STEW

2 medium-sized beef kidneys
1 oz. flour
2 slices bacon
1 oz. butter or dripping
3 ozs. raw celery
2 medium onions
1 large tin tomatoes (1¾ pts.)
1 green pepper
1 tsp. salt
½ tsp. cayenne pepper
⅛ tsp. curry powder

Scald the kidneys and soak them in salted water for 2 to 3 hours. Change the water 2 or 3 times during that period. Remove the fat, split the kidneys lengthways and take out the white centre and the tubes. Sprinkle the kidneys with flour. Mince the bacon and sauté it slowly until it is light brown. Add the butter. Brown the kidney, chopped into ½ inch slices, in this fat together with the onions and celery chopped fine. Cover the pan and simmer for 10 minutes. Bring to the boil and add the tomatoes, salt, pepper and curry powder. Seed and shred the green pepper and add it. Cover the pan again and simmer the stew for about 15 minutes or until the pieces of green pepper are tender. Stir it often.
Serve with rice or boiled noodles.

LAMB CHOPS WITH TOMATO SAUCE

4 lamb chops
1 oz. butter or dripping
2 medium onions
¼ pint tomato juice or soup
¼ pint water
flour
salt
pepper

Trim the chops, sprinkle them with salt and pepper and roll in flour. Brown them lightly in the butter. Put them in a fireproof baking dish. Peel the onions, slice them finely and then sprinkle them over the chops. Mix the tomato juice with the water and heat to boiling point. Pour it over the chops. Cover the baking dish and bake in a slow oven for about 1½ hours. Serve with new potatoes or creamed potatoes sprinkled with parsley.

BAKED CANADIAN BACON

2 lbs. gammon
¼ pt. grapefruit or pineapple juice
½ tsp. dry mustard
4 ozs. brown sugar

Combine the brown sugar and the mustard and spread them over the gammon. Bake uncovered for 1 hour in a moderately hot oven and baste with the fruit juice. Add further fruit juice if necessary. Peel off the skin (if the gammon is cooked the skin will peel off easily). Serve with the juice from the pan as sauce.

BREAKFAST SAUSAGE

¼ lb. beef
¼ lb. pork or bacon
¼ lb. breadcrumbs
black pepper
salt
1 egg, beaten

Mince the meat finely. Beat in the breadcrumbs, egg and seasoning. Shape into a thick roll, tie in a very well greased and floured cloth and boil for 2½ hours. Remove from the cloth and drain. Serve hot or cold.

CHICKEN PUDDING

PASTE:
1 lb. flour
2 tsp. baking powder
8 ozs. lard or butter
water to mix

FILLING:
1 medium chicken
salt
1 tbsp. flour
black pepper
2 ozs. butter

Make a paste with the flour, baking powder, lard or butter, salt and water. Roll out rather thick and line a greased pudding basin with it, saving enough paste for the lid. With a sharp knife cut the chicken meat into small pieces. Sprinkle with flour, salt, and pepper. Fill the prepared pudding basin with the chicken, add a little water and butter. Cover with the paste lid, then with greased paper, then tie down with a cloth. Steam for 2 hours. Meanwhile simmer the chicken bones and the giblets with seasoning. Add the resulting stock as necessary to the pudding when it is served.

EGGS BENEDICT

4 crumpets
4 slices ham or gammon
hollandaise sauce
butter
4 eggs

Toast and butter the crumpets and set aside to keep hot. Fry the ham, and lay a slice on top of each crumpet. Poach the eggs and put one on top of each slice of ham. Cover the eggs with a hollandaise sauce (see p. 159).

EGG MOUSSE

6 hard-boiled eggs
¾ pint mayonnaise (see p. 159)
½ pint whipped cream
black pepper
2 lbs. skinned chopped tomatoes
1 tin crab or lobster
1¼ tbsp. granulated gelatine
salt

Dissolve the gelatine in a very little hot water and allow it to cool. Cut the hard-boiled eggs very fine and fold them into the mayonnaise. Fold in the gelatine, which should be cool but still liquid. Fold in the whipped cream and seasoning. Put the mixture into a ring mould and turn out when thoroughly set. The centre may be filled with a mixture of skinned and chopped tomatoes and tinned crab or lobster.

RAGOUT OF TOMATOES

4 large tomatoes (or ¾ pint tinned
   tomatoes)
1 oz. butter
1 green pepper
1 large onion
½ tsp. salt
1 tsp. paprika
2½ tsp. brown sugar
cream
½ oz. flour

Chop the onion. Seed and shred the pepper. Peel and slice the tomatoes. Melt the butter in a saucepan. Add all the chopped vegetables and cook until they are tender. This should take about 15 minutes. Add the salt, paprika and brown sugar. Strain the juice from the saucepan. Add to the juice enough cream or evaporated milk to make ½ pint liquid. Combine this carefully with the flour and cook, stirring constantly, until it is thick and well blended. Add the vegetables, bring just to the boil and serve. This makes a good vegetable dish or may be served as a supper dish spread on toast or accompanied by bacon.

TOMATO AND ORANGE SALAD

6 small tomatoes, peeled and
   quartered
2 oranges
tomato ketchup
juice of ½ orange

Peel the oranges and divide into segments. Cut segments into halves if the oranges are large. Mix with the tomatoes and tomato ketchup diluted with the orange juice.

BACKWOODS PIE

½ lb. short crust pastry
4 oz. brown sugar
12 oz. syrup (maple if possible)
¼ pint milk
2 ozs. butter
3 eggs separated
nutmeg to taste

Beat all together exept the egg whites. Beat the egg whites stiff and fold them into the mixture. Line a flan tin with good short crust. Pour the mixture in. Bake in a moderate oven for 30 to 40 minutes.

MENNONITE TOAST

8 slices bread one inch thick with crusts
3 eggs
1 pint milk
salt

Beat the eggs well and add the milk and salt. Dip the bread slices into the egg and milk, fry in deep hot fat till brown on both sides. Sprinkle with icing sugar and serve hot.

POPOVERS

2 eggs
1 tbsp. sugar
1 tbsp. melted butter
½ pint milk
4 ozs. flour
1 tsp. salt
2 tsp. baking powder

Separate the egg yolks from the whites. Beat the whites until stiff and put aside. Make a batter with the yolks and the other ingredients. Then add the egg whites. Grease castle pudding tins and fill each tin half full of the mixture. Bake for 10 minutes in a hot oven. Serve hot with butter and maple syrup. A piece of fruit added to each tin as the batter is poured in makes a simple variation.

BLUEBERRY PIE

short crust pastry made with 12 ozs. flour
1 lb. bilberries
1 oz. flour
4 ozs. sugar
1 oz. butter

Line a greased flan tin with half of the pastry. Dredge the washed fruit with the flour. Pour it onto the pastry, sprinkle with the sugar and dot with butter. Cover with the rest of the pastry. Make a hole for the steam to escape. Bake in a hot oven for 25 to 30 minutes.

CREAM FINGERS

1 lb. flour
½ pint cream
1 oz. sugar
⅛ tsp. salt
½ oz. yeast
1 tbsp. sugar ⎫ *for glaze*
2 tbsp. milk ⎭

Cream the yeast with a teaspoonful of sugar. Scald the cream, add sugar and salt, cool to lukewarm, add the yeast mixture. Meanwhile warm the flour and make a well in the centre. When the yeast mixture is ready, add to the flour with the hand, and knead well. Stand the dough in a warm place, covered with a cloth, until it has doubled its bulk. Knock down the dough and roll it out to a quarter of an inch thickness. Cut into strips, 4½ in. long by 1 in. wide, rounded at the corners. Cover and stand in a warm place again. When light, brush over with the milk and sugar. Bake for 20 to 30 minutes in a moderate oven. Cool on a rack, dust with icing sugar when cold.

BROWNIES

8 ozs. sugar
4 ozs. flour
4 ozs. plain chocolate
8 ozs. butter
4 eggs
¼ tsp. salt
¼ lb. ground or chopped nuts

Melt the butter and chocolate and set aside to cool. Beat the eggs and sugar until thoroughly light and creamy. Fold in the chocolate and butter mixture, add the flour sifted with a pinch of salt and beat until smooth. Fold in the ground nuts. Bake in a 9 × 13 inch tin lined with heavy waxed paper or tinfoil in a slow oven for about 45 minutes. Cut into fingers when cold. Brownies should be crisp outside and sticky inside.

PEANUT WAFERS

½ lb. chopped peanuts
2 eggs (well beaten)
4 ozs. white sugar
½ tsp. salt
1 oz. melted butter
1 tbsp. milk
8 ozs. flour

Mix all the ingredients together, adding more flour if necessary. Roll out the dough ½ inch thick. Cut into strips 4 × 1 inches and cook on a greased baking sheet for 20 minutes in a moderate oven.

CHOCOLATE CAKE

4 ozs. butter
4 ozs. sugar
2 eggs
½ pint milk
8 ozs. flour
½ tsp. salt
2 tsp. baking powder
3 ozs. plain chocolate or cocoa
1 tsp. vanilla

Cream the butter and sugar, adding sugar gradually. Melt the chocolate over water, add this. Sift together the dry ingredients, and add alternately with liquid and egg yolks to first mixture. Fold in the stiffly beaten egg whites. If a finer grained cake is wanted, the eggs should be added whole and unbeaten. Bake this cake in a shallow pan or 2 9-inch layer-cake pans in a moderate oven for about 30 minutes. Ice with chocolate frosting (see p. 89).

CANADIAN GINGERBREAD

6 ozs. plain flour
¼ pint sour milk
4 ozs. sugar
6 ozs. black treacle (molasses)
3 ozs. butter
1 egg
1 tsp. bicarbonate of soda

Sift the flour. Add all the other ingredients including the unbeaten egg, mix thoroughly. Pour the mixture into a shallow well-greased cake tin, and bake in a moderate oven for 20 minutes.

MANITOU BLACK CAKE

3 ozs. chocolate
yolk of one egg
¾ pint milk
1 oz. butter
8 ozs. sugar
1 tsp. vanilla
½ tsp. bicarbonate of soda
2 tsp. baking powder
6 ozs. flour
salt

Melt the chocolate over hot water, and gradually add it to the well-beaten yolk of egg beaten up with ½ pint of milk. Cook until it thickens slightly. Cream the butter and sugar, add the chocolate mixture and stir well. Add the mixed and sifted dry ingredients alternately with the remaining quarter pint of milk and the vanilla. Mix well. The batter should be quite thin. Pour into a greased tin and bake in a moderately hot oven for 45 to 60 minutes.

CANADIAN BUNS

½ oz. yeast
8 ozs. plain flour
2 eggs
1 tbsp. sugar
4 ozs. soft butter
4 ozs. shredded coconut
water
1 tsp. salt

Dissolve the yeast in the water and stir this into the flour. Set it to rise over night. In the morning add the eggs, coconut, sugar and salt. Beat all together with a wooden spoon; if necessary, add extra flour to make a stiff dough. Knead well for 15 minutes, then stand in a warm place and leave it to rise until it has doubled its bulk. With the hands, work in the soft butter. Allow it to rise again, and when light shape it into buns. Put the buns close together in a baking pan, and set to rise once more. When light, bake in a moderate oven till brown, about 20 minutes. While still hot, brush the tops with sugar dissolved in milk.

JOHNNY CAKE (1)

1½ pints buttermilk
8 ozs. sugar
2 eggs
1 tsp. salt
2 small tsp. bicarbonate of soda
1 lb. ground maize or polenta meal
6 ozs. flour
1 tsp. cream of tartar
3 tbsp. lard

Mix the buttermilk with the soda, sugar, eggs and salt. Add the ground maize. Sift the cream of tartar with the flour and add to the mixture. Heat 3 tbsp. of lard and pour them boiling hot over the mixture. Beat well. Put into a greased tin and bake in a hot oven. Johnny Cake should always be eaten hot and served with butter.

JOHNNY CAKE (2) (with molasses)

½ pint sour milk
6 ozs. black treacle (molasses)
pinch of salt
3 ozs. lard
6 ozs. ground maize or polenta meal
1 tsp. bicarbonate of soda

Mix the sour milk with the soda. Then add the black treacle, sugar, eggs and salt. Add the ground maize and flour. Melt the lard and pour it hot into the mixture. Beat well. Put the mixture into a greased cake tin and bake in a hot oven until it is a delicate brown. Johnny Cake should always be eaten hot and served with butter.

RAILROAD CAKE

1 lb. flour
6 ozs. butter and lard mixed
6 ozs. sugar
2 eggs
½ pint milk
1 tsp. bicarbonate of soda
1 tsp. cream of tartar

1 oz. caraway seeds
2 ozs. candied peel

Rub the fat into the flour, add all the other ingredients. Mix well, pour into a well-greased cake tin and bake in a hot oven for 1 hour.

ALMOND MERINGUES

2 egg whites
4 ozs. caster sugar
vanilla
nut brittle (see p. 88)
1 oz. shredded almonds

Beat the egg whites until very stiff, gradually fold in 3 ozs. sugar, add the pounded nut brittle and vanilla to taste, fold in the remaining sugar. Arrange spoonfuls on a baking tray covered with waxed paper. Sprinkle the shredded almonds onto it and sift sugar over them. Bake for 25 minutes in a moderately slow oven.

MEAT PASTE FOR SANDWICHES

½ pint milk or cream
1 oz. flour
2 egg yolks
1 oz. butter
½ tsp. salt
½ tsp. made mustard
black and paprika pepper to taste
½ cup lemon juice
1 lb. meat, veal tongue, chicken or pork very finely minced

One of the following very finely chopped: olives, watercress, parsley, lettuce, green pepper

Beat the egg yolks well then mix with the milk, flour, butter and seasonings. Cook in a double boiler until thick, stirring constantly to prevent lumps. When cool, beat in the lemon juice, minced meat and chopped olives, watercress etc.

CHICKEN SANDWICH FILLING (1)

½ lb. cold roast chicken
3 stuffed olives
1 tbsp. mustard pickle
1 tbsp. capers
¼ pint mayonnaise (see p. 159)

Mince the above ingredients together and pound to form a paste.

CHICKEN SANDWICH FILLING (2)

1 lb. cold roast chicken
¼ lb. blanched almonds
¼ pint thick cream
1 tsp. lemon juice
black pepper
salt

Mince the chicken and almonds finely, blend them with the cream, lemon juice and seasoning.

NASTURTIUM SANDWICHES

brown bread
nasturtium petals
mayonnaise (see p. 159)
butter

Wash the nasturtium petals and lay them in iced water for 5 minutes. Spread the thinly sliced bread with mayonnaise and a thick layer of the prepared petals. Cover with a thin slice of buttered bread. Serve at once with a few fresh blossoms strewn over the plate.

CHEESE SANDWICH FILLING

½ lb. cream cheese
½ tbsp. paprika
salt
black pepper

¼ lb. chopped walnuts
chopped watercress to garnish

Blend the above ingredients thoroughly, add cream if the paste is too dry.

NUT BRITTLE

1 lb. sugar
8 ozs. roasted Jordan almonds
pinch of salt

Melt sugar in a heavy pan, stirring constantly until it is a thin syrup. Add the nuts and salt. Stir until well coated, and spread thinly on an oiled pan. When it is cold it may be broken up.

CHOCOLATE FROSTING

8 ozs. sugar
5 tbsp. water
⅛ tsp. cream of tartar
1 egg white beaten stiff
1½ ozs. chocolate grated finely
few drops oil of peppermint

Put sugar, chocolate, water, cream of tartar or lemon juice in a saucepan, stir until sugar is dissolved and bring to boiling point. Beat the egg white and add 3 tbsp. of the syrup to it, beating constantly after adding each spoonful. Add the oil of peppermint to the syrup in the saucepan. Boil this syrup without stirring until it spins to a long thread. Pour it slowly over the egg white, beating constantly, until thick enough to stand up in peaks. Spread quickly on the cake before it becomes too stiff.

MOCK MAPLE SYRUP

1½ lbs. small potatoes
sugar
½ tsp. vanilla

Wash the potatoes thoroughly without breaking the skins. Cover with water and boil until done, being careful that the potatoes do not break. Drain off the water and measure it, then take half a pint of sugar to each half pint of the liquid. Boil this mixture for 15 minutes without a lid on the pan. Season with vanilla.

PUMPKIN SYRUP

Take a good sized pumpkin which is thoroughly ripe, wash well and remove most of the seeds and the soft centre. Cut the flesh with skin on into small cubes, and nearly cover them with water. Boil until soft, then put into a jelly bag. When all the juice has drained, put it in a pan and boil for 30 minutes; then measure the juice and put a cup of sugar to each cup of juice and boil again until thick. Serve with toast or pancakes.

China & Japan

CHINESE EGG AND PEA SOUP

½ lb. lean raw pork or
½ lb. raw chicken
½ lb. raw green peas
2 eggs
¼ tsp. Ve-Tsin (flavouring)
1 tsp. brandy or dry sherry
1 small knob green ginger
2½ pints cold water
salt

Slice the pork or chicken into thin strips, add the cold water, the peas and ginger. Bring to the boil and simmer for 30 minutes. Beat the eggs, add the brandy or sherry and the Ve-Tsin. Pour this into the soup, bring once more to the boil and serve, having added salt to taste.

CHINESE LOBSTER WITH NOODLES AND VEGETABLES

6 ozs. lobster meat
8 ozs. noodle pastry cut in strips
    ¼ × 1½ inches
1 8-oz. tin bean sprouts
3 ozs. tinned bamboo shoots
1 oz. mushrooms
6 ozs. onions
1 tsp. cornflour
water
salt
pepper
sweet sour sauce
deep fat or oil for frying

Soak the mushrooms in hot water for 15 minutes. Drain and cut in very thin slices. Slice the onions thinly, also the bamboo shoots and lobster meat. Bring the fat or oil to boiling point, plunge the noodles in and cook for 5 or 6 seconds, till crisp. Remove, drain well and place on hot serving dish and keep warm. Heat a little oil in a large frying pan, cook the lobster, onions, bamboo, beans and mushrooms all together for 1 minute, season with salt and pepper. Stir well. Mix the cornflour to a smooth paste in cold water, add two more tbsp. water and pour over the lobster, etc. Cook for 1 minute. Add 1 tsp. sweet sour sauce. Pour over the noodles, and serve with sweet sour sauce.

CHINESE BEAN AND MEAT ROLLS

8 ozs. minced pork or veal
2 ozs. butter
1 tin bean sprouts
1 dsp. soy sauce
1 clove of garlic, chopped
8 ozs. plain flour
¾ pint water
salt, pepper
fat for deep frying

Heat the butter in a frying pan, add the meat, bean sprouts and garlic, fry all together for 5 minutes. Stir in the soy sauce and salt to taste. Leave to cool. Mix the flour and water to a smooth batter, season with salt and pepper.

Heat a 6 inch frying pan, rub with butter, pour in 1 tablespoon of the batter, spread over the pan and cook quickly for a few seconds till set. Turn out on a board. Repeat until all the batter is used up, about 12 times. Put about a dessertspoon of the meat mixture on each round, damp the edges with water and seal tightly, making a neat little 'parcel'. Drop into smoking fat until golden brown and crisp.

SWEET AND SOUR SLICED FISH

½ lb. fillet of cod
1 egg
2 ozs. cornflour
1 tbsp. lard
sweet sour sauce

Slice the fish into small thin slices. Beat the egg, dip in the fish slices and roll in cornflour. Heat the oil, till smoking, add the slices and cook for 3 minutes, till brown on all sides. Lower the heat. Pour over sweet sour sauce and cook for 2 minutes more, stirring gently all the time.

CHINESE EGGS

6 eggs
1 oz. butter
3 tbsp. soy sauce

Boil the eggs for 7 minutes, put in cold water and shell them. Melt the butter in a saucepan, add the soy sauce and the eggs. Cook gently for 5 minutes, basting and turning all the time until the eggs are dark brown. Serve cold, cut in slices.

PRAWN OR CRAB CHINESE OMELETTE

3 eggs
½ pint milk
¼ tsp. salt
4 ozs. crab meat or
4 ozs. shelled prawns
2 ozs. mushrooms
2 ozs. finely chopped spring
   onions or onions
¼ tsp. Ve-Tsin (flavouring)
2 tsp. lard
pepper

Peel the mushrooms and plunge into boiling water. Leave for 3 minutes. Remove and slice thinly. Beat the eggs, milk and salt together. Heat the oil in a large thick frying pan, add the prawns or crab meat and the sliced mushrooms. Fry lightly for 3 minutes. Add the onions and a pinch of pepper to the egg mixture. Make the pan containing the prawns, etc., very hot, pour in the egg mixture, and cook quickly for 2 or 3 minutes, lifting the edges of the omelette to let any uncooked mixture run under on to the hot pan. Fold over and serve with Chinese brown omelette sauce poured over (see p. 97).

CHINESE BOILED CHICKEN

1 medium boiling fowl
boiling water
½ wine glass of sherry
4 tsp. salt
1 tsp. soy sauce
½ lb. spring onions

Have the bird plucked, cleaned and trussed. Place in large saucepan, add the sherry, salt, soy sauce, and spring onions. Pour over enough boiling water to cover the bird. Cover the pan and simmer for 1½ hours, or until the bird is cooked. Leave the chicken in the soup till cold. Remove and carve it, arrange in a shallow dish. Put the carcase, etc., back in the saucepan, pour off half the liquid and simmer for 45 minutes. Strain and pour over the carved meat. Chill thoroughly to set the jelly if served cold.

CHINESE FRIED SAVOURY RICE

6 cups cold cooked rice (12 ozs. uncooked)
1 egg
½ lb. pork
4 ozs. shelled prawns
4 tbsp. chopped spring onions or onions
1 dsp. soya sauce ⎱ mixed
1 dsp. water ⎰
1 dsp. oyster sauce
1 dsp. minced cooked ham
2 tbsp. lard
½ tsp. salt

Shred the pork into fine strips, about 1 × ⅛ inch. Heat the fat in a large thick bottomed pan, add the shredded pork, rice and salt. Fry gently for 10 minutes, stirring with a fork. Add the prawns, mix well. Make a hole in the mixture and drop in the egg, unbeaten, cook for a few minutes in the heat of the rice, till set. Break up with the fork and stir through the mixture. Add the oyster sauce, the soya and water mixture, and the onions. Sprinkle the ham over the dish and serve hot.

CHICKEN CHOP SUEY ('Chop Suey' means mixture)

the breast of a cooked chicken
1 pint chicken stock
¼ lb. spring onions
1 celery stick
2 slices bamboo shoot
2 Jerusalem artichokes
¼ lb. heart of white cabbage
6 water chestnuts
2 ozs. mushrooms
2 ozs. bean sprouts
1 dsp. soy sauce
3 tbsp. oil
2 ozs. butter
1 oz. cornflour

Slice all the vegetables except of course the bean sprouts, in thin small strips, also the chicken meat. Mix the cornflour and butter well together. Heat the oil, add all the vegetables, fry quickly stirring all the time for 3 minutes. Add the stock and the soy sauce, bring to the boil and boil for 3 minutes. Add the cornflour mixture, stir well, then the chicken meat. Cook for 3 minutes longer. Serve hot. As the secret of this dish is the taste of each separate vegetable they *must* be very finely sliced, and cooked quickly.

FRIED KOW TZE WITH SWEET SOUR SAUCE

1½ lbs. finely minced pork
4 ozs. shelled shrimps, crab meat or shredded lobster
2 eggs
½ tsp. Ve-Tsin flavouring
2 tsp. soy sauce
2 tsp. dry sherry, or brandy
1 tsp. oil
2 tsp. cornflour
4 tbsp. finely chopped spring onions

salt, pepper
Dimsum pastry (see p. 97) cut in four 4-inch squares
sweet sour sauce

Mix all the ingredients — except of course the pastry — well together with one egg. Put a quarter of the mixture on each piece of pastry, fold in two, brush the edges with beaten egg, seal tightly. Fry each packet in very hot deep oil or lard till crisp and brown.

Serve with sweet sour sauce (see p. 96).

CHINESE PORK AND CELERY

8 ozs. pork
1 tsp. cornflour
1 tbsp. water
1 tbsp. soy sauce
3 ozs. mushrooms, sliced
2 hearts of celery, chopped finely

2 ozs. butter
¼ tsp. salt

Prepare and cook exactly as for the 'Chinese Veal with Cucumber' recipe.

CHINESE PORK WITH MUSHROOMS

2 lbs. pork
½ pint water
½ lb. mushrooms, sliced
1 tbsp. soy sauce
1 tsp. sugar
1 tsp. sherry
½ tsp. salt

Cut the pork meat into 1 inch cubes. Cover with the cold water, bring to the boil, and simmer for 30 minutes. Strain, keeping the stock. Add the soy sauce to the meat in the saucepan, mix well; now add the sugar, sherry, mushrooms and salt, pour on the stock, mix well. Cover the pan and cook very slowly for 40 minutes. Eat hot, or cold—when it will be a thick jelly.

CHINESE VEAL, LAMB, OR PORK WITH CUCUMBER

8 ozs. meat
1 tsp. cornflour
1 tbsp. water
1 tbsp. soy sauce
3 ozs. mushrooms, sliced
1 peeled cucumber cut in cubes
2 ozs. butter
¼ tsp. salt

Mix the cornflour with the water to make a smooth paste. Slice the veal into strips, about ¼ × 2 inches. Mix well in the paste. Heat the butter in a frying pan, add the sliced mushrooms and cucumber cubes, fry for 3 minutes, stirring and turning all the time; now add the veal strips, fry gently for a further 10 minutes. Pour on the soy sauce, stir all together, lower the heat and cook gently for 5 minutes more.

CHINESE SWEET SOUR SAUCE

1 tsp. oil, lard or butter
2 tbsp. finely chopped mixed
  pickles
½ tsp. minced green ginger
1 tsp. vinegar
3 tsp. sugar
1 tsp. tomato sauce
2 tsp. cornflour
1 tsp. brandy or sherry
¼ pint cold water

Heat the fat in a saucepan, fry the pickles and ginger for two minutes. Mix the cornflour with the sugar, vinegar, tomato sauce, brandy or sherry to make a smooth paste, pour in the water, mix well. Pour over the pickle mixture and cook fairly briskly for 5 minutes, till the sauce thickens.

CHINESE BROWN OMELETTE SAUCE

¼ *pint cold water*
1 *tsp. soy sauce*
2 *tsp. oyster sauce*
1 *tsp. cornflour*

Mix the cornflour with the sauces to a smooth paste in a small saucepan, add the water gradually, bring to the boil and cook gently for 5 minutes, stirring all the time.

DIMSUM PASTRY

8 *ozs. plain flour*
1 *egg*
water
¼ *tsp. salt*

Mix the flour and salt with the beaten egg and add enough cold water to make an elastic, but not sticky dough. Roll out on a floured board as thinly as possible. Leave to dry out for 1 hour before cutting into whatever sizes required.

CHINESE NOODLE PASTRY

8 *ozs. plain flour*
½ *tsp. salt*
2 *eggs*
2 *egg yolks*
water

Beat the 2 whole eggs, mix with salt and flour, then add the 2 egg yolks, knead lightly to a smooth elastic dough, adding a little water if necessary. Turn out on to a floured board, and roll out very thinly, like paper, twice. Leave for 2 hours, before cutting into squares or strips for whatever dish required.

CHINESE BOILED RICE

1 *lb. rice*
cold water
2 *tsp. salt*

Wash the rice in 4 changes of cold water till the last water is clear. Put the rice and salt in a large saucepan, pour over cold water to cover, plus 1 inch above the level of the rice, whatever the quantity. Cover with a tight lid. Bring rapidly to the boil, lower the heat, simmer till the water has evaporated, lower the heat again to almost nothing and leave the rice to cook and swell in its steam for 20 minutes. Keep the lid on all the time. The best way to test the cooking processes is either to put your ear close to the pan and listen for any sounds of bubbling, or to hold the saucepan lid and feel for any vibration. If there is none, all the water will have evaporated and the rice is ready for the 20 minutes swelling process. If this process is successful each rice grain will be separate.

JAPANESE BOILED WATERCRESS

4 or 6 bundles watercress
2 tsp. 'shoyu' sauce

Chop the watercress coarsely, put in a saucepan, bring to the boil and simmer in its own juice till tender, about 10 minutes. Drain well, stir in the sauce and serve as a green vegetable.

JAPANESE PICKLED LETTUCE, CUCUMBER AND TURNIPS

2 lettuce hearts
1 cucumber
1 turnip
1 tsp. salt

Cut the lettuces in half, peel the cucumbers and turnip, and slice thinly lengthwise. Sprinkle with the salt and leave for 2 days. This is eaten as a separate vegetable course with rice.

JAPANESE SAVOURY RICE

¾ lb. boiled rice (see 'Chinese Boiled Rice', p. 97)
½ lb. cooked chicken
¼ lb. tinned bamboo shoots
¼ lb. mushrooms
2 ozs. butter or oil
½ pint chicken stock
¼ tsp. sugar
½ tbsp. 'shoyu' (soya bean) sauce

Chop the chicken in $\frac{1}{2}$ inch squares. Slice the mushrooms and bamboo shoots thinly and fry in butter for 2 minutes. Add the chicken, mushrooms and bamboo shoots to the rice, sprinkle in the sugar, add the stock, stir gently. Cover the pan and simmer very gently for 30 minutes till the stock is absorbed. Add the 'shoyu' sauce, mix well and serve.

JAPANESE BLACK NOODLES (Soya Bean)

1 lb. soya bean flour
1 egg yolk
1 tsp. salt
cold water

Mix the flour, egg, salt with enough cold water to make a thick paste. Leave for 30 minutes. Roll out paper thin and fold in a roll about 14 inches long. Cut in $\frac{1}{8}$ inch strips or slices. Throw into boiling water, boil for 5 minutes. Drain and serve.

Creole Cookery

CREOLE LES ACHARDS (Hors d'Œuvre)

3 tsp. salt to 1 pt. water
1 medium finely chopped onion
1 pinch saffron
Raw vegetables, cut in dice, carrots, French beans, onions,
  cauliflover, cabbage, peas,
  coconut, pimentos, etc.

¼ tsp. salt
¼ tsp. pepper   } to ¼ pt. olive oil
¼ tsp. chilli pepper

Soak each vegetable separately in salted water for 24 hours. Drain and place in mounds in a shallow dish. Add the onion, saffron, salt and peppers to the oil and bring to the boil. Pour over the raw vegetables and leave for 48 hours.

CREOLE AUBERGINE (Hors d'Œuvre)

2 aubergines
2 chilli peppers
2 tsp. lemon juice
¼ tsp. salt
1 tbsp. olive oil
toast, bread or plain biscuits

Peel the aubergines and chop finely. Heat the oil and fry the aubergines gently, till soft. Put in a mortar with the other ingredients and pound to a smooth paste. Pile on small pieces of toast, bread or small biscuits.

CREOLE POTATO SALAD (Hors d'Œuvre)

1 lb. potatoes
½ pint shrimps
3 hard boiled eggs, sliced
6 tbsp. French dressing
2 chilli peppers, sliced or
  1 pimento

Boil the potatoes and slice them, mix with the prawns and while still warm pour over the dressing, garnish with the hard boiled egg and chillies.

PIMENTADE (Creole Boiled Fish)

1½ lbs. thick white fish, cod, hake,
  turbot, haddock, etc., cut in
  thick slices
juice of 1 lemon
1 lemon cut in slices
1 sprig parsley
1 sprig thyme
¼ tsp. cinnamon
3 chilli peppers, chopped

3 cloves
¼ tsp. salt
2 pints water

Rub the fish slices all over with the lemon juice and leave for 1 hour. Boil all the other ingredients together and simmer for 30 minutes. Add the fish and cook gently for 20 minutes or till soft.

ROUGAIL DE CREVETTES (Creole Prawn Hors d'Œuvre)

4 ozs. shelled prawns
2 chilli peppers
2 tsp. lemon juice
1 dsp. olive oil
¼ tsp. salt
bread or toast or biscuits

Chop the chillies finely and pound in a mortar with the prawns, oil, lemon juice and salt to a smooth paste. Pile on small pieces of bread, toast or biscuits.

CREOLE LES ACRATS

fat or oil for deep frying
1 lb. salt cod, or smoked haddock, or smoked cod
2 chilli peppers, chopped
1 clove of garlic, chopped pinch of salt and pepper
4 ozs. flour
1 egg
¼ pint milk or water

Salt cod is difficult to buy in England, so smoked fish is used instead. Soak the fish in cold water for 12 hours. Take off the fish from the bones and skin, and pound the fish in a mortar with the garlic, chillies and seasoning. Make a batter of the flour, egg and liquid, mix well with the pounded fish. Drop a dsp. of this mixture in to the boiling fat and fry to a golden brown. Drain and serve.

CREOLE CHICKEN

1 chicken cut in joints
2 medium onions, sliced
3 ozs. butter
a pinch of saffron
1 tbsp. curry powder
1 chopped chilli pepper
¼ tsp. salt
cold water
4 tbsp. coconut milk
boiled rice

Melt the butter in a casserole, fry the chicken joints and the onions till brown, add the curry powder, saffron, chilli and salt, add 2 tbsp. coconut milk. Cover the casserole and simmer very gently till tender, turning occasionally. Add the rest of the coconut milk and stir well. Serve with cooked rice.

CREOLE DAUBE DE PORC

2 lbs. pork fillet
3 ozs. butter or lard
1 large finely sliced onion
1 tbsp. water
2 large peeled aubergines, sliced
salt, pepper

Melt the fat in a casserole, add the pork and onion and brown well on all sides. Add salt and pepper to taste, and the water. Cover the casserole tightly and simmer gently, turning the meat occasionally for 50 minutes. Add the aubergines, season with salt and pepper, put the lid back and cook gently for 20 minutes longer.

CREOLE CHICKEN WITH PIMENTOS

1 or 2 chickens, jointed
6 large tomatoes, peeled and sliced
2 large onions, sliced
2 cloves of garlic, chopped
6 red and green pimentos
1 tsp. chopped parsley
¼ tsp. chopped thyme
1 bay leaf, chopped
3 ozs. butter
2 ozs. flour
1 pint chicken stock
salt, pepper
boiled rice

Rub the chicken joints with salt and pepper. Heat the butter in a large saucepan and fry the chicken till brown all over. Add the onion and fry for 2 minutes. Add the flour, stir well and cook till it begins to brown. Add the tomatoes, herbs, pimentos and simmer gently with the lid on for 20 minutes. Pour on the stock, season with salt and pepper and simmer, covered, for 45 minutes. Serve with the hot rice.

CREOLE CHICKEN AND RICE

1 chicken
2 medium carrots, sliced
2 medium onions, sliced
1 medium turnip, sliced
1 bouquet garni
4 ozs. rice, washed in 4 fresh
*   waters*
salt, pepper
cold water

Put the chicken in a saucepan with the vegetables, herbs and seasoning. Pour in cold water to cover two-thirds of it. Bring to the boil and simmer till tender: 45 minutes if a young bird; up to 3 hours if old. When done remove the bird and strain the stock. Put the vegetables round the bird on the dish and keep warm, covered with buttered paper. Replace the stock in the saucepan, add the rice and simmer till tender and dry, about 15 minutes. Heap onto the serving dish.

CREOLE JAMBALAYA WITH SAUSAGES

8 ozs. Patna rice, boiled
1 lb. chipolata or Vienna sausages
1 large onion, chopped
1 clove of garlic, chopped
½ lb. tomatoes, peeled and
*   quartered*
½ a chilli pepper or pimento,
*   seeded and chopped*
salt, pepper, cayenne
butter

Heat 2 ozs. butter in a large casserole and fry the onion and garlic till light brown. Add the tomatoes, and crush with a wooden spoon to make the mixture juicy. Fry the sausages separately in butter, if possible; when done cut in 2 inch lengths, pour these and their butter over the tomatoes and onion mixture, add the chilli or pimento, season with salt and pepper and a pinch of cayenne pepper. Fill the casserole with the cooked rice, cover and cook very gently for 35 minutes. Serve hot.

CREOLE STUFFED CABBAGE

1 white cabbage
¾ lb. sausage meat
1 large onion, finely chopped
2 tomatoes, peeled and chopped
1 clove of garlic, finely chopped
1 tsp. chopped parsley
½ tsp. chopped thyme
¼ a chilli pepper, or pimento
½ bay leaf, chopped
10 rashers of bacon
2 ozs. butter
salt, pepper
cooked rice

Remove the best of the coarse outer leaves of the cabbage, put the rest of the cabbage in boiling salted water and boil for 10 minutes. Drain well. Fry the onion and garlic in the butter till brown, add salt and pepper, the tomato and the sausage meat, then the herbs and chilli, stir well and cook gently for 20 minutes. Open the cabbage and stuff inside the leaves with the sausage mixture. Wrap the outer leaves round the stuffed cabbage, put 4 rashers on top and tie together with string. Put 6 rashers in the bottom of a covered pan or casserole, put the tied cabbage on top, add ⅛ pint cold water, cover tightly and cook very gently for 1½ hours. To serve, remove the string and the outer leaves, and pour the remaining liquid over the cabbage and bacon rashers. Eat with cooked rice.

JAMBALAYA WITH PRAWNS

Cook this as for Sausage Jambalaya (see p. 103) but add 1 pint of shelled prawns instead of the sausages.

BŒUF CREOLE

3 lbs. rump steak
6 rashers fat bacon
2 finely chopped chilli peppers
2 lbs. finely sliced onions
2 lbs. peeled tomatoes
salt, pepper

Put the rashers in the bottom of a large casserole, place the steak on top, sprinkle with the chillies, salt and pepper. Cover with the onions and tomatoes. Cover the casserole with a tight fitting lid and simmer very gently for 5 hours. No water is used for this recipe: the meat cooks in its own juices and the tomato and onion juice.

CREOLE LIVER (Chanfaina)

1 lb. calves' liver, cut in slices
3 ozs. butter or 3 tbsp. oil
1 tbsp. water
1 lb. peeled sliced tomatoes
2 chopped chilli peppers
1 clove of garlic, chopped
1 tbsp. chopped parsley
salt, pepper

Melt half the fat in a casserole, add the liver slices, salt, pepper, chillies, garlic, parsley and water; cook very gently, turning round and round with a wooden spoon for 5 or 6 minutes or till done. Remove from the heat and keep warm. Fry the tomatoes in the rest of the fat and add to the casserole, having seasoned with salt and pepper.

CREOLE BAKED SWEET POTATOES

Scrub the potatoes well. Bake in their skins in a moderate oven for 1 to 1½ hours till soft throughout. Serve with butter, salt and pepper.

CREOLE CORNFLOUR CAKE PUDDING

¼ lb. cornflour
2 pints milk
2 eggs, beaten
3 ozs. butter, warmed till soft
1 oz. sugar
a few drops of vanilla essence

Boil the milk, add the cornflour and stir quickly till smooth. Leave to cool. When cold add the soft butter, sugar, eggs and vanilla. Mix all well together. Pour into a buttered fireproof dish and bake in a moderate oven for 10 or 15 minutes till light brown.

CREOLE FRIED BANANAS

deep fat or oil
6 bananas
4 tbsp. rum
1 tbsp. brown sugar
¼ pint batter

Peel the bananas and cut in 4 pieces. Place in a shallow dish, sprinkle with the sugar and pour over the rum. Leave for 30 minutes, turning occasionally. Drain any rum and sugar left into the batter. Mix well, dip each banana piece into this mixture and fry in the boiling fat till light brown. Sprinkle with sugar and serve.

CREOLE RICE PUDDING

1 pint milk
2 tbsp. rice
1½ ozs. butter
6 lumps sugar
a few drops of vanilla essence
4 tsp. grated cinnamon

Put the milk, rice, butter, sugar and vanilla in a deep casserole, sprinkle the cinnamon on top. Cook in a very slow oven for 5 hours.

CREOLE SWEET POTATO PUDDING

5 baked sweet potatoes
3 eggs
8 ozs. sugar
3 ozs. butter
½ pint milk
½ tsp. black pepper
¼ tsp. salt

Peel the potatoes and rub through a sieve. Separate the eggs, beat the whites till stiff. Add the egg yolks and milk to the potato, then the sugar, butter, salt and pepper. Fold in the whites. The mixture should be smooth and 'runny'. Pour into a buttered pie dish and bake in a moderate oven for 1 hour, till brown on top, and eat as a sweet course.

CREOLE COCONUT CAKES

¼ lb. finely grated fresh coconut
¼ lb. caster sugar
2 egg whites, beaten stiffly

Add the coconut and sugar to the egg whites and beat again till stiff.

Butter a thick baking tin and put spoonfuls of the mixture on it. Bake in a slow oven for 35 minutes, or till they begin to brown.

CREOLE PEANUT PRALINES

1 lb. brown sugar
1 lb. peanuts
4 tbsp. water
1 tbsp. butter, melted

Shell the peanuts and chop them coarsely. Mix with melted butter.

Add the sugar to the water, bring to the boil and cook till it forms a syrup. Add the peanuts, stir till the mixture bubbles, remove from the heat. Take a tbsp. at a time, place on a buttered slab or large dish press into a round ¼ inch thick and 4 inches in diameter. Work fast, leave till dry, lift with a knife. They should be light, crisp and flaky.

Czechoslovakia

TOMATO SOUP

1 lb. tomatoes, chopped
4 ozs. rice
1 oz. butter
1 dsp. tarragon vinegar
salt
pepper
sugar
4 ozs. grated cheese
1½ pints stock

Fry the rice in the butter, add 2 pints boiling water and 1 teaspoonful salt. Simmer until the rice is just cooked. Pour the rice into a strainer and steam it gently over the pan in which it was cooked. Cook the tomatoes in very little water until tender. Season with salt, pepper and sugar. Pass through a sieve. Put the tomatoes and rice together in a pan with the vinegar, add hot stock gradually. Serve with grated cheese.

BOILED BACON

1½ lbs. boiling bacon (collar is good)
1 onion
1 lb. French beans
1 oz. butter
salt
pepper
bay leaf

Soak the bacon for 3 hours, or longer if it seems very salt. Drain off the water. Put it in a saucepan with the onion, the bay leaf and 1 pint water. Simmer until tender (about 1½ hours). Cook the beans in boiling salted water. Drain and toss in the butter. Serve the bacon on a dish with the beans around it. Hand the broth separately. Serve with baked spaghetti (see p. 112).

CAULIFLOWER WITH EGGS

1 small cauliflower
4 eggs
1 small onion, sliced
1 oz. butter
salt
pepper
caraway seeds

Cook the cauliflower in salted water until just tender. Break into flowerets. Fry the onion in the butter until transparent. Add the cauliflower and caraway seeds. Mix with the onion and fry for 3 minutes. Pour the beaten and seasoned eggs into the pan. Cook slowly, stirring all the time, until the eggs are set.

POTATO PIE (Bramborák)

1 lb. potatoes
2 tbsp. milk
2 ozs. flour
1 clove garlic, crushed
1 onion, finely chopped
salt
pepper

marjoram
1 oz. butter

Peel, grate and drain the potatoes. Stir the milk into the flour and add it to the potatoes with the potatoes with the garlic, onion and seasoning. Bake, dotted with butter, in a greased pan for 30 minutes in a hot oven.

POTATO PANCAKES

Use the same mixture as for Bramborák, but drop spoonfuls of it into hot fat and fry quickly on both sides.

SPINACH ROLLS

½ lb. spinach
½ pint white sauce
1 slice bread
1 oz. butter
½ pint milk
2 eggs
2 ozs. grated cheese

Wash the spinach, reserve 8 large leaves. Cook the rest, drain and chop. Mix with the white sauce, season with salt and pepper. Cut the bread into small dice, fry quickly in the butter. Mix with the spinach mixture. Spread the mixture on the blanched spinach leaves, roll and arrange in a shallow fireproof dish. Beat the eggs with the milk, cook slowly until the mixture thickens, stir in the grated cheese. Pour over the spinach rolls. Bake in a moderate oven for 20 minutes.

BRAISED BEEF

1½ lbs. topside
2 ozs. butter
4 ozs. streaky bacon
1 onion, sliced
juice of 1 lemon
cayenne pepper
salt

Sprinkle the meat with lemon juice, cover with onion. Leave for 12 hours. Season with salt and cayenne pepper. Brown on all sides in the butter. Lay bacon rashers on the bottom of a casserole, put the meat on top of them. Cover it with more bacon. Put in ½ pint water. Cover with a lid and cook in a moderate oven for 2 hours. Serve with sharp sauce poured over it (see p. 111).

CABBAGE

1 savoy cabbage
2 ozs. butter
1 oz. flour
1 small onion
1 clove garlic
1 blade mace
salt
pepper
½ pint stock

Remove hard stalks and shred the cabbage. Blanch it in boiling water and drain. Melt the butter, cook the flour in it, gradually add the stock. Add the mace and the crushed garlic, season with salt and pepper. Put the cabbage into the sauce, with the onion. Simmer for 20 minutes.

CELERIAC PICKLED

1 celeriac
1 large onion
salt
ginger
vinegar

Clean the celeriac and cut it into thick slices. Slice the onion. Put alternate layers of onion and celeriac into an earthenware dish. Sprinkle each layer with salt and ginger. Cover the vegetables with vinegar and water (4 parts vinegar to 1 part water). This will keep for some time.

APPLE TART

pastry as in 'Heavenly Favours'
   (see below)
2 ozs. butter
2 large cooking apples, sliced
2 ozs. sugar
2 ozs. seeded raisins

Line a greased square baking tin with half the pastry. Brush with melted butter. Cover with sliced apples sprinkled with sugar and raisins. Lay the rest of the pastry on top. Brush with melted butter. Bake in a hot oven for 20 minutes.

HEAVENLY FAVOURS

½ lb. flour
2 ozs. mixed butter and lard
2 eggs
2 tbs. milk
cinnamon
sugar
fat for frying

Cut the fat into the sifted flour, mix in the beaten eggs and the milk. The mixture should have become an elastic dough. Knead until smooth. Leave in a warm place for 1 hour. Roll on a floured board, fold into 3. Repeat this twice. Roll out to ¼ inch thick. Cut into diamonds, fry in very hot fat. Drain and sprinkle with cinnamon and sugar.

SHARP SAUCE

½ carrot sliced
½ celeriac sliced
2 onions sliced
3 tomatoes quartered
4 juniper berries
parsley
1 glass red wine
juice of 1 lemon
½ bay leaf
½ pint stock
6 capers

cayenne pepper
salt
2 ozs. butter
½ oz. flour

Cook the vegetables, parsley, juniper berries and bay leaf in 1 oz. butter until tender, adding stock if necessary. Add the wine, lemon juice, capers and stock. Season with salt and cayenne pepper. Rub through a sieve. Thicken with a roux made from 1 oz. butter and the flour.

111

BAKED SPAGHETTI

½ *lb. long spaghetti*
2 ozs. butter
2 ozs. breadcrumbs
salt

Cook the spaghetti in the usual way (see p. 258). Drain and put into a buttered fireproof dish. Fry the breadcrumbs in the butter until golden. Spread on top of the spaghetti. Bake in a moderate oven until very hot.

France

SALADE NIÇOISE

1 large lettuce heart
1 seeded green pepper cut in rings
12 stoned black olives
4 medium peeled sliced tomatoes
4 ozs. cooked French beans
2 hard boiled eggs
1 tin tunny fish
8 anchovy fillets
2 tbsp. chopped fresh herbs,
    parsley, chives, etc.

1 tbsp. chopped onions
1 clove of garlic
3 tbsp. olive oil ⎱
1 tbsp. wine vinegar ⎰ *French dressing*
salt, pepper

Rub the salad bowl with the garlic. Make the dressing and pour into the bowl. Add the lettuce leaves, green pepper, onions, beans, olives, herbs. Mix well in the dressing. Arrange the tunny fish, eggs, tomatoes, anchovies on top. Eat at once.

SALADE DE BŒUF (Cold Beef Salad)

4 slices lean cold cooked beef
6 medium cold cooked potatoes
3 peeled seeded tomatoes
3 tsp. chopped mixed herbs
    (parsley, chives, chervil, etc.)
3 chopped spring onions or
    1 medium onion
2 or 3 tbsp. French dressing

Cut the beef in ½ inch squares. Cover with the dressing and leave for 1 hour. Slice the potatoes and onions. Add the herbs. Mix all together with the cold beef. If 'dry' looking add another tablespoon of dressing.

HARDBOILED EGGS

6 eggs
1 tbsp. French dressing
1 oz. butter
4 spring onions, finely chopped
4 lettuce leaves

Boil eggs till hard, peel and cut in half. Remove yolks, mash these with the blade of a knife with the dressing and the butter. Fill whites, sprinkle with onion. Stand three per person on a crisp lettuce leaf.

POTATO AND EGG SALAD

1 lb. potatoes (not the 'floury'
    kind)
4 hardboiled eggs
¼ pint French dressing
4 tsp. chopped herbs (chives,
    parsley, tarragon, etc.)

Boil the potatoes in their skins. Peel and cool. Remove egg yolks and mash till smooth with the herbs and dressing. Add this mixture to the potatoes and egg whites coarsely chopped, and mix all together. Serve very cold.

FOND D'ARTICHAUTS A L'ORIENTALE

6 globe artichokes
3 tbsp. water
3 tbsp. olive oil
1 small onion
2 tender carrots
4 ozs. cooked green peas
4 ozs. cooked new potatoes
½ lemon
½ tsp. sugar
1 tsp. chopped herbs (fennel and
   parsley)
salt, pepper

Strip the stalk and leaves from each artichoke, keeping the heart. Mix the oil with the water, add the onion and carrots, finely chopped, and boil for 3 minutes. Put in the artichoke hearts, sugar, lemon juice, a pinch of salt and pepper, cover the saucepan and simmer very slowly for 40 minutes. Add the cooked peas and potatoes. When cold sprinkle the herbs on top.

All the vegetables for this hors d'œuvre must be young and tender.

POTATO, HARDBOILED EGG, ANCHOVY SALAD

potato and hardboiled egg salad
   (see p. 115)
8 anchovy fillets

Cut up the fillets and mix with the potato and hardboiled egg. Serve very cold.

ŒUFS MIMOSA

6 hard boiled eggs
6 tsp. foie gras
2 tbsp. mayonnaise
6 tbsp. cold Béchamel sauce

Halve the eggs and fill with *foie gras*. Mix the mayonnaise and Béchamel. Pour over. Chop the yolks and sprinkle on top.

MACÉDOINE NIÇOISE

Ravigote sauce (see p. 160)
½ lb. cold chicken
½ lb. cooked lean ham
1 kipper fillet
¼ lb. Mortadelle sausage
1 peeled chopped eating apple
   (Cox's Orange if possible)
1 head of celery (use only the
   inner sticks)
salt and pepper
3 hard boiled eggs
1 sweet pepper, very finely sliced,
   having removed the seeds

12 green olives
3 medium cold boiled potatoes
1 lettuce heart, chopped
1 medium chopped cooked
   beetroot

Remove yolks and chop the whites. Cut all the 'meats' into thin strips. Mix the 'meats' with all the chopped vegetables and the egg whites. Salt and pepper the mixture. Pour over this the Ravigote sauce, put all in a shallow dish, sprinkle with the chopped egg yolks.

CUCUMBER SALAD

½ tsp. salt
1 cucumber
1 tbsp. wine vinegar
black pepper

Peel and slice thinly the cucumber. Spread out on a flat dish and sprinkle with the salt.

Leave for 1 hour and squeeze in a clean cloth. Add the vinegar and a good sprinkling of black pepper.

TOMATOES AND BLACK OLIVES

8 medium ripe tomatoes
16 black olives
1 clove of garlic
pepper
6 tbsp. mayonnaise

Peel the tomatoes. Scoop out the seeds and pulp. Put this in a bowl, mix with the crushed garlic, add the mayonnaise and pour all over the tomatoes, filling them. Sprinkle very lightly with black pepper. Stone the olives, chop them coarsely and scatter on top of the filled tomatoes.

STUFFED EGGS WITH SARDINES

6 eggs (hard boiled)
1 tin sardines
1 oz. butter
12 capers
1 tsp. lemon juice
salt, pepper

Cut the eggs lengthways. Chop the yolks. Mash the sardines, having boned and skinned them, with the butter and lemon juice; season with salt and pepper. Fill the whites with the mixture and sprinkle with the chopped yolks.

MUSSELS WITH SAFFRON

1½ pints mussels
2 leeks
1 small onion
2 medium tomatoes
1 clove of garlic
pinch of saffron
pinch of thyme
1 bay leaf
2 small glasses white wine
3 tbsp. olive oil
1 tsp. chopped parsley
salt, pepper

Scrub the mussels under a running tap, very carefully, to remove ALL sand, soak in cold water. Slice all the vegetables. Use only the white parts of the leeks. Melt the oil in a large stew pan, add the leeks and onion, cook for 3 minutes then add the tomatoes and garlic, thyme, bay leaf and saffron; stir together. Put in the wine, season with salt and pepper. Simmer till somewhat reduced, about 20 minutes, stirring now and then.

Add the mussels, put the lid on and toss occasionally. They will soon open; after opening, cook very slowly for 5 minutes more. Remove from their shells and put in a shallow dish. Strain the liquid over them. When cold sprinkle with the parsley.

TUNNY FISH

8 ozs. fresh cooked tunny fish or
   1 tin
2 hard boiled eggs
2 ozs. butter
3 tsp. chopped herbs (mixed
   parsley, chives, tarragon)
¼ pint mayonnaise
sliced lemon or parsley sprigs
buttered brown bread cut in
   rounds

Mash the fish, butter, eggs, chopped herbs very finely with a fork until creamy. Pile the mixture on the small rounds of buttered bread, cover with the mayonnaise. Sprig with parsley, or small pieces of lemon. Serve three to each person.

TUNNY FISH WITH CELERY

8 ozs. fresh cooked tunny fish
   or 1 tin
1 tbsp. wine vinegar
¼ tsp. mustard
1 heart of chopped celery head
3 tsp. chopped herbs (chives,
   tarragon, parsley, fennel)

salt, pepper
lettuce

Cut the fish in tiny pieces, add the inner white parts of the celery head, very finely chopped, also the herbs. Mix all together with the vinegar, mustard, salt and pepper. Fill the inner leaves of a lettuce, three to each person.

POT-AU-FEU

2 lbs. beef (the cheaper cuts)
1 lb. shin bones
the remains of a chicken—bones,
   neck, skin, etc.
2 large carrots
1 turnip
1 head of celery
1 tomato
1 leek
1 large onion stuck with cloves
bouquet garni
½ tsp. salt
pepper
4 pints cold water

This is the classic consommé 'bouillon', stock or broth, the basis for many dishes and soups. Some cooks make a week's supply at a time and keep it in the refrigerator. Beef or chicken cubes available today, especially the Swiss makes, are a substitute unless you are the better sort of cook.

Prepare all the ingredients and put in the water, bring to the boil. Boil, skim, skim and skim until no more scum appears. This skimming is the secret of a clear stock. Continue to simmer for 5 hours. Strain and remove the fat — far easier when cold. Of course the vegetables and beef can be eaten as a meal in themselves with boiled potatoes.

BOUILLABAISSE

2 lbs. mixed pieces of fish (cod
    fillets, whitings, mullets, smelts,
    turbot, eel, small crabs, lobster)
3 finely sliced onions
4 finely sliced cloves of garlic
3 peeled and seeded tomatoes
1 bouquet garni (with a fennel
    sprig added)
1 slice orange peel
½ glass olive oil
¾ pint hot water
½ glass white wine
¼ tsp. nutmeg
¼ tsp. saffron
2 tsp. chopped parsley
salt, pepper
slices of stale bread or stale rolls

This classic Mediterranean fish dish can be termed either a soup or a fish recipe. It is a meal in itself. There are many ways of making it, but this is as good as any. The fishes should be cut up in fairly equally sized pieces (easy for eating).

  Cut up the lobster and/or crabs, cover with water and simmer for 20 minutes. In a large pot, put the vegetables, garlic, *bouquet*, saffron, nutmeg, orange peel. On this bed place the pieces of firmer fish all washed and cleaned — such as cod, eel, turbot — add olive oil and wine and the water. Bring to the boil and cook fiercely for 5 minutes. Now put in the softer fish pieces—red mullet, whiting, smelt, etc. Add ½ a cup of the lobster and crab liquid and boil again as before, fiercely for another 5 minutes, or until the pieces of fish are done, but not overcooked or disintegrating. Season with salt and pepper.

Pick out the *bouquet* and the orange peel.

Put the sliced bread or rolls cut lengthways into one dish and pour the liquid over them (you can, if you like, fry the bread or rolls first in olive oil), put the fish pieces in another dish and sprinkle with parsley.

Eat both dishes together.

The lobster and crab are not essential, as most extravagant unless you catch them yourselves, but little, otherwise useless, crabs will do.

The secret of bouillabaisse lies in the fierce cooking, to which is due the smooth mixture of oil and the liquid.

MUSSEL SOUP

2 dozen mussels
2½ pints cold water
1 glass dry white wine
1 medium onion
1 tsp. chopped parsley
1 sprig thyme
1 clove
4 tbsp. cream
salt, pepper

See that the mussels are cleaned, completely free of sand. Put them in the pot with the onion, sliced, ½ tsp. of the parsley, the thyme, clove, salt and pepper. Pour on the water and the wine. Boil for 15 minutes. Strain the liquid through a fine sieve or muslin in another pot. Take the mussels from their shells and put them in the warmed tureen. Simmer the liquid until reduced by a quarter. Pour over the mussels in the tureen and stir in the cream, and sprinkle on the parsley. Taste and add more salt and pepper if you think fit.

CONSOMMÉ MADRILÈNE

2½ *pints beef stock*
4 *tomatoes*
3 *ozs. lean raw minced beef*
1 *egg white*
salt, pepper

Peel and slice the tomatoes, add to the minced beef, salt, pepper. Stir. Pour on the stock, add the well beaten egg white, stir again, and simmer for 1 hour. Strain and serve.

CONSOMMÉ A LA CHIFFONADE

3 *lettuce hearts*
3 *handfuls sorrel or spinach*
  leaves
2 *ozs. butter*
1½ *pints boiling water*
1 *pint milk*
3 *ozs. vermicelli*
1 *tsp. chopped chervil*

Wash the sorrel or spinach and the lettuce hearts, chop them very small. Melt the butter, add the vegetables and cook for 4 minutes, stir, add salt and pepper. Pour on the water and milk, bring to the boil, then throw in the vermicelli, stir from time to time and simmer till the vermicelli is soft — about 20 minutes. Sprinkle the chervil on top before serving.

SARDINES

1 *tin sardines*
2 *ozs. butter*
juice of 1 lemon
salt, pepper

Mash the sardines and the butter till very smooth with a fork, add the lemon juice and pepper plus a tiny pinch of salt. If the bones and skin seem tough take them out before mashing.

This mixture can be served on rounds of buttered bread, or filling lettuce leaves. Also stuffing the whites of hard boiled eggs.

POTAGE A LA PURÉE DE GIBIER (Giblet Soup)

remains of cooked game bird
  (pheasant, partridges, grouse,
  etc.)
2½ *pints cold water*
3 *carrots*
2 *onions*
½ *head of celery*
1 *bouquet garni*
2 *ozs. white breadcrumbs*
2 *tbsp. cream*
salt, pepper

Take whatever you have left of your bird—carcase, bones, skin, giblets, neck, etc.—and put in the pot. Add the chopped vegetables, the *bouquet*, salt and pepper. Pour the water over, bring to the boil and simmer for 1 hour. Strain. Remove any pieces of meat left on the bones and pass them through a sieve, pound them, or 'rub' them as finely as possible on a plate with a wooden spoon. Return this 'paste' to the liquid, add the breadcrumbs, re-heat, but do not boil. Stir in the cream. Serve croutons with this soup.

SIEVED WATERCRESS SOUP

1 lb. potatoes
1 bunch watercress
2 pints cold water
¼ pint milk or cream
½ oz. butter
salt, pepper

Peel and boil the potatoes in the water till nearly done, then add the chopped watercress. Cook again till the potatoes are soft. Sieve. Re-heat and add the milk or cream, butter, salt and pepper to taste.

A sprinkling of chopped watercress on top makes this soup look interesting.

LOBSTER SOUP (Potage à la Bisque d'Homard)

1 lobster
1 pint cold water
1 onion
1 carrot
2 ozs. butter
¼ pint Madeira or white wine
1½ pints stock
4 slices stale white bread
salt, pepper
bouquet garni

Dice the vegetables, add the water, salt, pepper and *bouquet*. Bring to a fierce boil, put in the lobster, simmer for 15 minutes. Strain, but keep the liquid. Take the meat out of the lobster tail and put the shell through the mincer, then pound it to a paste. Put this paste in to 1 pint of the liquid, simmer for 5 minutes. Strain once more. Now put in the bread (crusts removed) and mash with a wooden spoon till free of any lumps, pour on the stock, the wine and the rest of the liquid, bring to the boil stirring the whole time. Take off the heat, put in the butter and the tail meat. Serve immediately.

WATERCRESS SOUP WITH LEEK

1½ lbs. potatoes
2 leeks
1 bunch watercress
2 ozs. butter
2 pints water
1 egg yolk
1 tbsp. milk
salt, pepper

Chop the prepared vegetables and cook in the melted butter for 4 minutes. Add the salt, pepper and water. Bring to the boil then simmer for 20 minutes. Beat the egg yolk in the milk and add to the hot soup before serving.

POTAGE VELOURS

6 cooked carrots
2 pints stock
1 oz. tapioca
1 oz. butter
½ tsp. chopped parsley
salt, pepper

Mash the carrots. Boil the stock, throw in the tapioca, cook for 6 minutes stirring all the time. Add the mashed carrots, butter, salt, pepper. Stir, boil up once more, stirring quickly the whole time. Sprinkle on the parsley.

SOUPE DE CHASSE

4 medium onions
1 leek
1 head celery
1 clove of garlic
2 ozs. butter
bouquet garni
2½ pints cold water
salt, pepper, sugar
1 clove
8 slices thin stale bread fried
   in butter

1 oz. potato flour mixed in ½ cup
   stock
3 egg yolks

Melt the butter, add the chopped vegetables, stir, add clove, salt, pepper and a pinch of sugar. Pour on the water, add the *bouquet garni* and simmer for 2 hours. Just before serving stir the egg yolks quickly into the potato flour and stock till smooth and add to the hot soup.

Put the fried bread slices in the tureen and pour the soup over them.

TURNIP SOUP

6 young turnips
1 oz. butter
2½ pints boiling water
½ tsp. salt
¼ tsp. sugar
pepper
1 egg yolk
1 tbsp. cream

Slice the turnips, melt the butter in the soup pot, and cook slowly for 5 minutes, tossing once or twice. Add the salt, sugar and pepper. Stir. Pour on the boiling water and let the soup simmer till the turnips are soft. Pass through a sieve or mash well with a wooden spoon. Beat the egg yolk in the cream and add to the soup to 'bind' it, just before serving.

TOMATO SOUP

1 lb. tomatoes
¼ of a bay leaf
¼ tsp. dried thyme or 1 sprig
1 medium onion
2½ pints cold water
¾ tsp. salt
½ tsp. sugar
2 ozs. butter

Quarter the tomatoes and put in a heavy pot, add the bay leaf, thyme, sliced onion. Crush the tomatoes with a wooden spoon and cook very gently for 30 minutes, stirring often to prevent sticking. Sieve. To this purée add the water, salt, sugar, butter. Stir well, bring to the boil and take off heat.

Pour over croutons and serve at once.

MUSHROOM JULIENNE

Prepare vegetables as for Soupe Julienne (see p. 123), but add ½ lb. mushrooms, washed and very thinly sliced (use both caps and stems) 5 minutes before the soup is cooked.

Serve with croutons.

SOUPE JULIENNE (Vegetable Soup)

2 carrots
2 small turnips
2 medium potatoes
2 leeks
4 cabbage leaves
2 ozs. butter
2½ pints stock
¼ lb. green peas (or ¼ lb. French
  beans)
salt, pepper

Cut all the vegetables into very thin strips about 1½ inches long, except of course the peas. Melt the butter in the soup pot and add the vegetables and fry for 4 minutes. Stir them about, gently. Pour on the stock and bring to the boil. Simmer for 15 minutes, add the peas (or beans) and simmer for a further 15 minutes. Add salt and pepper.

The special character of this soup is the look of the vegetables, which should be almost like matchsticks.

TOMATO SOUP WITH TAPIOCA

tomato purée
1½ pints cold water
½ pint hot milk
¼ tsp. salt
1¼ ozs. tapioca
2 ozs. butter

Make the purée as in Tomato Soup (see p. 122).

Boil the water, add the salt and throw in the tapioca, cook for 5 minutes, stir all the time, heating as it thickens; now add the milk slowly, still stirring the mixture. Add the purée and the butter (if too thick add more milk). Stir all together and serve, without croutons.

POTAGE BOURGUIGNON

3 ozs. cooked haricot beans
2 medium onions
4 sticks of celery
½ pint cold water
2 pints stock
1 oz. butter
salt, pepper

Chop up the onions and celery finely, add the cooked beans, salt and pepper, pour on the water and simmer for 20 minutes. Sieve or mash the vegetables thoroughly with a wooden spoon. Add the stock, boil up again, skimming if necessary.

Add the butter before serving, stir and serve with croutons, fried in bacon fat.

ONION SOUP WITH CHEESE

6 medium onions
2½ pints water
8 slices French bread
¼ lb. grated cheese
2 ozs. butter
salt, pepper

Slice the onions finely and fry in the melted butter in a thick pot until brown, but not burnt. Pour in the water and simmer till reduced by a quarter. Add the salt and pepper, be generous with the latter. Ladle into separate fire-proof, or earthenware, soup bowls, float 2 slices of bread in bowl, cover generously with the grated cheese (Gruyère is best, but not essential) and brown in a hot oven.

ONION SOUP 'SAVOYARDE'

6 medium onions
2 ozs. butter
1½ pints beef stock
1 pint boiling water
1 clove of garlic
1 bouquet garni
1 beaten egg
wine vinegar
salt, pepper

Melt the butter, when sizzling add the sliced onions and chopped garlic, cook till soft. Pour on the boiling water, stir, then the stock. Put in the *bouquet*, add salt and pepper. Boil gently for 20 minutes. Remove the herbs. Draw the pot away from the heat and stir in the beaten egg plus 3 or 4 drops of vinegar.

WHITE ONION SOUP

6 medium onions
2 ozs. butter
1 tbsp. flour
½ pint boiling water
1½ pints milk
salt, pepper

Melt the butter; when sizzling, add the sliced onions, cook for 3 minutes. Add the flour, stir, add the hot water, stir. Reduce the heat, season with salt and pepper. Cook for 10 minutes to reduce. Stir again and add the milk. Simmer very gently for 15 minutes or until the onions are soft. This soup may be sieved, but is very good as it is. As in all soups it may be made richer with a beaten egg yolk or a tablespoon of cream added at the last, AFTER it has stopped cooking.

ONION SOUP WITH VERMICELLI

onion soup
4 tbsp. vermicelli

Follow the recipe for White Onion Soup. Add the vermicelli broken in ½ pieces as the soup begins to simmer after the addition of the milk. Stir constantly to prevent sticking, and simmer for 20 minutes.

PEA POD SOUP

1 lb. young green peas
1 lettuce
1 small onion
1 handful spinach
1 sprig mint
1 tbsp. flour
1 oz. butter
1½ pints boiling water
½ pint milk
salt, pepper, sugar

Chop the mint and all the vegetables, pea pods included. Melt the butter in the pot, add the vegetables, cook for 4 minutes, stirring once or twice. Add the flour and stir till absorbed. Pour on 1½ pints of boiling water gradually, stirring all the time, then the milk. Add the salt and pepper and a pinch of sugar. Simmer for 20 minutes.
This soup must be sieved.

ONION SOUP WITH SEMOLINA

onion soup (see p. 124)
2 tbsp. semolina

Follow the recipe for White Onion Soup. Add the semolina with the milk and simmer for 30 minutes, stirring occasionally.

GARBURE

1 large cabbage
½ lb. cooked haricot beans
  or dried peas
3 large carrots
3 large potatoes
1 ham bone or 4 ozs. bacon
2 pints cold water
bouquet garni
salt, pepper
1 tbsp. goose fat

Shred the cabbage, slice the potatoes and carrots. Put these in a large soup pot with the haricot beans, the bone or bacon, and the *bouquet*. Pour the cold water on and bring to the boil. Simmer for 40 minutes. Take out the *bouquet*. Add the salt and pepper to taste, not too much salt. Remove the meat. Cut the rind off the bacon and chop the meat in pieces, pick any meat off the ham bone and do likewise. Return to the soup. Mash the 'solids' with a wooden spoon to a mush, and just before serving add the goose fat.

SOLE NORMANDIE

2 large soles, filleted
1 pint mussels
1 chopped shallot
12 oysters
½ pint shrimps
½ pint dry white wine
½ pint cold water
4 ozs. butter
2 ozs. flour
¼ pint thick cream
½ lb. mushrooms, peeled and sliced
salt, pepper

This is a complicated dish, but sole *par excellence*.

Cook the mushrooms in 2 ozs. butter very slowly till tender. Open the perfectly cleaned mussels by heating gently in a covered frying pan. Keep any liquid. Open the oysters, keep any liquid. Peel the shrimps, keep the shells and heads. Pour the wine and water, the mussel and oyster liquid into a small saucepan, add salt and pepper, shrimp heads and tails, the shallot and the butter from the cooked mushrooms. Simmer slowly for 30 minutes. Strain through muslin, re-heat and poach the fillets in this liquid for 10 minutes. Remove the fillets and place lengthwise in a buttered fireproof or baking dish. Keep warm.

Make a sauce of 2 ozs. butter, 2 ozs. flour, ½ pint of the fish stock as you would a Béchamel sauce, add the cream, taste for seasoning. Pour this over the fish, decorate with mussels, oysters, shrimps and mushrooms. Put under a hot grill till slightly brown and serve.

SOLE MEUNIÈRE

4 medium soles
½ oz. flour
4 ozs. butter
2 tsp. lemon juice
salt, pepper

Dust the fishes with the flour, salt and pepper. Heat the butter, when sizzling hot put in the fish and cook for 30 seconds, turn over and cook for another ½ minute, or till a skewer goes through the thickest part easily.

Arrange in the serving dish, add a pinch of salt and pepper, pour over lemon juice and any butter left in the pan. Serve immediately.

FILLETS OF SOLE FLORENTINE

2 large or 4 medium filleted soles
4 ozs. butter
juice of 1 lemon
salt, pepper
½ pint Béchamel or Mornay sauce
  (see pp. 161, 163)
1½ lbs. cooked spinach. tossed
  in 1 oz. butter

Melt the butter, add salt, pepper, lemon juice and when hot put in the fillets. Turn each one. Cook till tender, about 5 minutes in all. Line a shallow fireproof dish with the cooked spinach, put in the cooked fish, pour over the sauce, and brown quickly under a hot grill.

SOLE AU VIN BLANC

2 medium soles
2 tbsp. finely chopped shallots
5 ozs. butter
3 ozs. white breadcrumbs
¼ pint dry white wine
salt, pepper

Have your fishmonger prepare the fish and take off the black skin.

Butter a flat fireproof dish, add the fishes, sprinkle with the shallots, salt, pepper, dabs of butter. Pour over the wine. Add the breadcrumbs and dot with the rest of the butter. Cook uncovered in a moderate oven for 25 minutes. Serve in the dish.

You may put the cooked dish under a hot grill to brown if wished.

SOLE MORNAY

4 medium soles, filleted
¼ pint fish stock
2 ozs. butter
½ pint Béchamel sauce
  (see p. 163)
3 ozs. grated cheese (Parmesan
  or Cheshire)
salt, pepper

Arrange the fillets in a buttered flat fireproof dish, add salt and pepper and the stock. Bake in a moderate oven for 15 minutes. Pour off the liquid and add to the Béchamel mixed with the cheese. Pour over the fillets, lifting them up to let the sauce run underneath. Put back in the oven for 4 minutes.

SOLE BONNE FEMME

4 medium soles
1 tsp. chopped parsley
4 ozs. butter
1 chopped shallot
½ lb. mushrooms
½ tsp. lemon juice
2 egg yolks

SAUCE:

4 tbsp. fish stock
½ oz. butter
½ oz. flour
salt, pepper

Chop the mushrooms very finely. Melt the butter in a small saucepan, add the mushrooms, shallot, parsley, lemon juice and cook, covered, very slowly for 10 minutes. Make a sauce with the wine, fish stock, butter and flour as you would White Sauce, put the soles in a flat fireproof dish, pour on this sauce. Cover the dish and cook till the soles are tender, about 15 minutes.

Pour this sauce over the mushrooms, etc., boil for 3 minutes, remove from heat, add salt and pepper and the beaten egg yolks. Pour back again over the fish, put under a hot grill for 3 minutes. Serve.

BAKED CODFISH

1 small whole cod
1 quart fish stock or water
1 bouquet garni
salt, pepper
1 oz. flour
3 ozs. brown breadcrumbs
2 ozs. butter
1 pint shrimps, shelled
1 tbsp. anchovy essence
1 sliced lemon
parsley sprigs to decorate

Wash and dry the fish. Put it in a baking tin, add the fish stock, or water, the bouquet, salt and pepper. Cover with the mixed flour and breadcrumbs and dot with butter. Bake in a moderate oven, basting frequently, till done, about 30 minutes. Take 4 tbsp. of fish liquid out of the dish in the oven, pour over the shrimps, with the anchovy essence, stir and pour over the fish and return to the oven for 7 minutes. Decorate the fish with the lemon slices and sprigs of parsley and serve in the dish it is cooked in.

PROVENÇAL CRUSHED SALT COD (Brandade)

2½ lbs. salt cod
1 clove of garlic
½ pint olive oil
½ pint milk
1 tsp. lemon juice
pepper
a few truffles (optional)
fried bread triangles

This dish is salt cod crushed to a creamy paste.
Soak the fish in cold water for 12 hours, change water twice. Cover with cold water, bring to the boil, remove at once from the heat. Drain, remove bones but not skin. Crush the garlic, and put in a warm large saucepan. Add the fish pieces and place over very low heat. In two other pans warm the milk and the olive oil—only tepid, not hot. (Fish, oil and milk must all be of the same low warmth throughout the making). With a wooden spoon pound and crush the fish and garlic, add a spoon of milk, stir fiercely, add a spoon of oil, stir fiercely. Continue thus until the mixture is smooth and creamy. Season with pepper and lemon juice. Decorate with truffles, if any. Serve with the fried bread.

SCALLOPS (Coquilles St-Jacques)

8 scallops
1 large peeled sliced tomato
1 small finely chopped onion
¼ lb. finely sliced mushrooms
2 ozs. butter
⅛ pint Béchamel sauce

Ask your fishmonger to open and clean the scallops and give you the shells.

Wash the scallops, cover with cold salted water, bring to the boil and simmer for 7 or 8 minutes till soft. Drain and chop white and red part together and mix with the tomato, onion, mushrooms, salt and pepper. Cook in the butter in a small saucepan, for 3 minutes. Add the Béchamel sauce, mix and fill 4 shells. Brown under a hot grill for a few minutes.

SCALLOPS AU GRATIN

8 scallops
¼ lb. mushrooms finely chopped
2 ozs. breadcrumbs
2 ozs. butter
⅛ pint Béchamel sauce
1 sherry glass white wine
2 ozs. grated cheese
pepper

Prepare and cook the scallops as in previous recipe.

Melt the butter and cook the mushrooms till soft, about 5 minutes, add the breadcrumbs, pepper, wine and Béchamel sauce, plus the finely chopped cooked scallops. Sprinkle with the cheese, and brown under the grill.

MULLET EN PAPILLOTE

1 medium mullet
2 ozs. breadcrumbs
2 ozs. melted butter
1 tsp. chopped fennel
salt

Cut off head, tail and fins. Rub in melted butter, mix the breadcrumbs, salt and fennel, put ½ of this in the fish and the rest sprinkled over. Wrap it up well in buttered paper, and cook under a moderate grill for 25 minutes.

BAKED RED MULLET

2 mullets
2 ozs. breadcrumbs
salt, pepper
2 tsp. chopped parsley
2 ozs. butter
2 tsp. lemon juice

Ask your fishmonger to clean the fish, keeping the liver. Score the fish on both sides. Butter a shallow fireproof dish, put in the fish, sprinkle with the breadcrumbs, salt, pepper, parsley and lemon juice. Dot on the rest of the butter, bake in a moderate oven for 20 minutes, basting from time to time.

LOBSTER THERMIDOR

2 small boiled lobsters
2 tbsp. butter
½ tsp. finely chopped onion
dash of cayenne pepper
½ glass dry white wine
¼ lb. finely chopped mushrooms
1 tbsp. tomato purée
½ pint Béchamel sauce
2 tbsp. grated Parmesan cheese
salt

Pick the meat out of the claws, etc. Chop into dice, coral included, if any.

Heat the butter in a saucepan, add the lobster meat, coral, onion, cayenne and wine. Simmer for 5 minutes, stirring constantly. Add the mushrooms, tomato purée, salt, if necessary, simmer for 5 minutes more. Fill the shells with this mixture and put in serving dish. Cover with the Béchamel sauce, sprinkle on the cheese. Heat thoroughly in a hot oven, then put under a hot grill for 2 minutes.

MUSSELS MARINIÈRE

1 quart mussels
¼ pint cold water
¼ pint dry white wine
1 finely sliced carrot
1 sliced onion
1 crushed garlic clove
bouquet garni
2 ozs. butter
salt, pepper
3 tsp. chopped parsley

Wash and scrub the mussels carefully till no sand is left. A long business, but essential.

Add the carrot, onion, garlic, *bouquet*, butter, salt and pepper to the water and wine. Bring to the boil and simmer for 30 minutes. Strain and put the liquid in a large saucepan. Add the mussels, cover the pan and place over a strong heat, shaking the pan the whole time; after 5 minutes turn the mussels gently so that the top ones go to the bottom, cook for another 4 or 5 minutes till all are open. Take out the mussels, remove top shell, put in a deep serving dish or tureen and pour the liquid over. Sprinkle with the parsley. Serve hot.

LOBSTER A L'AMÉRICAINE

1 hen lobster
4 tbsp. olive oil
1 green pepper, seeded and sliced
2 large ripe tomatoes seeded, peeled and quartered
1 small onion, finely chopped
1 pint dry white wine
4 ozs. butter
½ tsp. lemon juice
1 tsp. meat glaze or ¼ tsp. Bovril
1 tsp. chopped parsley
1 tsp. chopped tarragon
salt, pepper

Cut the lobster in even pieces. Carefully keep the coral and water. Heat in a saucepan the olive oil, add the lobster and cook for 3 or 4 minutes. Add salt, pepper, the pimento, tomatoes and onion and the wine. Simmer for 20 minutes. Remove the lobster and keep warm in the serving dish. Put the saucepan back on a fierce heat and boil to reduce the liquid by half. Meanwhile knead together the butter, coral and lobster water with a wooden spoon. Add this to the reduced liquid, over a low heat stir till creamy and smooth. Add the meat glaze, lemon juice and herbs, stir for another minute and pour over the lobster and serve.

TRUITE AU BLEU

4 trout
2 tbsp. wine vinegar
1½ pints fish stock
2 tsp. chopped parsley
Hollandaise or Ravigote sauce
   (see pp. 159, 160)

Clean the trout, put in a shallow dish and pour over the vinegar, turn the fish over so that all sides are coated with the vinegar to 'blue' the fish. Boil the stock, put in the fish, bring to the boil again and at once take off the heat, cover the pot, and leave for 5 minutes. Remove the trout, put in the serving dish, sprinkle with parsley and serve with either Hollandaise or Ravigote sauce.

TRUITE MEUNIÈRE

4 trout
1 tbsp. flour
4 ozs. butter
2 tsp. chopped parsley
½ tsp. lemon juice
salt, pepper

Clean and wash the trout. Dry and roll them in the flour, salt and pepper. Heat 3 ozs. of butter in a frying pan, put in the trout and fry gently for 10 to 12 minutes, or until the fish is soft all through. Remove from pan and put on warm dish, sprinkle with parsley and lemon juice, add 1 oz. butter to the butter hot in frying pan, mix well and pour over the fishes.

HERRINGS A LA LORRAINE

4 large herrings
1 tbsp. flour
salt, pepper
3 ozs. butter
1 small onion finely chopped
juice of 1 lemon
2 tbsp. cream
4 tbsp. breadcrumbs

Ask the fishmonger to clean the herrings and cut off the heads. Wash and dry the fish. Mix flour, salt and pepper and roll the fish in this. Melt the butter in a large frying pan, add the chopped onion and cook gently till transparent. Add the herrings and fry gently on both sides for 4 or 5 minutes. Dust with the breadcrumbs, add the cream and lemon juice, stir the fish gently about in the pan, turn each fish over, spoon on some of the liquid over each and cook gently with a lid on until the fish are soft through the thickest part.

WHITE FISH IN CUSTARD

4 fillets turbot, halibut, cod,
   plaice
1 pint milk or ½ milk, ½ cream
3 eggs
1 oz. butter
salt, pepper

Butter a shallow fireproof dish and place the fish in it. Beat the eggs, add the milk or milk and cream, salt and pepper, pour over fish. Stand the dish in a baking dish with 1 inch water in it, cook in a very slow oven for 1 hour.

Any white filleted fish, cod, plaice, halibut, etc. can be cooked in this simple delicious way.

MACKEREL A LA NANTAISE

2 large mackerel
1 tbsp. olive oil
1 finely chopped onion } marinade
salt, pepper
1 pint fish stock
2 tsp. vinegar
½ pint Béchamel sauce
1 tsp. chopped chives
1 tsp. chopped capers

1 tsp. lemon juice
1 oz. butter

Take off heads and tails of already cleaned fish and cut open lengthwise. Soak in the marinade for 2 hours. Heat the stock till simmering gently, add vinegar, put in the mackerel and simmer for 30 minutes. Make the Béchamel sauce, add the chives, capers, lemon juice and butter. Pour over the cooked fish and serve.

BAKED TURBOT

4 slices of turbot
3 tbsp. butter
½ tbsp. finely chopped onion
½ tbsp. chopped parsley
2 ozs. white breadcrumbs
1 sherry glass white wine
salt, pepper
1 sliced lemon
few parsley sprigs } garnish

Grease a flat fireproof dish with 1 oz. butter, sprinkle over half the chopped onion and parsley, salt and pepper, place the fish slices on this, dot with the rest of the butter, onion, parsley, another pinch of salt and pepper and the breadcrumbs. Pour the wine over, cover with greaseproof paper, and bake in a moderate oven for 25 minutes. Garnish with lemon slices and parsley.

EEL WITH WINE AND MUSHROOM SAUCE

1 eel
¾ pint dry white wine
1 bouquet garni
1 chopped onion
salt, pepper
2 ozs. butter
2 ozs. flour
¼ lb. chopped mushrooms
12 very small onions or shallots
1 egg yolk
12 shrimps
  croutons } fried in butter

Cut the cleaned skinned eel in 3 inch pieces and put in a saucepan with the wine, chopped onion, *bouquet*, salt and pepper. Bring to the boil and boil for 30 minutes. In a small saucepan melt the butter, add the flour, pour on ½ pint of the eel liquid, gradually stirring all the time till smooth. Add the small onions and mushrooms and cook till soft. Add more stock, if too thick. Remove from the heat and stir in the egg yolk. Put the cooked eel on the serving dish, pour over the sauce, decorate with the fried shrimps and croutons.

WHITINGS A LA BERCY

4 medium whitings
4 tsp. finely chopped shallots
1 liqueur glass white wine
1 liqueur glass cold water
juice of 1 lemon
2 ozs. butter
salt, pepper
2 tsp. chopped parsley

Split the whitings and cut along the backbone for easier cooking. Butter a shallow fireproof dish and lay the whitings side by side. Put 1 tsp. of the shallots in each whiting, salt and pepper them, add the lemon juice and the water and wine. Dot the rest of the butter over and put in a moderate oven for 25 minutes. Baste frequently until there is no liquid left.

CHICKEN MARENGO

1 2-lb. chicken
1 dsp. flour
6 tbsp. olive oil
1 clove of garlic
bouquet garni
½ lb. sliced mushrooms
salt, pepper
2 tomatoes
3 tbsp. stock
1 tsp. chopped parsley
2 slices white bread ⎱ croutons
2 ozs. butter ⎰
4 fried eggs

Carve the bird in seven pieces—wings, thighs, drumsticks and breast. Chop the garlic finely, heat the oil in a casserole. Put the legs in, plus garlic, salt and pepper, cook for 5 minutes, add the rest of the chicken and the *bouquet*. Cook till browned, add the mushrooms, the peeled and sliced tomatoes and the stock. Cover and simmer for 30 minutes. Make the croutons, fry the eggs meanwhile. Remove the *bouquet* and serve arranged on a flat dish.

CHICKEN A LA BOURGOGNE

1 young chicken — cut in 5 pieces
6 mushrooms
3 ozs. butter
1 dsp. flour
12 button onions
3 ozs. bacon
2 shallots
6 tarragon leaves
¼ tsp. nutmeg
1 liqueur glass brandy
1 pint red Burgundy
salt and pepper

Slice the mushrooms and fry gently in 1 oz. butter till done. Keep warm. Roll the chicken pieces in the flour, salt and pepper. Melt 2½ ozs. butter in a casserole, add the mushrooms and butter, plus the bacon cut into small cubes. Put in the onions, fry for 3 minutes, now add the chicken and fry till brown all over. Add the shallots, tarragon and nutmeg. Stir well. Pour in the wine and brandy. Simmer for 30 minutes. Add the fried mushrooms.

POULET A LA VALENCIENNE

1 3-lb. chicken
3 tbsp. olive oil
2 medium onions
2 medium tomatoes
2 cloves of garlic
2 small red chillies
1 pinch of saffron
1 tsp. chopped parsley
4 ozs. Patna rice
½ pint stock
salt, pepper

Cut up the chicken as for Chicken Marengo. Peel the tomatoes and chop finely, also the onions, garlic, chillies. Heat the oil in a casserole or thick stewpot, add the garlic, cook for 3 minutes. Add the chicken pieces and the chopped parsley, onions, tomatoes, chillies, salt and pepper. Fry all till browned, stirring all the time. Put in the rice and saffron, pour over the stock. Boil up once, skim, and simmer with no lid for 30 minutes, or until rice grains are tender. Stir in with a fork. Serve with chutney sandwiches.

COQ AU VIN

1 young chicken
2 ozs. butter
2 ozs. lean bacon
¼ lb. sliced mushrooms
1 clove of garlic
bouquet garni
1 liqueur glass brandy
1 pint red wine
pepper

The blood of the chicken plus ¼ tsp. vinegar should be kept.
Divide the chicken into 6 pieces. Melt the butter in a saucepan, add the diced bacon, the mushrooms, pepper. Fry all for 5 minutes till browned. Add the chopped garlic and the *bouquet*. Pour the brandy over and set it alight, add the wine, cover the pot and simmer for 20 minutes. Now pour in the chicken blood to thicken the gravy. Serve very hot with pieces of toast.

POULET AU BLANC

1 2-lb. chicken
2 medium onions
bouquet garni
1 tsp. salt
1 oz. butter
1 tbsp. flour
¼ pint milk
¼ pint chicken stock
3 egg yolks
2 lemons
pepper
½ pint cold water

Carve the bird as for Chicken Marengo. Slice the onions, add the salt, *bouquet* and chicken pieces. Pour on the water and simmer covered for 30 minutes. Remove the chicken and put on serving dish. Keep warm. Make a sauce by melting the butter, add flour, ¼ pint hot chicken stock, ¼ pint milk. Boil and stir for 10 minutes. Remove from heat, stir in the beaten egg yolks, the juice of the lemons, pepper. Stir well and pour over the chicken.

CUISSE DE POULET A LA MOUTARDE

4 chicken legs
½ oz. butter
½ tsp. prepared mustard
1 oz. white breadcrumbs
pinch of salt

Skin the legs, rub in the butter and mustard and salt, roll in breadcrumbs. Grill on both sides till tender. Serve with Mousseline sauce (see p. 160).

DUCK WITH ORANGE

1 4-lb. duck, trussed
1 tbsp. wine vinegar
2 ozs. sugar
2 oranges, squeezed
the grated rind of 1 orange
1 wine-glass Grand Marnier
salt, pepper

Dust the duck with salt and pepper and roast for 1 hour. Ten minutes before the duck is cooked make the sauce — take a thick saucepan, boil the sugar and vinegar till it caramels. Add the orange juice, Grand Marnier, grated rind. Stir gently. Pour in the duck gravy, boil once and pour over the duck.

ALICOT

Any parts of uncooked chicken, duck, goose, turkey, you may have or remains of cold birds
2 lbs. poultry meat
2 ozs. goose fat
2 large onions
2 ozs. raw ham
5 medium tomatoes
bouquet garni

1½ pints stock
salt, pepper

Slice all the vegetables, add the ham, *bouquet*, salt, pepper, cover with the hot stock. Boil for 20 minutes. Meanwhile fry the meat in the goose fat till brown. Put the meat in a casserole. Strain the vegetable stock, pick out the ham, add the ham to the casserole plus the strained liquid. Cover and simmer for 2 hours.

CONFIT D'OIE PÉRIGOURDINE (Preserved Goose)

1 goose
enough salt to rub all the pieces
¼ pint cold water

The goose must be cut in quarters. Cut away all fat from the inside. If not enough fat, use pork or beef dripping later on.

Rub the goose pieces all over with salt. Leave for 24 hours. Melt the fat, add the pieces plus the water. Cover the pot and simmer very slowly for 3 hours.

Sprinkle salt inside a deep glazed jar or basin, pour in some of the fat; when congealed, add the goose, cover completely with the rest of the fat. Store in a cool place. This will keep for months and may be used in Cassoulet or heated in its fat and eaten with cooked haricot beans or lentils.

PARTRIDGES WITH CABBAGE

2 partridges, trussed
1 oz. butter
1 medium cabbage
1 medium carrot, sliced
1 medium onion, sliced
2 ozs. fat bacon, diced
1 dsp. flour
bouquet garni
½ pint stock
6 chipolata sausages
salt, pepper

Boil the cabbage, having cut it in 4. Keep warm. Melt the butter in a large casserole, add the bacon, onion, carrot, stir for 3 minutes on a quick heat. Dredge the birds with flour, add them to the casserole, cook, turning occasionally till brown all over. Season, put in the sausages and the *bouquet*. Pour the stock over, cover, and simmer for 20 minutes. Place the boiled cabbage on top, press down till covered by the stock. Cover and simmer for 1 hour or more, until the partridges are tender.

PARTRIDGE WITH WHITE GRAPES

2 trussed partridges
1 oz. bacon fat
6 rashers of bacon
bouquet garni
1½ lbs. white grapes
salt, pepper

Peel and seed the grapes. Cut each rasher in 3. Melt the fat in a casserole, just large enough to hold the birds, add the rashers, the birds and the *bouquet*, salt and pepper. Press in the grapes to cover the birds and simmer for 1 hour. The casserole lid must fit well: seal with flour paste if necessary.

SADDLE OF HARE BOURGUIGNON

1 saddle of hare
3 ozs. butter or dripping
¼ pint cream
¼ pint chestnut purée
salt, pepper
red currant jelly

Cover the hare with the fat, salt and pepper it. Cover with greaseproof paper and roast for 45 minutes in a fairly hot oven. Keep warm on the dish. Pour off excess fat from the gravy, add the cream and purée, stir well, re-heat but do not boil. Pour over the saddle and serve with Red Currant Jelly.

CIVET DE LIÈVRE LANDAIS

1 cut-up hare
3 ozs. goose fat or lard
12 chopped shallots
3 chopped cloves of garlic
¼ lb. diced raw ham or bacon
2 ozs. butter
1 glass red wine
¼ pint stock

1 tbsp. tomato purée or 6 peeled
  cooked tomatoes
¼ lb. sliced mushrooms or cepes
salt, pepper

Fry the hare pieces in the fat till slightly brown. Fry the shallots, garlic, bacon or ham in the butter in a casserole till brown. Add the wine, stock, tomato, mushrooms, salt and pepper. Add the fried hare pieces. Simmer for 3 hours. Serve.

RABBIT WITH LENTILS

1 lb. cooked lentils
1 cut-up rabbit
4 rashers of bacon
2 ozs. bacon fat or butter
¼ pint cider
bouquet garni
salt, pepper

Halve the rashers, add to the melted fat, plus the rabbit pieces, and fry till brown. Pour on the cider, cook for 3 minutes, add the *bouquet*, salt and pepper. Cover and simmer for 45 minutes or until the rabbit is tender. Pour the liquid over the lentils, re-heat, cook to reduce. Add the hot rabbit and bacon.

BŒUF A LA PROVENÇALE

3 lbs. lean beef
½ cup olive oil
2 medium onions
2 bacon rashers
1 tbsp. flour
bouquet garni
¼ pint white wine
¼ pint cold water
3 large tomatoes
12 green olives
salt, pepper

Chop the onions, cut up the rashers (always remove the rinds). Peel and quarter the tomatoes, stone the olives. Cut the beef in pieces 2×3 inches. Heat the olive oil in the stew pot and when fairly hot add the meat, onions, salt and pepper. Stir and add the flour, stir all the time and cook for 3 minutes. Add the *bouquet*, wine and water. Bring to the boil and simmer very gently for 3 hours. Now lift out the beef and put in another pot, add the bacon, the tomatoes and the olives. Strain the liquid over and cook again slowly for 30 minutes, shaking the pot occasionally.

BŒUF A LA MODE

3 lbs. lean beef
2 ozs. fresh pork skin — with
    ¼ inch of fat left on
3 ozs. butter
3 shallots
1 clove of garlic
6 medium carrots
1 calf's foot — split in 4
2 ozs. fat bacon — cut in cubes
½ pint claret or white wine
1 liqueur glass brandy
12 small or button onions
bouquet garni
½ tsp. salt and pepper

Melt the butter in a thick pot large enough to take the meat; when hissing hot put in the piece of meat and brown it on all sides quickly to 'close' it. Turn it with wooden spoons or tongs so as not to prick it and let the juices escape. Take the beef out and in the same pot put the pork skin cut in 2 strips. Now add all the ingredients except the carrots. Cover the pot tightly and simmer very slowly for 3 hours. Lift the lid and put in the carrots, sliced, and cook for a further 3 hours, covered. Take out the *bouquet*, the calf's foot and the pork skin. Put the beef on a dish and pour the vegetable liquid over.

FILET DE BŒUF FLAMBÉ A L'AVIGNONAISE

4 small thick fillet steaks
1 clove of garlic
5 ozs. butter
1 liqueur glass brandy
4 slices white bread
4 sprigs watercress
salt, pepper

Cut the crusts off the slices of bread. Cut the garlic clove in half and rub both halves over the steaks to get full flavour, season with salt and pepper.

Fry the bread slices in 2 ozs. butter, till golden, arrange on the serving dish and keep warm. In the cleaned frying pan melt another 2 ozs. butter; when sizzling put in the steaks and quickly brown all over, use a spoon to turn. When brown add the last 1 oz. of butter, when melted pour on the brandy. Set it alight. Cook another ½ minute. The whole steak frying should only take 3 minutes. Arrange the steaks on the fried bread and pour over the gravy. Serve at once.

TOURNEDOS SAUTÉ

1 lb. fillet steak
3 ozs. butter
¼ pint stock
1 small glass sherry
1 tsp. flour
salt, pepper

Mix ½ oz. butter with the flour in a small basin. Cut the steak across in ½ inch strips, dust with salt and pepper. Melt 2½ ozs. butter in a frying pan and when sizzling add the pieces of meat. Toss these and cook very quickly till brown, only for 2 or 3 minutes. Remove them and keep warm. Pour the sherry and the stock into the frying pan, heat, add the mixed butter and flour, stir and scrape the sides and bottom of the pan to get all the meat essence. Keep stirring quickly until the mixture is smooth, taste and add more salt if necessary, let it simmer for 3 minutes. Pour over the fillets.

PORC AU MARÉCHAL

4 pork chops
2 ozs. butter
1 tsp. chopped parsley
salt, pepper
1 small orange
1 liqueur glass Madeira or sherry
½ cup cold water

Cut the orange peel into tiny strips, boil in a small pan with the water for 5 minutes. Add the wine, and leave.

Mix the parsley on a plate with 1 oz. butter to make a paste. Leave.

Salt and pepper the chops spread with 1 oz. butter. Grill, when well done (pork must be well cooked), put on the serving dish and keep warm.

Pour the orange and wine liquid on to the juices and fat that have come from the chops. Slit each chop, rub in the parsley butter, and serve, with the sauce served separately.

RUMPSTEAK A LA HUSSARDE

2 lbs. lean rumpsteak
2 medium onions
¼ lb. mushrooms
1 pint stock
2 tbsp. milk
3 ozs. white breadcrumbs
3 ozs. calves' liver
2 egg yolks
6 ozs. butter
salt, pepper

Pick a thick square steak. Chop the liver and onions finely. Soak the breadcrumbs in the milk, squeeze dry, and mix all together, add salt and pepper. Melt 2 ozs. butter in a small saucepan, add the mixture and cook till it begins to brown. Cool and then add the egg yolks, stir well and set aside: this is the stuffing.

With a very sharp knife cut five deep slits in the steak in rows, open out like the pages of a book. Fill these with the stuffing up to ½ inch of each slit. Tie with string securely. Fry in a stew pot using the rest of the butter, quickly, till brown all over. Add a little more salt, pour the stock on gradually, add the mushroom caps and any stuffing left over. Bring to the boil, cover and then simmer very gently for 4 hours. Serve with mashed potatoes or spaghetti.

PORC A LA MARSEILLAISE

4 loin pork chops
1 egg
2 ozs. breadcrumbs
3 ozs. butter
2 lbs. onions
½ pint stock
salt, pepper

Chop the onions finely and boil in the stock till quite soft. Mash them well. Dust the chops with salt and pepper, then egg and breadcrumb them and fry in the butter till cooked.

Pile the onion purée in the middle of the dish and arrange the chops around.

AGNEAU JARDINIÈRE

1 small leg or shoulder of lamb
4 small onions, or 2 large ones
2 medium turnips
2 ozs. lard or pork fat
2 glasses dry white wine
1 tbsp. chopped parsley
1 tsp. chopped tarragon
3 tbsp. cream
salt, pepper

Quarter the vegetables. Melt the lard or pork fat in the casserole or pot, fry the vegetables till they brown. Add salt and pepper. Put in the meat and turn to 'close' it. Pour on the wine, cover tightly and simmer for 2½ hours. Lift out meat and vegetables, keep warm. Remove excess fat from the gravy, add the parsley, tarragon and stir in the cream.

This dish should be served in slices on a plate surrounded by the vegetables with the gravy poured over.

PORK IN CASSEROLE

2 lbs. pork
2 ozs. butter
1 clove of garlic
½ tsp. chopped sage
¼ pint hot water
salt, pepper

Old, lean pork will do for this dish.

Cut up the meat in 2 inch cubes. Melt the butter in the casserole, add the pork pieces, salt and pepper, stir till browned. Add the sage and chopped garlic, stir again. Cook very slowly in the covered casserole, turning the meat with a wooden spoon occasionally for 2 hours. Add the hot water and stir thoroughly.

Cooked chestnuts are good with this dish.

GIGOT A LA PROVENÇALE

1 leg mutton
1 clove of garlic
1 oz. butter
salt, pepper
3 anchovy fillets
3 chopped gherkins

Slit the meat next the bone and push in the garlic about 1 inch down. Dust with salt and pepper and rub with the butter. Roast the meat, 20 minutes to the lb. Keep the meat gravy, to which you add the anchovy fillets and the gherkins, all very finely chopped. Pour over the roast joint.

GIGOT A LA BRETONNE

1 small leg of mutton
1 clove of garlic
2 ozs. butter
5 ozs. haricot beans
1 large onion
1 large tomato
1 shallot
bouquet garni
salt, pepper
water

Soak the haricot beans over night. Take the beans and the whole onion, add the *bouquet*, salt and pepper, cover with water and boil till soft, skimming frequently. Strain. Keep the beans and the onion warm.

Slit the meat and press the garlic in next the bone. Dust with salt and pepper and rub with 1 oz. butter. Roast the ordinary way, 20 minutes to the lb. Keep warm in the serving dish. Keep the gravy in the pan. Make a sauce by melting 1 oz. butter, salt and pepper, add the chopped shallot, the tomato peeled and quartered and the boiled onion. Cook till soft. Stir this mixture into the gravy left in the roasting pan, add the cooked beans and pour over the roast joint.

LAMB CUTLETS A LA MINUTE

8 lamb cutlets
4 ozs. butter
½ tsp. lemon juice
salt, pepper

Beat the cutlets very flat, or ask the butcher to do it.

Sprinkle with salt and pepper. Fry in the sizzling butter for 1 minute each side. Put in the serving dish. Add lemon juice to the butter in the pan, stir and pour over the cutlets.

ROAST LAMB A LA NICOISE

1 leg of lamb
6 small vegetable marrows
　(courgettes)
1 large tomato
12 small potatoes
½ tsp. salt
pepper
¼ pint olive oil

Halve the courgettes, do not peel them; peel and slice the tomato, peel the potatoes. Put these in the flat roasting pan, add salt and pepper. Put the joint on top, pour over the olive oil, cover with grease-proof paper and roast 15 minutes to the lb.

AGNEAU RÔTI PERSILLÉ

1 leg of lamb
2 ozs. white bread-
　crumbs
2 tsp. chopped parsley
1 clove of garlic,
　chopped
pinch of salt, pepper
} persillade

Roast the lamb, 15 minutes to the lb. When three-quarters cooked, spread the breadcrumbs, parsley, garlic, salt, pepper mixed together on top. Baste once or twice until the meat is cooked and the persillade golden brown.

ROAST LAMB A LA BORDELAISE

1 leg lamb
3 ozs. butter
3 tbsp. olive oil
½ lb. mushrooms
1 tsp. chopped parsley

1 chopped clove of garlic
pinch salt, pepper

Roast the lamb in a large casserole or covered stew pot adding all the ingredients, 15 minutes to the lb.

LAMB STEW

2 lbs. best end neck of lamb
1 tbsp. flour
2 medium onions
1 oz. butter
1 pint stock
3 large tomatoes
3 medium turnips
1 dsp. mushroom catsup
1 glass dry sherry
salt, pepper

Have the meat cut up by the butcher. Trim excess fat. Peel and slice the tomatoes, chop the onions and turnips. Melt the butter in the stewpan, add the meat and fry till brown on all sides. Remove the meat. Add the flour to the butter, stir till brown, pour on the stock and stir till the mixture boils. Add the meat, the vegetables, salt and pepper. Cover closely and simmer gently for 2 hours. Before serving stir in the sherry and catsup.

More carrots and turnips should be served as a vegetable.

ROAST LAMB A LA BONNE FEMME

1 leg of lamb
3 rashers fat bacon
12 small onions
¼ lb. butter
pinch salt, pepper

Cut 10 or 12 larding strips of bacon and lard the joint. Cook in a covered casserole, 15 minutes to the lb. with the butter, salt, pepper and onions whole.

PAUPIETTES DE VEAU CLEMENTINE

1 lb. veal cut in very thin slices
½ bacon rasher to each slice
1 medium onion
1 tbsp. flour
½ tsp. lemon juice
2 ozs. butter
salt, pepper
1 glass white wine
¼ pint cold water
½ tsp. chopped parsley
pinch of thyme
1 small strip lemon peel
6 capers

Dust the veal slices in flour, salt and pepper and add a few drops of lemon juice to each slice. Put ½ bacon rasher on top of each slice and roll up, peg or tie securely — these make the paupiettes. Slice the onion finely and fry in the butter till soft, add the paupiettes and brown, turning gently. When brown add the parsley, thyme, lemon peel and capers, pour on the wine water and simmer very gently for 10 minutes. Strain the liquid over the paupiettes and serve — of course remove pegs or cotton.

ESCALOPES DE VEAU AUX OLIVES

4 veal escallops
1 dsp. flour
2 ozs. butter
12 black olives
1 glass white wine
salt, pepper
½ tsp. lemon juice

Dust the escallops in the flour, salt and pepper, brown quickly in the butter, lower the heat and cook very slowly for 8 minutes. Stone the olives and add them to the meat, cook together for 2 minutes, then lift the meat and olives out of the pan. Keep warm on the serving dish. Add the wine and lemon juice, stir and scrape round the pan, cook till the gravy begins to thicken, pour over the escallops.

ESCALOPES DE VEAU CHASSEUR

4 veal escallops
1 dsp. flour
salt, pepper
3 ozs. butter
2 tomatoes
¼ lb. mushrooms
½ tsp. chopped tarragon

Dust the escallops in flour, season with salt and pepper and brown quickly in butter. Keep warm. Peel and slice the tomatoes and mushrooms and cook till soft, in 1 oz. butter, add the tarragon. Put in the cooked veal, stir gently and cook slowly for 6 minutes more.

ESCALOPES DE VEAU AU BEURRE D'ANCHOIS

8 veal escallops
6 ozs. butter
1 oz. flour
salt, pepper
¼ cup white wine
¼ cup hot water
8 slices stale white bread
2 anchovy fillets
a few drops of lemon juice
parsley

Mash the anchovies and lemon juice in 1 oz. butter to make a paste. Fry the bread (crusts removed) in 2 ozs. butter till golden. Take out and spread with the anchovy paste and keep warm, arranged on the serving dish.

Ask your butcher to flatten the escalopes, or beat them with a wooden spoon. Dust with the flour, salt and pepper.

Heat the 3 ozs. butter in the frying pan, and fry the escalopes till brown on both sides, quickly, taking about 8 minutes all told. Remove the escalopes and put one on each piece of fried bread, keeping warm in the oven. Pour the wine and water into the pan, and scrape the sides and bottom and stir till the gravy thickens. Cook for 2 minutes more. Pour over the escallops. Before serving decorate with parsley sprigs.

ESCALOPES DE VEAU A LA ROYALE (A recipe from Dijon)

4 slices white bread fried in butter
4 large veal escallops
1 tbsp. olive oil
2 medium onions
4 tbsp. cold water
2 tbsp. cream
2 egg yolks
2 tbsp. brandy
2 tbsp. port
salt, pepper

Put the escallops in the heated oil. Add the sliced onions; cook, turning frequently till brown. Now add the cold water, salt and pepper. Stir and leave to cook very slowly for 8 or 10 minutes. Lift out the escallops and place one on each slice of fried bread on the serving dish. Keep warm. Beat the egg yolks and stir into the cream, add this to the gravy, also the brandy and the port. Cook very gently, stirring all the time until the sauce begins to thicken, pour at once over the escallops and serve.

VEAL CUTLETS A LA MARÉCHALE

4 veal cutlets
1 oz. breadcrumbs
1 oz. grated Parmesan cheese
1 egg
2 ozs. butter
1 orange
salt, pepper

Pepper and salt each cutlet, brush with the egg and roll them in the mixed cheese and breadcrumbs. Fry in the butter till golden brown. Squeeze the juice of the orange over them. As a vegetable serve spinach.

BLANQUETTE DE VEAU AU RIZ

2 lbs. shoulder of veal
½ lb. mushrooms, chopped
4 medium onions
3 ozs. butter
1 egg yolk
¼ pint cream
¼ pint dry white wine
1 tsp. lemon juice
2 tbsp. flour
1 liqueur glass dry vermouth
bouquet garni
salt, pepper
4 cups hot water
cooked rice

Melt the butter in the stewpan; when hot, put in the veal cut in 1½ inch cubes, stir and cook till slightly brown. Add the chopped onions, stir, then the flour, stir and lower the heat. Cook gently for 3 minutes, stir again, add the wine and the vermouth, salt and pepper and the *bouquet*. Pour on the water, cover the pan, simmer for 1¼ hours, add the sliced mushrooms and simmer for another ¼ hour. Meanwhile heat the egg yolk in the lemon juice, and add two minutes before serving, also the cream. Remove *bouquet*. Keep warm but do NOT boil, as this will curdle the gravy. Serve with cooked rice.

VEAL AU BOULANGER

4 veal cutlets
2 ozs. butter
1 tsp. chopped parsley
salt, pepper
1 lb. apples
1 small strip lemon rind
1 dsp. sugar
¼ pint water

Peel and chop the apples, add the water and lemon rind. Stew till soft, add the sugar. Mash them or put through a sieve.

Mix 1½ ozs. butter with the parsley to make a paste. Salt and pepper the cutlets, spread with ½ oz. butter and grill till done. Slit each cutlet and press in the parsley butter. Serve the cutlets sitting on a bed of the apple purée.

FRICANDEAU DE VEAU

3 lbs. fillet veal
salt, pepper
8 medium carrots or 12 small ones
4 rashers of fat bacon for larding
1 slice fresh pork fat, enough to
  wrap round the veal
6 medium onions
2 cups stock
bouquet garni

Roll the larding pieces of bacon in salt and pepper and lard the meat, and wrap in the piece of pork fat. Put it in a heavy stew pan, add the sliced carrots and onions, the *bouquet* and pour over the stock. Simmer gently for 3½ hours with the lid on.

Now take out the meat, remove the pork fat, and strain the liquid. Put the meat and the liquid back in the pot and cook quickly to reduce by a quarter. Skim off excess fat. Press the vegetables through a sieve into the pot, stir, re-heat and serve. The veal should be soft enough to cut with a spoon. Spinach is the best vegetable to have with this dish.

FOIE DE VEAU SAUTÉ (Fried Calves' Liver)

½ lb. calves' liver
2½ ozs. butter
4 rashers of bacon
2 medium onions
1 tsp. chopped parsley
2 tbsp. water
salt, pepper

Melt 2 ozs. butter in a frying pan, add a pinch of salt and pepper, when hot put in the pieces of liver and fry quickly for 3 minutes, turning the pieces till brown all over. Cover the pan and remove from the heat.

Butter a shallow fireproof dish with ½ oz. butter, add the finely sliced onions and bacon cut in ½ inch squares (always remove the rinds), the parsley, salt and pepper. Slip the liver out of the frying pan plus all the juices and butter onto this mixture, add the water. Cover the dish tightly and in a moderate oven cook for 20 minutes.

CALVES' LIVER

½ lb. calves' liver
1 tbsp. flour
salt, pepper
3 ozs. butter
1 tsp. lemon juice
1 small glass white wine
1 tsp. chopped parsley

Have the liver cut in slices ¼ inch thick. Roll the pieces in a mixture of the flour, parsley, salt and pepper: Melt 2½ ozs. butter in a frying pan and fry quickly for 2 minutes on each side, lower the heat, cover the pan and cook very gently for 10 minutes more without disturbing. Remove the liver and put on the serving dish; keep warm.

Pour the wine in the frying pan, stirring and scraping to collect all the juices, add ½ oz. butter and the lemon juice. Stir and pour over the liver.

OX TONGUE WITH MUSHROOMS

1 ox tongue
1 large onion
1 stick celery
1 bay leaf
½ tsp. salt
½ tsp. pepper
enough cold water to cover
1 oz. butter
1 oz. flour
½ pint tongue stock ⎫
1 dsp. French mustard ⎬ sauce
¼ lb. mushrooms ⎭
1 oz. butter
3 pickled gherkins, chopped

1 glass dry white wine
3 tbsp. cream

Put the tongue (previously soaked for 12 hours in cold water) in enough water to cover it, add the onion, celery, bay leaf, salt and pepper. Bring to the boil, skim if necessary, and simmer for 4 hours.

Take the tongue out of the pot, skin it and remove hard root and nerve. Keep warm on the serving dish.

Now for the sauce. Slice the mushrooms and fry in butter. Make the sauce as for Brown Sauce, adding the mustard. Be careful with the salt. Add the fried mushrooms, the gherkins and the wine and cream. Pour over the tongue and serve.

BEEF KIDNEY A LA PARISIENNE

1 very fresh beef kidney
1 clove of garlic
2 ozs. butter
1 tsp. wine vinegar
1 tsp. chopped parsley
1 tsp. chopped chives or onion
1 tsp. flour
1 cup stock
salt, pepper

Skin and core the kidney, cut in ¼ slices. Melt the butter in a small pan, add the kidney, chive or onions, salt, pepper, fry for 3 or 4 minutes till brown, lower heat, stir in the flour, add the vinegar, stir again. Cook for 1 minute then add the stock. Stir till the gravy begins to thicken, and serve. Do not boil or the kidney slices will become hard.

ROGNON DE VEAU A LA LIÈGEOISE (Calves' Kidney à la Liègeoise)

4 veal kidneys
2 ozs. butter
1 small glass dry white wine
16 juniper berries
½ tsp. lemon juice
salt, pepper

Skin the kidneys, leaving on a little of the fat. Melt 1½ ozs. butter in a small saucepan; when sizzling, add the whole kidneys, salt and pepper, turn each kidney till brown — a matter of seconds. Lower the heat and add the wine. Cover with a tight lid and cook extremely slowly for 5 minutes. Add the juniper berries, lemon juice, ½ oz. butter, stir, and continue stirring over a very low heat for 5 minutes more. Serve on toast if you wish.

TÊTE DE VEAU VINAIGRETTE (Calf's head with Sauce Vinaigrette)

1 calf's head
1 tbsp. flour
2 large carrots
1 large onion
2 lemons or 2 tbsp. wine vinegar
2 cloves
1 bouquet garni
½ tsp. salt
½ tsp. pepper
5 quarts boiling water

Ask the butcher to split the head and remove the tongue and brains. Soak altogether in cold water for 12 hours.

Put the flour, salt, pepper, chopped onion, chopped carrot, the juice of the 2 lemons, or the vinegar, the cloves and the 'bouquet' in a pan large enough to hold the head. Pour on the boiling water and simmer for 15 minutes. Add the head, brains and tongue. Boil for 30 minutes and take out the tongue and brains (easier if previously tied in muslin). Peel the tongue and keep warm with the brains, on a plate over hot water. Simmer the head for another 1½ hours. Cut the hot meat from the head and arrange on the serving dish with the tongue cut in slices and the brains. Serve with Sauce Vinaigrette (see p. 162).

ROGNONS AU MADÈRE (Sheep's Kidneys in Dry Sherry)

4 sheep's kidneys
2 ozs. butter
½ glass dry sherry
¼ lb. mushrooms
½ tsp. flour
few drops of lemon juice
1 tsp. chopped parsley
salt, pepper
4 pieces toast

This is a good entrée. Make the toast and put in the serving dish. Skin and halve the kidneys. Cut each half in three pieces. Slice or chop the mushrooms.

Melt the butter in a small saucepan, add the pieces of kidney, the mushrooms, flour, salt and pepper. Cook fairly quickly, for 3 or 4 minutes, stirring all the time. Pour on the sherry, stir again, then the drops of lemon juice and the parsley. Stir to mix, pour over the toast and serve at once. This whole job must be done very quickly to keep the kidneys tender.

CALVES' BRAINS WITH BLACK BUTTER

4 calves' brains
boiling water
½ cup wine vinegar
1 medium onion
¼ tsp. salt
bouquet garni
4 ozs. butter
¼ tsp. vinegar
2 tsp. chopped parsley

Soak the brains in cold water for 1 hour. Throw into boiling water for 5 minutes, drain, skin and clean.

Put them in a saucepan, add ½ cup of vinegar, the salt, chopped onion, and the *bouquet*. Simmer for 30 minutes. Remove, drain and keep warm in the serving dish. Melt the butter till dark brown, cook for 2 minutes, add ¼ tsp. vinegar, stir and pour over the brains. Sprinkle parsley over and serve.

CALVES' FEET A LA MENAGÈRE

3 calves' feet
cold water
1½ ozs. butter
1 large onion
1 large tomato
bouquet garni
salt, pepper
1 dsp. flour

¼ pint stock
1 liqueur glass white wine

Have the feet split in three. Cover with cold water, boil for 2 hours. Bone carefully. Melt the butter, add the flesh off the feet, the onion chopped, tomato peeled and seeded, the *bouquet*, salt, pepper; stir, add the flour, stir again; then add the stock and wine, and simmer for 20 minutes.

SWEETBREADS (Ris de Veau, Ris d'Agneau)

Preparation of Sweetbreads: The 'heart' round ones are best. Remove all blood, hard tubes, etc., soak in cold water for 4 hours.

Remove and put in a stewpan, cover with cold water or stock, bring to the boil, simmer for 2½ minutes. Throw into cold water, drain, trim to a tidy shape, and set between two plates or boards with a weight on top till cold.

ASPARAGUS

1½ lbs. asparagus
3 ozs. butter
boiling water
salt, pepper

Asparagus should be cooked standing up, as the stalks take longer than the tips.

Trim the stalks, wash gently and tie in a tidy bundle. Stand in a jug or deep jar, add a little salt, pour in boiling water two-thirds of the way up. Stand this in a pan of boiling water. Cover the pan and boil for 30 minutes. Serve with melted butter, pepper and salt.

TRIPE A LA MODE DE CAEN (1)

2½ lbs. tripe, cut in 2 inch squares
1 leek washed and trimmed ⎤
1 small onion stuck with 3 cloves ⎬ *bouquet garni*
1 bay leaf |
1 sprig thyme ⎦
4 large onions
1 calf's foot split in 4
½ lb. chopped beef suet
1 tsp. salt
½ tsp. pepper
½ pint cider
2 tbsp. Calvados
cold water
1 cup flour
2 or 3 tbsp. cold water

Tie the *bouquet* together firmly, or tie up in a piece of muslin. Make a stiff paste with the flour and water.

Slice the onions. Put a layer of onions in the bottom of a large casserole, then a layer of tripe, the calf's foot, a layer of suet, another layer of onions, tripe, the *bouquet* and finish with a layer of suet. Add the Calvados, the cider, salt and pepper and enough water to cover the layers. Put on the lid and seal the edges tightly with the flour paste. Cook in a very slow oven for 12 hours.

When cooked, remove the *bouquet*, and the calf's foot. Pick the flesh off this and put in the casserole. Skim off any excess fat. Serve boiling hot, with boiled potatoes.

TRIPE A LA MODE DE CAEN (2)

2 lbs. tripe cut in 1 inch squares
1 cow heel or *2 calves' feet cut in 1 inch pieces*
4 leeks
2 large carrots
3 large onions
2 bay leaves ⎤
6 cloves ⎬ *bouquet garni*
2 sprigs of thyme ⎦

1 pint cider or dry white wine
½ port glass of brandy
2 tsp. chopped parsley
enough water to cover everything
salt, pepper

Put all these ingredients, except the chopped parsley, in a large casserole, or stewpan, covered with a very tight lid. Simmer for 11 hours. Take out the *bouquet*, sprinkle with chopped parsley and serve boiling hot.

SWEETBREADS A LA MINUTE

4 sweetbreads
1½ oz. butter
2 tsp. lemon juice
1 tsp. chopped parsley
salt, pepper

Melt the butter; when sizzling, put in the prepared sweetbreads, fry for 2 or 3 minutes, turning to brown. Remove to serving dish. Add pinch of salt, pepper, lemon juice and parsley to the gravy and pour over the sweetbreads.

JERUSALEM ARTICHOKES

2 lbs. artichokes
1 pint cold water
1½ oz. butter
or
1 pint Béchamel sauce
salt, pepper

Scrub the unpeeled artichokes thoroughly. Cover with cold salted water, boil till tender, about 20 minutes. Drain, keep the liquid. Cool slightly then rub the skin off. Serve with melted butter, salt and pepper, or Béchamel sauce made with half milk and half the artichoke liquid.

ARTICHOKES (Globe)

Cut off the stems and the top. Remove the very hard outer leaves. Plunge them, stem end down, into boiling water, boil for 30 minutes, uncovered. Drain well upside down. Serve with melted butter, French dressing or Hollandaise sauce (see p. 159).

AUBERGINES WITH HERBS

4 aubergines or breadfruit
2 rashers bacon, diced
2 cloves of garlic
½ tsp. mixed chopped marjoram
  and basil
salt, pepper
4 tbsp. olive oil

In each unpeeled aubergine cut two slits lengthways. Chop each clove of garlic into 4, roll in salt and herbs. Fill the slits with the bacon dice and garlic. Pour over the oil. Put the aubergines in a shallow covered fireproof dish and bake in a slow oven for 1 hour.

BRAISED CELERY

3 heads of celery
2 ozs. butter
2 tbsp. meat glaze or
½ tsp. Bovril

Cut each thoroughly clean head in half, throw into boiling water and boil for 10 minutes. Drain till dry. Melt the butter in a covered shallow fireproof dish, add the celery and cook slowly for 30 minutes or more, till tender. 5 minutes before serving add the glaze or Bovril.

CREAMED SPINACH

2 lbs. young spinach
4 ozs. butter
¼ pint cream
¼ tsp. nutmeg
½ tsp. sugar
salt, pepper

Wash and chop the spinach finely. Melt the butter, add the spinach, stir over a good heat until there is no juice left. Add the cream, nutmeg, sugar, salt and pepper. Stir well and simmer gently for 10 minutes.

CREAMED BEETROOT

8 small young boiled beetroots
8 grapes, peeled and pipped
2 tbsp. cream
a few drops of lemon juice
1 pint Béchamel sauce
  (see p. 163)

Peel and slice the boiled beetroots, add them to the hot sauce with the grapes. Simmer for 5 minutes. Just before serving stir in the cream and the lemon juice.

CREAMED CUCUMBERS

2 cucumbers
½ tsp. chopped mint
salt, pepper
½ pint thick Béchamel sauce
  (see p. 163)

Peel and cut the cucumbers in fingers. Season and steam for 20 minutes till soft. Add the chopped mint to the sauce and the cucumbers.

GREEN BEANS MAÎTRE D'HÔTEL

2 lbs. French beans
2 pints boiling water
3 ozs. butter
1 tbsp. chopped parsley
salt, pepper

Pick dark green small young beans. Wash and trim the ends. Boil whole uncovered in salted water for 20 minutes. Drain. Melt the butter, re-heat the beans in it. Sprinkle parsley, salt and pepper over.

SALSIFY

1 lb. salsify
½ tsp. vinegar
1 oz. butter
salt, pepper

Wash, trim and scrape each root, put in cold water plus the vinegar to prevent turning black. Throw into boiling salted water, boil for 20 minutes. Drain. Heat the butter and toss the cooked vegetables in it, season and serve hot.

GLAZED TURNIPS

12 small very young turnips
1 pint boiling salted water
1 tsp. caster sugar
2 ozs. butter

Prepare the turnips, pour over the water and boil for 15 minutes, till soft.

Butter a flat fireproof dish, add the drained turnips, sprinkle with sugar and put dabs of butter on top. Cook very slowly till the sauce turns brown and sticky. Do not burn. Stir the turnips round in the glaze and serve.

GREEN PEAS WITH LETTUCE

2 lbs. peas in pod
or
1 large packet frozen peas
1 tbsp. warm water
1 small lettuce
3 small chopped onions
1 oz. butter
salt, pepper

Shell the peas — thaw if the frozen sort. Wash and pull apart the lettuce.

Melt the butter, cook the onions till soft, add the lettuce leaves, salt, pepper, peas, warm water; stir, cover the pan and cook gently for 20 minutes, shaking the pan occasionally.

PURÉE OF CHESTNUTS

2 lbs. chestnuts
½ pint water
pepper
1 oz. butter
3 tbsp. cream
3 tbsp. stock

Prick each nut and bake in a moderate oven for 20 minutes. Peel off both skins.

Put the chestnuts in a casserole, pour on the water, add pepper, cover and cook slowly for 1½ hours.

When done, sieve or mash very finely, add the butter, cream and stock, stir and re-heat slowly.

ENDIVES IN BUTTER

4 endives (or chicory)
2 ozs. butter
½ tsp. lemon juice
salt

Prepare the endives, but do not cut them. Melt the butter in a casserole with a tight lid, add the endives. Turn well in the butter. Cook slowly till tender for about 20 minutes and golden brown. Add salt and lemon juice.

ROAST ONIONS

8 or 12 medium onions

Do not skin the onions. Bake them in a hot oven for 1½ hours. Peel off the skins.

Serve with butter, salt and pepper.

POTATOES A L'ÉCHIRLETE

1½ lbs. small potatoes
½ pint stock or cold water
2 cloves of garlic
1 tbsp. goose or pork fat
salt, pepper

Put the peeled potatoes in a large pan. Add the liquid, salt, pepper, plus the garlic. Cover the pan and cook till the liquid is absorbed. Melt the fat in a frying pan, add the potatoes and cook slowly, turning from time to time till brown all over.

GALETTE OF POTATOES

1½ lbs. potatoes
1 tbsp. olive oil
1 tbsp. butter
¼ tsp. ground nutmeg
salt, pepper

Peel and slice the potatoes very thinly, wash well in cold water. Dry them well.

Melt the oil and butter in a large frying pan. When hot arrange the slices flatly. Add nutmeg, salt and pepper. Fry for 5 minutes. Lower the heat, cover the pan and cook gently for 15 minutes. Turn them over, continue for 4 minutes.

Serve whole as a pancake or cut in 4.

PUFF PASTRY FOR VOL-AU-VENT

1 lb. plain flour
1 tsp. salt
⅜ pint water
11 ozs. washed butter

Squeeze the butter in your hands under a running tap for 3 minutes. Put the flour on a board, make a hole in the middle, put in the salt and some of the water, work with your finger tips, adding the rest of the water, very quickly, until it forms a ball. Flatten it with your hand. Leave for 10 minutes. Roll the butter into a ball half as big as the dough and put it on top of the dough. Flour the rolling pin and roll quickly and lightly into a strip 8×24 ins. by ¼ inch thick. Fold each end towards the middle to make a square. Leave for 15 minutes. Now roll again, having turned the strip round; fold as before and leave for 15 minutes. Repeat these two processes 4 times. Work in a cool place.

PROVENÇAL TOMATOES

4 large tomatoes
2 cloves of garlic
4 tsp. chopped parsley
salt, pepper
2 tbsp. olive oil

Do not peel the tomatoes. Halve them. Pound the garlic salt and pepper together. Score the pulp of each tomato half and press in the garlic mixture. Sprinkle with parsley, pour on the oil. Arrange in a flat fireproof dish and put under the grill for 6 or 7 minutes. Increase the heat and slightly blacken the surfaces.

POMMES ANNA

2 lbs. potatoes
3 ozs. butter
salt, pepper

FLOUR PASTE:
2 ozs. flour
1 tbsp. cold water
salt, pepper

Butter a straight-sided fireproof dish. Cut the peeled potatoes in very thin rings, soak in cold water for 10 minutes. Drain and dry them thoroughly. Fill the dish with the rings in layers, dotting each layer with dabs of butter, salt and pepper. Spread the top layer with butter. Seal the lid with the paste. Bake in a moderate-to-slow oven for 45 minutes, take out the 'cake' and put back upside down. Re-cover and bake another 45 minutes. Pour off excess butter and turn out the golden cake.

VOL-AU-VENT

Roll out the puff pastry $\frac{1}{2}$ inch thick. Cut out 4 rounds, say 7 inches in diameter. Keep 2, and cut out a circle 4 inches across in the other two. Moisten each round ring with water and build up in layers. Keep one 4 inch circle to make the lid. Put in a refrigerator or cold place for 20 minutes. Beat 2 egg yolks with 2 tbsp. water and brush the whole case, sides top and lid. Moisten the baking sheet with water, put on the case with the lid on top, bake in a very hot oven for 5 minutes, then in a moderate oven for 30 minutes longer. Scoop out the soft middle to make room for the stuffing.

MUSHROOM, CHICKEN, LOBSTER, SHRIMP OR HAM VOL-AU-VENT

Take enough cooked chopped mushrooms, ham, chicken or lobster meat or shrimps and mix with a thick Béchamel sauce, make a fairly thick mixture (see p. 163). Fill the vol-au-vent, place the lid on top and re-heat gently in the oven.

PLAIN OMELETTE

8 eggs
2 ozs. butter
½ tsp. salt
black pepper
1½ tsp. cold water

Break each egg into a cup first before putting in the mixing bowl; if any egg looks even slightly 'off', discard it. Add the salt, pepper and water. Beat with a fork for ½ a minute, not longer. Meanwhile, the frying pan, a heavy iron one not less than 8 inch diameter at base, should be heating slowly. Put in the butter, or butter and lard, turn up the heat. In a moment when the butter stops frothing, stir the egg mixture and pour it into the pan. Reduce the heat a little, and with a fork loosen the edges and let the excess mixture flow under; do this for 2 minutes. Fold the omelette over, press round the unfolded edges with the fork and slip onto serving dish. Rub some butter on the top and eat at once. If cooked quickly like this the omelette will be brown outside and wet inside.

MUSHROOM OMELETTE

6 eggs
¼ lb. mushrooms
2 ozs. butter

Slice the mushrooms finely, fry till soft in the butter, add salt and pepper. Cool, then add to the beaten eggs and cook as for plain omelette.

OMELETTE AUX FINES HERBES

6 eggs
salt
pepper
1 tsp. water
1 tbsp. chopped parsley

1 tbsp. chopped chives or
    tarragon

Mix the herbs into the egg mixture, add salt, pepper and water and cook as for plain omelette.

QUICHE LORRAINE (1) (Cream Custard and Bacon Tart)

6 ozs. flour
2 ozs. butter
1 oz. dripping
6 rashers bacon
½ pint cream
2 eggs
salt, pepper
⅛ pint water

Make a pastry with the flour, butter, dripping, salt and water. Roll it 2 or 3 times, leave in a ball for 1 hour.

Line a flan tin (6—8 inches in diameter) with the pastry. Dice the bacon, of course having taken off the rind, and fry for 1 minute. Spread over the bottom of the pastry. Now beat the eggs into the cream, add salt and pepper, pour over the bacon and bake in a moderate oven for 25 minutes. Serve with tomato salad, dressed with French dressing.

QUICHE LORRAINE (2) (Cheese Custard and Bacon Tart)

pastry
6 bacon rashers
1 cup grated cheese, Parmesan
1 cup grated cheese, Gruyère
2 eggs
¼ pint milk

black pepper
watercress salad

Make the pastry and line the tin with the bacon as in the previous recipe. Mix the cheese with the eggs, milk and pepper, pour over the bacon. Bake in a slow to moderate oven till brown, about 20 minutes. Serve with watercress salad, with French dressing.

PISSALADIÈRE

1 lb. dough
2 lbs. onions
20 stoned black olives
12 anchovy fillets
¼ pint olive oil

Ask the baker to give you the dough. Pull it out and spread on a baking dish. Slice the onions and cook in the oil very slowly for 40 minutes, till they make a thick purée. Pour the purée over the dough, decorate with the olives and anchovies. Bake in a moderate oven for 30 minutes.

If dough is hard to get, unsweetened pastry can be used or slices of a sandwich loaf cut lengthways 1 inch thick with the crusts removed. If bread is used, fry each slice on one side only, spread the purée, etc. and cook for only 10 minutes.

Serve with lettuce salad and French dressing.

SAVOURY RICE WITH CABBAGE

1 small white cabbage
¼ lb. peeled, sliced tomatoes
¼ lb. sliced onions
2 ozs. bacon fat
1 oz. sultanas or currants
2 rashers bacon, diced
1 tin tomato juice
½ tsp. nutmeg
½ tsp. thyme chopped
2 sugar lumps
⅛ of rind of 1 lemon chopped
*   finely*
1 clove of garlic

salt, pepper
½ lb. rice

Undercook the rice in boiling salted water for only 15 minutes. Fry the onions and mushrooms in the bacon fat. Slice the cabbage thinly. Mix together the tomatoes, mushrooms, onions, sultanas or currants, nutmeg, thyme, pinch of salt and pepper with the rice. Put a layer of cabbage in a deep casserole, then a layer of the rice mixture. Repeat this till the casserole is ¾ full. Add the garlic, lemon rind, salt and pepper to the tomato juice, and pour this into the casserole. Cover. Cook in a very slow oven for 2 hours.

ONION TART LORRAINE

8 ozs. plain flour
4 ozs. butter
¼ tsp. salt
4 tbsp. cold water
2 lbs. sliced onions
3 ozs. bacon fat
2 eggs

2 ozs. grated Gruyère cheese
salt, pepper

Make the pastry of the flour, butter, salt and water. Roll out and line tart tin. Melt the bacon fat, add the onions, salt and pepper. Cook gently, stirring now and then, for 30 minutes till soft, in a covered pan. Cool, add the beaten eggs, cheese, stir well. Pour into the tart tin and bake in a moderate oven for 20 minutes.

STUFFED LOAF

1 sandwich loaf
½ lb. chicken livers ⎫
1 pair sweetbreads ⎬ fried
½ lb. mushrooms ⎭
½ pint Béchamel sauce
  (see p. 163)
½ tsp. chopped parsley
½ tsp. chopped chives
½ tsp. chopped tarragon
16 rashers bacon

Scoop the crumb out of the sandwich loaf by opening one end. Mix the finely chopped fried chicken livers, sweetbreads and mushrooms previously fried, with the Béchamel and herbs. Line a deep casserole with 8 bacon rashers, of course no rinds, put in the stuffed loaf and put 8 more rashers on top. Cover the casserole and bake in a slow oven for 40 minutes. Serve cut in slices with a vegetable. Spinach, cabbage or cauliflower are good with this dish.

STUFFED MARROWS

STUFFING:
4 ozs. cooked pork
2 ozs. cooked beef or mutton
4 ozs. white breadcrumbs
salt, pepper
1 medium onion, chopped
1 shallot
1 clove of garlic
2 eggs
2 tsp. chopped parsley

4 small young marrows
2 medium peeled sliced tomatoes
3 ozs. grated Gruyère cheese
1 oz. butter

Wash and cut the marrows lengthways. Scoop out the seeds and flesh, leaving ¼ inch on edge. Butter a shallow fireproof dish and put in the 8 pieces. Make the stuffing and fill each half marrow. Sprinkle with the cheese and bake in a moderate oven for 20 minutes, place the tomato slices on top and bake 10 minutes longer.

STUFFED RED CABBAGE LANDAIS

1 medium red cabbage, sliced
1 lb. cooking apples, peeled, cored
  and sliced
1 lb. onions, sliced
2 red peppers, de-seeded and
  sliced
¼ of peel of 1 orange cut in strips
1 clove of garlic, chopped
1 tbsp. mixed herbs, chopped
1 tsp. pepper
1 tsp. salt
1 tsp. ground cloves

1 tsp. ground nutmeg
8 smoked frankfurter sausages
¼ pint red wine
¼ pint wine vinegar

In a large casserole put a layer of cabbage, then a layer of onions then one of apples. Sprinkle with some of the sugar, red peppers, orange peel, garlic, herbs, salt, pepper, cloves and nutmeg. Repeat this until everything is used up. Pour in the wine and vinegar. Cover and cook for 3½ hours. Now, bury the sausages deep in the dish and cook for a further 20 minutes.

CHEESE SOUFFLÉ

4 ozs. butter
2 ozs. flour
1 pint milk, hot
¼ tsp. salt
4 eggs
5 ozs. grated Parmesan cheese

Butter a soufflé dish. Separate the eggs, beat the whites till stiff. Melt the butter in a saucepan, add the flour and salt, add the hot milk gradually, stirring all the time, cook for 3 minutes, stirring, till smooth. Remove from the heat, beat in the yolks one at a time, add the cheese, stir well. Fold in the whites. Mix carefully. Bake in the buttered dish in moderate oven for 20 minutes. Eat immediately.

FISH SOUFFLÉ

Proceed as for Cheese Soufflé, but add 6 ozs. cooked flaked white fish instead of cheese.

RATATOUILLE (Provençal Vegetable Stew)

2 aubergines
2 large onions, sliced
4 medium tomatoes, peeled and
  quartered
2 red or green pimentos, sliced
¼ pint olive oil
2 cloves of garlic, finely chopped
salt, pepper

Slit the pimentos in the side and pull out seeds and core, wash thoroughly to remove every seed. Cut the aubergines into 1 inch squares.

Warm the oil in a large frying pan, add the chopped onions and stew gently for 8 minutes. Now add the sliced pimentos, aubergines, stew gently for 10 minutes. Add garlic, salt and pepper, then the quartered tomatoes. Cover the pan and simmer gently for another 10 minutes, or until all the oil has been absorbed.

RATATOUILLE WITH FRIED EGGS

1 lb. potatoes
¾ lb. onions
2 cloves of garlic
3 small young marrows
3 tomatoes
3 green or red peppers
¼ pint olive oil
2 tbsp. lard
salt, pepper
4 fried eggs

Peel all the vegetables, of course de-seed the peppers, slice thinly. Melt the lard in a large heavy frying pan, add the oil, salt and pepper and all the cut-up vegetables. Mix well together, cover the pan and simmer gently for 45 minutes, take the lid off and simmer for another 30 minutes.

Fry the eggs and place on top of the vegetables on the serving dish. If a substantial dish is wanted, serve with boiled rice.

FROGS' LEGS A LA PROVENÇALE

2 lbs. medium size frogs' legs
8 ozs. butter
1 tbsp. olive oil
1 tbsp. chopped parsley
2 cloves of garlic, finely chopped
¼ pint milk
2 tbsp. flour
juice of ½ lemon
1 tsp. chopped chives
½ tsp. salt, pepper

Add salt and pepper to the milk, dip in the legs and roll in flour. Heat 2 ozs. butter and the olive oil, add the floured legs, gently fry for 12 minutes, till browned. Add the lemon juice, parsley, chives and a pinch of pepper, stir and keep warm in the serving dish. Melt the remaining butter, add the garlic and brown quickly, pour over the dish. Cut slices of lemon may be used as a garnish.

PÂTÉ OF PIGS' LIVER PÉRIGORD

6 rashers of bacon
½ lb. pigs' liver
½ lb. bacon
½ tsp. black pepper
2 cloves of garlic
3 shallots
1 liqueur glass brandy
¼ tsp. nutmeg
¼ tsp. ground cloves
1 pig's foot cut in two
2 medium sliced carrots
2 medium sliced onions
1 sprig thyme ⎤
1 sprig rosemary ⎬ *bouquet*
1 bay leaf ⎦

1 wine glass white wine
1 wine glass cold water
lard for sealing

Mince the liver and bacon with the garlic and shallots. Pound to a smooth paste, add pepper, nutmeg and cloves. Line a deep small casserole or terrine with the bacon rashers, put in the mixture, pour in the brandy. Put on top the pig's foot, carrots, onions, *bouquet*, and add wine and water. Cover the casserole tightly, stand in a dish of water and cook very slowly for 4 hours. Take out the pig's foot, carrots, onions, *bouquet*. Seal the pâté with melted pure lard.

SNAILS

50 snails
1½ pints Chablis or 1½ pints salt
 water
a small handful of thyme
a large handful of fennel

Add the thyme and fennel to the wine or water, simmer the snails in this for 1 hour. Strain. Keep snails warm.

4 ozs. butter
2 cloves of garlic
a handful of parsley, finely
 chopped
¼ tsp. ground nutmeg
salt, pepper

Pound the garlic to a pulp in a mortar, remove any hard pieces that refuse to be pulped, add the butter and the parsley, salt, pepper and nutmeg. With a wooden spoon work thoroughly till everything is mixed well together. Put over the warm snails in the serving dish and let the garlic butter melt and run into the snails.

MIROTON

6 or 8 slices of cold boiled beef
3 ozs. butter
1 tbsp. wine vinegar
1 tsp. chopped parsley
2 ozs. breadcrumbs
4 medium onions, sliced
1 oz. flour
¾ pint meat stock
1 tbsp. tomato purée
salt, pepper
1 tbsp. tomato sauce

Melt 2 ozs. butter in a stewpan, add the onions, cook gently till turning brown, add the flour, stir and cook for 2 minutes. Add the vinegar, stir well, then gradually pour in the meat stock and stir till smooth. Add the tomato sauce, parsley, season generously with salt and pepper. Pour half this mixture into a shallow fireproof dish, arrange the meat slices on top, add the other half. Sprinkle with breadcrumbs, dot with the rest of the butter and brown in a moderate oven.

CASSOULET

1½ lbs. haricot beans
3 medium onions, sliced
2 large tomatoes, peeled and
 sliced
4 cloves of garlic, chopped
½ lb. bacon cut in 1 inch squares
2 ozs. white breadcrumbs
1 lb. garlic sausage
2 pints stock
1 leg and 1 wing preserved goose
bouquet garni
salt, pepper

Any good pieces of duck, chicken or turkey can be used as well.

Soak the beans overnight, and simmer for 2½ hours. Melt the bacon in a stewpan, add the onions, garlic, tomatoes, *bouquet*, salt and pepper. Pour over the stock and simmer for 30 minutes.

Take a large casserole, rub with garlic. Put the goose, sausage and any other pieces of poultry in the bottom, with plenty of goose grease. Pile the beans on top and pour in the strained stock. Bring slowly to the boil, lower the heat, and spread the breadcrumbs over all. Cook in a slow oven for 1 hour.

Serve exactly as it is, with a green salad and red wine. This is a meal in itself and should be the only course, except perhaps cheese or fruit as dessert.

FRENCH DRESSING

3 tbsp. olive oil
1 tbsp. wine vinegar
½ tsp. salt
¼ tsp. pepper

Mix all together. You can if you like add a pinch of sugar and ¼ tsp. of made mustard.

MAYONNAISE

1 egg yolk
½ pint olive oil
1 dsp. wine vinegar
salt, pepper

Make this sauce in a cool place, use cool ingredients and utensils. Stir with a silver spoon and 'keep cool' as you work.

Put a carefully broken yolk (no white at all) into a basin. Add the oil, drop by drop, stirring gently all the time. When the sauce begins to thicken stir in the vinegar, salt and pepper. Add more oil drop by drop till it once again thickens, when the oil can be poured in slowly, stirring always, until finished. Taste and add more salt and pepper if you wish.

Should the mayonnaise refuse to thicken and look curdled when finished, do not panic. Break a new yolk into another basin and stir the mixture on to it slowly. Taste and if it has not enough 'bite' stir in a few drops of vinegar to sharpen the extra yolk.

HOLLANDAISE SAUCE

3 egg yolks
2 ozs. butter
1 tbsp. wine vinegar
salt, pepper

The secret of this sauce is that it must not ever boil; also good fresh butter must be used.

Melt the butter in a double saucepan or in a basin over hot water. Mix the egg yolks, vinegar, salt and pepper, add to the melted butter, stir briskly without stopping until the sauce is smooth and thick. Taste and add more salt and pepper if you think it needs it.

TARTARE SAUCE

mayonnaise sauce
3 shallots or very small onions
green herbs — parsley, chives,
    chervil, tarragon, watercress,
    etc.
½ tsp. mustard

Chop the shallots, all or any of the herbs very finely, stir these, plus the mustard, into the mayonnaise sauce.

BÉARNAISE SAUCE

2 shallots
1 sprig tarragon
3 stalks chervil
2 tbsp. dry white wine
1 tbsp. wine vinegar
2 egg yolks
2 ozs. butter
1 tsp. cold water
salt, pepper

Chop the shallots and herbs extremely finely. Put the wine and vinegar in a saucepan, add the chopped shallots and herbs. Simmer till reduced by two thirds. Strain and cool.

Put the egg yolks in a basin over very hot but *NOT* boiling water, add the cold water and the herbs and wine mixture. Whip with an egg whisk, gently but steadily, adding the butter bit by bit, as you whip, until the sauce is thick and creamy. Season with salt and pepper.

Should the sauce curdle try adding another tsp. of cold water to it, remove from the heat and whip furiously.

RAVIGOTE SAUCE

½ a bunch of watercress
4 tsp. chopped parsley, chives, tarragon, chervil
1 clove of garlic
½ tsp. mustard
2 tbsp. wine vinegar

¼ pint olive oil
salt, pepper

Pound or squash the herbs with a wooden spoon in a basin, add the oil, vinegar, salt and pepper.

Good with cold meats.

MOUSSELINE SAUCE

¼ pint Hollandaise sauce
(see p. 159)
¼ pint fresh cream
salt, pepper

Whip cream till stiff and add to Hollandaise sauce, already made, and heat extremely carefully in a bowl over hot water. If it gets too hot it will be a failure. Season to taste.

SAUCE PIQUANTE

½ pint brown sauce already made
(see p. 163)
3 tbsp. wine vinegar
1 chopped shallot or grated onion
1 tsp. chopped parsley

1 oz. butter
2 tbsp. chopped gherkin

Heat everything slowly in the butter, except the gherkins. When melted, add the lot to the brown sauce. Last add the chopped gherkins.

SAUCE MADÈRE (1) (Madeira Sauce)

½ pint brown sauce
bouquet garni
1 wine glass of Madeira

Add the *bouquet garni* to the sauce when thickened and cook very gently for 10 minutes, then take it out. Add the Madeira.

If the sauce should need thinning, add another tbsp. of stock.

SAUCE MADÈRE (2) (Madeira Sauce)

½ pint brown sauce already made
4 medium mushrooms, finely sliced
2 tbsp. gravy
1 wine glass Madeira wine

Add the mushrooms and gravy to the brown sauce. Five minutes before serving add the Madeira and simmer very gently with the lid on the pan till the mushrooms are tender, for 5 or 6 minutes.

MAÎTRE D'HÔTEL SAUCE

4 ozs. butter
2 tsp. finely chopped parsley
2 tsp. lemon juice
salt, pepper

With a wooden spoon knead the butter, parsley, strained lemon juice, salt and pepper together, till smooth.

MORNAY SAUCE

½ pint Béchamel sauce
  (see p. 163)
2 ozs. grated Parmesan cheese or
  4 ozs. 'cooking' cheese (Cheddar or Cheshire)
cayenne pepper

Make the Béchamel and stir in the cheese. A tiny pinch of cayenne pepper is an improvement.

MAYONNAISE AU RAIFORT

2 tbsp. grated horseradish
mayonnaise (see p. 159)

Add the horseradish to the mayonnaise. Bottled horseradish will do, but fresh is better by far.

BLACK BUTTER SAUCE (Beurre Noir)

4 ozs. butter
2 tbsp. wine vinegar
1 tsp. chopped parsley

Melt the butter until dark brown, but do *NOT* burn, put in the parsley and cook for 1 minute. Pour this over the cooked dish (fish, brains, etc.). Put the vinegar in the used saucepan, heat for half a minute or less, till hot, and pour this too over the dish.

SAUCE AU FENOUIL (Fennel Sauce)

½ pint Béchamel sauce
 (see p. 163)
½ tsp. finely chopped fennel

Fennel is delicious with fish.
 Add ½ tsp. finely chopped fennel to ½ pint Béchamel sauce, mix well. Fennel is strong, do not use too much.

AILLOLI (Garlic Mayonnaise)

3 cloves of garlic
½ pint mayonnaise sauce
 (see p. 159)

Crush or pound the garlic as finely as possible, in the bowl in which you make the mayonnaise.

GARLIC SAUCE

2 cloves of garlic
1 slice white bread
2 tbsp. milk
½ pint mayonnaise sauce
 (see p. 159)

Remove the crust from the bread, soak in the milk, mash with a fork. Chop or pound the garlic and crush into the mashed bread, drain excess milk. Add this mixture to the mayonnaise.
 Good, if you like the taste of garlic, with all cold meats and poultry.

SAUCE VINAIGRETTE

4 tbsp. olive oil
2 tbsp. wine vinegar
1 tsp. salt
1 tsp. black pepper
1 tsp. chopped onion

1 tsp. chopped chives
1 tsp. chopped parsley

Mix the herbs, salt and pepper with the vinegar. Stir thoroughly, add the oil.

BÉCHAMEL SAUCE

2 ozs. butter
2 ozs. flour
½ pint hot milk
salt, pepper

Melt the butter. Add the flour gradually, stir over a slow-to-medium heat until the mixture leaves the sides of the pan. Add the hot milk slowly, stirring all the time, till thick and creamy. Add salt and pepper. Flour and butter must be of equal quantities always: this, with the continual stirring and fairly slow cooking is the secret of a smooth creamy 'white' sauce, and not a paste full of lumps.

BROWN SAUCE

2 ozs. butter
1 oz. flour
½ pint hot meat stock or water
salt, pepper

Melt the butter, stir in flour and cook gently until it browns. Add the hot liquid gradually, stirring all the time until the sauce thickens. Add salt and pepper to taste.

MEAT GLAZE

any pieces of meat, bones,
   carcases, etc.
1 sliced carrot
1 sliced onion
1 sliced leek
1 bouquet garni
1 clove of garlic
salt, pepper

Chop any bones, break up carcases. Put the vegetables, *bouquet*, salt, pepper and garlic in a baking dish, add the meat, etc., and put in the oven till brown and shrivelled, but *not* burnt. Take out, cover with boiling water and simmer for 15 minutes, remove all bones, simmer again, stirring and scraping the pan to collect essence which may stick to the pan, until reduced to one third. Strain through muslin. This glaze will keep in a cool place almost indefinitely.

TOMATO SAUCE

8 large ripe tomatoes
1 medium finely sliced onion
1 bouquet garni
1 clove of garlic chopped
1 oz. butter
1 tsp. cornflour
salt, pepper

Cut up the tomatoes and crush them with a wooden spoon in a thick saucepan. Add the sliced onion, garlic and the *bouquet*. Simmer gently till soft for 10 minutes. Sieve this purée. Mix the cornflour with the butter, add to the purée, return to the pan and simmer for 15 minutes. Season with salt and pepper.

LARDING

bacon
a larding needle

Cut the bacon in strips, ¼ inch square, 3 to 4 inches long. Thread the needle and stitch into the meat in 1 inch 'tacking' stitches going down about ½ an inch; pull through till the needle is empty each time, leaving the lardons embedded in the meat.

BOUQUET GARNI (Herbs of various kinds)

2 or 3 heads of parsley
1 sprig of thyme
1 bay leaf

This recipe is the basic *bouquet garni*: the herb or spice flavouring often used in cookery.

Tie the ingredients together firmly with string or cotton. If cloves, fennel, lemon peel or other herbs are included in any recipe, they are specially mentioned.

Some cooks find it better to tie all together in a small piece of clean muslin.

COURT-BOUILLON (for boiled fish)

1 large onion sliced in rings
1 bouquet garni
1 clove garlic
1 shallot
1 carrot sliced
1 clove
8 peppercorns
pinch of curry powder

1 tbsp. coarse salt
2½ quarts water
1 tumbler dry white wine

Simmer spices and vegetables for 1 hour in the water and wine. Then poach your fish in the court-bouillon until it is cooked. This stock may be used as a basis for soup.

CROUTONS

Bread, toast, or croutons are served with French soups: bread or toast with meat or fish soups, croutons with vegetable soups

Cut the crusts off slices of stale white bread, then cut the bread in 1 inch squares. Fry in butter or oil, or bacon fat till golden. 1 slice of bread per person is ample. Serve separately on a warm plate or scatter on top of the soup if to be served immediately, or put in the bottom of the tureen and pour the soup over them.

FRENCH APPLE SAUCE

8 cooking apples
2 ozs. butter
4 ozs. sugar
½ tsp. grated lemon rind
3 tbsp. water
1 tbsp. mixed candied peel

Peel, core and quarter the apples. Put the apples, butter, sugar, and rind, water and candied peel in a thick saucepan. Cook slowly over a low heat, stirring frequently until the apples are quite soft, about 20 minutes.

APPLE SAUCE MERINGUE

½ oz. butter
2 egg whites
2 tbsp. caster sugar
apple sauce

Butter a soufflé dish, pour in the apple sauce. Whisk the egg whites till stiff, sieve in the sugar gradually beating continually. Spread the meringue over the apple mixture and bake in a moderate oven for 20 minutes.

BANANA TRIFLE

7 bananas
2 tbsp. apricot jam
3 tbsp. sherry
½ pint cream

Peel and cut 6 bananas lengthways. Spread with the jam and pour on the sherry. Leave for 1 hour. Whip the cream for 4 minutes, spread over and decorate with 1 banana cut in thin slices.

CREAMED BANANAS

3 large bananas
2 ozs. caster sugar
½ pint cream
¼ pint sherry

Peel the bananas, sieve them. Add the sugar, stir, add the cream and whisk for 10 minutes or until thick, beat in the sherry gradually. Chill for 2 hours.

BANANAS AU RHUM

6 large bananas
3 tbsp. Demerara sugar
juice of 1 lemon
3 tbsp. water
1 sherry glass rum
1 nut butter
cream to serve

Butter a shallow fireproof dish. Cut the bananas in half lengthways and arrange overlapping in the dish. Sprinkle the sugar over, add the lemon juice and water. Bake in a moderate oven for 20 minutes or till brown. Add the rum 5 minutes before the end. Serve with whipped cream, which may be flavoured with rum, if wished.

CHOCOLATE MOUSSE (1)

4 ozs. bitter chocolate
4 tbsp. water
6 ozs. caster sugar
5 eggs
1 tbsp. brandy

Separate the eggs — whip whites till stiff.
Melt the chocolate over a very low heat, add water and sugar, stir till sugar is dissolved. Remove from heat. Add the yolks one by one, beating vigorously, then the brandy. Stir. Fold in the egg whites, stir till thoroughly mixed. Serve in separate small moulds or glasses. Serve very cold.

CHOCOLATE MOUSSE (2)

3 heaped tbsp. cocoa powder
3 ozs. caster sugar
3 eggs
3 tbsp. cream or milk top
1 tbsp. very strong coffee

Separate the eggs — whip whites till stiff.
Melt the cocoa, sugar, cream or milk top on a very low heat. Take off the heat. Add the eggs, one by one, stir quickly, also the coffee. Fold in the whites, whip all together till well mixed. Serve in separate moulds, glasses, or failing these a soufflé dish or glass bowl. Chill and serve. All chocolate mousse improves with keeping, so make the day before if wished.

APPLE TART

2 lbs. apples
5 ozs. sugar
apple peels
rind of 1 lemon
2 ozs. sugar
¼ pint cider
pastry case

Pastry tart case as in Cold Cheese Tart (see p. 170). Prick the bottom of the pastry. Peel, core and slice the apples very finely. Fill the tart tin in layers of apple and sugar. Bake in a moderate oven for 30 minutes. Boil the peels, lemon rind, cider till syrupy and pour over the cooled tart.

RASPBERRY AND RED CURRANT TART

1 cooked flan or tart case
1½ lbs. raspberries
½ lb. red currants
6 ozs. caster sugar
1 tbsp. red currant jelly

Prepare the fruit, add the sugar, and cook stirring gently for 4 minutes, or until the sugar has melted and made a syrup. Keep the fruit whole. Strain the fruit and put in the cooked case. Bake in a moderate oven for 10 minutes. Add the red currant jelly to the juice, pour over the cooled fruit.
Eat cold, with cream, of course, if possible.

PEARS WITH CHOCOLATE

8 pears
¼ pint water
2 ozs. sugar
one-third of a vanilla pod
4 ozs. chocolate
½ oz. butter

Peel and quarter the pears. Put the pears, water, and vanilla pod in a saucepan and stew till nearly cooked. Place in a shallow fireproof dish.
Melt the chocolate in 1 dsp. pear liquid, add the butter, stir. Pour over the pears, cover and bake in a moderate oven for 15 minutes till the pears are quite soft.

PEACH MELBA

8 ozs. vanilla ice cream
4 ripe peaches
½ lb. raspberries
2 ozs. sugar

Melt the raspberries and the sugar, stir and bring to the boil, simmer till the fruit is soft, about 4 minutes, stirring all the time. Sieve to make the purée. Cool.

Peel and stone the peaches. Put 2 halves on 2 ozs. ice cream, pour ¼ of the cold purée on each.

BOMBE GLACÉE

½ lb. sugar
¼ pint water
3 egg yolks
1 pint thick cream
½ tbsp. powdered coffee essence

Beat the cream till it begins to thicken, add the coffee essence. Dissolve sugar and water, add beaten egg yolks. Stir all the time in a double boiler over simmering water until mixture thickens. Do *NOT* overcook. Whip for 15 minutes. Fold in the flavoured cream. Pour into a chilled mould and freeze.

CHESTNUT MOULD

2½ lbs. chestnuts
cold water
¼ pint milk
6 ozs. caster sugar
2 tbsp. brandy
6 egg whites
3 tbsp. water
½ pint cream

Roast the chestnuts in a slow oven for 20 minutes. Skin and peel them. Cover with cold water and boil till soft. Drain and sieve or mash very finely. Add 2 ozs. sugar and the brandy to the purée, stir well, then fold in the egg whites.

Make a caramel of 4 ozs. sugar with the water. Coat the bottom and sides of a cake tin. Pour in the chestnut mixture and cook in a moderate oven for 1 hour. Turn out on serving dish. Serve very cold with the cream, whipped.

PLUMS ON BUTTERED BREAD

4 large slices white bread
2 ozs. butter
24 ripe plums
2 ozs. brown sugar

Butter the bread on one side only, stone the plums, put six on each buttered side, press down well, dab with the rest of the butter and sprinkle with sugar. Arrange the slices flatly in a buttered fireproof dish, plum side up, cover with buttered paper and bake in a moderate oven for 30 minutes, when the plums should be cooked in a syrup on golden crisp bread.

ST. ÉMILION AU CHOCOLAT

¼ lb. butter
¼ lb. sugar
1 egg
½ lb. chocolate
1 tbsp. water
½ pint milk
2 lbs. macaroons
1 liqueur glass rum

Soak the macaroons in the rum. Cream the butter and sugar. Scald the milk and when cool beat in the egg yolk. Melt the chocolate in the water over a low heat, stir in the milk and egg mixture, then the creamed butter and sugar. Stir till quite smooth.

In a soufflé dish put a layer of rum-flavoured macaroons, then a layer of the chocolate cream; repeat until the dish is full, finishing with macaroons. Chill for 12 hours or more and serve.

JACQUES — (These pancakes are special to the Périgord)

4 ozs. flour
¼ pint milk
¼ pint water
1 dsp. olive oil
2 ozs. sugar
2 eggs
3 eating apples
1 tsp. lemon juice

Peel and core the apples, slice them very thinly, spread on a dish, sprinkle each one with 2 tsp. sugar and lemon juice.

Make the batter, but using only 1 tsp. sugar. Grease a small very hot frying pan with lard or butter and pour in a little batter, about 1 tbsp. Place 2 apple slices on the pancake, cook ½ minute, pour in another tbsp. of batter, cook ½ minute, turn, and cook for another minute or till the apple is soft. Serve the pancake flat, sprinkle over the rest of the sugar. Keep warm and work quickly. Serve at once when all cooked.

CRÊPES OR FRENCH PANCAKES

6 ozs. flour
2 ozs. sugar
3 eggs
2 ozs. melted butter
¾ pint milk
2 tbsp. brandy or rum
1 tsp. grated lemon rind
⅛ tsp. salt

Sift the dry ingredients, add the eggs one at a time, beating well till quite smooth. Add the sugar, brandy or rum, lemon rind and salt plus the melted butter, and mix well. Now gradually pour in the milk, beating all the time. Always make the batter 2 hours before using.

The frying pan should be rubbed with butter and lard and the pancakes cooked very quickly on both sides with only enough batter to cover the pan very thinly. Keep pancakes warm in a covered dish over hot water, never in the oven as this dries and hardens them.

CARAMEL RICE

4 ozs. rice
1 pint milk
1 slice lemon rind or vanilla pod
4 tbsp. cream
6 ozs. caster sugar
juice of 1 lemon
2 ozs. candied peel

Put the milk, 4 ozs. sugar, lemon rind or vanilla pod in a double saucepan. Simmer for 2 hours, when the mixture will be creamy. Stir in the lemon juice and cream and the candied peel. Pour into a soufflé dish and chill thoroughly. Spread 2 ozs. sugar on top evenly, and put under a very hot grill for about 1 minute or till the sugar looks like toffee; watch it all the time, as it burns easily. Serve very cold.

CRÊPES SUZETTE

3 oz. butter
3 oz. sugar
grated rind of 1 orange or lemon
2 tsp. brandy, or cointreau,
   or curaçao or kümmel
1 liqueur glass brandy, or
   cointreau, or curaçao
   or kümmel

Make the pancakes. Keep warm. Cream the butter and sugar, add the grated rind and the 2 tsp. brandy or liqueur. Spread each warm pancake with this mixture, fold, and arrange on warmed serving dish. Pour the liqueur glass of brandy or liqueur over the top of the pancakes as they are put on the table and set alight.

PASTRY FOR FRUIT, CUSTARD OR CHEESE TARTS

6 ozs. flour
4 ozs. butter
3 ozs. sugar
1 egg
a pinch of salt

Sieve the flour, add the sugar and the butter in small pieces, work till crumby, add the beaten egg, work as quickly as possible. Roll out on greaseproof paper, large enough to fit bottom and sides of the tin, place the flan or tart tin on top and turn upside down otherwise you will find the pastry will break in handling. Fill with beans or crusts and bake in a moderate oven for 20 minutes, covered with greaseproof paper to prevent burning.

ALMOND TART

3 eggs
2 ozs. sugar
4 ozs. ground almonds
⅛ pint milk
1 cooked pastry flan case

Mix all the ingredients thoroughly. Fill the case and bake in a moderate oven for 15 minutes.
   Serve with whipped cream and sugar.

CREAM CHEESE TART

1 cooked pastry flan or tart case
6 ozs. Pommel cheese or demi-sel,
  or home-made cream cheese
2 egg yolks
4 tbsp. sugar

grated rind of 1 orange
¼ pint milk, cream or milk top

Mix the cheese, egg yolks, sugar, rind, milk together thoroughly. Add the stiff beaten egg whites, pile into the already cooked pastry case and bake for 15 minutes in a very moderate oven.

COLD CHEESE TART

8 ozs. flour
4 ozs. butter
1 egg
¼ tsp. salt
2 tbsp. cold water
6 ozs. cream cheese
3 eggs
4 ozs. caster sugar

2 tbsp. cream
2 tbsp. chopped angelica

Make a pastry of the flour, butter, salt, egg and water. Leave for 2 hours, roll and line the tart or flan tin.
    Mix the cream cheese, eggs, sugar, cream and angelica well together, fill the flan tin and bake in a slow oven for 40 minutes. Eat it cold.

CUSTARD (1)

3 egg yolks
1 egg white
¾ pint milk
1 oz. sugar

Heat the milk. Beat the eggs. Pour the hot, not boiling milk over in a double saucepan or basin above simmering water. Stir until the mixture thickens, add the sugar. Never boil custard or the mixture will curdle. This is proper custard, quite unlike the custard powder variety usually served.

CUSTARD (2)

1 pint milk
4 ozs. sugar
3 egg yolks
1 vanilla pod

Scald the milk, in which is the vanilla pod. Take out pod and cool milk till warm. Beat the yolks with the sugar, add the milk gradually, stirring all the time. Put in a double boiler over simmering, *NOT* boiling, water and cook till it thickens, stirring gently all the time.

HOME-MADE MILK CHEESE WITH FRESH FRUIT

5 pints milk
sugar and fresh raspberries or red currants to serve

This is a favourite French sweet dish for the pudding course and an excellent way of using surplus milk.

Pour 5 pints of milk into a large bowl and leave overnight. Skim off the cream and keep cold. Leave the milk for 12 hours more, pour into muslin and hang up to drip in the usual way for several hours until all the liquid has run out. Fill separate little moulds, pour cream over each and serve with sugar and the prepared fruit. 5 pints of milk should make 1 lb. cheese and 6 ozs. cream.

Germany

ANCHOVY SALAD

8 anchovy fillets
¼ lb. ham sausage
¼ lb. smoked salmon
¼ pint prawns
pickled cucumber
capers
½ lemon

2 tbsp. olive oil
1 tbsp. wine vinegar

Mix the oil and vinegar well. Arrange the anchovy fillets in the middle of a dish, surround them with slices of ham sausage and smoked salmon and prepared prawns. Pour the oil and vinegar over them. Garnish with pickled cucumber, capers and slices of lemon.

LEEK AND LETTUCE HORS D'ŒUVRES

1 round lettuce
2 leeks
½ rasher gammon
½ oz. lard
2 tbsp. wine vinegar
salt

Shred the lettuce, finely chop the leeks. Cut the gammon into small pieces and fry lightly in the fat. Stir the vinegar into the fat in the pan, season with salt. Pour over the lettuce and leek.

POTATO SALAD WITH ROLLMOPS

2 medium potatoes
4 rollmops
gherkins
2 tbsp. olive oil
1 tbsp. wine vinegar
parsley

salt
pepper

Boil the potatoes in their skins, peel and slice them when still warm and dress with olive oil and vinegar. Slice the gherkins and add them to the salad. Season with salt and pepper and sprinkle with chopped parsley. Serve with rollmops.

ROLLMOPS

herrings
capers
shallots
gherkins
wine vinegar
pickling spice
peppercorns
onion
lemon

Fillet the herrings. Mix sliced gherkins and sliced shallots and capers and spread a layer of this mixture on each fillet. Roll and secure with cocktail sticks. Put them in a glass preserving jar with wine vinegar, a teaspoonful of pickling spice, a little sliced onion and a squeeze of lemon juice. Screw down the lid and leave for 4 days or longer.

BEER SOUP

1 pint dark lager
1 pint milk
juice of ½ lemon
2 egg yolks
cinnamon
sugar
salt

Heat the lager in a saucepan with the lemon juice and a pinch of cinnamon. Heat the milk and beat in the egg yolks, add them to the beer. Season with sugar and salt.

CABBAGE SOUP

1 cabbage
1 onion
1 lemon
½ lb. tomatoes
2 pints stock
2 apples
sugar

salt
pepper

Shred the cabbage, mince the apple and onion. Cook the tomatoes with a little water and pass through a sieve. Cook the cabbage, onion, apple and tomato purée in the stock for 30 minutes. Season with salt, pepper, lemon juice and sugar.

KIDNEY SOUP

1 calf's kidney
2 pints stock
2 onions
1 oz. flour
1 oz. butter
parsley
thyme
½ bay leaf

1 egg yolk
1 gill milk

Blanch the kidney, skin it and remove the core, slice thinly. Brown the kidney in the butter with the sliced onion and the herbs, stir in the flour and cook till brown. Add the stock, season with salt and pepper. Simmer for 30 minutes. Mix the beaten egg yolks with warm milk, add to the soup just before serving.

LENTIL SOUP

½ lb. lentils
1 onion
2 sticks celery
bacon bones
1 dsp. wine vinegar

salt
pepper

Soak the lentils for 12 hours. Chop the celery and onion and cook with the strained lentils and bacon bones in 3 pints water until tender. Season with salt and pepper. Stir in the vinegar.

FISH BALLS

2 lbs. white fish (bream, fresh
    haddock or cod)
2 eggs
2 onions
1 carrot
1 stick celery
1 oz. ground almonds
1 oz. breadcrumbs
parsley
salt
pepper

Remove the skin, head and bones from the fish. Cook them with the onion, sliced, half the carrot, sliced, and the celery in 1½ pints of water for 30 minutes. Strain.

Mince the fish and the remaining onion, add the ground almonds, some chopped parsley and season with salt and pepper. Beat the eggs into this mixture and blend well. Add the breadcrumbs, shape into balls. Slice the rest of the carrot, add it to the strained stock. Bring the stock to the boil, simmer the fish balls in it for 1 hour. Arrange the fish balls on a dish with a little stock strained over each. Serve cold.

FISH CAKES WITH SPINACH

2 lbs. cod on the bone
1 slice bread
1 onion
1 egg yolk
1 gill milk
2 ozs. breadcrumbs
8 anchovy fillets
salt
pepper } 1 lb. spinach
butter

Dot the fish with butter and cook slowly in a covered fireproof dish. Chop the onion and fry it in a little butter until transparent. Soak the bread in milk. Remove the skin and bones from the fish, pound it with the onion and bread, from which the milk has been squeezed. Season with salt and pepper. Shape into balls, roll in egg and breadcrumbs and fry quickly in hot fat. Chop the anchovy fillets, mix with the cooked spinach and serve with the fish balls.

BRUNSWICK STEW

1 rabbit cut into pieces
1 lb. tomatoes, peeled and
    quartered
1 lb. runner beans, sliced
3 spring onions, chopped
1 lb. small new potatoes
1 glass red wine
½ bay leaf
thyme

salt
pepper
2 ozs. dripping

Dredge the rabbit in seasoned flour. Fry lightly in the dripping until browned. Transfer to an oven-proof dish, add the vegetables, wine, herbs and seasoning. Cover the pan. Cook in a moderate oven for 1½ hours.

HAMBURG STEAK

1 lb. raw beef finely chopped
¼ lb. raw pork, finely chopped
chopped parsley
1 small onion chopped
1 slice bread soaked in milk
5 eggs
salt
pepper

breadcrumbs
fat for frying

Mix the meat with the parsley, onion and soaked bread (from which the milk has been squeezed) and 1 egg, season with salt and pepper. Shape into 4 flat cakes. Roll in breadcrumbs. Fry fairly slowly on both sides. Fry the eggs lightly and place one on top of each meat cake.

HAM WITH POTATOES

1½ lbs. cooked ham
6 raw potatoes, sliced
4 green peppers
2 large onions
½ pint milk
1 egg
¼ lb. grated cheese
salt
pepper
butter

Peel and slice the potatoes. Remove the seeds and slice the green peppers. Slice the onion. Cut the ham into 1 inch dice. Put a layer of potatoes in the bottom of a fireproof dish, cover with layers of onion, green pepper and ham. Repeat the layers until the dish is full, ending with a layer of potatoes. Beat up the egg with the milk. Season with salt and pepper and pour into the dish. Dot with butter. Cook in a moderate oven for 1½ hours. Sprinkle with grated cheese and brown in the oven or under a grill.

PANCAKE PUDDING

¼ lb. minced cooked meat
1 oz. butter
2 shallots or small onions, finely
  chopped
2 tbsp. stock
½ oz. flour
salt
pepper
oil for frying
½ pint pancake batter (see p. 183)

Fry the shallots in the butter, stir in the flour, add the stock and cook slowly until the onions are soft. Add the meat, season with salt and pepper and mix well together, and keep hot. Make the pancakes in the usual way. Put the first one on a fireproof dish, spread a little of the meat mixture over it. Continue with alternate layers of meat and pancakes. Put in a moderately hot oven to reheat if necessary.

POTATOES WITH COTTAGE CHEESE

2 lbs. potatoes
½ lb. cottage cheese
½ pint thick sour cream
1 bunch spring onions, chopped
1 oz. caraway seeds
salt

Boil the potatoes in their skins in salted water. Peel. The potatoes should be served hot. The cheese, cream, onions and caraway seeds should be handed separately in individual dishes. Each person takes as much of the side dishes to eat with the potatoes as he fancies.

FRANKFURTERS WITH SAUERKRAUT

½ lb. sauerkraut
½ lb. haricot beans
bacon bones
4 rashers bacon
4 frankfurters
salt
pepper

Soak the beans overnight. Drain and cook with the bacon bones and 2 pints water until tender, pass through a sieve, season with salt if necessary and pepper. Fry the bacon and remove to keep warm. Heat the sauerkraut in the bacon fat. Arrange the bean purée in the middle of a dish, surrounded by the sauerkraut, and put the bacon and frankfurters on top. Put in a moderate oven until the frankfurters are hot.

PRAWNS WITH MIXED VEGETABLES

1 pint prawns
½ lb. cooked peas
½ lb. cooked new carrots
1 small cauliflower, cooked
¼ lb. mushrooms
½ lb. asparagus
2 ozs. butter
1 oz. flour
sugar
salt

Remove the heads and tails of the prawns, cook them in the butter until tender. Remove and keep hot. Separate the cauliflower flowerets, fry them lightly in the butter with the peas, carrots and prawns. Season with salt and a little sugar and add to the mushrooms. Cook the asparagus in boiling salted water until tender. Break off the tips and put them with the other ingredients. Stir the flour into the butter and gradually add enough of the water in which the asparagus was cooked to make a fairly thick sauce. Arrange the vegetables and prawns on a dish and pour the sauce over them.

RABBIT

1 rabbit cut into pieces
1 pint mild beer
2 onions
1 tbsp. flour
½ lb. prunes
2 ozs. dripping

salt
pepper

Dust the pieces of rabbit with seasoned flour. Brown them in the dripping. Add the sliced onions and the prunes (previously soaked if necessary). Cover with water, cook with a lid on the pan in a slow oven for 1½ hours.

MEAT BALLS

½ lb. beef
¼ lb. pork
¼ lb. liver
1 slice bread
chopped parsley
½ lemon
1 teaspoonful Worcester sauce
2 pints stock
2 ozs. dripping
1 oz. flour
1 onion
2 eggs
½ oz. butter
capers

salt
pepper

Mince the onion, fry it lightly in a little butter. Mince the meat and the bread (previously soaked in water and the water squeezed out). Mix the onion, minced meat, bread and eggs and beat well. Add the parsley, grated lemon rind, lemon juice and sauce and beat again. Shape the mixture into balls and poach them in the stock for about 15 minutes. Remove them and drain. Put aside to keep hot. Melt the dripping, cook the flour in it for 1 minute, gradually add enough stock to make a fairly thick sauce. Season with salt and pepper and capers. Pour the sauce over the meat balls.

BRAISED TOPSIDE. SAUERBRATEN

3 lbs. topside
2 ozs. lard
salt
6 peppercorns
1 teaspoon dry mustard
1 bay leaf
1 sprig thyme
4 cloves
1 onion sliced
1 carrot sliced
2 glasses red wine
1 tbsp. wine vinegar

1 oz. flour
½ pint sour cream
¼ pint stock

Put the wine, vinegar, carrots, onion, cloves, bay leaf, thyme, salt and mustard into a pan. Marinate the meat in this mixture for 48 hours, turning it every 12 hours. Drain the meat and fry it lightly on all sides in the lard. Pour the marinade over it and cook, covered with a lid, in a slow oven for 3 hours. Strain the sauce and thicken with the flour, add stock if necessary and the cream. Slice the meat and pour the sauce over it. Serve with noodles.

GOULASH WITH SAUERKRAUT

2 lbs. veal
2 ozs. dripping
2 onions
½ lb. tomatoes
½ pint sour cream
¼ teaspoonful paprika
1 lb. sauerkraut
salt

Cut the veal into 1 inch squares. Slice the onion and brown in the dripping, add the meat and fry it, turning the pieces so that all sides are browned. Add the peeled and quartered tomatoes, season with salt and paprika. Cover with water, put a lid on the dish and simmer for 1½ hours. Strain the sauce, simmer it gently to reduce it, add the cream and simmer for 34 minutes. Pour the sauce over the meat, reheat and serve with sauerkraut.

MEAT CAKES WITH SAUERKRAUT SAUCE

½ lb. beef
½ lb. pork
2 slices bread
1 gill milk
1 onion chopped
6 anchovy fillets
1 egg
2 ozs. butter
1 oz. flour
½ pint stock
1 glass white wine
1 tsp. capers
1 tsp. French mustard
1 dsp. sugar
juice of ½ lemon
2 egg yolks

salt
pepper

Soak the bread in the milk, squeeze it gently and mix it with the minced meat, chopped onion and minced anchovies. Season with salt and pepper. Bind with the egg. Shape into flat cakes and fry in the butter; keep warm.

FOR THE SAUCE:

Melt the butter, cook the flour in it for 1 minute, gradually add the stock and the wine. Add the capers, mustard, sugar, lemon juice, salt and pepper. Pour the sauce over the rissoles, cook slowly for 15 minutes. Mix the beaten egg yolks with a little melted butter and stir carefully into the sauce just before serving.

PORK CHOPS WITH MADEIRA SAUCE

4 large pork chops
¼ pint white wine
½ tbsp. wine vinegar
½ bay leaf
1 clove garlic
1 glass Madeira
salt
pepper

Rub the chops with the garlic and put them in a shallow fireproof dish, pour the wine and vinegar over them and enough water to cover the meat. Season with salt and pepper. Cover the dish and cook in a moderate oven for 1 hour. Strain the sauce and add the Madeira and simmer for 2—3 minutes. Pour it over the meat. Serve with cooked slices of apple.

PORK CHOPS WITH PLUMS

4 pork chops
½ lb. plums
1 oz. sugar
cinnamon
4 cloves
1 glass red wine
salt
pepper

Trim the chops and fry lightly in the surplus fat. Stew the plums with the sugar in a little water. Pass through a sieve. Put the chops in a shallow fireproof dish. Mix a pinch of cinnamon and the cloves with the strained plums. Pour on top of the chops. Add the wine. Season with salt and pepper. Cover with a lid and bake in a moderate oven for 1 hour, adding a little water from time to time if necessary.

PORK WITH SAUERKRAUT

1 lb. pork fillets
caraway seeds
1 lb. sauerkraut
¼ pint sour cream

Cook the pork with the sauerkraut for 40 minutes. Remove the meat and keep it hot. Stir the cream into the sauerkraut, flavour with a few caraway seeds. Put the sauerkraut onto a hot dish, arrange the pieces of pork on it, serve immediately.

PORK CHOPS WITH SOUR CREAM

4 pork chops
¼ pint sour cream
juice of ½ lemon
1 teaspoon sugar
thyme
flour
salt
pepper

Trim the chops and melt the surplus fat. Season the chops, and dust with flour. Fry lightly on both sides in the fat. Transfer to a casserole, add the sour cream, lemon juice, sugar and a pinch of thyme. Pour in enough water to cover the chops. Put a lid on the casserole. Cook in a moderate oven until tender (about 1 hour).

MIXED VEGETABLES STEAMED

peas
new carrots, sliced
small new potatoes
cauliflower, broken into flowerets
broad beans
celeriac, sliced

salt
1 oz. butter

Mix all the vegetables together, put them in a pudding basin with the butter and a pinch of salt. Steam until tender.

RED CABBAGE

1 red cabbage
1 onion
2 rashers streaky bacon
1 oz. dripping
2 glasses red wine
1 dsp. vinegar
salt

pepper
allspice

Shred the cabbage and blanch it in boiling water, drain. Fry the sliced onion in the fat, add the bacon, the wine, the shredded cabbage, the vinegar; season with salt and pepper. Add a little allspice in a muslin bag. Cook slowly in a covered pan for 1 hour. Remove the allspice before serving.

PORK WITH PRUNES

loin of pork weighing about 3 lbs.
½ lb. prunes
1 clove garlic

Rub the boned pork with a cut clove of garlic. Soak and stone the prunes and stuff the pork with them. Roll the meat. Roast it in a hot oven for ½ hour per lb.

SAUERKRAUT

2 lbs. sauerkraut
1 grated potato, raw
1 onion chopped
4 ozs. butter
10 juniper berries
¾ pint stock
1 small glass kirsch or white wine

Lightly brown the onion in the butter. Add the sauerkraut and the juniper berries. Pour in a little stock, simmer for 1½ hours, adding a little stock every 15 minutes. Add the potato 15 minutes before serving. If white wine is used, it should be substituted for some of the stock during the cooking.

SAVOY CABBAGE

1 savoy cabbage
1 onion
1 apple
1 dsp. wine vinegar
pepper
½ tsp. sugar

¼ pint stock
2 ozs. dripping
salt

Fry the sliced onion lightly in the dripping. Add the shredded cabbage, sliced apple and all the other ingredients. Simmer in a covered pan for 30 minutes.

APPLE PANCAKES

6 ozs. flour
½ pint milk
1 egg
1 oz. melted butter
salt
3 apples
cinnamon
2 ozs. sugar
juice of 1 lemon

Break the eggs into the sifted flour, pour on the milk and beat the batter well. Add the melted butter and a pinch of salt just before using. Slice and chop the apples, flavour them with the lemon juice, sugar and a pinch of cinnamon. Heat a very little fat in a heavy pan, put in a tbsp. of the batter, cover with the apple mixture, fry quickly, turn and fry the other side.

APPLE TART

½ lb. pastry (see p. 276, Apricot
   tart, Italian)
1 lb. apples
2 ozs. sugar
nutmeg
cinnamon
½ lemon
1 egg
¼ pint milk

1 oz. melted butter
2 ozs. almonds

Cut the apples into thin slices. Beat the egg in the milk, add the sugar, melted butter and flavourings. Put the apple slices in the mixture and leave to stand for 2 hours. Roll out the pastry and line a Swiss Roll tin with it. Fill it with the apple mixture, sprinkle the top with chopped almonds and bake in a hot oven for 30 minutes.

CHESTNUT MOUSSE

1 pint milk
4 egg yolks
2 ozs. sugar
1 lb. chestnuts
1 oz. gelatine
½ pint whipped cream

Make a thick custard by cooking the eggs and milk very slowly in a double saucepan. Peel and sieve the chestnuts (see p. 384, Spanish section). Stir them and the sugar into the custard. Add the gelatine, dissolved in a little warm water. Whip the cream and fold it into the mixture. Pour it gently into a glass dish. Serve cold.

FRUIT KUCHEN

½ pint milk
4 ozs. flour
1 egg
1 oz. sugar
2 ozs. melted butter
fruit

2 ozs. almonds
cinnamon

Beat the eggs into the flour, beat in the milk, sugar and lastly the melted butter. Pour into a shallow greased pie dish. Put small pieces of tinned or fresh fruit in the batter, sprinkle with cinnamon and chopped almonds. Bake in a moderate oven for 45 minutes.

FRUIT PANCAKE

½ pint milk
3 ozs. flour
3 eggs
1 oz. sugar
1 oz. stoned chopped raisins
1 oz. ground almonds
2 ozs. butter

Beat the egg yolks into the flour, beat in the milk, add the sugar, raisins, ground almonds and the stiffly beaten egg whites. Heat the butter in a large frying pan, pour in the mixture. Cook quickly until the underside is brown, brown the top under a hot grill and serve sprinkled with sugar.

TRIFLE

½ *pint thick rice pudding*
½ *pint boiled egg custard*
damson cheese
vanilla
½ *pint cream*

Cover the bottom of a glass dish with damson cheese, or with a thick purée of any sharp tasting fruit. Cover this with the rice pudding and pour the egg custard over the top. Add a drop of vanilla to the cream, beat it and arrange it on the custard and serve chilled.

ANISEED CAKES

4 ozs. sugar
3 eggs
6 ozs. flour
1 tsp. baking powder
1 tbsp. aniseed, crushed
vanilla

Beat the eggs and sugar until white and creamy. Sift the flour with the baking powder and fold it into the egg mixture. Flavour with a few drops of vanilla and the aniseed. Drop teaspoonfuls of the mixture onto greased baking tins, leave to stand for 12 hours. Bake in a moderate oven for 10 minutes.

CINNAMON STARS

8 ozs. icing sugar
6 egg whites
1 tsp. cinnamon
1 tsp. grated lemon peel
1 lb. ground almonds
salt

Whisk the egg whites stiffly with a pinch of salt. Fold in the sugar, cinnamon and lemon peel. Put aside one third of the mixture. Fold the ground almonds into the rest. Roll out the mixture to ¼ inch thick. Cut into star shapes, cover with spoonfuls of the meringue. Bake on a greased tin for 15 minutes in a slow oven.

GERMAN COFFEE CAKE

8 ozs. sugar
2 ozs. butter
2 ozs. lard
5 eggs
4 tsp. baking powder
salt
1 lb. flour
½ *pint milk (scant)*
4 ozs. sultanas
1 tsp. grated lemon peel

1 tsp. vanilla
4 ozs. flaked almonds
icing sugar

Cream the butter and sugar. Beat the eggs in one at a time. Fold in ½ the flour sifted with the baking powder. Beat in ½ the milk. Repeat with the rest of the flour and milk. Add the sultanas, lemon peel and vanilla. Bake in a moderate oven for 40 minutes. Ice with very thin white icing, sprinkle with almonds.

ORANGE CAKE

3 ozs. sugar
3 eggs
3 ozs. flour
2 ozs. melted butter
1 tbsp. rum
1 orange

Beat the egg yolks and the sugar until white. Beat in the orange juice and the rum. Add the sifted flour and the butter. Fold in the stiffly beaten egg whites. Bake in a greased and floured tin for 40 minutes in a slow oven. Ice with rum icing (see p. 187).

PRETZELS

½ lb. flour
2 ozs. butter
2 egg whites
2 egg yolks
milk
salt

pepper
coarse salt

Work the creamed butter, beaten egg whites and egg yolks into the flour with a little salt and pepper. Roll out on a floured board, shape into figures of eight. Brush with milk, sprinkle with coarse salt. Bake in a moderately hot oven for 10 minutes.

SPICED BISCUITS

4 ozs. butter
7 ozs. sugar
3 eggs
6 ozs. flour
vanilla
cinnamon
¼ lb. almonds

Cream the butter with 3 ozs. sugar. Beat in the egg yolks and then the sifted flour. Roll out between sheets of grease-proof paper until ¼ inch thick. Cut into rounds with a small pastry cutter. Put into greased baking tins. Cover with meringue made as follows:

Whisk the egg whites stiffly, fold in the sugar, flavouring and finely chopped almonds. Bake in a moderate oven for 15 minutes.

TARTELETTES

4 ozs. sugar
6 ozs. butter
6 ozs. flour
2 egg yolks
1 egg white
4 ozs. almonds
2 ozs. sugar
cinnamon

nutmeg
lemon peel

Cream the butter with the sugar and a little grated lemon peel. Beat in the egg yolks, fold in the sifted flour. Drop small spoonfuls of the mixture onto greased baking tins. Beat the egg white with 1 tbsp. water. Brush the biscuits with it. Mix the almonds with the sugar, cinnamon and nutmeg. Sprinkle over the biscuits. Bake in a moderate oven for 10 minutes.

RUM ICING

½ lb. icing sugar
2 ozs. lump sugar
1 strip lemon peel
1 tbsp. rum

Rub the lump sugar with the lemon peel. Heat the icing sugar, the lump sugar and the rum slowly with a little water until it thickens.

SPICED CAKES

8 ozs. brown sugar
4 ozs. butter
2 eggs
¼ pint sour milk
flour
2 tsp. baking powder
cinnamon
nutmeg

salt
4 ozs. currants

Cream the butter and sugar. Beat in the eggs one at a time. Add the sour milk, fold in the flour sifted with the baking powder, a pinch of salt, a little cinnamon and nutmeg. Beat well, add the currants and beat again. Bake in 24 small greased tins for 20 minutes in a moderate oven.

EGG DUMPLINGS

2 eggs
6 ozs. flour
salt
½ tsp. baking powder
2 ozs. breadcrumbs
4 ozs. butter

Beat the eggs, beat in the flour sifted with salt and baking powder. Cut very small pieces off the dough and poach in boiling water. Roll in bread crumbs as for potato dumplings (see p. 188).

SAUSAGE BALLS FOR SOUP

½ lb. sausage meat
1 egg white
parsley
basil
1 tbsp. fine breadcrumbs

Mix the ingredients well together, shape into balls about 1 inch in diameter. Poach them in boiling stock for 15 minutes. Drain and serve with pea, bean or lentil soup.

POTATO DUMPLINGS

6 medium potatoes
2 eggs
4 ozs. flour
2 ozs. butter
salt
2 ozs. breadcrumbs

Steam the potatoes in their skins until tender. Leave to cool, peel, pass through a sieve. Beat in the eggs, then the flour and a good pinch of salt. Shape into balls and poach for 10 minutes in gently boiling salted water. Melt the butter, brown the breadcrumbs in it. Roll the dumplings in the browned breadcrumbs. Traditionally served with Sauerbraten (see p. 180).

Great Britain

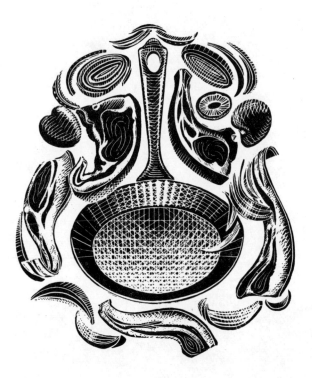

CABBAGE SOUP

8 ozs. streaky bacon, diced
2¼ pints boiling water
1 large cabbage, chopped
1 large onion
1 large carrot
4 sticks of celery
½ pint dried peas, soaked
   overnight

salt, pepper to taste
rolls or slices of bread (optional)

Put everything in a large saucepan, pour over the boiling water, simmer for 4 hours. Serve, if liked, with a roll or a slice of bread in each soup plate with the hot soup poured over.

CAULIFLOWER, CREAM OF

1 medium cauliflower
1 pint milk
1¼ pints vegetable stock
2 ozs. butter
4 celery sticks finely chopped
1 small onion finely chopped
1 oz. flour
1 bay leaf
salt, pepper
croutons

Cook the cauliflower in boiling salted water for 20 minutes. Cut in half. Save half of the white flower and coarsely sieve the rest. Fry the celery and onion in the butter for 5 minutes in a large saucepan, add the flour, mix well, add the stock and the bay leaf, bring to the boil and simmer for 10 minutes. Strain. Add the sieved cauliflower and the milk to the stock. Add salt and pepper to taste. Separate the cauliflower into small heads, add to the soup, re-heat and serve with croutons.

COCK-A-LEEKIE SOUP (Scotch)

1 small fowl
salt, pepper
6 leeks
3 ozs. butter
2 tbsp. rice (optional)
2½ quarts stock or water
a few sprigs of thyme and parsley
   tied together

Joint the fowl. Wash the leeks thoroughly and chop finely.

Heat the butter in a large saucepan and add the pieces of fowl lightly seasoned with salt and pepper. Fry gently on all sides till brown, add the leeks and fry for a further 3 minutes. Pour on the stock, add the thyme and parsley, bring to the boil, skim if necessary, and simmer for 2 hours, or until the bird is tender.

Remove the pieces of fowl, take out any bones and chop the meat, return to the soup, remove the thyme and parsley. If rice is used add after 1 hour's cooking. Add more salt and pepper to taste.

This soup is better if made 24 hours before eating and re-heated when wanted.

COD, CRIMPED

1½ lbs. cod cutlets
3½ pints water
2 tsp. salt
1 tsp. vinegar
1 medium chopped onion
1 bay leaf
2 peppercorns
1 oz. butter
juice of a lemon
parsley

Put 1½ tsp. salt in 2 pints of water and the vinegar, add the fish and leave for 3 hours.

Add the onion, peppercorns, bay leaf and ½ tsp. salt to 1½ pints of water. Bring to the boil and simmer for 20 minutes. Boil up, put in the fish, lower the heat and simmer for 10 minutes or till tender. Drain well, place on a hot dish, squeeze a little lemon juice on each cutlet, dab with butter. Serve with ½ pint white sauce to which you can add 2 tsp. chopped parsley, or 1 chopped hard boiled egg.

HADDOCK SAVOURY

2 1½-lb. smoked haddocks
8 rashers of bacon
4 ozs. butter
3 ozs. flour
2½ pints milk
6 peeled tomatoes, sliced
1 onion, finely chopped
pepper
3 ozs. grated cheese (Parmesan
  is best)

Soak the fish in cold water for 30 minutes.

Drain, this will have got rid of excess salt. Put the fish in the milk, bring to the boil and simmer for 15 minutes. Strain the milk into a basin. Pick all the skin and bones off the fish and flake the flesh. Cut the bacon rashers in half, fry them with the chopped onion.

Make a white sauce with milk the fish has cooked in, flour, butter; season with pepper. Add the grated cheese. Arrange the fish, bacon and onion and tomatoes in layers in a fireproof dish, pour over the sauce, brown in the oven and serve hot. This is a substantial dish, and with a green salad and brown bread and butter makes a very adequate supper for four or six hungry people.

FRIED HERRINGS

4 large herrings
2 ozs. medium oatmeal
salt, pepper
1 oz. butter
fat for frying
parsley and cut lemon garnish

Take the head off the fish, already scaled and cleaned, but with the roes left in. Split down the back, take out the backbone and as many smaller bones as possible. Season with salt and pepper. Rub with oatmeal, pressing in to make as much adhere as possible. Heat the fat and fry the fish for 3 or 4 minutes on each side or till soft right through. Put a pat of butter on each fish and decorate with parsley and lemon slices.

STUFFED HERRINGS

4 large herrings, with soft roes
3 ozs. fresh breadcrumbs
2 tsp. chopped parsley
salt, pepper
2 ozs. butter
1 egg
2 tbsp. milk
1 tsp. lemon juice

Split the fish, remove the roes.

Mix the roes, parsley, breadcrumbs, salt and pepper together. Melt 1 oz. butter in a saucepan, add the egg and the breadcrumbs mixture, stir well together and cook gently till the egg is just cooked in the mixture. Cool and stuff the fish with this. Place the stuffed fish in a shallow fireproof dish, dot with 1 oz. butter, sprinkle with lemon juice, salt and pepper. Pour the milk in the dish, cover with grease-proof paper and bake in a moderate oven for 20 minutes, or till soft throughout. Serve with lemon slices.

HERRING PIE (Yorkshire)

4 herrings, boned and filleted
salted water
1 oz. butter
4 medium potatoes, cut in thin
   slices
2 medium cooking apples, peeled
   and finely chopped
salt, pepper

Having prepared the fish leave them to soak in salted water for 1 hour. Drain. Rub the butter over the sides and bottom of a straight sided pie dish. Line sides and bottom with some of the potato slices. Arrange the fillets and chopped apple in layers in the dish, season each layer with salt and pepper, finish with a layer of potatoes.

Cover with a well-buttered paper. Bake in a moderate oven for 45 minutes. 15 minutes before the end remove the paper to brown the top.

MACKEREL AU GRATIN

4 cleaned mackerel, heads and
   tails removed
4 shallots
2 medium onions
2 tsp. chopped parsley
2 ozs. white breadcrumbs
1½ oz. butter
salt, pepper

Butter a shallow fire-proof dish. Chop the onions, shallots very finely. Arrange the fish in the dish, sprinkle with the onions, shallots, breadcrumbs, a sprinkling of salt and pepper and the parsley. Pour over enough white wine to come up to one third of the fish, dot with butter. Cover with a buttered paper and bake in a moderate oven for 25 minutes.

BOILED MACKEREL WITH GOOSEBERRY SAUCE

4 fresh cleaned mackerel, heads
   and tails removed
boiling water
¼ tsp. salt

Have enough boiling water to cover the fish, add the salt. Make several incisions in the back of each fish, put into the boiling water, simmer very gently for 15 minutes. Drain and serve with the hot sauce.

SOUSED MACKEREL

4 cleaned mackerel, heads and
   tails removed
1 large onion, cut in thin rings
½ tsp. salt
¼ tsp. black pepper
a pinch of dried thyme
1 cut up bay leaf
1 carrot, finely sliced
1 tsp. olive oil

enough cold water mixed with
1 tbsp. vinegar to cover

Put the fish in a shallow fire-proof dish, add all the other ingredients. Bake in a cool oven until the vegetables are tender, basting frequently. Leave to cool in the liquor if eaten cold; but they are good eaten hot.

White wine and a good squeeze of lemon juice may be used instead of the vinegar and water.

CASSEROLE OF HARE WITH PRUNES AND RAISINS

1 hare, with the blood
2 ozs. butter
6 medium onions, chopped
½ lb. prunes
¼ lb. seedless raisins
¾ pint meat stock
½ tsp. salt
¼ tsp. pepper
¼ tsp. sugar
1 sherry glass red wine
1 tbsp. red currant jelly
fried croutons of bread

Separate the front from the back part of the hare. Cut up the front part in egg-sized pieces. Roast the back part in the usual way, so that it will be done by the time (1½ hours) it takes the casserole to cook. Fry the cut-up pieces in the butter till brown, add salt, pepper, the onions, prunes, raisins and the stock. Bring to the boil and simmer for 1½ hours with the lid on the casserole. Add the sugar, wine and jelly and cook uncovered for 30 minutes. Now add the blood and the roasted back.

Heat and serve with the croutons in the gravy.

JUGGED HARE

1 hare, well hung
salt, pepper
¼ pint red wine, preferably port
1 pint meat stock or water
2 ozs. butter
2 ozs. bacon, chopped small
1 tbsp. lemon juice
1½ tbsp. flour
1½ tbsp. butter

TIED IN MUSLIN:

4 cloves
4 bay leaves
4 sprigs of parsley
1 sprig thyme, or marjoram
¼ tsp. nutmeg powder

¼ tsp. cinnamon powder
12 peppercorns

Ask your butcher to skin, clean and cut up the hare in pieces the size of an egg. Dust these with salt and pepper. Fry these in the 2 ozs. butter and bacon till browned. Put the pieces in a jar or deep casserole and pour over the wine. Cover tightly and cook in a moderate oven for 30 minutes. Now add the lemon juice, stock and herbs. Stand the jar or casserole in a pan of water, cover and cook in a moderate to cool oven for 3 hours or simmer very gently on top of the stove. Strain the gravy. Mix the 1½ tbsp. butter with the flour, pour on the hot gravy, bring to the boil, stirring all the time, pour over the hare and serve hot.

FRICASSÉE OF RABBIT

1 young rabbit, cut in joints
3 ozs. butter
¼ lb. bacon rashes, chopped small
4 medium onions, chopped
4 cloves
a small bunch of mixed
herbs, parsley, thyme, marjoram,
    etc.
¼ tsp. nutmeg
½ tsp. salt
¼ tsp. pepper
½ pint water
1 oz. flour
1 sherry glass white wine

2 egg yolks
grated rind of ½ a lemon

Heat the butter and bacon in a stew pan, add the rabbit pieces and chopped onions, fry for 3 minutes, add the cloves, herbs (tied in a muslin bag), nutmeg, pepper, salt and water, bring to the boil and simmer for 50 minutes with the lid on.

Mix the flour with 2 ozs. butter, pour on some of the stock from the saucepan to make a thick gravy, return this to the pan, stir well and simmer for 5 minutes. Beat the yolks, add the wine, the lemon rind and pour over the hot, but not boiling, dish. Stir well and serve.

PIGEONS IN CASSEROLE

4 pigeons or 2 wood-pigeons
2 ozs. butter
4 ozs. bacon, diced
4 medium onions, chopped
4 medium carrots, chopped
1 oz. flour
1 bay leaf
2 tsp. chopped parsley
¼ tsp. dried thyme
½ tsp. salt
¼ tsp. pepper

½ pint meat or chicken stock
2 sherry glasses red or white wine

Fry the diced bacon in a thick saucepan for 2 minutes, add the butter and the pigeons and brown quickly on all sides. Remove them and add the chopped vegetables, the herbs, salt, pepper and flour. Mix well. Replace the birds, pour on the stock and the wine, bring to the boil and simmer very gently for 1½ hours or until the birds are tender. Serve with red currant jelly.

CORNISH PASTIES

1 lb. short pastry
½ lb. raw steak
¼ lb. kidney
½ lb. potatoes or a mixture of
    onions, turnips and potatoes
salt, pepper
1 beaten egg

Cut the steak, kidneys and peeled potatoes, etc. into ½ inch dice, season with salt and pepper. Roll out the pastry and cut in six rounds the size of a saucer. Place a sixth of the mixture on each round, moisten the edges with cold water, fold over and seal tightly. Brush with the beaten egg.

Cook on a baking sheet in a hot oven for 15 minutes, lower the heat to moderate and cook for a further 40 minutes.

TOAD IN THE HOLE

1 lb. steak, cut in 1 inch pieces
4 ozs. flour
½ pint milk
1 egg
salt, pepper
1 oz. dripping

Mix the flour, milk, beaten egg and ½ tsp. salt to make a smooth batter and leave for 1 hour or longer. Heat the dripping in a flat tin or fireproof dish in a hot oven, when smoking hot pour in a quarter of the batter and bake till set, for about 10 minutes. Now put in the meat, seasoned with salt and pepper. Pour over the rest of the batter and bake quickly till risen, for 25 minutes. Lower the heat to moderate and cook for a further 20 minutes. Cut up kidney, small rolls of bacon may be added to the meat. Any of these are far better than the usual sausage.

ROAST BEEF

1 sirloin or middle rib
salt, pepper
dripping

Sprinkle the joint all over with salt and pepper and rub well in. If the joint has not much fat put 2 ozs. dripping on the fat side.

Make the oven very hot, stand the joint in a roasting dish or on the oven bars with the pan underneath and cook for 20 minutes. Reduce to a moderate heat and cook; for underdone beef 16 minutes to the pound, 22 minutes for medium and even 30 minutes for those who like it overdone. Serve with Horseradish Sauce and Yorkshire Pudding and potatoes, peeled (halved if too big), cooked round the joint for 30 to 40 minutes in the roasting dish, or until quite soft inside when pricked with a skewer or fork and crisp and brown outside.

IRISH STEW

2 lbs. neck or loin of mutton
3 large onions
2 lbs. potatoes
¾ pint cold water
1 tsp. salt
¼ tsp. pepper

Remove any excess fat from the meat and cut the rest into 2 × 1 inch pieces, or smaller. Peel and slice the onions and potatoes into ⅛ inch thick rounds. Fill a casserole or thick pan with alternate layers of meat, then onions, then potatoes, with a sprinkling of salt and pepper on each. Pour in the water and bring to the boil, skim if necessary, reduce the heat, cover the casserole or pan tightly, cook very slowly in the oven or on the stove for 3 to 4 hours until the meat is tender and almost all the liquid has disappeared. Serve hot, straight from the pot.

WELSH RABBIT

4 slices of thick toast (crusts
   removed)
8 ozs. grated cheese
2 ozs. butter
¼ pint beer or stout
½ tsp. paprika
1 tsp. mustard
2 beaten egg yolks

Make the toast, keep warm. Melt the butter in a double-boiler or over a very low heat, add the cheese, stir, then add the beer or stout slowly, stirring all the time till smooth, now the paprika and the eggs. Keep stirring till warm throughout, pour over the toast and serve. Never let this mixture boil or bubble; if you do it will become 'stringy' and lumpy.

SCOTCH EGGS

4 ozs. minced ham
3 anchovy fillets
2 ozs. fresh breadcrumbs
¼ tsp. pepper
1 beaten egg
4 hard boiled eggs
fat for frying

Chop the anchovies very finely, add to the minced ham, breadcrumbs and pepper, stir in beaten egg. Cover each egg with a coating of this forcemeat and fry in hot fat until brown all over. Cut in half and serve on fried bread, if wished.

DEVILLED KIDNEYS

4 pieces toast
8 sheep's kidneys
2 ozs. butter
1 tbsp. dry mustard
1 dsp. Worcester sauce
salt, pepper

Skin the kidneys, cut them in half and core them. Mix the sauce and the mustard together. Heat the butter in a saucepan, add the kidneys, season with salt and pepper, brown quickly for 2 minutes, lower the heat and cook very gently for 6 minutes with the pan covered, add the mustard mixture, stir well and cook slowly for 2 minutes more. Stir and serve on the hot toast.

LANCASHIRE HOT POT

2 lbs. neck of mutton
2 lbs. potatoes
3 large onions
8 ozs. mushrooms
3 sheep's kidneys
1 pint meat stock
2 ozs. butter
12 oysters (optional)
salt, pepper

Cut the meat into cutlets and remove excess fat. Peel and slice the potatoes fairly thickly, slice the onions thinly. Wash, but do not peel, the mushrooms and cut in two. Skin and core the kidneys, cut in halves. Take a deep casserole and place in each ingredient in layers, finishing with potatoes on top. Season each layer with salt and pepper, pour in the butter, melted, and the stock. Cover the casserole tightly and cook very slowly for 3 hours.

BOILED MUTTON WITH DUMPLINGS AND CAPER SAUCE

1 3- to 4-lb. leg of mutton
1 tsp. salt
1 large turnip
3 medium carrots
3 medium onions
2 tbsp. pearl barley
2 tsp. chopped parsley

Boil enough water to cover the meat, put in the meat best side down. Bring again to the boil, skim, add the vegetables cut in medium sized pieces and the salt. Lower the heat and simmer for nearly 2 hours for a 4 lb. joint, 20 minutes less for a 3 lb. joint. Garnish with chopped parsley over the joint and the vegetables round the dish.

MUTTON AND HARDBOILED EGG PIE

4 lean mutton chops
4 hardboiled eggs
6 whole allspice
1 oz. butter
1 oz. flour
½ pint meat stock
salt, pepper
short crust pastry
fat for frying

Fry the chops in hot fat till brown all over, season with salt and pepper and pack into a pie dish. Add the eggs, cut in half and the allspice. Mix the butter and flour with a little of the stock to form a paste, pour the rest of the warmed stock over and mix well. Add this to the pie-dish. Cover with short crust pastry, sealing the edges well, make a hole in the top and bake in a moderate oven for 40 minutes.

ROAST STUFFED SHOULDER OF MUTTON

4 lb. shoulder of mutton
1½ lbs. potatoes
2 ozs. dripping

STUFFING OR FORCEMEAT:
3 ozs. breadcrumbs
1 finely chopped small onion
¼ lb. finely chopped mushrooms

1 egg
pepper, salt

Ask your butcher to bone the shoulder.
Mix all the stuffing ingredients together and stuff the meat. Skewer or tie into a neat shape. Peel and cut the potatoes in halves, if too big. Arrange the potatoes round the joint in the roasting tin, add the dripping and roast in a moderate-to-hot oven for 1½ hours. Serve with onion sauce.

POT ROAST

2½ lbs. rump or rolled rib of beef
1 large chopped onion
2 tbsp. beef dripping
½ pint hot water or beef stock
2 peeled chopped tomatoes
1 chopped head of celery
3 medium sliced carrots
1 bay leaf

1 tsp. salt
¼ tsp. pepper

Take a thick bottomed pot and melt the dripping in it, add the onion and fry till brown. Put in the meat and brown it all over, pour in the hot liquid, add the vegetables, bay leaf, salt and pepper. Bring to the boil, cover the pot tightly and simmer very slowly for 3 hours.

STEWED OXTAIL WITH TOMATOES

1 oxtail, jointed
1 oz. dripping
1 large onion, sliced
1 lb. tomatoes
1 oz. flour
parsley, thyme, bay leaf or other
herbs tied together
cold water or stock
2 cloves
2 tsp. lemon juice
salt, pepper
2 tsp. flour
2 tsp. butter

Wash the tail well. Heat the dripping in a stew pan or casserole, add the oxtail pieces, fry till browned, add the onions, sprinkle in the flour, stir well. Pour in enough water or stock to cover the meat, add the cloves and herbs, salt and pepper. Bring to the boil, cover and simmer very gently for 2 hours. Skin the tomatoes, add them, re-cover and simmer for another 30 minutes. Leave until cold, then lift off the fat formed on top.

Melt the butter in a small saucepan, add the flour, stir, pour on enough of the meat stock to thicken, add this to the stew plus the lemon juice. Bring again to the boil and simmer for 15 minutes longer. If the oxtail is old this dish may take longer to cook — it is essential that the meat should be just falling off the bone.

PORK PIE

1 lb. lean pork
1 lb. flour
½ tsp. salt
6 ozs. lard
1 egg, beaten
¼ pint cold water
salt, pepper

Cut the pork in ½ inch squares, put in a pan with the water, bring to the boil. Pour off the water onto the lard. Sieve the flour and salt in a basin, pour on the lard and hot water slowly, stirring all the time to make the dough. Leave till cool, turn on to floured board and knead for 4 to 5 minutes. Cut off ¼ of the dough. Roll out to about ⅛ inch thick and line a buttered piedish, which should be round with straight sides. Season the meat with salt and pepper and fill the pie. Roll the ¼ of dough into a round and cover the top, moisten and seal the edges. Cut leaves out of any left-over rolled pastry, make a small hole in the middle of the top, decorate with the leaves. Brush well with beaten egg and bake in a moderate oven for 2 hours.

BOILED SILVERSIDE AND DUMPLINGS

3 to 4 lbs. silverside
2 lbs. carrots cut in two
lengthways
2 lbs. medium onions
1 bay leaf
cold water

Put the meat in a large saucepan, add the prepared vegetables and bay leaf, cover with cold water. Bring to the boil gradually, skim if necessary, cover the pan and simmer gently for 2½ to 3 hours.

Serve with hot dumplings.

TERRINE OF PORK, VEAL AND LIVER

1 lb. fat pork (belly)
1 lb. lean veal
½ lb. liver
2 tbsp. brandy
6 tbsp. dry white wine
1 clove of garlic
6 black peppercorns
6 juniper berries
¼ tsp. ground mace or nutmeg
4 ozs. fat bacon
2 tsp. salt

Mince the pork, veal and liver. Mix well. Add 2 ozs. of the bacon cut into ¼ dice, chop the garlic very fine and the berries, add these, the salt, the brandy and the wine. Mix thoroughly and leave for 2 hours. Put into a 2 pint size terrine dish or a straight-sided casserole. Cut the rest of the fat bacon into ¼ wide long strips and arrange on the top of the pâté or terrine decoratively. Place the dish in a roasting tin filled with water. Cook uncovered in a slow oven for 1½ hours. When the mixture begins to come away from the sides of the dish it is done. Remove and cool. They are better if pressed down with weights when half cold.

Cover with melted lard or butter when cold, if to be kept more than a week.

STEAK AND KIDNEY PUDDING

suet crust
1½ lbs. rump steak
½ lb. kidney
1 clove of garlic (optional)
2 ozs. flour
1 tsp. salt
¼ tsp. pepper
½ lb. mushrooms
½ pint meat stock

Cut the steak into thin slices, 4 × 3 inches. Cut the kidney in ½ inch squares. Slice the mushrooms. Mix the flour, salt and pepper together, and roll the steak, kidney and mushrooms in it. Wrap a piece of kidney and mushrooms in a slice of meat. If using garlic, cut it in two and rub the inside of the basin well with it. Roll out the suet crust, line the basin with it, sides and bottom and cut a round for the top. Pack the steak rolls in the lined basin, add any extra pieces of kidney or mushroom, pour over the stock, cover with the round of pastry, damp the edges and seal tightly. Tie two pieces of greased paper tightly over the top. Steam for 4 hours.

JUGGED PEAS

2 lbs. shelled peas
1 tbsp. butter
½ tsp. salt
1 tsp. caster sugar
12 mint leaves
a pinch of pepper

Put everything in a screw-top jar. Screw the lid on tightly and stand in a saucepan of boiling water coming half way up the jar. Boil for 30 minutes. Take out the mint leaves before serving. If the peas are old they may take a little longer, but cooked in this way peas are delicious and tender.

VEAL AND HAM PIE

2 lbs. veal
¼ lb. ham
2 hard boiled eggs
salt, pepper
pinch of dried herbs
enough meat stock to cover the
    meat, etc.
6 ozs. flour
2 ozs. lard
⅜ pint hot milk
½ tsp. salt

Cut the veal into slices 1 × 2 inches, also the ham. Slice the eggs. Arrange these ingredients in layers in a pie-dish, season with salt, pepper and a sprinkling of herbs. Pour over the stock.

Make the pastry by melting the lard in the warmed milk, stir slowly into the sieved flour and salt, mix to a soft dough. Turn on to a floured board, roll out fairly thinly, cover the pie-dish, moisten and seal the edges. Decorate with any left-over pastry, make a hole in the middle and bake in a moderate to hot oven for 1 hour.

APPLE AND QUINCE SAUCE

1 quince
4 small or 2 large cooking apples
½ pint cider
3 ozs. sugar
1 oz. butter

Peel, core and grate the fruit coarsely or chop very fine. Put the grated quince in a small saucepan, pour in the cider, bring to the boil and simmer for 10 minutes, till tender. Add the apple and simmer for 10 minutes longer, till tender. Stir well with a wooden spoon to make a thickish pulp (if too thin drain off some of the liquid), add the sugar and cook gently till melted, stir well and add the butter. Stir again. Serve hot with roast pork or roast goose.

BRANDY BUTTER

4 ozs. butter
1 oz. sugar
brandy

Work the sugar into the butter till smooth. Add enough brandy (or rum) into the mixture gradually stirring all the time until the mixture will absorb no more brandy while remaining stiff.

BREAD SAUCE

½ pint milk
1 small onion
2 cloves
1 blade mace or a good pinch
    of ground nutmeg
2 ozs. white fresh breadcrumbs
½ oz. butter
1 tbsp. cream
½ tsp. salt
pinch of pepper

In a double boiler heat the milk, add the onion stuck with the cloves and nutmeg or mace until just not boiling, for 30 minutes. Remove the mace, if used, add the breadcrumbs, stirring and beating with a fork, now the salt, pepper and half the butter. Cook gently, beating frequently, for 20 minutes. Remove the onion, add the other half of butter and the cream. Serve hot.

CAPER SAUCE

2 ozs. butter
2 ozs. flour
¼ pint milk
¼ pint mutton stock
salt, pepper
1 tbsp. capers
1 dsp. vinegar

Heat the milk and mutton stock till nearly boiling. Melt the butter in the saucepan, add the flour, stir well, pour in the nearly boiling liquid and, stirring all the time, simmer for 3 minutes. Add salt and pepper to taste. Just before serving stir in the capers and the vinegar. Serve hot.

CUMBERLAND SAUCE

1 lemon rind and juice
1 orange rind and juice
½ gill port wine (⅛ pint)
½ gill water
2 tbsp. red currant jelly
2 tbsp. vinegar
½ tsp. made mustard
pinch of salt
pinch of cayenne pepper
2 ozs. glacé cherries, chopped

Shred the lemon and orange rinds very finely, no white pith must be attached. Squeeze the juice of both fruit and strain. Boil the shredded rinds in the water for 5 minutes, strain and put the liquid back in the saucepan. Add the wine, red currant jelly, mustard, cayenne, salt, the fruit juice and the vinegar. Boil all together for 3 minutes. When cold, add the chopped cherries.

CUMBERLAND RUM BUTTER

1 lb. dark brown soft sugar
¼ tsp. grated nutmeg
1 sherry glass rum
½ lb. best fresh butter
icing sugar for dusting

Melt the butter very slowly, do not let it froth. Put the sugar in a bowl, add the nutmeg. Pour in the rum and mix well. Pour the melted butter over the sugar mixture and beat for 10 minutes until it begins to set. Turn into a pretty china bowl and sprinkle with icing sugar. Delicious with unsweetened biscuits and bread and butter at tea time.

GOOSEBERRY SAUCE

½ pint young green gooseberries
¼ pint water
1 oz. butter
1 oz. sugar
salt, pepper
¼ tsp. ground nutmegs
cooked sorrel or spinach leaves

Boil the gooseberries in the water for 4 or 5 minutes, till tender and mushy. Drain and sieve them. Add a tablespoon of sorrel leaves chopped finely, the butter, sugar, salt and pepper to taste and the nutmeg. Re-heat and serve with mackerel or other fish.

If wished, this concentrated sauce may be mixed with ¼ pint white sauce.

HARD SAUCE

4 ozs. caster sugar
2 ozs. butter
1 egg white, stiffly beaten
2 tbsp. brandy

Cream the sugar and butter. Add the egg white, mix well, then the brandy. Stir all together. Serve very cold.

HORSERADISH SAUCE (1)

4 tbsp. finely grated horseradish
1 tsp. sugar
1 tsp. salt
1 tsp. mustard
½ tsp. pepper
2 tbsp. vinegar
3 tbsp. cream

Heat the vinegar in an enamel saucepan, add the sugar, salt, mustard and pepper, stir over a very low heat for 2 minutes, add the horseradish and cook for a further 2 minutes, cool, then add the cream. Stir well and serve cold.

HORSERADISH SAUCE (2)

2 tbsp. finely grated horseradish
¼ tsp. made mustard
¼ pint cream
1 tbsp. white wine vinegar
2 tsp. caster sugar
½ tsp. salt
¼ tsp. pepper

Mix the horseradish with the sugar, salt and pepper, mustard and vinegar. Whip the cream and stir gradually into the mixture. Serve very cold.

ONION SAUCE

2 ozs. butter ⎫
2 ozs. flour ⎬ white sauce
1 pint hot milk ⎭
¼ tsp. ground nutmeg
3 large finely chopped onions
salt, pepper

Cover the onions with water, salt and pepper to taste, bring to the boil and simmer till tender. Add to the white sauce, season with salt and pepper, if necessary, add the nutmeg. Stir well. Serve hot.

MINT SAUCE

2 level tbsp. finely chopped mint
¼ pint white wine vinegar
3 ozs. sugar
½ tsp. salt
2 tbsp. water

Boil the sugar, vinegar, water and salt for 4 minutes, pour over the chopped mint, cover tightly while cooling. Stir well before serving, when quite cold.

RED CURRANT JELLY

1 lb. sugar to 1 pint juice

Pick the fruit off the stems and wash it. Put it in a large basin or casserole, stand this in a saucepan of simmering water and steam for several hours until all the juice has run out of the currants or leave in a cool oven: the length of time depends, naturally, on how many pounds of fruit you have.

Pour the currants into a jelly bag—one made of thick flannel is best—and leave them to drain until they stop dripping. Measure the juice. For each pint take 1 lb. sugar. Put both in the preserving pan, bring to the boil and boil for 5 minutes, or until the jelly sets. Bottle at once in warm jars and seal.

SAGE AND ONION STUFFING

1 lb. chopped onions
boiling water
1 tsp. salt
pinch of pepper
4 ozs. breadcrumbs
1 tsp. finely chopped sage
1 oz. butter

Put the onions and salt in a small pan and just cover with boiling water, simmer for 8 to 10 minutes till tender, add the breadcrumbs, sage and pepper, and butter, stir to make a smooth 'dryish' mixture.

PUFF PASTRY

1 lb. flour
2 ½-lb. blocks of butter
* or margarine*
1 egg yolk
the juice of 1 lemon
¼ pint cold water

Ingredients, utensils and hands must be cold. Sieve the flour into a basin. Beat the egg. Cut the butter into small dice and with the finger tips mix with the flour, but do not rub it in. Add the beaten egg, water and lemon juice spoon by spoon, mix quickly and lightly until the dough leaves the sides of the basin. Turn on to a floured board and roll quickly all over into an oblong, rolling with quick short pushing strokes away from you. Fold the pastry in three, top edge a third down, and bottom edge over the two thicknesses, making three thicknesses. Turn the pastry round on the board, folded edges at the sides, and repeat the process of rolling. Repeat twice more, four times in all. Put into a very cold place and leave for at least an hour before using.

WHITE SAUCE

(This is the basis for many sweet and savoury sauces)

2 ozs. butter
2 ozs. flour
1 pint hot milk
½ oz. butter

Melt the butter in a saucepan, stir in the flour with a wooden spoon on a low heat, pour over the hot milk gradually, stirring all the time, till smooth and creamy, cook gently for a further 2 or 3 minutes. Stir in the ½ oz. butter before serving.

DUMPLINGS

4 ozs. flour
2 ozs. chopped suet
¼ tsp. baking powder
1 medium finely chopped onion
1 tsp. finely chopped parsley
1 tsp. salt
¼ tsp. pepper
cold water to mix
plenty of boiling water or stock to boil

Mix all the ingredients together in a basin, add a little cold water, tsp. by tsp. to make a soft but firm dough: when it comes cleanly away from the sides of the basin it is right. Roll into 12 small balls. Have the water or meat stock, as in Boiled Silverside, boiling; put in the dumplings and cook, uncovered, for 20 to 30 minutes till dry inside and nicely swollen in size.

SHORT CRUST PASTRY

½ lb. flour
¼ tsp. baking powder
¼ tsp. salt
4 ozs. butter, lard or dripping
cold water

Sieve the flour, baking powder and salt together, rub the fat in lightly with the fingers till the mixture looks like breadcrumbs. Add enough—only a little—cold water to make stiff paste that comes cleanly away from the sides of the basin. Roll out at once. Work quickly throughout the proceeding.

SUET CRUST

8 ozs. flour
4 ozs. chopped suet
1 level tsp. baking powder
½ level tsp. salt
cold water

Sift the flour, salt and baking powder, add the suet and mix well. Add a little cold water gradually and mix well until the paste forms a soft dough. When it leaves the sides of the basin cleanly, it is done.

YORKSHIRE PUDDING

1 pint milk
4 ozs. flour
2 eggs, beaten
½ tsp. salt
1 oz. dripping

Sift the flour and salt, add the milk gradually, stirring all the time till quite smooth, then stir in the beaten eggs. Always make this batter at least an hour before it is to be cooked.

Melt the dripping in a shallow baking tin in the oven; when smoking hot, stir the mixture and pour in the batter. Cook in a moderate-to-hot oven for 30 minutes. A most delicious way of cooking this batter is to place the tin in which it is to be cooked under the meat which is roasting on the oven shelf. The essence of the meat drips into the pan and the batter is put in the tin 30 minutes before the meat is fully cooked. This however means a roast with no separately served meat gravy.

APPLE CHARLOTTE

1 lb. cooking apples, peeled
*   and cored*
8 ozs. sugar
rind and juice of ½ a lemon
2 ozs. butter
3 tbsp. apricot jam
¼ tsp. cinnamon
2 ozs. almonds, skinned
puff pastry (see p. 204)

Cut the apples in ½ inch dice, put in a saucepan, add the sugar, lemon rind and juice, butter, jam and cinnamon. Cook very slowly, stirring all the time until the apples are soft. Add the almonds.

Line a pie-dish, preferably one with straight sides, with puff pastry. Pour in the mixture. Bake in a moderate oven for 45 minutes. Serve with cream or hard sauce.

APPLE DUMPLINGS

4 cooking apples, peeled, cored
*   and halved*
2 tsp. sugar
1 tsp. cinnamon
½ oz. butter
8 ozs. self raising flour
¼ tsp. salt
2 ozs. butter
milk

Sift the flour and salt, add the 2 ozs. butter and mix till the mixture is like fine breadcrumbs. Add enough milk to make a soft dough. Roll till ⅜ inch thick. Cut 4 squares large enough to hold half an apple. Mix the sugar, cinnamon and ½ oz. butter. Put an equal amount on each apple half. Wrap the apples in the dough, moisten and seal well. Steam for 45 minutes or till the apple is soft. Serve with cream or hard sauce (see p. 203).

AUNT NELLY PUDDING

½ lb. chopped suet
½ lb. golden syrup
½ lb. plain flour, sifted
the juice and grated rind of
   1 lemon
3 tbsp. milk
2 eggs, beaten

Add the syrup to the suet and stand in very hot water, or in a cool oven till the suet begins to melt. Beat well till the mixture forms a smooth cream. Add the rind and the juice of the lemon, stir in the flour, the eggs and the milk. Pour into a buttered basin and cover tightly with greased paper. Steam for 4 hours.

A sauce made with 3 tablespoons warmed syrup diluted with 1 tablespoon warm water may be served with this.

BREAD AND BUTTER PUDDING

4 slices of bread
2 ozs. butter
2 ozs. currants
2 ozs. sultanas
3 tbsp. sugar
4 eggs, well beaten
1⅛ pints milk
grated lemon rind to taste
½ tsp. nutmeg

Remove the crusts and butter each slice of bread. Cover the bottom of a greased dish with slices, sprinkle over some of the fruit and 2 tbsp. sugar. Repeat until bread and fruit and sugar are finished. Mix the eggs well into the milk, add the lemon rind and pour into the dish. *And,* this is important, leave for 2 hours. Sprinkle 1 tbsp. sugar and nutmeg on top and bake in a very slow oven for 1 hour or till the custard is set.

COLD LEMON WHIP (uncooked)

3 eggs
2 tsp. powdered gelatine
1 tbsp. cold water
2 tbsp. hot water
6 ozs. caster sugar
grated rind of 1 lemon
5 tbsp. lemon juice

Soak the gelatine in the cold water for 10 minutes. Separate the eggs. Beat the yolks with the lemon rind and sugar till creamy, add the lemon juice. Pour the hot water over the gelatine, stir till dissolved and add to the yolk mixture. Mix well. Whip the egg whites till stiff, fold lightly, into the yolk mixture until completely mixed. Turn into a mould or glass dish. Chill and serve with sweetened cream, if possible.

LEMON SOUFFLÉ

5 eggs
2 lemons
8 ozs. icing sugar

Sieve the sugar. Separate the eggs, beat the whites until stiff. Grate 1 lemon, and squeeze the juice of both. Add the peel and the juice to the egg yolks, stir in the sugar and whip till creamy. Fold in the stiff whites. Put in a buttered soufflé dish and bake in a moderate-to-hot oven for 20 minutes. Serve at once.

DUKE OF CAMBRIDGE PUDDING

short crust or puff pastry
  (see pp. 204, 205)
3 ozs. butter
3 ozs. caster sugar
2 egg yolks
2 oz. finely chopped candied peel

Line a shallow dish or flan ring with the pastry. Cover the bottom with the candied peel. Melt the butter in a saucepan, add the sugar, stir till melted, add the egg yolks and bring to the boil. Pour, at once, over the candied peel and cook in a slow oven till the top is nicely browned and crinkled.

GOOSEBERRY FOOL

1 lb. green gooseberries
4 ozs. sugar
¼ pint water
½ pint cream or 2 bottles of yoghourt (in which case use 6 ozs.
  sugar)

Stew the gooseberries, water and sugar till tender. Sieve them and add the cream, whipped, or the yoghourt. Sponge fingers or digestive biscuits are good served with this.

QUEEN OF PUDDINGS

4 ozs. fine white breadcrumbs
3 eggs, the yolks and whites
  separated
1 whole egg, beaten
1 pint milk
3 or 4 tbsp. raspberry jam
3 tbsp. caster sugar

Beat the 3 yolks and the 1 egg, add to the milk and mix well. Add the breadcrumbs. Put the jam on the bottom of a pie dish, making a layer of about ½ inch. Pour over the milk, egg and crumb custard and leave for 30 minutes. Bake in a very cool oven for 1 hour, till set. Whip the whites very stiffly, add the sugar. Pile on top of the custard, sprinkle a little sugar on top and put back in the very cool oven till the meringue is set and delicately browned.

GUARDS PUDDING

4 ozs. butter
4 ozs. caster sugar
2 eggs
2 ozs. white breadcrumbs
2 tbsp. sieved raspberry jam
  or raspberry jelly
pinch of bicarbonate of soda

SAUCE:
3 tbsp. raspberry jam
3 tbsp. water
1 tsp. lemon juice

Butter a soufflé dish and put a round of buttered paper on the bottom. Cut another round of paper to be over the top of the dish.

Cream the butter and sugar till quite white and fluffy. Beat in 1 egg, half the flour and half the breadcrumbs, then the other egg and the rest of the flour and breadcrumbs and the bicarbonate. Add the sieved jam or jelly. Pour into the dish. Tie over the buttered paper. Steam for 1½ hours. When done leave cooling for 8 minutes before turning out.

Make the sauce by heating all the ingredients mixed together. Sieve and serve separately.

RHUBARB PUDDING

short crust pastry
¾ lb. rhubarb, finely chopped
2 ozs. flour
4 ozs. soft brown sugar
grated rind of ½ lemon
3 tbsp. thick cream

Line a plate with pastry. Cover with the rhubarb mixed with the cream, sugar and rind. Bake in a moderately hot oven for 10 minutes, lower the heat and cook till the mixture is firm and the top crisp, about 25 minutes. Serve with whipped cream if possible.

PLUM PUDDING

10 ozs. chopped suet
10 ozs. breadcrumbs
5 ozs. flour
8 ozs. raisins, seedless and washed
10 ozs. sultanas, washed
5 ozs. chopped apples
4 eggs
5 ozs. candied peel chopped small
1 oz. chopped almonds
grated rind and juice of ½ a lemon
½ tsp. nutmeg
3 ozs. brown sugar
¼ tsp. salt
1 sherry glass rum

½ sherry glass sherry
1 sherry glass stout

Soak the raisins and sultanas in the rum and sherry. Sieve the flour, add the breadcrumbs, suet, salt, sugar, lemon rind, almonds, nutmeg, peel, apples and the fruit and rum mixture. Beat the eggs, add to the stout and lemon juice, stir well. Add gradually to the flour mixture, stirring for a long time till completely and well mixed. Put the mixture into a greased basin or basins. Tie two layers of grease-proof paper firmly over the top of each basin and tie the whole in a cloth. Boil for 6 hours.

This pudding will keep for months. Before using boil again for 3 hours.

Serve with brandy butter.

RUM BUMBLE PUDDING

¾ tbsp. gelatine
water
4 ozs. sugar
¼ pint rum
2 tbsp. whisky
2 egg whites, beaten stiff
¼ pint cream
almonds, skinned and chopped

Soak the gelatine in a basin in 1 tbsp. cold water then dissolve in 3 tbsp. boiling water. Add the sugar, rum and whisky. Stir till the sugar is dissolved. Strain and leave to cool.

When the mixture begins to set, whisk until frothy, add the egg whites and the cream gradually, whisk all together. Chill and serve sprinkled with almonds.

Skin the almonds by placing in boiling water for 1 or 2 minutes, when the brown skins will come off easily.

GOOSEBERRY PUDDING

FRUIT MIXTURE:
¾ *lb. gooseberries*
3 *ozs. butter*
3 *ozs. soft brown sugar*
1 *oz. chopped nuts*

CAKE MIXTURE:
4 *ozs. self-raising flour*
¼ *tsp. salt*
4 *ozs. caster sugar*

4 *ozs. butter*
2 *eggs, beaten*

Wash and prepare the fruit. Melt the 3 ozs. butter, add the brown sugar, stir well, add the nuts. Butter a deep fireproof dish and pour in this mixture. Place the gooseberries in a layer on top. Sieve the flour and the salt. Cream the 4 ozs. butter with the caster sugar, add the eggs and flour gradually, stirring well. Pour over the fruit and bake in a moderate oven for 35 minutes. When done turn the pudding on to a dish so that the gooseberries are on top.

SUMMER PUDDING

currants, black, red or white, strawberries, raspberries. 1½ *lbs. ought to be enough for 4 people*
slices of stale white bread, crusts removed
sugar to taste

Choose a soufflé dish or basin that will half fill with the fruit. Butter the bottom and sides and line with the slices of bread, so that they just overlap. Add enough sugar to taste to the fruit in a saucepan and heat until the sugar melts and the juice begins to run, but do not boil. Pour the fruit into the lined dish, cover the top with bread. Put a plate or saucer on top and a heavy weight on this. Leave overnight in a cold place.

Serve very cold with whipped cream.

TRIFLE

3 *small sponge cakes*
6 *macaroons*
1 *oz. ratafias*
¼ *pint medium sweet sherry*
3 *tbsp. brandy*
2 *ozs. blanched almonds, cut in strips*
strawberry jam
½ *pint custard*
¼ *pint cream*

¾ *oz. sugar*
1 *white of egg*

Put the sponge cakes, macaroons and ratafias in a dish, pour over the brandy and sherry, keeping back 1 tsp., leave to soak for 10 minutes. Cover with a thick layer of strawberry jam. Pour over the cooled custard. Whisk the cream, sugar, egg white and 1 tsp. sherry till fluffy, cover the cake and jam mixture. Stick the almond strips all over the cream mixture. Serve cold.

WHIPPED RASPBERRIES

1 lb. raspberries
1 lb. sugar
2 egg whites

Bruise the fruit with a wooden spoon, add the sugar. Stir well. Beat the egg whites till stiff, stir into the raspberry mixture and beat with the egg whisk till everything is well mixed. Serve cold with cream.

CHRISTMAS CAKE

1 lb. seedless raisins
1 lb. currants
2 ozs. almonds, shredded
3 ozs. glacé cherries, chopped
4 ozs. mixed peel, chopped
½ lb. flour
½ lb. butter
½ lb. soft brown sugar
1 tbsp. black treacle
grated rind of 1 orange and
    1 lemon
¼ tsp. mixed spice, cinnamon,
    nutmeg and ginger
a few drops of vanilla essence
4 eggs
¼ pint brandy or sherry
almond paste
royal icing

Line an 8 inch cake tin with 1 layer of brown and 2 layers of greaseproof paper to come 2 inches higher than the tin.

Wash and dry the fruit. Take a large basin, put in the fruit, almonds, cherries, peel and 1 tbsp. flour. Mix well.

In another basin cream the butter and sugar, add treacle, orange and lemon rinds, essence and the spices. Beat well, then add the eggs, one by one, beating between each. Sieve the flour and add with the fruit mixture. Pour in 2 tbsp. of brandy or sherry and mix well. Pour into the tin, make a hollow in the middle, for a flat top result. Tie a band of newspaper round the tin and bake in a slow oven for 1½ hours, reduce the heat to very slow and cook for a further 4 hours. Test with a skewer or knife, which will come out clean if the cake is done.

Leave the cake in the tin for 40 minutes, turn upside down, prick deeply with a skewer and pour over the remaining sherry or brandy and let it run into the cake.

Cover with almond paste and royal icing (see p. 212).

ALMOND PASTE

2 eggs
4 ozs. caster sugar
4 ozs. icing sugar
8 ozs. ground almonds
4 drops lemon juice
3 drops almond essence
1 dsp. brandy or sherry
2 tbsp. warm apricot jam

Spread the warm jam on top of the cake. Beat the eggs with the sugars in a basin over hot water till light and fluffy. Cool, add the almonds, lemon juice, almond essence and brandy.

Roll out to fit the top of the cake, an 8-inch diameter cake.

ROYAL ICING

½ lb. icing sugar
1 egg white
1 tsp. lemon juice
a drop of laundry blue (optional)

Sieve the icing sugar, beat the egg white not stiffly, but till no longer slimy. Add gradually to the sugar, beating all the time, also the lemon juice and blue, if any. Beat for 20 minutes. Spread over the cake, smoothing on at the end with a stainless steel knife dipped in boiling water.

CORNISH SPLITS

1½ lbs. flour
4 ozs. butter
1 oz. lard
1 oz. yeast
½ tsp. sugar
¼ pint warm water
¼ pint milk
cream
jam

Put the yeast, sugar and 1 tsp. flour in a basin, pour on the warm water, mix well and leave in a warm place for 15 minutes. Sieve the flour in a large basin and leave in a warm place. Heat the milk gently, add the lard and butter, leave to melt.

Make a well in the middle of the flour and gradually pour in the yeast water and the warmed milk, and butter and lard, mixing all to a soft dough. Leave in a warm place for 1½ hours to rise. Knead for 4 minutes, roll out ½ inch thick. Cut in pieces and form small balls about the size and shape of a tangerine, or small rissole. Bake in a moderate oven for 20 to 30 minutes till golden brown. Serve cold, split in half, filled with Cornish cream and jam, especially raspberry.

SPONGE CAKE

8 eggs
the weight of the eggs in caster
    sugar
the weight of 5 eggs in flour
the grated rind and juice of
    1 lemon

Butter a large cake tin and sift sugar all over the inside. Put the sieved flour on a piece of paper in a cool oven to warm.

Put the sugar in a basin, add the yolks of 4 eggs and 4 whole eggs. Beat the 4 whites very stiffly in another basin. Stand the basin with the sugar and egg yolks over nearly boiling water, grate the lemon rind on to them and whisk for 15 minutes, add the lemon juice, then the stiff whites and lastly the flour stirring it in as lightly and quickly as possible. Bake in a moderate oven for 1¼ hours.

DIGESTIVE BISCUITS

4 ozs. butter
1 lb. whole-meal flour
1 beaten egg
1 oz. sugar
pinch of bicarbonate of soda
½ pint cold water
1 tsp. milk

Rub the butter well into the flour. Mix the soda in the milk. Add this to the eggs and the sugar, mix well. Gradually pour in the water, mixing quickly. Roll out on a floured board as thick as a penny. Cut into rounds, prick all over with a fork and bake in a moderate-to-cool oven for 25 minutes.

VICTORIA SANDWICH CAKE

6 ozs. flour, self raising
6 ozs. caster sugar
6 ozs. butter
3 eggs
grated rind and juice of ½ a lemon
2 tbsp. raspberry, strawberry
    or apricot jam

Grease two cake tins and dredge them with flour. Sieve the flour. Cream the butter and sugar till fluffy, add the flour and eggs spoonful by spoonful, beating all the time, and add the lemon rind. Pour into the tins, bake in a moderate oven for 20 minutes. When done turn out on a wire rack. Spread one cake with jam and place the other on top.

JUMBLES

5 ozs. sugar
5 ozs. butter
1 egg
10 ozs. flour
1 tsp. grated lemon rind
2 ozs. ground almonds

Cream the butter and sugar, add ½ the egg, stir in the sieved flour, lemon rind, almonds and the rest of the egg. Form the mixture into rolls the thickness of a finger, shape as the letter 'S', place on a greased baking sheet and bake in a moderate oven for 10 minutes.

PARKIN

1 lb. flour
¾ lb. medium oatmeal
¼ lb. butter
1 tsp. salt
2 ozs. sugar
½ lb. syrup
½ lb. treacle
½ pint milk
½ tsp. bicarbonate of soda
1 tsp. ground ginger
1 egg

Dissolve the soda in the milk. Melt the treacle syrup and butter together. Beat the egg. Mix all the dry ingredients together, pour in the melted butter and treacle and syrup, stir well, add the egg, then the milk, stirring all well together.

Bake in a flat square greased tin for 45 minutes in a moderate oven. Turn out of the tin when cold. Half these quantities may be used, as this makes a big cake, but it keeps well and matures by keeping.

CRANBERRY CHEESE

1 pint cranberries
½ pint water
¾ lb. sugar
2 ozs. seedless raisins, chopped
2 ozs. walnuts, chopped
1 orange, peeled and thinly sliced

Cook the cranberries in the water till soft. Sieve them. Add the sugar, raisins and walnuts. Bring slowly to the boil, stirring all the time, add the orange. Simmer for 20 minutes. Pour into jars and seal.

DAMSON OR BULLACE CHEESE

¾ lb. sugar to 1 pint pulp

Cook the fruit slowly till soft, either in a saucepan, no water added, or in a slow oven. Sieve the fruit. Add ¾ to 1 lb. sugar to every 1 pint of pulp. Bring to the boil stirring all the time, until it stiffens and grows thick. Pour into warm jars and seal.

Crack the stones and boil the kernels with the sugar and pulp to make it most delicious.

LEMON CURD OR CHEESE

6 ozs. caster sugar
4 egg yolks
1 egg white
grated rind and juice of 1 large
    lemon
2 ozs. butter

Whip the egg yolks and white very well. Melt the butter, sugar, lemon rind and juice in a saucepan, add the eggs, mix well and cook very slowly, stirring all the time till thick, for about 15 minutes preferably over boiling water in a double saucepan. If overheated or not stirred, the eggs will scramble and the curd be ruined.

Pour into pots and seal with paper if not to be eaten at once.

DARK COARSE MARMALADE

1 lb. Seville oranges
2 pints water
2 lbs. Demerara sugar
1 tsp. lemon juice

Wash the oranges. Put in the preserving pan, cover with the water and cook very slowly till the oranges are soft throughout. Remove, cool and cut into ½ inch squares. Save the pips, add these to the orange liquid and simmer for 10 minutes. Strain, throw away the pips. Add the sugar and orange pieces and lemon juice to the liquid. Stir gently till the sugar has dissolved, bring to the boil, boil rapidly for 15 minutes. Test for setting. When 'jelled' leave to cool for 15 minutes. Stir well, pour into warm jars and seal.

JAPONICA JELLY

These fruits of the garden shrub make a tart amber coloured jelly. They are of the quince family, and are excellent eaten with cold meats.

Cut the fruits in quarters, unpeeled and uncored, cover with water and cook till soft. Strain overnight or for 12 hours in a flannel jelly-bag. Take 1 lb. sugar for 1 lb. juice. Warm the sugar, bring the juice to the boil, add the sugar, stir till the sugar is dissolved, bring to the boil and boil for 15 minutes. Test, pour into jars and seal.

RHUBARB WINE

5 lbs. rhubarb
1 gallon water
3 lbs. loaf or preserving sugar
$\frac{3}{8}$ oz. isinglass
grated rind and juice of 1 lemon

Wash the rhubarb and cut into $\frac{1}{2}$ inch slices. Put into a large basin and press and pound them well, pour in the water. Cover the basin, leave for 10 days, stirring once a day. Strain it, add the sugar and stir till dissolved, with the lemon juice and rind. Add the isinglass, stir well and pour into the cask. Leave uncorked for 10 days, but cover the bung hole with a folded cloth. After 10 days cork tightly. Drink it after 12 months.

HOT CIDER AND RUM

3 quarts cider
$\frac{3}{4}$ pint rum
4 tbsp. brown sugar
1 lemon
1 orange
1 tsp. ground cinnamon
1 tsp. ground ginger
8 cloves

Peel the fruit very thinly and chop the rind. Slice the fruit. Put $\frac{1}{2}$ pint cider in a small saucepan with the sugar and spices, cover and simmer for 30 minutes. Pour the rest of the cider into a large saucepan, add the strained fruit and spice liquid. Heat slowly to a comfortable drinking temperature, add the rum and warm once more. Never over-heat any alcohol mixture or all the 'power' will disappear. Taste, and if more sugar is wished add more, as the sweetness of cider varies. Sufficient for 10 or 12 people.

RUM PUNCH

3 parts rum
2 parts brandy
1 part lemon juice
6 parts hot, not boiling, water
sugar to taste

Mix the rum, brandy, lemon juice, together. Heat the water, add the sugar, stir till dissolved and pour over the rum, etc.

WASSAIL BOWL

3 quarts beer
1 lb. sugar
1 grated nutmeg
1 tsp. grated ginger
4 glasses sherry
3 slices of lemon
3 slices of toast, crusts removed

Warm to comfortable drinking temperature 1 quart of beer, add the sugar, nutmeg and ginger, stir till sugar is dissolved. Add the sherry, the rest of the beer and the lemon slices. Warm once more. Serve with the toast floating on top.

SLOE GIN

sloes
white sugar
gin

Wash and prick the sloes. Mix with an equal weight of white sugar. Half fill the bottles with this and fill up with the gin. Cork tightly. Drink in 3 months' time.

SYLLABUB

This is an old English rich frothy drink, originally made from the milk straight from the cow. This is a modern version:

$\frac{1}{4}$ pint lemon or orange juice
1 tbsp. sherry (optional)
sugar to sweeten
$\frac{1}{4}$ pint cream
$\frac{1}{4}$ pint milk
2 egg whites stiffly beaten

Put the sweetened juice and sherry in a large bowl, add the cream and milk and whisk till fluffy, be careful not to over-whisk and make buttery. Add the egg whites, whisk again, chill and serve in glasses. This will keep in a cold place for several days.

MULLED CLARET

2 nutmegs, grated
2 pints claret
2 oranges
12 sugar lumps
12 cloves
$\frac{1}{2}$ tsp. ground cinnamon
1 pint boiling water
1 sherry glass curaçao
1 sherry glass brandy

Slice one unpeeled orange finely, pare the rind thinly off the other. Add these to the claret in a saucepan, plus the sugar, cloves and cinnamon. Heat slowly to comfortable drinking temperature, add the boiling water just off the boil, stir well, add the curaçao and the brandy. Pour into glasses and sprinkle the nutmeg over each. Serve at once.

Holland

BROWN BEAN SOUP

8 ozs. brown beans
1 onion
2 ozs. dripping
1 oz. flour
bouquet garni
nutmeg
salt
pepper

Soak the beans for 12 hours. Simmer in 2 pints of water with the *bouquet garni* until tender. Cook the chopped onion in the dripping until tender, stir in the flour. Cook for 1 minute. Add to the soup. Season with salt and pepper and grated nutmeg. Pass through a sieve. Serve with croutons of fried bread.

PEA SOUP

½ lb. dried peas
2 leeks
1 stick celery
1 pig's trotter
½ lb. boiling sausages
salt
pepper

Soak the peas for 12 hours. Put into a pan with the sliced leeks, chopped celery, pig's trotter and 4 pints water. Simmer for 4 hours, add the sausages 30 minutes before serving. Season with salt and pepper.

SPINACH SOUP

1 lb. spinach
2 ozs. butter
1 oz. flour
¼ pint cream
salt
pepper
nutmeg

Cook the spinach in a little salted water until tender. Pass through a sieve. Melt the butter, cook the flour in it for 1 minute, gradually add the spinach purée or some hot milk if necessary. Season with salt, pepper and nutmeg. Stir in the cream just before serving. Serve with croutons of fried bread.

DRIED COD

1½ lbs. dried cod
potatoes
4 onions
2 ozs. butter
1 oz. flour
1 teaspoon mustard
½ lb. cooked rice

Soak the cod for 24 hours. Remove the skin and bones. Cut into slices, roll and secure with a cocktail stick. Cook in boiling salted water for 45 minutes. Remove the fish from the water. Melt the butter, stir in the flour and the mustard, cook for 1 minute, gradually add the fish water to make a medium thick sauce. Put the fish and the rice in a shallow fireproof dish, pour the sauce over them. Bake in a moderate oven until the top browns. The same recipe can be used for fresh cod or any other white fish.

FISH CAKES

1 lb. fish fillet
2 ozs. butter
2 slices bread
1 egg
chopped parsley
nutmeg
salt
pepper
flour

milk
fat for frying

Cook the fish in a court bouillon (see p. 164) until tender. Flake the fish. Soak in a little milk the bread. Mash the fish and soaked bread well together, beat in the egg and the butter. Season with salt, pepper and nutmeg. Shape into flat cakes, dust with flour. Fry quickly in hot fat.

HERRINGS WITH RED CABBAGE

4 herrings
salt
pepper
flour
fat for frying

Split the herrings. Dust with seasoned flour. Make the fat very hot. Fry the insides first and then the outsides. Serve with red cabbage (see p. 223).

MACKEREL, STEWED

4 small mackerel
2 tomatoes, peeled and quartered
1 onion finely chopped
salt
pepper
juice of ½ lemon
1 tbs. chopped parsley

2 ozs. breadcrumbs
1 oz. butter

Put the mackerel in frying pan with a little water and the tomato, onion and parsley. Season with salt and pepper. Sprinkle with lemon juice. Spread the breadcrumbs over the top. Dot with butter. Simmer for 34 minutes.

HUNTSMAN PIE

1 lb. minced meat fresh or cooked
2 lb. cooked potatoes diced
2 onions sliced very thin
2 large cooking apples sliced
½ pint stock
salt
pepper
nutmeg

4 ozs. breadcrumbs
2 ozs. butter

Arrange alternate layers of potatoes, cooked meat, onion and apple in a deep casserole, beginning and ending with a layer of potato. Season the stock with salt, pepper and grated nutmeg. Pour this into the dish. Sprinkle with breadcrumbs. Dot with butter. Bake in a moderate oven for 1 hour.

MEAT AND BEETROOT SALAD

1 cooked beetroot
½ lb. chopped cooked meat
2 cooked potatoes
1 hardboiled egg
1 cooking apple
parsley
2 tbsp. olive oil
1 tbsp. wine vinegar
salt

pepper
pickled onions

Mix the cold sliced potatoes, sliced beetroot, chopped meat and peeled and chopped cooking apple. Mix the oil and vinegar well together, season with salt and pepper and pour over the salad. Garnish with chopped parsley, slices of hardboiled egg and pickled onions.

MINCED MEAT BALLS

½ lb. minced beef
½ lb. minced veal
½ lb. minced pork
1 large onion minced
2 ozs. breadcrumbs
1 egg
salt
pepper
lard for frying
2 tbsp. concentrated tomato purée

¼ pint sour cream
½ pint stock

Mix the minced meats with the onion and breadcrumbs. Bind with the egg. Season with salt and pepper. Form into small balls and fry quickly in the lard. Gradually add the tomato purée and the stock, simmer for 15 minutes. Leave to stand for several hours. Reheat and stir in the cream just before serving.

MINCED MEAT SCALLOPS

½ lb. minced beef fresh or cooked
½ pint espagnole sauce
2 ozs. breadcrumbs
1 oz. butter
parsley

Mix the meat with the sauce. Fill 4 scallop shells with the mixture. Sprinkle with breadcrumbs. Dot with butter. Bake in a moderate oven for 30 minutes. Garnish each one with a sprig of parsley.

SAUSAGE WITH CURLY KALE

2 lbs. curly kale cooked
2 lbs. potatoes cooked
½ pint stock
½ lb. smoked sausage sliced or
    frankfurters
2 ozs. rolled oats
2 ozs. butter
salt
pepper

Put the curly kale and potatoes together in a saucepan with ½ pint stock. Add the rolled oats and simmer for 15 minutes without a lid; the stock should almost all have evaporated. Remove the sausage, mash the vegetables with the butter. Season with salt and pepper. Arrange on a flat dish, garnished with the sausages.

MIXED SALAD

½ lb. peas
½ lb. new carrots
2 new potatoes
½ onion
½ lb. cooked meat, minced
gherkins
salt
pepper
parsley
1 tbsp. wine vinegar
2 tbsp. olive oil

Cook the peas and diced carrots in boiling salted water until just tender. Steam the potatoes in their skins, peel and chop them. Mix lightly together with the raw chopped onion. Arrange the meat in the middle of a flat dish, surround it with the mixed vegetables. Garnish with gherkins and chopped parsley. Mix the vinegar and olive oil well together season with salt and pepper. Pour over the vegetables.

SAUSAGES WITH RICE, ONION AND POTATOES

8 small pork sausages
2 lbs. onions
1 lb. potatoes
4 ozs. cooked rice
salt
pepper

Cook the potatoes and roughly chopped onion together in boiling salted water until tender. Drain and mix with the rice. Season with pepper and salt if necessary. Arrange the fried sausages on a dish with the rice and vegetable mixture round them. Serve with vinegar or Worcester sauce.

SCRAMBLED EGG SALAD

3 eggs
1 oz. butter
2 grated raw carrots
½ onion chopped
2 tomatoes sliced
cucumber sliced
mint
parsley
marjoram
salt

pepper
2 tbsp. olive oil
1 tbsp. vinegar

Beat the eggs lightly, season with salt and pepper and the chopped herbs. Scramble with the butter in the usual way. When cold, cut into small pieces, mix with the carrot and onion, surround with the sliced tomatoes and cucumber. Mix the oil and vinegar well together and pour over the tomato and cucumber.

VEAL OLIVES

8 slices lean veal (4 ozs. each)
2 ozs. butter
½ pint stock
1 lemon
salt
pepper

Beat the veal, season with salt and pepper. Roll and secure with string. Brown all over in the butter. Arrange in a shallow fireproof dish, put a slice of lemon on each roll. Pour the stock over. Cover and cook in a moderate oven for 1 hour. Remove the string before serving.

STUFFED BREAD ROLLS

8 long bread rolls
8 ozs. meat, minced or ham
½ pint stock
1 oz. butter
parsley
1 oz. flour
salt
pepper

Make a sauce with the butter, flour and stock. Mix the meat with it. Season with salt, pepper and chopped parsley. Scoop out the insides of the rolls and fill with the mixture, brush with melted butter. Replace the lid and bake for 10 minutes in the oven or under the grill.

PORK CHOPS WITH CHESTNUTS AND RED CABBAGE

4 pork chops
2 ozs. butter
½ pint chicken stock
½ small red cabbage
16 chestnuts
salt
pepper

Shred the cabbage and remove the hard stalks. Soak in cold water for 1 hour. Peel and cook the chestnuts (see p. 384, Spain). Lightly fry the chops on both sides in the butter. Drain the cabbage and place at the bottom of a deep casserole, put the chestnuts on top of it and then the chops. Season with salt and pepper. Pour in the stock. Cover with a lid, bake in a moderate oven for 1½ hours.

STEWED STEAK

1½ lbs. beef steak
1 onion
½ bay leaf
2 cloves
nutmeg
salt
pepper
lard

Cut the meat into 8 slices. Season with salt and pepper. Brown the meat on both sides with the fat. Add the sliced onion and the flavourings and ½ pint water. Cover the pan and stew slowly for 2 hours, or longer if necessary. 1 tbsp. vinegar is cooked with this stew.

RED CABBAGE

½ red cabbage
1 onion
1 cooking apple
1 oz. butter
salt
pepper
3 cloves
1 dsp. wine vinegar

Shred the cabbage and remove the hard stalks. Soak in cold water for 1 hour or longer. Drain. Fry the sliced onion in the butter for a few minutes. Add the cabbage, sliced apple and flavourings. Stew very slowly for 2 hours, adding a little stock or water if necessary.

APPLE OR PLUM CAKE

8 ozs. flour
2 tsp. baking powder
3 ozs. sugar
2 ozs. butter
2 tbsp. milk
1 lb. plums or cooking apples
cinnamon

Sift the flour with the baking powder, rub in the butter lightly, mix in 2 ozs. sugar. Add enough milk to make a stiff paste. Roll it out to $\frac{1}{4}$ inch thick, lay it on a greased Swiss Roll tin. Peel and slice the apples or halve and stone the plums. Arrange them on top of the pastry. Sprinkle with sugar and cinnamon. Bake in a hot oven for 25 minutes.

SEMOLINA WITH SULTANAS

1 pint milk
1 oz. semolina
1 oz. butter
1 egg
cinnamon
1 oz. sugar
2 ozs. sultanas

Bring the milk to the boil, stir in the semolina and the sugar. Cook very slowly, stirring from time to time. Add a pinch of cinnamon, the butter, beaten egg and sultanas when the mixture thickens.

Hungary

FISH SOUP

½ lb. skate
½ lb. pike
1 onion
1 tomato
1 oz. butter
4 potatoes
salt
1 tsp. paprika
pepper

Fillet the fish and cut into small pieces. Boil the heads, tails, bones and skin to make fish stock. Chop the onion and cook it in the butter until it is golden, add the peeled and chopped tomato, the paprika and the fish. Fry the fish until all pieces are well browned. Pour in 2 pints of strained fish stock, add the potatoes, cut into long pieces. Simmer for 20 minutes. Season with salt and freshly ground pepper.

HARICOT BEAN SOUP

½ lb. haricot beans
1 pint bacon stock
2 carrots
1 parsnip
1 oz. bacon fat
1 tbsp. flour
½ pint sour cream

Soak the beans overnight. Pour off the water and substitute bacon stock made by boiling bacon bones, rinds or a small knuckle. Add the sliced carrot and parsnip. Season with salt and pepper. Simmer until tender. Sieve the soup and mix it with the flour, cooked and slightly browned in the fat. Reheat and sprinkle with chopped parsley. Serve with croutons of fried bread.

POTATO SOUP

2 lbs. potatoes
1 onion
2 ozs. lard
¼ pint sour cream
1 green pepper
2 pints stock
nutmeg
salt
pepper

Fry the diced potatoes and the chopped onion in the lard, until well covered with fat. Add the chopped flesh of the green pepper. Pour in the stock and simmer until all vegetables are tender. Season with salt, pepper and nutmeg. Stir in the sour cream and bring to the boil. Serve with croutons of fried bread.

BACON AND POTATO CASSEROLE

2 lbs. potatoes
8 rashers bacon
1 onion
¼ pint milk
1 tsp. paprika
salt
butter

Arrange alternate layers of thinly sliced potato, chopped bacon and sliced onion in a well-buttered fireproof dish, ending with a layer of potato. Mix the paprika with the milk, add a pinch of salt and pour over the potatoes. Dot with butter. Cook in a moderate oven for 1½ hours.

SAUERKRAUT SOUP

1 lb. sauerkraut
1 lb. bacon bones
1 onion chopped
1 oz. lard
2 ozs. flour
1 tsp. paprika
salt
caraway seeds (optional)
½ cup sour cream
½ lb. boiling sausage

Simmer the sauerkraut with 2 pints water and the bacon bones for 30 minutes. Fry the onions in the lard until transparent, stir in the flour and cook for 1 minute. Add the paprika and caraway seeds, mix them well with the flour. Pour in the stock from the sauerkraut, stirring all the time, add the sauerkraut and the sausage cut into small pieces. Simmer for 10 minutes.

HAM AND PANCAKE PUDDING

12 small pancakes
½ lb. minced cooked ham
½ pint thick white sauce
2 ozs. grated cheese
salt
pepper

Make 12 small pancakes (see p. 267). Line a greased pudding basin with one of them and reserve one for the top, cut the rest into strips. Mix with the ham and sauce, season with salt and pepper, pour into the basin. Cover with the remaining pancake. Sprinkle with grated cheese. Bake in a moderate oven for 15 minutes.

MUSHROOM PAPRIKASH

½ lb. mushrooms
½ onion
½ tsp. paprika
½ oz. butter
¼ pint sour cream
1 dsp. flour

Fry the chopped onion in the butter until golden. Stir in the paprika, add the thinly sliced mushrooms, cover the pan and cook slowly for 10 minutes. Stir in the flour and gradually add the sour cream. Re-heat but do not boil.

SMOKED SAUSAGE WITH SCRAMBLED EGG

¼ lb. smoked sausage
2 rashers bacon
1 green pepper
1 small tomato
4 eggs
1 oz. butter
salt
pepper

Peel the tomato and cut into small pieces. Remove the seeds from the pimento and cut it and the sausage and bacon into small dice. Fry all these lightly together in the butter. Beat the eggs and stir them into the mixture. Season with salt and pepper. Cook fairly slowly, stirring from time to time until the mixture thickens. It should have the consistency of lightly scrambled egg.

STUFFED AUBERGINES

4 aubergines
2 ozs. breadcrumbs
1 small onion
1 clove garlic
1 tbsp. olive oil
½ lb. cooked minced pork
1 rasher bacon minced
parsley
salt
pepper

Scoop out the insides of the aubergines and chop the flesh. Fry the finely chopped onion and the garlic in the olive oil, add the pork and bacon and cook for 10 minutes. Mix with the chopped aubergine and a little chopped parsley. Fill the aubergines with this mixture, cover with bread crumbs and bake in a moderate oven for 20 minutes.

CHICKEN PAPRIKASH

1 large chicken
1 onion
1 green pepper
2 tomatoes
2 ozs. lard
1 tbsp. paprika
¼ pint sour cream
1 tbsp. flour
salt
½ pint water

Cut the chicken into pieces and dust with flour. Fry the finely chopped onion in the lard until golden, fry the chicken pieces until browned on all sides. Add the peeled and chopped tomatoes, the chopped flesh of the green pepper, paprika and water. Cover the pan and simmer until the chicken is tender. Strain off the liquid, season with salt and stir in the sour cream. Heat but do not boil the sauce, arrange pieces of chicken on a hot serving dish and pour the sauce over them. Serve with sauté potatoes and watercress.

PORK CHOPS (1)

4 pork chops
½ bottle white wine
2 carrots, sliced
1 onion, sliced
1 bay leaf
1 sprig parsley
1 clove garlic
1 sprig rosemary
2 ozs. butter
2 ozs. breadcrumbs
1 tsp. paprika

1 oz. flour
salt
pepper

Put the carrots, onion, bay leaf, parsley, rosemary, garlic and wine into a shallow dish and marinate the chops in it for 12 hours. Drain the chops and brown them in the butter. Stir in the flour, cook for 1 minute and add the strained marinade. Simmer for 20 minutes. Add the paprika and simmer for another 5 minutes. Arrange the chops in a shallow dish, pour the sauce over them, cover with breadcrumbs and brown them in the oven.

PORK CHOPS (2)

4 pork chops
1 oz. lard
1 onion, chopped
1 tsp. paprika
juice of ½ lemon
salt
pepper
small savoy cabbage
¼ pint sour cream

Fry the onion lightly in the lard. Add the chops and brown them on both sides. Stir in the paprika and lemon juice, season with salt and pepper. Add a little water. Cook, covered with a lid, in a moderate oven for 45 minutes. Cook the shredded cabbage in boiling salted water for 8 minutes. Drain and stir in the sour cream. Arrange the chops on a hot dish, pour the sauce over them and surround them with the cabbage.

GOULASH

1½ lbs. stewing beef
1 oz. dripping
1 onion, sliced
4 medium potatoes
½ lb. tomatoes
1 tsp. paprika
salt

Cut the beef into 1 inch pieces. Cook the sliced onion in the dripping until golden, add the meat, the peeled and quartered tomatoes and ½ pint water. Season with salt and paprika. Cover the dish and cook in a moderate oven for 1 hour. Peel the potatoes and cut them into long pieces, add them to the stew and simmer for another 30 minutes. Serve with plain boiled rice.

GOULASH WITH RUNNER BEANS

2 lbs. pork
1 onion
2 ozs. dripping
1 lb. tomatoes
1 tsp. paprika
salt
2 lbs. runner beans

Cut the pork into cubes, brown them in the dripping, add the chopped onion and brown it with the meat. Peel and quarter the tomatoes and cook them slowly with a little water until tender, rub through a sieve. Add them and the sliced beans to the meat. Season with salt and paprika and cook slowly in a covered pan for 1½ hours. Serve with mashed potatoes.

PÖRKÖLT: PORK STEW

2 lbs. pork, goose or duck
1 onion
2 potatoes
1 tsp. paprika
salt
1 oz. dripping

Fry the chopped onion in the dripping. Cut the meat into 2 inch cubes and brown it in the dripping with the onion. Stir in the paprika, season with salt, cover with water and cook in a moderate oven with a lid on the pan for 1½ hours. Add the potatoes, cut into ½ inch cubes, and cook for another 30 minutes.

TOKAY GOULASH

2 lbs. shoulder of pork
2 tomatoes
1 green pepper
1 lb. sauerkraut
1 tsp. paprika
salt
½ pint sour cream
1 oz. butter

Peel and quarter the tomatoes, remove the core and seeds of the pepper and cut it into slices. Melt the butter and cook tomatoes and pepper in it slowly until tender. Cut the pork into 1 inch pieces and add them to the vegetables. Brown slightly and add the sauerkraut, the salt and the paprika. Put a lid on the pan and cook slowly for 1½ hours. Stir in the sour cream and serve immediately.

TOKANY (Beef Stew)

2 lbs. stewing steak
1 onion
¼ lb. mushrooms
parsley
1 tsp. paprika
2 ozs. butter
salt
½ pint sour cream (optional)

Cut the meat into strips about 1 inch wide and 3 inches long. Brown them in the butter, add the finely chopped onion and fry until it is golden. Slice the mushrooms and add them to the meat. Season with paprika and salt, cover the pan and cook in a moderate oven for 1½ hours. Stir in the sour cream before serving.

VEAL CUTLETS

4 veal cutlets
2 ozs. butter
1 tsp. paprika
1 oz. flour
8 rashers streaky bacon
salt
pepper
¼ pint sour cream

Season the flour with salt and pepper. Dust the cutlets with it. Fry them on both sides in the butter until golden. Remove the cutlets and keep warm. Stir the paprika into the fat in the pan, cook for 1 minute, add the cream and heat gently. Pour this sauce over the cutlets and heat in a slow oven for 5 minutes. Roll the bacon rashers and cook them separately in the oven while making the sauce. Arrange them round the cutlets.

APPLE FOOL

2 lbs. cooking apples
2 egg whites
¼ lb. sugar
4 fresh plums

Peel and core the apples. Cook with very little water until tender. Rub through a sieve. Beat the egg whites until very stiff. Fold in the sugar, gradually add the apple purée. Decorate with fresh plums, stoned and cut in half, or with any fresh fruit in season. Serve cold.

CHOCOLATE ICE CREAM

5 ozs. cooking chocolate
½ pint double cream
2 tbsp. black coffee

Melt the chocolate in the coffee. Whip the cream and beat in the melted chocolate. Pour into the freezing tray of a refrigerator and leave to freeze.

PANCAKES WITH CHOCOLATE SAUCE

8 pancakes
2 ozs. ground almonds
2 ozs. seeded raisins
3 ozs. caster sugar
vanilla
1 oz. butter
¼ lb. cooking chocolate
1 tbsp. strong black coffee
¼ pint milk

Pound the raisins with the ground almonds, 2 ozs. sugar and a drop of vanilla. Put one pancake into a greased round fireproof dish, cover with a layer of the almond mixture, repeat the layers until all the pancakes have been used. Sprinkle with sugar, dot with butter and bake in a moderate oven for 10 minutes. Serve with chocolate sauce made by melting the chocolate in the coffee and milk.

CHOCOLATE CAKE

4 ozs. sugar
5 eggs
2 ozs. flour

FOR THE FILLING:

4 ozs. sugar
4 eggs
4 ozs. cooking chocolate
vanilla
2 ozs. butter

FOR THE GLAZE:

3 ozs. sugar

Beat the eggs, beat in the sugar until white and creamy. Beat in the finely sifted flour. Fold in the stiffly beaten egg whites. Grease and flour 2 8-inch baking tins. Fill with the mixture. Bake in a moderate oven for 5 minutes.

MAKE THE FILLING:

Pour the sugar and eggs into the top of a double saucepan, cook slowly, stir until thick. Melt the chocolate and a drop of vanilla in a little water. Cream the butter and beat the chocolate into it. Add this gradually to the egg mixture. Spread this between the layers of cake. Dissolve the sugar in a little water, cook gently until it begins to colour. Spread over the top of the cake. The cake should not be cut for at least 12 hours.

RICE SOUFFLÉ

2 ozs. rice
1 pint milk
4 ozs. sugar
2 eggs
strawberry jam
apple purée
1 small glass brandy

Put the rice and milk in a double saucepan and cook slowly until thick and creamy. Beat the egg yolks with 1 oz. sugar and add them to the rice. Put one third of the rice mixture into a buttered fireproof dish, cover it with a thin layer of jam, repeat these layers twice. Cover the top layer with apple purée. Whip the egg whites stiffly, fold in 3 ozs. sugar, arrange this on the top and bake in a moderate oven for 20 minutes. Warm the brandy, pour it over the pudding, set light to it and serve immediately.

India

INDIAN BOILED RICE

8 ozs. Patna rice
2 tsp. salt
3 pints cold water

Wash the rice in two changes of water. Soak in cold water for 30 minutes. Drain the rice and put in a large saucepan, add the salt and pour over 3 pints of cold water. Bring to the boil quickly and simmer for 20 minutes or more until each grain is soft, but not mushy. Drain in a colander and rinse under the cold tap for one minute. Cover the colander with a clean cloth only, no lid, and stand over simmering water till the rice is warmed throughout.

MULLIGATAWNY SOUP

2 pints chicken or meat stock
1 oz. butter
1 medium minced onion
1 minced clove of garlic
1 heaped dsp. mulligatawny paste
1 heaped dsp. tomato purée
*   or paste*
salt, lemon juice

Heat the fat in a saucepan, fry the onion, garlic, paste and purée very gently for 3 minutes. Pour on the stock, add salt and lemon juice to taste, bring to the boil and serve.

If a thicker soup is liked, add 1 tbsp. flour to the mixture and mix well, before the stock is poured over.

MADRAS FRIED FISH

4 cod cutlets, 2 filleted plaice
*   or other white fish*
1 egg, beaten
1 tsp. ground turmeric
¼ tsp. ground chillies
1 medium finely chopped onion
1 finely chopped clove of garlic
juice of ½ a lemon

salt to taste
fat for deep frying

Make a pickling mixture of all the ingredients and leave the fish in it for 1 hour, turning from time to time. Fry in the very hot fat till golden brown, drain and serve. Garnish with parsley and a cut lemon if wished.

KEDGEREE

1½ lbs. cooked fish (the flaky sort)
*   haddock, cod, turbot, etc.*
8 ozs. cooked rice
2 ozs. butter
2 medium chopped onions
1 clove of garlic chopped
1 tsp. ground turmeric
2 hard boiled eggs
pepper
salt

a few red and green chillies
*   cut lengthwise*

Heat the butter in a large pan, fry the onions and garlic till transparent. Add the turmeric and fry gently for 3 minutes. Add the flaked fish and the rice. Turn over and over gently with a fork or knife till warmed through, add pepper and salt to taste.

Pile on a warm dish and decorate with slices of egg and the chillies.

PLAIN PEPPER WATER

the juice of 1 large lemon
1 tsp. vinegar
2 pints hot water
1 oz. butter
2 cloves of garlic, finely chopped
2 tsp. ground coriander
1 tsp. ground turmeric
½ tsp. ground cummin seed
½ tsp. ground mustard seed
6 peppercorns

2 dry chillies
salt to taste

In a large saucepan melt the butter, and fry gently all the other ingredients for 2 or 3 minutes. Add the lemon juice and vinegar and hot water, add salt to taste, and simmer for 15 minutes.

This is to be used to moisten the rice served with dry curry.

PORK VINDALOO (Hot Curry)

1 lb. fat pork cut into ½ inch
  squares
4 medium finely chopped onions
1 clove of garlic finely chopped
2 tbsp. vindaloo mixture, mixed
  to a paste with vinegar
2 ozs. butter
salt to taste
cold water

Fry the onions and garlic in the fat until transparent, add the vindaloo paste, fry very gently for 3 minutes. Add the pork, mix well, cover the pan lightly and cook on the lowest possible flame, as it easily burns, for 30 minutes or until the pork is tender. Add enough cold water to make a thick gravy, stir well, add salt to taste.

TOAST CURRY

1 medium onion, sliced
2 cloves of garlic chopped
2 bay leaves
8 cardamom seeds } *tied in muslin*
12 cloves
2 ozs. butter
1 tbsp. curry powder
½ pint tomato ketchup
1 tsp. tarragon vinegar

Heat the butter, add the onions, garlic and fry till brown. Stir in the curry powder, pour over the tomato ketchup, vinegar, and the bag of spices. Simmer gently for 20 minutes, until thick.

This paste can be spread warm on hot buttered toast, or cold on biscuits for a picnic.

COOKED VEGETABLE CURRY

1½ lbs. cooked mixed vegetables
  cut into small pieces
2 ozs. butter
1 medium finely sliced onion
1 tbsp. curry powder
½ pint meat stock

Heat the butter in a saucepan, fry the onion till brown, stir in the curry powder, add the vegetables, pour over the stock, simmer for 30 minutes.

VEGETABLE CURRY

½ lb. green beans, sliced
½ lb. potatoes, cut in 1 inch cubes
½ lb. tomatoes, peeled and
    chopped
2 ozs. fat
1 large finely chopped onion
1 clove of garlic finely chopped
1 heaped tbsp. curry powder
salt

a squeeze of lemon juice
cold water

Heat the fat, fry the onions and garlic till transparent, add the curry powder, fry gently for 3 minutes. Add the tomatoes, stir well. If too dry add a little cold water to make a thick gravy. Now add the beans, simmer for 12 minutes, add the potatoes and simmer for another 6 or 7 minutes. Season with the lemon juice and salt, to taste.

VINDALOO CURRY

6 medium sliced onions
5 ozs. butter
2 tbsp. medium hot curry powder
1 lb. chopped rump steak
¼ pint wine vinegar
½ tsp. salt

Heat 4 ozs. butter in a saucepan and fry the onions till brown, add the curry powder. Have the steak cut in ½ inch cubes and brown these in 1 oz. butter. Add to onion mixture. Put on a low heat and add the vinegar drop by drop, stirring all the time, add the salt, cover and simmer very gently for 2 hours.

BENGAL CURRY

1 young chicken or rabbit or
    2 lbs. mutton cutlets
4 ozs. butter
4 medium thinly sliced onions
1 clove of garlic, chopped
2 tbsp. medium hot curry powder
    or
1 tbsp. hot curry powder
2 tbsp. tomato juice
1 tbsp. milk
1 tsp. salt
¾ pint meat stock

Parboil the chicken, rabbit or mutton for about 20 minutes. Cut in small pieces, about ½ inch square. Heat the butter in a saucepan, add the onions and garlic, fry till brown, add the chopped meat, curry powder, tomato juice, milk and salt. Cook for 35 minutes, stirring all the time with a wooden spoon, until the butter separates from the curry and the liquid has been absorbed. Serve on a hot dish, eat off hot plates with boiled rice served separately.

PISH-PASH

8 ozs. rice
1 chicken cut in pieces
2 pints water
1 tbsp. milk
2 tsp. salt
2 ozs. raisins
2 medium finely chopped onions

Boil the chicken pieces in the water, milk and salt till quite tender. Remove the chicken meat and keep warm. Add the washed rice and onion to the chicken stock and boil for 25 minutes until the stock is absorbed. Put in the chicken meat and the raisins, cover with a clean cloth. Keep warm.

DHALL RISSOLES

4 ozs. lentils
1 large minced onion
1 clove of garlic minced
¼ pint boiling water
2 ozs. breadcrumbs
¼ tsp. ground turmeric
a pinch of ground chillies
1 beaten egg
1 oz. flour

salt
fat for deep frying

Put the lentils, minced onions and garlic in boiling water and simmer gently; stir till the mixture cooks to a stiff paste. Cool and add the rest of the ingredients, mix well. Flour your hands and form into rissoles. Have the fat smoking hot and fry the rissoles till golden brown. Drain on paper and serve.

COLD MEAT 'KOOFTAH' CURRIED RISSOLES

2 tsp. 'Kooftah' mixture
1 lb. minced cooked meat
4 medium finely chopped onions
1 beaten egg
2 cloves of garlic finely chopped
1 oz. flour
2 ozs. butter, oil or fat
1 tbsp. curry powder
1 dsp. tomato paste
½ pint cold water
salt to taste
juice of 1 lemon

Mix the meat, 1 tbsp. chopped onion, Kooftah mixture, flour, salt with the beaten egg and make with floured hands into small balls, the size of a walnut. Put aside. Heat the fat and fry the onion and garlic till transparent, add the curry powder and tomato paste, mix well and cook slowly for 4 minutes, add the cold water gradually to make a thick gravy, stirring all the time, add salt and lemon juice to taste. Add the meat balls and simmer for 10 minutes more.

PILLAU RICE

1 lb. Patna rice
boiling water
8 ozs. butter
1 large onion, chopped finely
2 cloves of garlic chopped finely
½ tsp. saffron (soaked in ¼ pint
    warm water)
12 cloves
12 whole cardamoms
2 2-inch cinnamon sticks
½ tsp. whole allspice
4 ozs. sultanas

2 ozs. skinned almonds, fried in
    butter
salt

Boil the rice in a large pan. Heat the butter, add the onions, garlic and dry spices, fry but do not brown. Add the rice, cook for 5 minutes, stirring with a fork. Pour in the saffron and water, add salt to taste and pour in boiling water to cover and come 2 inches above. Cover the pan and cook very slowly till the liquid is absorbed and each grain is separate — for about 35 minutes. Add the sultanas and fried almonds and stir all together.

'KOOFTAH' PILLAU RICE

cooked Pillau rice
1 lb. minced mutton or beef
1 tbsp. finely chopped onions
1 clove of garlic finely chopped
1 heaped dsp. 'Kooftah' mixture
1 oz. flour
1 beaten egg

salt to taste
fat for frying

Mix all these ingredients well together, make into walnut sized balls and fry in fat till brown all over. Add to the prepared Pillau. Keep the pan covered till ready to eat to preserve the flavour.

CHICKEN CURRY

1 chicken, cut in pieces
½ pint sour milk
1 tbsp. ground coriander
1 tbsp. desiccated coconut
1 level tsp. ground turmeric
½ tsp. ground cummin seed
½ tsp. ground chillies
2 tsp. ground almonds
2 ozs. butter, oil or other fat

1 large finely chopped onion
2 cloves of garlic, finely chopped
salt to taste
juice of 1 lemon

Fry the onions and garlic in the butter, but do not brown. Add everything else and simmer gently in a covered pan for 30 minutes, or until the chicken is tender. Serve with Pillau rice.

COCONUT CURRY

1 chicken
2 ozs. butter
1 coconut, or an equal amount of
   desiccated coconut
2 medium onions, sliced
1 tbsp. hot curry powder
½ pint meat or chicken stock,
   or gravy

Joint and skin the chicken. Heat the butter and fry lightly till brown. Crack open the coconut and pour off the milk, keep it. Chop very finely or pound the flesh of the nut and put it, or the desiccated coconut, in a heated frying pan, add the onions and the curry powder and fry till brown. Put the fried chicken in a stew pan, add the coconut mixture, pour in the stock and simmer gently for 45 minutes.

EGG CURRY

8 eggs, hard boiled
3 medium onions sliced
½ tbsp. curry powder
3 ozs. butter
½ pint meat or chicken stock

Fry the onions in butter till brown, add the curry powder and stock, bring to the boil and simmer for 5 minutes, add the shelled hard boiled eggs, and simmer for 30 minutes. Cut the eggs in halves, and pour the curry gravy over them on a bed of boiled rice.

HOOSEINEE COOKED MEAT CURRY

cooked lamb or mutton or beef
green ginger, sliced
onions, sliced
2 ozs. butter
1 tbsp. hot curry
2 small sliced onions
1 tbsp. cold water
1 tbsp. cold milk
½ pint meat stock

Cut the cold meat in 1 inch squares and put on skewers, one slice of meat, one of ginger, one of meat, one of onion, until the skewers are packed tight. Pound the 2 small onions with the curry powder and moisten with water to form a paste. Heat the butter and cook this paste gently for 3 minutes. Add the milk and the water and cook for 10 minutes more, stirring all the time. Add the skewered meat and cook gently for 2 minutes, pour in the stock. Cover the saucepan and cook gently until the butter separates from the curry — for about 30 minutes.

KHEER

1 pint milk
1 oz. ground rice
1 oz. sugar
2 ozs. chopped almonds
2 ozs. chopped pistachio nuts
coconut milk
a few drops of rose, orange or
    lemon flavouring

Boil the milk, sprinkle in the ground rice, lower the heat and stir till it begins to thicken, add the nuts, flavouring and gradually pour in enough coconut milk to make as thin as an ordinary custard. Cook gently for 3 or 4 minutes longer. This dish is sometimes decorated with gold and silver leaf.

RHUBARB CHUTNEY

2 lbs. rhubarb
1 lb. sultanas
2 lbs. sugar
2 lemons
8 cloves of garlic
1 tbsp. salt
1 oz. ginger
1 pint vinegar

Cut up the rhubarb in 1 inch pieces. Peel the lemons, remove seeds, chop pulp and skin finely. Chop or crush the garlic finely. Bruise the ginger. Put everything in a large saucepan, bring to the boil slowly, stirring all the time, stir and cook until the mixture turns to a thick pulp. Take out the ginger, put into jars and seal. Keep for a month before using.

GREEN TOMATO CHUTNEY

2 lbs. green tomatoes
2 ozs. mustard powder
1 oz. cinnamon
1 oz. ground cloves
1½ lbs. brown sugar
3 pints vinegar
a pinch of cayenne pepper

Slice the tomatoes, put in a saucepan, add all the other ingredients, bring slowly to the boil and cook till thick. Pour into jars and seal. Eat after one month.

JELLABIES

BATTER:
4 ozs. flour
1 pint cold water
deep fat for frying

SYRUP:
8 ozs. sugar
½ pint water
2 sprigs of saffron
3 inner seeds of cardamoms

Make a smooth batter of the flour and water and leave in a warm place for 24 hours to ferment.

Put the sugar, saffron, cardamom seeds and water in a saucepan, bring to the boil slowly, and boil gently till a heavy syrup is formed. Keep warm. Heat the fat in a large deep pan till smoking. Stir the fermented batter. Take an ordinary funnel, put your finger over the hole and fill the funnel; let the batter run into the boiling fat in figures of eight or double circles. When set turn them over in the fat. They should be joined together. When crisp and golden brown, remove and drain them of fat. Separate them and put them in the syrup for 3 minutes. Remove and drain. The syrup will run through the tubes and the jellabies should keep crisp.

CHIPATTIES

4 ozs. plain flour
4 ozs. wholemeal flour
1 oz. butter or ghee salt
⅛ pint water (approximately)

Make a dough with the flour, butter, pinch of salt and water. It must be elastic, but not sticky. Knead well, cover and leave for 1 hour, then separate into six balls. Roll out on a floured board as thinly as possible. Have a slightly greased frying pan very hot, put in the chuppatie, remove from the heat and cook on the hot metal until a light brown skin has formed, turn and do the other side. Keep in a warm oven. Immediately re-heat the pan till very hot, put in the chuppatie last cooked side down and wait till it puffs up the top skin, but do not let it burst. Put at once in a warm oven. Each of the six balls of dough must be cooked like this.

TO MAKE SOUR MILK DHYE OR TYRE

Warm 2 pints of milk to blood heat, add the juice of 3 lemons. Cover the pan and set aside for 24 hours to set. Put the curd in a clean cloth and hang up to drip for several hours till dry.

This can be kneaded into little balls, which are often served in rose-flavoured sugar syrup as a sweet meat called Rasgollah.

BHUGIAS

4 ozs. flour
1 tsp. ground turmeric
¼ tsp. ground chillies
1 medium minced onion
1 clove of garlic, minced
2 small finely chopped chillies
4 ozs. finely chopped cooked vegetables—peas, carrots, turnips, etc.
2 eggs, beaten
milk
salt
fat for deep frying

Mix the flour, turmeric, chillies, minced onion and garlic well together, add the beaten egg and mix into a thick batter. If too thick add a little milk. Add the vegetables and salt to taste and stir gently so as not to break the vegetables.

Heat the fat till smoking and drop in dessertspoons of the mixture. The Bhugias will swell up like doughnuts; when golden brown, drain well and serve hot.

DHALL

8 ozs. lentils
1 medium onion
2 ozs. butter
½ tbsp. curry powder
1 pint meat or chicken stock
½ tsp. salt

Soak the lentils in cold water for 1 hour. Chop the onion very finely. Drain the lentils and put them, with the onion, butter, curry powder and stock in a saucepan, bring to the boil, cover the pan and simmer for 30 minutes. Add the salt and cook a little longer until the mixture looks like thick soup.

BAHMI (Indonesia)

½ lb. vermicelli (Chinese mie if possible)
1 tsp. salt, pinch of pepper
2 large finely chopped onions
2 cloves of garlic finely chopped
4 tbsp. oil
½ lb. pork
2 lbs. mixed vegetables, chopped small (cauliflower, cabbage heart, beans, peas, sprouts, spinach)
2 lbs. leeks, chopped
2 heads of celery, chopped
4 ozs. shelled shrimps
an omelette made from 2 eggs

soy sauce, tomato salad, cucumber salad
cut lemon served separately

Throw the vermicelli in plenty of salted boiling water and boil for 10 minutes. Fry the onion and garlic in the oil until brown. Remove and keep warm. Fry the meat in the same oil, quickly at first on both sides, then more slowly for 10 minutes, cool, and cut in ½ inch cubes. Put all the finely chopped vegetables, the pork cubes, shrimps and vermicelli in a large saucepan, mix well, cover the pan and heat slowly for 10 minutes. Meanwhile make an omelette with the eggs, pepper and salt; when done, cut in strips. Serve the Bahmi in a shallow dish; decorate with criss-cross strips of omelette.

TO COOK BOMBAY DUCK

Fresh or tinned Bombay Ducks

These salt dry fishes are either roasted in the oven with 2 ozs. fat, or fried till crisp. The fish should be held down while cooking as otherwise it will curl up; weighted in the oven or held down with a spoon or slice while frying. It has a strong smell but is a great appetiser to be eaten with curries.

NARRI GORENG (Javanese Fried Rice)

1½ lbs. rice
2 pints boiling water
½ tsp. salt
3 large onions, finely chopped
2 cloves of garlic, finely chopped
1 tsp. finely chopped red chillies
4 ozs. lard
½ lb. cooked meat, ham or chicken
  chopped in ½ inch cubes
½ tbsp. ground coriander seed
4 ozs. shelled shrimps
an omelette made from 2 eggs

Boil the rice, drain and keep warm over hot water with a clean cloth over the colander.

Heat 3 ozs. of the fat in a frying pan and fry gently for 10 minutes the onions, garlic and chillies. Remove and keep warm. Fry the meat in 1 oz. lard for 5 minutes in a large pan, add the coriander and the cooked rice, onion mixture and the salt. Mix with a fork till everything is well blended, lower the heat, add the shrimps, cover the pan and heat slowly for 10 minutes. Meanwhile make the omelette, cut in strips, serve the rice mixture in a shallow dish and decorate with the omelette strips.

BOMBAY PUDDING

2½ tbsp. semolina
½ tsp. salt
1 pint milk
2 ozs. butter
½ oz. flour
fat for frying

SAUCE:
juice of 3 lemons
2 tbsp. sugar

Boil the milk, sprinkle in the semolina and cook until the semolina becomes clear and thick. Stir in the butter. Spread thinly on two or three plates. Leave to cool and harden. Dust each piece with flour and fry in butter or lard. Cut in segments and serve with the sugar melted in the warmed lemon juice.

COCONUT MILK

Grate the kernel of a fresh coconut or take the same amount of desiccated coconut and pour over enough boiling water to cover the coconut. Leave for 20 minutes. Squeeze the milk out with a vegetable presser or by the hands. Save this milk and do exactly the same again with the coconut pulp. This milk is excellent for cooking rice for curries, or for making the sweet meat Kheer. Cows' milk and water mixed will make an even better 'milk'.

PINEAPPLE BALLS (Anglo-Indian)

2 eggs
4 ozs. sifted flour
a pinch of salt
¼ pint milk
2 tbsp. finely chopped pineapple
fat for deep frying
caster sugar

Make a thick batter of the flour, eggs, salt and milk, add the pineapple, mix well. Have the fat smoking hot, drop in the mixture a dessertspoonful at a time. Fry till golden brown, drain well and serve with caster sugar sifted over them. They should puff up into golden balls.

Italy

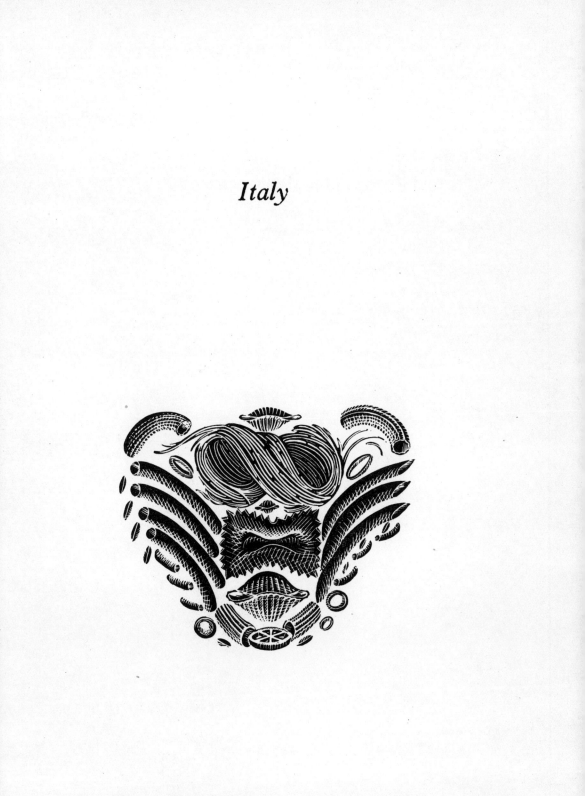

ANCHOVIES AND CAPERS

4 unsweetened biscuits
8 anchovy fillets
8 stoned olives
12 capers
1 tbsp. olive oil

Soften the biscuits with a little water. Chop the anchovies and olives. Mix them with the softened biscuits, the capers and the olive oil. Spread on bread or biscuits.

ANTIPASTO

tomato salad (see p. 251)
potato salad (see p. 250)
1 green pepper
2 hardboiled eggs

Slice the pepper. Arrange it and the tomato and potato salads on a dish. Cover with sliced hard boiled eggs.

MUSHROOMS AND SCAMPI

1 packet frozen scampi or prawns
½ lb. mushrooms
3 tbsp. olive oil
1 tbsp. lemon juice
chopped parsley
salt

pepper
garlic

Slice the raw mushrooms thinly. Mix olive oil, lemon juice, salt, pepper and crushed garlic. Pour half of the dressing over the mushrooms and half over the scampi. Mix the two together just before serving.

PESTO

8 anchovies chopped
¼ lb. grated Parmesan cheese
2 ozs. pine kernels or walnuts,
   chopped
1 clove garlic chopped

basil
1 tbsp. olive oil

Put all the ingredients in a bowl. Beat with a wooden spoon until they form a smooth paste. Serve spread on bread or dry biscuit.

POTATO SALAD

4 potatoes
2 tbsp. olive oil
1 dsp. wine vinegar
salt
pepper
garlic
parsley

Steam the potatoes until cooked but very firm. Peel and slice them. Dress them while still warm with the oil and vinegar, add crushed garlic, chopped parsley, salt and pepper.

RADISH, TOMATO AND YELLOW PEPPER SALAD

2 yellow peppers
2 tomatoes
3 radishes
1 stick celery
2 tbsp. olive oil
salt
pepper

Peel and slice the tomatoes. Cut the peppers into rings. Slice the radishes and the celery. Mix together. Pour the olive oil over them. Season with salt and pepper.

RICE AND SCAMPI

¼ lb. Patna rice
1 packet frozen scampi
3 tbsp. olive oil
1 tbsp. wine vinegar
chopped chives
salt
pepper

Cook the rice in boiling salted water. Drain and mix with the olive oil, vinegar, salt and pepper while still warm. When cold add the scampi and sprinkle with chopped chives.

RICE AND TUNNY FISH

¼ lb. Patna rice
¼ lb. tunny fish
3 tbsp. olive oil
1 tbsp. wine vinegar
½ onion, finely chopped
garlic
parsley

salt
pepper

Cook the rice in boiling salted water. Drain and dress with oil and vinegar while still warm. Mix with onion, salt, and crushed garlic. Sprinkle with freshly ground pepper. When cold add the tunny fish.

TOMATO SALAD

½ lb. tomatoes
2 tbsp. olive oil
salt
pepper
sugar

basil (optional)
chopped onion (optional)

Slice the tomatoes. Pour the olive oil over them, season with salt and pepper. Add sugar, onion or basil to taste.

TUNNY FISH WITH FRENCH BEANS

1 lb. cooked French beans
¼ lb. tunny fish
3 tbsp. olive oil
1 tbsp. lemon juice
salt
pepper

Mix the olive oil and lemon juice, season with salt and pepper. Pour over the beans while they are warm. Cut the tunny fish into ½ in. squares, arrange them on top of the beans before serving.

TUNNY FISH SALAD

potato salad (see p. 250)
¼ lb. tunny fish

Add tunny fish broken into fairly large pieces to potato salad, half an hour before serving.

BACON SOUP

1 bacon knuckle
1 onion sliced
1 oz. butter
4 peppercorns
2 ozs. flour
¼ lb. grated Parmesan cheese

¼ lb. Patna rice
salt

Cook the bacon, rice and peppercorns in 2 pints of water for 1 hour. Cook the onion in the butter until golden, add the flour, finely chopped bacon from the bone, the bacon stock and the rice. Reheat and serve with grated cheese.

CHICKEN SOUP WITH EGGS (for two people)

¾ pint chicken stock
2 eggs
2 ozs. grated Parmesan cheese
2 slices bread
2 ozs. butter

Fry the bread in the butter. Spread with grated cheese. Cut each piece into 3 strips. Bring the stock to the boil, poach the eggs in it. Pour into warmed soup bowls. Arrange 3 strips of bread round each plate.

CREAM OF CHICKEN SOUP

1½ pints rich chicken stock
 (a bouillon cube will not do for
 this)
1 oz. ground rice
2 eggs
1 dsp. lemon juice
nutmeg
½ gill milk
pepper

Mix the ground rice with the milk and a little of the stock. Heat the stock and add it to the ground rice paste. Simmer for 20 minutes. Season with the lemon juice, nutmeg and pepper. Beat up the eggs in a basin, pour a little of the hot soup over them, being careful not to allow the egg to curdle. Pour back into the pan and reheat carefully.

HARICOT BEAN SOUP

1 lb. haricot beans
⅓ a small red cabbage
2 or 3 onions
2 leeks
a small head of celery
a crushed clove of garlic
a sprig of thyme
salt
pepper

4 tbsp. olive oil
2 tbsp. concentrated tomato purée
3 pints of beef stock

Soak the haricot beans for 12 hours. Put them in a casserole with the olive oil, tomato purée, and the chopped vegetables, season with salt, pepper and herbs. Add the stock and simmer slowly for at least 2 hours.

MINESTRONE (1)

1 small head celery, chopped
1 small marrow, sliced
2 carrots, sliced
½ a small cabbage, shredded
⅓ lb. tomatoes, skinned
2 leeks, sliced
¼ lb. spaghetti
1 small onion, sliced
4 pints stock
¼ lb. streaky bacon

¼ lb. grated cheese
parsley
salt
pepper

Put the bacon, celery and carrots into the boiling stock. Simmer for 30 minutes. Add the other vegetables and the spaghetti, cook for a further 30 minutes. Stir the grated cheese into the soup before serving.

MINESTRONE (2)

½ lb. bacon
3 pints stock
½ lb. broad beans
½ lb. peas
1 small head celery, chopped
1 onion, sliced
½ lb. spinach
2 carrots, sliced
½ lb. tomatoes, peeled and
    quartered

¼ lb. Patna rice
¼ lb. grated Parmesan cheese
salt
pepper
parsley

Cut the bacon into 1-inch squares, put it into the boiling stock with all the vegetables and the rice, season with salt and pepper, add the parsley. Simmer for 1 hour. Stir in the grated cheese before serving.

MUSHROOM SOUP

½ lb. mushrooms sliced
2 ozs. butter
2 ozs. flour
1 pint milk
¼ pint stock
1 clove garlic
½ glass Marsala
salt

pepper
nutmeg
chopped parsley

Melt the butter and cook the mushrooms in it. Add the Marsala and cook gently for 2 minutes. Add the flour, cook for 1 minute, pour in the warmed liquids gradually. Season with salt, pepper and nutmeg. Sprinkle with parsley.

TOMATO SOUP (1)

2 lbs. ripe tomatoes chopped and
    skinned (or a large tin of Italian
    tomatoes)
2 pints stock
parsley
salt
pepper
tsp. of sugar
2 tbsp. ground rice

Cook the tomatoes slowly without water for 5 minutes. Add the stock and the parsley. Simmer for 10 minutes. Season with salt, pepper and sugar. Sieve the soup into the ground rice which has first been mixed with a little water. Return to the pan and simmer for 10 minutes.

TOMATO SOUP (2)

½ lb. tomatoes skinned and
   chopped
1 tbsp. olive oil
2 pints stock
1 clove garlic crushed with salt
½ tsp. sugar

parsley
basil or marjoram

Cook the tomatoes in the olive oil for 10 minutes.
Add the other ingredients and simmer for 5 minutes.
   This can also be served chilled.

THICK SPINACH SOUP

2 lbs. spinach
¼ pint stock
2 ozs. butter
¼ lb. grated cheese
2 eggs
nutmeg
salt
pepper

Cook the spinach without water for 30 minutes.
Strain thoroughly, put it into a casserole with the
stock and butter. Stir well, add the beaten eggs and
cheese. Season with salt, pepper and nutmeg. Cook
in a slow oven for 15 minutes. Serve with croutons
(see p. 164).

DRY SALT COD

5 large onions
6 anchovies (pounded until soft)
1 clove garlic
2 tbsp. olive oil
2 lbs. dry salt cod
a little milk
1 sprig parsley
salt
pepper
cinnamon

The fish should be soaked under running water for
24 hours and then steamed for 2 hours. Skin and
bone it and pound it to reduce toughness.
   Cook the onions with the parsley, crushed garlic
and the pounded anchovies in the olive oil until
they are soft. Add the fish and season with salt,
pepper and cinnamon. Cook for 20 minutes, then
cover with a little milk and simmer for 1 hour.

FRIED BREAM

1 lb. bream
olive oil for frying
¼ lb. flour
salt
pepper
1 lemon

Cut the bream into slices 1 inch thick. Mix the flour
with the salt and pepper. Dredge the fish slices. Cook
in smoking olive oil. Serve with slices of lemon.

GRILLED MACKEREL

4 *mackerel*
2 *ozs. olive oil or butter*
1 *lemon*

Score the fish across in two places and brush with oil or melted butter. Brush the grid with fat to prevent the fish from sticking to it. Place the fish under the grill and cook for about 3 minutes on each side. The fish should be placed very near the grill to start with and be moved further away when the skin is sealed and crisp. Serve with slices of lemon.

Herring can be cooked in the same way.

RED MULLET GRILLED

4 *red mullet*
2 *ozs. olive oil or butter*
maître d'hôtel butter for a garnish

Leave the liver in the fish and make two incisions across it. Brush it with olive oil or melted butter and grill it quickly for about 7 minutes on each side. Serve with maître d'hôtel butter (see p. 161).

RED MULLET WITH TOMATOES

1½ *lbs. tomatoes peeled and sliced*
red mullet (2 or 4 fish according to size)
1 *stick celery chopped*
salt
pepper
1 *clove garlic, chopped*

1 *tbsp. olive oil*
½ *tsp. sugar*

Cook the tomatoes, celery and garlic in the olive oil. Sieve and season with salt, pepper and sugar. Put this purée into a fireproof dish, lay the red mullet on it, cover with greaseproof paper and cook in a slow oven for 30 minutes.

RED MULLET IN PAPER CASES

4 *red mullet*
1 *onion*
1 *stick celery*
1 *tbsp. olive oil*
parsley
garlic

Slice the onion finely and chop the celery, fry them until golden in the oil and add chopped parsley and crushed garlic. Make several incisions in the fish and put the onion mixture into them. Wrap each fish separately in greaseproof paper and cook in a moderate oven for about 30 minutes. Serve in the paper so that the juices do not escape.

GRILLED SCALLOPS

4 scallops
2 tbsp. olive oil
½ onion chopped
pepper
1 tbsp. chopped parsley
1 clove garlic
salt

Remove the coral and grill the scallops under a hot flame for 5—10 minutes. Slice the coral, mix it with the butter, onion, parsley and crushed garlic. Pour over the scallops. Season with salt and pepper, and re-heat.

SHELLFISH RISOTTO

3 doz. scampi or prawns
8 ozs. Patna rice
1 onion, sliced
2 tbsp. olive oil
salt
pepper

Cook the shells and claws of the scampi. Drain and keep the water. Dip the shelled scampi in flour and fry in oil. Fry an onion until golden, add the rice, moving it about in the fat with a wooden spoon until each grain is cooked, which will be between 20 and 30 minutes, add the scampi, which should have been kept warm. Season with salt and pepper.

SOLE WITH PARMESAN CHEESE

4 soles
¼ lb. grated Parmesan cheese
2 ozs. butter
parsley
thyme } bouquet garni
bay leaf
salt
pepper

Remove the skins from the fish and put them in a fireproof dish, season with salt and pepper. Dot with butter. Cook in a moderate oven until one side is brown, turn fish over to brown the other side. Simmer the fish in ½ pint water with a *bouquet garni* for 10 minutes. Strain the liquid over the fish. Sprinkle with grated cheese. Cook for another 5 minutes until cheese is melted.

SOLE WITH WHITE WINE SAUCE

4 small soles
2 ozs. butter
4 tbsp. chopped mint
2 tbsp. chopped parsley
1 clove crushed garlic

SAUCE:
1 oz. butter
1 onion, sliced
1 glass white wine
salt
pepper

Skin the soles on both sides, make two crosswise incisions in the top of each fish. Fill these with butter, parsley, mint and garlic well mixed together. Wrap each sole in greaseproof paper and bake in a hot oven for 15 minutes. Serve with the following sauce.

Melt the butter, cook the onion in it until soft and golden. Add the wine and simmer for 10 minutes. Add a little water, season with salt and pepper. Simmer for another 10 minutes.

BROAD BEANS WITH BACON

2 lbs. broad beans, cooked
2 ozs. bacon
1 small onion
1 oz. butter

Chop the onion and bacon finely. Melt the butter, cook the onion and bacon in it for 5 minutes. Add the broad beans and cook gently for 5 minutes more.

NEW CARROTS WITH MARSALA

2 lbs. carrots
1 oz. butter
1 wine glass Marsala
salt

Cut the carrots lengthwise, put them in a pan and cook gently in the butter for 2 minutes. Pour in the Marsala, simmer for a minute or two, add ¼ pint of water, season with salt. Cover the pan and simmer for 30 minutes.

MUSHROOMS IN BATTER

½ lb. mushrooms
olive oil for frying

MAKE A BATTER AS FOLLOWS:
¼ lb. flour
1 white of egg
salt
3 tbsp. olive oil
1 gill warm water

Sieve the flour with a pinch of salt, mix in the olive oil, add the water and beat until smooth. Leave to stand for or 3 hours, stir in the beaten egg white immediately before the batter is to be used.

Cut the mushrooms into thickish slices, coat them in the batter and fry quickly in hot olive oil.

GRILLED MUSHROOMS

½ lb. field mushrooms
1 clove garlic
salt
olive oil

Put olive oil, chopped garlic, and a sprinkling of salt onto the underside of each mushroom. Cook quickly under the grill, in a heat-proof pan in which they can be served.

PEAS WITH HAM

2 lbs. peas
¼ pint stock
1 oz. lard
4 slices of ham

salt
pepper

Cut the ham into strips. Put all the ingredients into a double saucepan. Cook for 45 minutes.

PIPERONATA (Stewed Tomatoes and Pimentoes)

4 red pimentoes
6 tomatoes
1 onion
2 ozs. butter
salt
pepper

Melt the fat, slice the onions and cook until golden. Slice the pimentoes and remove the seeds. Add them to the onion and cook slowly for 15 minutes. Peel and quarter the tomatoes. Put them in the pan. Season with salt and pepper and cook for another 30 minutes.

POTATO CROQUETTES

2 lbs. potatoes
2 ozs. Parmesan cheese
2 eggs
salt
pepper
nutmeg
¼ lb. breadcrumbs
oil for frying

Cook the potatoes in boiling salted water. Sieve them and beat in the grated cheese and an egg, season with pepper and nutmeg. When the mixture is cool, shape into balls, roll in egg and breadcrumbs and fry quickly in olive oil.

SPAGHETTI

It is absolutely essential to have the genuine Italian spaghetti made in long unbroken pieces: the English imitations always become soft and mushy.

Put the spaghetti into a large pan of salted boiling water. If the pasta is too long to go in to start with, watch it until the parts under water begin to soften, and then gently push the rest under the water. The pasta is ready when it is soft but still very firm. Drain the water off by pouring the pasta gently into a large sieve. If the sieve is then balanced on top of the pan in which the pasta was cooked and put onto a very low gas, it will stay hot for some time without becoming overcooked. It is very important not to overcook the pasta in the first place: if it has been overcooked the pieces will stick together in a congealed mass.

The amount of pasta needed per head will vary according to circumstances: a 1 lb. packet is enough for 4 if it is to be the main course. All pasta should be cooked in this way.

RICE (for Risotto)

Italian rice is better than Patna for risotto but it is rather more expensive and not always obtainable. Patna rice is a good substitute. Melt a sliced onion gently in olive oil until it becomes soft and golden. Pour in the rice. Stir the rice about in the fat until each grain is covered, gradually add hot chicken stock, about a quarter of a pint at a time; continue adding stock until the rice is cooked.

A pound of rice will absorb about 2 pints of stock and take 20 to 30 minutes to cook. It should be stirred fairly continuously, particularly towards the end when the rice will become soft and likely to stick to the pan.

One Knorr chicken bouillon cube makes enough stock for 1 lb. of rice if it is diluted slightly more than is allowed for in the instructions.

BAKED GREEN NOODLES

¾ *lb. green noodles*
Bolognaise sauce (see p. 264)
Béchamel sauce (see p. 163)
¼ *lb. grated cheese*

Cook the noodles as described on p. 258 until they are nearly soft. Make half the amount of Bolognaise sauce described on p. 264 and the same amount of Béchamel sauce (p. 163).

Cover the bottom of a casserole with Bolognaise sauce, cover this with a layer of Béchamel sauce, and then a layer of green noodles. Repeat these layers until the dish is full. Spread the grated cheese on the top and bake in a moderate oven for 30 minutes.

CHEESE AND ANCHOVIES WITH BAKED BREAD

8 slices French bread
2 ozs. butter
8 anchovy fillets
¼ *lb. Bel Paese or Gruyère cheese*

Cut the bread into slices half an inch thick. Lay them in a shallow dish with a slice of cheese between each. Cook in a moderate oven for about 10 minutes until the bread is crisp and the cheese melted. At the same time melt the butter in a frying pan and heat the anchovy fillets in it. Pour them over the baked bread when it is ready.

BABY MARROWS IN BATTER

1 baby marrow per person
frying batter (see p. 257, recipe
   for mushrooms)
salt
olive oil for frying

Cut the marrows into thin slices. Sprinkle with salt and leave in a colander for an hour to drain. Coat with batter and fry quickly in olive oil.

CHICKEN RISOTTO

½ a boiling chicken (the whole
   chicken should weigh about 4
   lbs.)
1 onion
3 tomatoes
1 stick of celery
1 green pepper
¼ lb. mushrooms
1 glass white wine
¼ lb. butter
¼ lb. Parmesan cheese
salt
pepper
garlic
thyme
1 thick slice ham

½ lb. rice
basil

Skin the chicken and take the meat off the bones and slice it before cooking. Fry the sliced onion in 2 ozs. melted butter until it is golden. Add the chopped vegetables and the chicken and fry together for 2 to 3 minutes. Pour in the wine and cook for 2 minutes. Add thyme and basil or marjoram, season with salt and pepper. Cover with water, put a lid on the pan and cook slowly for 2 hours.

Cook the rice as for plain risotto (p. 259). Just before serving put in the chicken and sauce and stir in the grated cheese and 1 oz. butter.

Serve with watercress.

EGGS WITH GRATED CHEESE

4 eggs
1 oz. butter
1 tbsp. cream
1 oz. grated Parmesan cheese
salt
pepper

Melt the butter in a saucepan. Beat the eggs. Pour them into the butter, stirring as they cook. Add the cream. Season with salt and pepper. Stir in the grated cheese just before the eggs set.

CHEESE FONDUE

4 eggs
12 ozs. Gruyère cheese
½ oz. butter
¼ pint milk
salt
pepper

Cut the cheese into small cubes and soak them in the milk for 4 hours. Put the butter, beaten eggs and cheese in a double saucepan. Season with salt and pepper. Cook very slowly until creamy.

Serve with dry toast.

FORCEMEAT BALLS

½ *lb. minced veal*
1 *lb. minced gammon*
3 *onions chopped*
2 *sticks celery chopped*
2 *carrots chopped*
butter
parsley
thyme
basil
cinnamon
¼ *lb. flour*

eggs
salt
pepper

Mix the veal and gammon with the finely chopped herbs, cinnamon, salt and pepper. Bind the mixture with egg. Shape into balls. Roll in flour. Melt the butter, brown the vegetables in it. Add ½ pint of water, season with salt and pepper. Bring to the boil. Cook the meat balls in this sauce for 45 minutes. Arrange on a dish with the sauce poured round them.

HARICOT BEANS WITH BACON ROLLS

½ *lb. haricot beans (red or white)*
½ *lb. streaky bacon*
parsley
garlic
nutmeg
cinnamon
pepper

Soak the beans overnight. Chop the parsley, mix it with the crushed clove of garlic, a little grated nutmeg, cinnamon and pepper. Spread a little of it onto each rasher of bacon. Roll the rashers up and line the bottom of an earthenware casserole with them. Put the beans on top. Cover with water. Cook very slowly for 8 hours, adding more water if the beans get too dry.

STUFFED MARROWS

1 *medium sized marrow*
¼ *lb. rice*
¼ *lb. chopped bacon*
2 *ozs. mushrooms*
parsley
salt
pepper
1 *oz. butter*

Cook the rice in a lot of boiling salted water until it is cooked but still very firm. Drain it. Melt the butter, cook the sliced mushrooms slowly, add the bacon. Mix with the rice. Cut the top off the marrow, scoop out the inside. Fill with rice mixture. Replace the top. Put into a fireproof dish. Cook with the lid on in a moderate oven for an hour.

MEAT RISOTTO

½ lb. frying veal or beef
1 onion
1 carrot
1 stick celery
1 glass white wine
Cook rice as for risotto (p. 259)
¼ lb. grated Parmesan cheese
½ lb. rice
¼ lb. butter
salt
pepper

Melt 2 ozs. butter in a pan. Put in the carrot and celery finely chopped. When they are brown add the meat cut up into small pieces. Stir the meat about so that it is sealed on all sides, put the wine into the pan and simmer for 2 minutes. Season with salt and pepper, cover with a little water and cook slowly for an hour.

Mix this with the rice. Stir in grated cheese.

PASTRY PIZZA

MAKE THE DOUGH
AS FOLLOWS:

6 ozs. flour
2 ozs. butter
1 egg
¼ oz. yeast
salt
pepper

The tomatoes, cheese and anchovies are prepared as for the bread pizza (see p. 263)

Dissolve the yeast in a little water. Mix all the ingredients into a dough. Cover the bowl and leave to rise for 2 hours. Spread the dough in a greased shallow dish with the tomatoes and anchovies on top. Cook in a hot oven for 25 minutes. Add the cheese and cook for another 5 minutes.

SAUSAGES WITH TOMATO SAUCE

1 lb. pork sausages
½ lb. tomatoes
1 dsp. sugar
sage
salt
pepper
1 tbsp. olive oil

Peel and quarter the tomatoes. Season with salt, pepper, sugar and a little sage, and simmer for 10 minutes. Fry the sausages slowly until they are brown. Put them in the tomato sauce, simmer for 5 minutes.

PIZZA

¼ *lb. flour*
½ *oz. yeast*
water
salt
4 tomatoes
6 anchovy fillets
3 ozs. Bel Paese cheese
basil
1 tbsp. olive oil

Fresh yeast can be obtained from many bakers, and keeps for a considerable time (at least a month) in a refrigerator. The dough for pizza, like all bread mixtures, should be kept at room temperature while it is being made. Put the flour in a bowl, add a pinch of salt. Mix the yeast with a little warm water. Put the yeast into the flour and mix well. Add enough warm water (about a gill) to make a stiff dough. Knead it thoroughly, until the dough becomes elastic. Put it in a warm place, covered with a cloth until it has doubled its size. Roll the dough out on a floured board. It should be ¼ inch thick.

Prepare the tomatoes, cheese and anchovies while the dough is rising. Peel the tomatoes, and chop them into small pieces, cut the cheese into thin slices, halve the anchovies.

Put the pizza dough onto a baking tin, cover it with tomatoes, then arrange the anchovies on top. Sprinkle with basil. Pour a little oil over it and a little onto the baking dish. Bake in a hot oven for 25 minutes. Add the cheese and bake for another 5 minutes.

RAVIOLI

THE PASTE:
6 ozs. flour
1 tsp. salt
2 eggs

Sift the flour and salt onto a board. Pour the beaten eggs into a hole in the middle of the flour. Knead the eggs and flour to a soft dough. Divide the dough into halves.

THE FILLING:
½ *lb. minced beef*
¼ *lb. minced pork*
1 onion, sliced
1 carrot, sliced
1 stick celery, sliced
½ *glass white wine*
pepper
¼ *pint stock*
1 dsp. tomato purée
1 oz. butter
2 ozs. breadcrumbs
1 egg
salt

Brown the carrot, onion and celery in the butter. Add the minced meat and cook for 10 minutes. Put in the wine, tomato purée and stock and cook in a slow oven for 2 hours. Mix with the breadcrumbs and egg. Roll the two pieces of dough very thin. Put teaspoonfuls of the meat mixture onto one of the pieces at 1½ inch intervals. Cover with the other piece of dough. Cut into squares.

Cook in boiling stock until the pieces rise to the top. Serve in the stock with grated cheese.

SPAGHETTI BOLOGNAISE

¾ lb. spaghetti
1 onion sliced
1 carrot sliced
1 stick celery chopped
1 dsp. concentrated
   tomato purée
4 ozs. minced beef
2 rashers streaky bacon
2 ozs. chicken liver, chopped
1 glass white wine
½ pint stock
1 clove garlic
3 ozs. butter
¼ lb. grated cheese

salt
pepper

Melt 1 oz. butter, cook the onion in it until soft, add the bacon cut into small pieces, the carrot and the celery. When these are brown put in the meat and stir so that all the pieces are coated with fat. Add the liver, stirring in the same way. Put in the tomato purée, the wine and the stock. Season with salt, pepper and crushed garlic. Simmer for 40 minutes.

Cook the spaghetti as above (p. 258). Stir the sauce into it with 2 ozs. butter and the grated cheese.

SPAGHETTI WITH OIL AND GARLIC

¾ lb. spaghetti
2 tbsp. olive oil
1 clove garlic
¼ lb. Parmesan cheese
parsley
salt
pepper

Cook the spaghetti as described on p. 258. Put it into a pan with warm olive oil and chopped garlic. Stir it well. Season with salt and pepper and chopped parsley. Serve grated cheese separately.

SPAGHETTI WITH TOMATO SAUCE

¾ lb. spaghetti
1 tbsp. olive oil
1 onion, sliced
1 clove garlic, chopped
1 lb. tomatoes, peeled and
   quartered
¼ lb. Parmesan cheese
salt
basil (fresh or dried)
pepper

Cook the spaghetti as described on p. 258. Mix with the sauce just before serving, stirring in 2 ozs. melted butter and the grated cheese.

THE SAUCE:

Cook the onion with the garlic in the olive oil. When it is soft and transparent, add the tomatoes, a little basil, salt and pepper. Simmer for 30 minutes, sieve. Add sugar if the tomatoes are not very ripe.

SPAGHETTI WITH TOMATOES AND ANCHOVIES

¾ *lb. spaghetti*
1 *tbsp. olive oil*
3 *ozs. butter*
1 *lb. tomatoes*
6 *anchovy fillets*
¼ *lb. Parmesan cheese*
parsley
1 *onion*
1 *clove garlic*
salt
pepper

Cook the spaghetti as described on p. 258. Mix with the sauce and sprinkle with grated cheese before serving.

THE SAUCE:

Prepare the sauce in the same way as for the tomato sauce (p. 264), adding pounded anchovies and chopped parsley.

SPINACH WITH GRATED CHEESE

2 *lbs. spinach*
¼ *lb. grated cheese*
¼ *lb. butter*
salt

Put the spinach in a big saucepan. Cook without water with the lid on until tender. Sieve. Stir in the grated cheese and the butter cut into small pieces. Season with salt and serve hot.

STUFFED ARTICHOKES

4 *artichokes*
2 *ozs. breadcrumbs*
4 *chopped anchovies*
1 *clove garlic*
2 *tbsp. olive oil*

Make a stuffing by mixing the chopped anchovies and crushed garlic with the breadcrumbs.

Cut the outside leaves of the artichokes off, remove as much of the choke as possible and cut off the top part of the remaining leaves.

Put the stuffing into the artichokes. Put them into a pan with the olive oil. Cover the pan and cook slowly for an hour.

STUFFED MUSHROOMS

1 *lb. large mushrooms*
2 *ozs. ham or bacon*
2 *ozs. grated Parmesan or*
   Gruyère cheese
garlic
parsley
2 *ozs. breadcrumbs*
olive oil
salt
pepper

Make a stuffing by mixing the breadcrumbs with the stalks of the mushrooms finely chopped, the grated cheese, chopped parsley and garlic. Season with salt and pepper.

Spread the mixture on the tops of the mushrooms, place them in a fireproof dish, put a little olive oil on top of each. Cover the dish and cook in a moderate oven for 30 minutes.

TAGLIATELLI WITH BACON AND MUSHROOM SAUCE

¾ lb. tagliatelli (or any other
  pasta)
½ lb. mushrooms
¼ lb. bacon
¼ lb. butter
¼ lb. grated cheese
salt
pepper

Cook the pasta as described on p. 258. Stir in the sauce just before serving.

THE SAUCE:

Melt 2 ozs. of butter in a saucepan. Add the sliced mushrooms and the bacon finely chopped. Cook slowly until the mushrooms are soft (about 15 minutes). Stir in the cheese.

PRAWN RISOTTO

2 doz. prawns or 1 lobster
3 ozs. butter
1 small onion
½ lb. rice
¼ lb. grated cheese

Cook the rice as for plain risotto (see p. 259). Melt 1 oz. butter and heat the cooked prawns in it. Add them to the rice. Stir in 2 ozs. melted butter and the grated cheese. Season with salt and pepper.

STUFFED CABBAGE

½ white cabbage
stuffing (as for marrow - see
  p. 261)
2 pints stock

Blanch the leaves of the white cabbage in boiling salted water for 5 minutes. Fill each leaf with stuffing made of a mixture of meat, rice and onions as for stuffed marrow (p. 261), roll the leaf and tie it with string. Poach them gently in stock for an hour.

STUFFED LETTUCE

4 small round lettuces
2 anchovy fillets
1 tsp. capers
1 tsp. olive oil
1 clove garlic
1 glass white wine

STUFFING:

2 ozs. breadcrumbs
12 black olives
6 anchovy fillets
1 oz. sultanas
1 tsp. capers
1 clove garlic
parsley

1 tbsp. olive oil
salt
pepper

Stone and chop the olives. Chop 6 anchovy fillets, parsley and garlic. Mix these with the other stuffing ingredients. Moisten with olive oil, season with salt and pepper. Put a little of the stuffing between the leaves of the lettuces, tie the tops up with string. Melt the olive oil in a large pan, chop 2 anchovy fillets and garlic and put them in the pan with the capers. Add a little water, put the lettuces in the pan and cook slowly for 1 hour. Pour in the wine and cook for another 10 minutes.

STUFFED PANCAKES (1)

filling as for ravioli (p. 263)
¼ lb. flour
¼ pint milk
¼ pint water
1 oz. butter
1 egg
2 ozs. grated cheese
1 oz. butter
¼ pint stock

Put the flour into a bowl. Beat the egg into it and gradually stir in the milk and water. Add the melted butter, season with salt. Beat thoroughly and leave to stand for 2 hours.

Make the pancakes in the usual way. Fill each pancake with the filling, roll them up and arrange them in a shallow fireproof dish. Dot with butter, sprinkle with grated cheese and pour in the stock. Heat the dish in a moderate oven for 20 minutes.

STUFFED PANCAKES (2)

pancake mixture as for stuffed
   pancakes (1)
½ lb. spinach, sieved
1 egg
2 ozs. grated Parmesan cheese
2 ozs. cooked chicken liver
2 ozs. Bel Paese cheese
1 pint Béchamel sauce (see p. 163)

Make the filling by mixing the spinach, egg, chicken liver and grated cheese. Spread the mixture on the pancakes and roll them up. Pour the Béchamel sauce into a shallow dish, put the stuffed pancakes into it. Cover with slices of Bel Paese cheese, dot with butter. Bake in a moderate oven for 20 minutes.

VEGETABLE SOUFFLÉ

3 lbs. peas
3 eggs
1 small onion
2 ozs. ham
1 oz. grated cheese
2 ozs. butter
1 tbsp. flour
2 tbsp. stock

This can be made with any green vegetable and should be served alone or with fried meats. The following recipe for green peas can be adapted for other vegetables.

Fry the onion in butter, add the peas. Pour boiling water over them, season with salt and cook until the peas are tender. Pass through a sieve. Melt 1 oz. butter, add 1 tbsp. flour, stir until the flour is cooked. Add ¼ pint warm milk slowly, stirring all the time. Put the ham, cut into strips and the grated cheese into the sauce. Mix in the sieved peas. Add the egg yolks and the stiffly beaten egg whites.

Pour the mixture into a buttered cake tin, cover the top with greaseproof paper and steam it for an hour.

STUFFED PIMENTOES

1 pimento per person
stuffing as for stuffed marrow
(see p. 261)
2 ozs. olive oil or butter

If possible get yellow, red and green pimentoes. Cut off the tops, remove the seeds and core. Pour boiling water over them to soften the skins a little.

Fill with the stuffing, put a little butter or olive oil in a fireproof dish, arrange the pimentoes in it, cover the dish and cook in a moderate oven for 45 minutes.

FRIED CALVES' LIVER

1 lb. calves' liver
1 or 2 eggs
8 ozs. bread crumbs
4 ozs. butter
1 tsp. lemon juice
parsley

salt
pepper

Season the liver with salt, pepper and lemon juice. Leave for 1 hour. Roll in egg and breadcrumbs. Fry quickly in butter. Sprinkle with chopped parsley and serve with quarters of lemon.

CALVES' LIVER WITH ONIONS

1 lb. calves' liver cut in very
thin slices
2 lbs. Spanish onions, sliced
2 tbsp. olive oil
salt

Cook the onions in the olive oil until soft. Add the liver and fry quickly on both sides until cooked (about 3 minutes a side).

STEWED KIDNEYS

1 lb. veal or lambs' kidneys
1 glass white wine
parsley
2 ozs. butter
½ tsp. grated lemon peel
1 tsp. lemon juice

salt
pepper

Blanch the kidneys in boiling water and lemon juice. Skin and slice them. Season with salt and pepper. Cook slowly in the butter with the lemon peel for 30 minutes. Add the wine. Simmer for 2 minutes.

CHICKEN LIVER CROUTONS

1 lb. chicken livers
2 ozs. bacon or cooked ham diced
4 slices bread made into croutons
¼ lb. butter
1 dsp. lemon juice
¼ lb. flour
¼ pint stock
salt
pepper

Brown the ham in the butter. Add the chicken livers, diced and floured. Stir them in the butter until sealed. Put in the stock and lemon juice. Season with salt and pepper and cook slowly for 10 minutes. Pour the mixture over the croutons (see p. 164).

CHICKEN AND RICE

1 cold chicken
12 ozs. rice
¼ lb. mushrooms
2 sticks celery
salt
pepper
2 tbsp. olive oil
½ dsp. lemon juice

Boil the rice in a lot of salted water for 15 minutes. Drain and while still warm pour the oil over it. Season with nutmeg, pepper and salt. When cold mix in the cold chicken, cut into pieces, and the chopped celery.

CHICKEN STUFFED WITH HAM

1 boiling chicken 3—4 lbs.
6 ozs. cooked ham, minced
1 clove garlic
fennel, chopped
pepper

Mix the ham with fennel, pepper and crushed garlic. Stuff the chicken with the mixture. Cook in ½ pint water in a moderate oven for 3½ hours.

PIGEON WITH WHITE WINE

2 pigeons
2 ozs. tongue
1 onion
1 glass white wine
¼ pint stock
2 ozs. butter
2 lbs. peas
pepper
basil

Slice the onion and cook it in the butter. Add the ham and tongue cut into small pieces to the onion. Put in the pigeons and brown them. Add the wine. Simmer for 2 minutes, add the stock. Season with salt, pepper and nutmeg. Put a cover on the pan and cook slowly for 1½ hours. Add the shelled peas and cook for 20 minutes more.

FRIED BREAST OF CHICKEN

4 slices of chicken breast
2 tbsp. flour
4 ozs. butter
salt
pepper

Flour the chicken. Season with salt and pepper. Melt the butter in a frying pan, fry the chicken quickly for 3 minutes on each side. Cover the pan with a lid and cook more slowly for about 30 minutes.

RABBIT WITH MARSALA

1 rabbit
1 carrot
1 stick celery
1 onion
½ lb. tomatoes
1 aubergine
1 pimento
salt
pepper
marjoram
2 tbsp. olive oil
1 glass Marsala

Brown the sliced onion, carrot and celery in the olive oil. Cut the rabbit into pieces, flour them and brown them in the pan with the vegetables. Pour in the wine, simmer for 2 minutes. Add the tomatoes, peeled and quartered and ½ pint of water. Season with salt, pepper and marjoram. Cover the pan and cook slowly for 45 minutes. Cut the aubergine into cubes and the pimento into slices. Add them to the pan and cook for another 30 minutes.

ROAST TURKEY (STUFFED)

1 turkey
1 lb. liver
1 lb. chestnuts
½ lb. prunes
4 pears
1 glass white wine
1 oz. butter
salt
pepper
nutmeg

Make a stuffing for the turkey as follows:
Soak, cook and stone the prunes. Shell the chestnuts and cook them in water. Peel the pears and cut them into small pieces. Chop the prunes and chestnuts. Cook the chopped liver, prunes, chestnuts and pears for 10 minutes in the butter. Add the white wine, season with salt, pepper and grated nutmeg. Stuff the turkey with the mixture and roast it in the usual way.

BEEF AND PORK STEW

1 lb. beef, cut into pieces
¼ lb. lean pork, cut into pieces
1 carrot
1 onion
1 stick celery
2 ozs. butter
½ glass white wine
1 tbsp. tomato purée
½ pint stock

salt
pepper

Brown the sliced vegetables in the butter. Add the meats and brown them. Put in the tomato purée and the wine, boil for 1 minute, add the stock. Season with salt and pepper, cook slowly in a covered pan for 2 hours.

BEEF STEW WITH RED WINE

round of beef, weighing 2—3 lbs.
1 clove garlic
1 glass red wine
parsley
thyme
bay leaf
salt
pepper
1 onion
¼ lb. bacon
1 tbsp. olive oil

Marinate the meat for 2 to 3 hours in the red wine with the herbs, garlic and seasoning. Heat the olive oil in a pan just big enough to hold the meat, brown the onion, add the meat and brown it on both sides. Put in the bacon, cut into medium sized pieces, and brown it. Strain the marinade into the pan, boil for a minute or two, add a cupful of water and simmer, covered with a lid, for 3 hours.

BEEF STEW WITH WHITE WINE

round of beef weighing 2—3 lbs.
2 large onions
2 tomatoes, peeled and quartered
1 stick celery, chopped
1 carrot, sliced
2 ozs. butter
1 glass white wine
salt
pepper
basil

Melt the butter in a pan just big enough to hold the beef, fry the onions until golden, put in the beef, brown it on both sides, add the vegetables. Season with salt and pepper, add a little basil and the white wine. If necessary add a little extra stock or water and cook slowly for 3 hours.

FRITTO MISTO (Mixed Grill)

4 very small lamb chops (boned)
8 forcemeat balls (see p. 261)
8 slices chicken liver
8 slices young marrow
breadcrumbs
egg
basil
salt
oil for frying

All the ingredients should be in very small pieces. Small pieces of brain or sweetbreads can be added. Dip the pieces in fine breadcrumbs, coat with egg, season with salt, pepper and chopped basil. Fry quickly in a deep pan of smoking olive oil.

OSSO BUCO

4 pieces of veal cut from the leg
  across the bone about an inch
  thick
2 tbsp. olive oil
2 tbsp. butter
garlic
parsley
lemon rind
½ pint stock (a chicken bouillon
  cube will do)
½ glass dry white wine
2 ozs. flour
4 tomatoes

FOR THE MIREPOIX:

2 leeks, sliced
2 Spanish onions, sliced
1 head celery, chopped

¼ lb. lean bacon, diced
1 tbsp. olive oil
thyme
½ bay leaf

THE MIREPOIX:

Fry the onions in the olive oil until there is enough moisture to cook the rest of the vegetables. Add the leeks and celery, the thyme and the bay leaf. Season with salt and pepper. Stew slowly for 40 minutes. Melt the butter in a frying pan, flour the slices of veal and brown on both sides. Put the vegetables into a casserole, add the tomatoes peeled and quartered, the wine, the stock and lastly the meat, and cook slowly for 1½ hours. Before serving, add chopped or finely grated lemon peel.

   Serve with rice.

ROAST LAMB

1 leg of lamb
garlic
4 ozs. butter or 4 tbsp. olive oil
pepper
rosemary
salt

Put 1 or 2 cloves of garlic into the meat near the bone at the fillet end. Lay a sprig of rosemary on top of the meat. Sprinkle with salt and pepper. Baste with the butter or olive oil and cook in a hot oven for 30 minutes per lb.

LAMB WITH WHITE WINE

2 lbs. of leg of lamb
2 carrots
2 tomatoes
1 onion
1 stick celery
½ orange
1 wine glass of white wine
garlic
marjoram
salt
pepper
2 tbsp. olive oil

Heat the olive oil in a stewpan. Fry the sliced onion until golden. Rub the meat with garlic, salt, pepper and marjoram, brown it with the onions. Put in the peeled and quartered tomatoes and the chopped carrots and celery. Cook for 10 minutes. Add the white wine and cook for 1 minute. Cover the pan and simmer for 2 hours. Squeeze the juice of half an orange over the meat before serving.

MINCED MEAT BALLS

1 lb. minced meat (veal or beef)
2 eggs
1 thick slice of bread
lemon peel
1 clove garlic
milk
2 ozs. butter for frying
salt
pepper

Mince the garlic, parsley, lemon peel and the meat. Soak the bread in a little milk. Mix it with the meat. Stir in the beaten eggs. Season with salt and pepper. Shape into flat cakes on a floured board. Fry the cakes quickly in smoking butter for about 7 minutes on each side.

ROAST LOIN OF PORK

loin of pork weighing 3—4 lbs.
garlic
rosemary
salt
pepper

Rub the meat with a cut clove of garlic. Stick more garlic into it under the skin. Strew with rosemary, season with salt and pepper. Fill a roasting pan with water 2 inches deep. Put the pork in the water. Cook in a moderate oven for 45 minutes per lb.

GRILLED PORK CHOPS

4 pork chops
garlic
1 piece of fennel
12 juniper berries (optional)
3 tbsp. olive oil
salt
pepper

Stick a clove of garlic into each chop. Chop the fennel and mix it with a crushed clove of garlic and the juniper berries. Put some of the fennel mixture over each chop. Pour olive oil over the chops and leave to marinate for 2 hours.

Grill the chops for 25 minutes, turning them over once or twice. Season with salt and pepper.

PORK WITH RED WINE

loin of pork weighing about 3 lbs.
2 tbsp. olive oil
salt
pepper
2 cloves garlic, chopped
chopped parsley
1 glass red wine

Season the pork with salt and pepper. Brown in the olive oil. Add the garlic, parsley and wine. Cook in a moderate oven for $1\frac{1}{2}$ hours. Pour the sauce over the meat.

STEAK WITH TOMATO SAUCE

4 *thick slices of rump steak*
1½ *lbs. tomatoes, peeled and*
  quartered
1 *clove garlic*
2 *tbsp. olive oil*
parsley
salt
pepper

THE SAUCE:
Melt 1 tbsp. olive oil, cook the tomatoes in it with the garlic crushed with salt and the parsley.

Melt 1 tbsp. olive oil in a frying pan, season the steaks with salt and pepper, brown on both sides. Add the sauce, simmer for 10 minutes.

STUFFED BEEF

1 *lb. rump steak cut in a thick*
  slice
2 *ozs. good liver sausage or*
  chicken livers
2 *ozs. ham*
2 *ozs. tongue*
1 *oz. grated Parmesan cheese*
1 *egg*
1 *thick slice of white bread*
1 *onion*
1 *stick celery*
1 *small carrot*
parsley
salt
pepper

Soak the bread in water and squeeze the water out. Mix it with the chopped onion, carrot, celery, parsley, liver, ham and tongue, the grated cheese and the beaten egg. Season with salt and pepper and add basil or marjoram to taste.

Spread the stuffing on the meat, roll it up and tie it with string. Cover with dripping and roast in a hot oven for 45 minutes, basting once or twice. This can be made with less good meat and pot roasted in the usual way. Serve cold. If pot roasted it should be allowed to get cold in the pan in which it was cooked.

VEAL OLIVES (1)

8 *thin slices of veal*
8 *slices of ham*
1 *wine glass Marsala*
sage
2 *ozs. butter*
salt
pepper

Beat the slices of veal until they are very thin. Lay a slice of ham on each and a very little sage. Roll them and tie with string. Melt 2 ozs. butter in a pan, brown the rolls in this. Add the Marsala, cook gently for a minute. Season with salt and pepper. Cover the pan and simmer for 30 minutes.

VEAL OLIVES (2)

8 thin slices fillet veal
8 anchovy fillets
12 capers
¼ lb. flour
butter or olive oil for frying

Pound the anchovies and capers together. Spread the mixture on each fillet. Roll and tie with string. Flour the rolls. Fry quickly in olive oil.

VEAL CUTLETS (1)

4 cutlets on the bone
1 egg
4 ozs. breadcrumbs
salt
pepper
butter for frying
lemon
parsley

Trim the fat or gristle from the cutlets. Beat them, coat with egg and breadcrumbs. Fry rather fast in butter. Serve in a heated dish garnished with parsley and slices of lemon.

VEAL CUTLETS (2)

4 veal cutlets on the bone
1 egg
4 ozs. breadcrumbs
4 slices ham
¼ lb. grated Parmesan cheese
butter

Prepare and cook the cutlets as for plain veal cutlets. When they are cooked put a slice of ham, 1 oz. grated Parmesan cheese and 1 tbsp. melted butter on each cutlet. Cover the pan and cook until the cheese has melted (about 5 minutes).

VEAL STEW

1½ lbs. stewing veal (preferably
* from the shin)*
1 onion
2 tomatoes
2 pimentoes
1 glass white wine
2 ozs. butter
salt

Fry the sliced onion in butter until it is soft and golden. Cut the meat into fairly small pieces, put them in the pan and brown them. Pour in the wine and let it cook for a minute. Add the tomatoes, peeled and quartered and the pimentoes, sliced. Just cover the meat with water. Season with salt. Simmer, with a lid on the pan, for about 2 hours.

VEAL WITH TUNNY FISH AND ANCHOVIES

1½ lbs. fillet veal
4 whole anchovies
4 ozs. tunny fish
1 onion
2 carrots, sliced
1 stick celery, chopped
¼ pint olive oil
1 bay leaf
2 cloves
2 tbsp. lemon juice
2 tbsp. capers
salt
pepper

Remove all the fat from the meat. Cut 2 anchovies into strips and lay them on the meat. Roll it and tie with string. Put in a saucepan, add the onion stuck with cloves, carrots, celery, bay leaf and salt. Cover with water and simmer for 1½ hours. When cold, drain the meat and slice thinly. Fill a casserole with the slices. Cover with the following sauce: Pound 2 anchovies with the tunny fish, add the olive oil gradually and then the lemon juice. Strew capers over the top. Leave in a cold place for 24 hours.

To serve: Arrange the slices on a flat dish with the sauce poured over them.

SWEET PASTRY

½ lb. flour
¼ lb. sugar
¼ lb. butter
1 egg
1 tsp. baking powder
milk

Put the flour in a bowl. Rub in the fat. Add the other ingredients and work gently until a smooth dough is formed. Leave for at least an hour in a cool place.

APRICOT TART

2 lbs. apricots
2 ozs. sugar
vanilla
sweet pastry

Cook the apricots in a little water with the sugar and a drop of vanilla. Cut them in halves and stone them. Arrange them on the pastry. Cook in a hot oven for 20 minutes and more slowly for another 10 minutes.

CHESTNUT PYRAMID

1 lb. chestnuts
¼ lb. sugar
¼ pint double cream

Score the chestnuts and put them in a hot oven for 10 minutes. Peel them and cook in boiling water until soft. Drain off the water. Mix with the sugar. Put through a sieve directly onto the serving dish. Cover the top with whipped cream.

CHOCOLATE MOULD

3 ozs. cocoa
3 ozs. butter
3 ozs. sugar
3 ozs. ground almonds
3 ozs. petit beurre biscuits
1 egg
1 egg yolk

Beat the butter and cocoa, add the ground almonds. Dissolve the sugar in a little hot water. Add it to the butter mixture. Beat the egg and egg yolk and add them. Cut the biscuits into small pieces and stir into the mixture, being careful not to crumble them. Grease a mould, put the mixture into it and leave in a cold place to set.

CREAM CHEESE WITH ALMONDS AND DRIED FRUIT

¼ lb. unsalted cream cheese
1 oz. ground almonds
½ oz. candied orange peel thinly
  sliced
2 ozs. sugar
1 egg yolk

1 oz. mixed raisins and sultanas
1 tsp. grated lemon peel

Put the cream cheese into a bowl. Beat the egg yolk, stir it into the cheese together with the other ingredients. Hand granulated sugar separately.

SOUR CREAM WITH LIQUEUR

1 pint cream
1 small glass liqueur (rum, brandy
  or kirsch)
2 ozs. sugar

Pour the cream into a basin, leave it to thicken and turn slightly sour, or turn it sour with lemon juice. Strain it through muslin and beat in the sugar and liqueur. Serve slightly chilled. Unsalted cream cheese can be used instead of cream.

STUFFED PEACHES

4 large peaches
2 ozs. macaroons
1 small egg yolk
1 tbsp. sugar
½ oz. butter

Halve the peaches, remove the stones and a little of the fruit. Crush the macaroons, mix them with the extra fruit and other ingredients. Fill the holes left in the peaches with this mixture. Cook in a buttered fireproof dish for 30 minutes in a moderate oven.

APRICOT ICE CREAM

½ *pint single cream*
4 *egg yolks*
¼ *lb. caster sugar*
1 *lb. apricots*

Make the cream as for strawberry ice cream (see below).

Cook the apricots with the sugar and a little water. Sieve. Add to the cream and freeze.

CASSATA

½ *pint single cream*
¼ *lb. sugar*
2 *ozs. mixed glacé cherries, angelica, candied peel and walnuts finely chopped*
4 *egg yolks*
1 *strip lemon peel*

Make the cream as for strawberry ice cream (see below). Add the chopped lemon peel during the cooking and the other ingredients when it is cool. Freeze.

STRAWBERRY ICE CREAM

½ *pint single cream*
4 *egg yolks*
¼ *lb. caster sugar*
1 *lb. strawberries*

Put the beaten egg yolks into a double saucepan with the cream. Cook very slowly, stirring all the time until it thickens. Add the sugar and the crushed strawberries. Freeze in the ice tray of a refrigerator turned to its lowest temperature, stirring every half hour.

COFFEE SORBET

5 *tbsp. coffee*
3 *tbsp. sugar*
1 *pint water*

Put the coffee and sugar into an earthenware jug and pour boiling water over them. Strain through a fine sieve or muslin when cold. Pour into the ice tray of a refrigerator and leave to freeze.

LEMON SORBET

¼ *pint lemon juice*
2 *ozs. sugar*
½ *pint water*

Make a syrup by boiling the sugar with the water for 5 minutes. Mix with the lemon juice and freeze in the ice tray of a refrigerator.

Jamaica

RICE AND RED PEAS

½ lb. red peas
½ pint of coconut milk (see p. 246)
2 ozs. salt pork or bacon
1 lb. rice

The peas are the oval red seeds of large runner or French beans. Boil the peas until tender, drain and set aside. Grate the coconut flesh, add a little water and hang in a muslin bag to drain. Add the liquid to the peas. Fry the salt pork, add the rice, peas, coconut milk and about a pint of water. Cook slowly until all the water is absorbed. Serve with fried bananas.

FRIED BANANAS

Choose large, rather unripe bananas for this. Peel the bananas, cut them in slices lengthwise and fry quickly in hot fat.

STAMP-AND-GO FRITTERS

1 lb. dried salt cod
1 onion
1 tomato
1 small chilli
2 ozs. flour
fat for frying

Soak the fish for 12 hours. Boil gently in unsalted water until tender. Drain, flake the flesh when cool. Mince the onion, tomato and chilli. Pound with the fish until smooth. Shape into cakes, fry on both sides in hot fat. Serve with yams, sweet potatoes or ockra. The Jamaicans always serve a variety of vegetables with each main dish.

Jewish Cookery

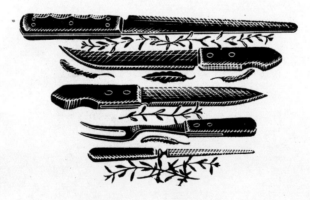

CHOPPED LIVER

1 lb. chicken's or calves' liver
1 onion
2 hardboiled eggs
2 ozs. breadcrumbs
1 oz. chicken fat
salt
pepper

Fry the liver lightly in the chicken fat. Mince finely with the onion and hardboiled eggs. Season with salt and pepper. Mix in the breadcrumbs and beat all together until smooth. Serve cold with thin toast.

CHOPPED LIVER WITH MUSHROOMS

8 ozs. cooked chicken liver
4 ozs. mushrooms
4 ozs. chicken fat
1 small onion finely chopped
salt
pepper

Fry the sliced mushrooms in 2 ozs. chicken fat until tender. Mix with the onion and liver, season with salt and pepper and rub through a sieve. Pour the rest of the chicken fat over it.

BREAM WITH SWEET SOUR SAUCE

2 lbs. bream
2 sticks celery
1 carrot
1 onion

FOR THE SAUCE:
½ onion chopped
1 oz. sultanas
1 oz. sugar
juice of 1 lemon
½ ozs. flour

Cut the fish into slices 1½—2 inches thick. Cook slowly with just enough water to cover, with the chopped celery, carrot, onion, salt and pepper. Serve hot or cold with the following sauce:

Cook the sugar with a little water until it starts to brown, gradually add the strained fish stock, the chopped onion and the lemon juice. Stir in the flour carefully, simmer for 10 minutes.

COLD FRIED FISH

2 lbs. plaice or bream
egg
breadcrumbs
olive oil

Cut the bream into slices 1½ inches wide or fillet the plaice. Coat with egg and fine breadcrumbs. Fry quickly in a little very hot olive oil, on both sides. Drain carefully onto absorbent paper. Serve with slices of lemon.

FRIED FISH A LA JUIVE

2 lbs. fish fillets
2 eggs
flour
salt

pepper
oil for frying

Coat the fish with beaten egg and dredge with seasoned flour. Cook quickly in a little olive oil.

GEFILLTE FISH

3 lbs. mixed bream, cod, fresh
haddock
3 eggs
3 onions
2 carrots
1 stick celery
1 tbsp. chopped parsley
1 oz. ground almonds
breadcrumbs
salt
pepper

Simmer the heads, skins and bones of the fish in ½ pint water with 1 carrot sliced, the chopped celery, salt and pepper for 45 minutes. Strain.

Mince and chop the fish, mix well with the parsley, ground almonds, beaten eggs and enough breadcrumbs to bind the mixture. Roll into balls. Simmer these gently in the fish stock with the other sliced carrot for 1 hour. Remove the balls from the stock, arrange a slice of carrot on top of each. Reduce the stock if necessary, and pour a little over each ball. It should set when cold. Serve cold.

BRUSSELS SPROUTS WITH CHESTNUTS

1 lb. Brussels sprouts
½ lb. chestnuts
salt
1 oz. butter

Peel the chestnuts (see p. 384) and simmer them in salted water until tender. Boil the Brussels sprouts rapidly in salted water for 10—15 minutes. Drain, mix with the drained chestnuts, lightly fry in the butter. This is particularly good with roast turkey.

POTATO PANCAKES

4 potatoes
3 ozs. flour
½ tsp. baking powder
2 eggs
salt
pepper
2 ozs. lard

Peel the potatoes and soak them in cold water for 1 hour. Grate them, add the beaten eggs, sifted flour and baking powder and salt and pepper. Cook tablespoonfuls of the mixture in hot fat, first on one side then on the other.

SCRAMBLED EGGS WITH MATZOS

4 eggs
1 oz. butter
2 matzos
salt
pepper

Break the matzos into small pieces. Put them in a strainer, pour boiling water over them. Drain. Break the eggs, beat lightly with the matzo pieces. Season with salt and pepper. Melt the butter, scramble the eggs slowly in the usual way.

ALMOND SOUFFLÉ

4 ozs. ground almonds
5 ozs. caster sugar
4 eggs
1 tsp. grated lemon peel

Beat the egg yolks and sugar until white and creamy. Mix with the almonds and lemon peel. Fold in the stiffly beaten egg whites. Cook in a very slow oven for 40 minutes. Serve with lemon sauce (see p. below).

CHAROSETH

1 lb. apples
4 ozs. sultanas
4 ozs. almonds
cinnamon

Peel and finely chop the apples. Mix them with the other ingredients and roll into small balls.

LEMON SAUCE

4 ozs. sugar
2 eggs
juice and grated rind of ½ lemon

Beat the eggs; cook slowly in a double saucepan with the sugar, lemon peel, lemon juice and a little water until the sauce thickens.

LEMON WHIP

4 eggs
juice of 2 lemons
5 ozs. caster sugar
1 oz. almonds, blanched and
  chopped

Beat the eggs with the sugar until white. Strain the lemon juice and dilute it with ¼ pint water, add this gradually to the egg mixture. Cook very slowly in a double saucepan until it thickens. Pour into custard glasses. Serve cold, sprinkled with chopped almonds.

HAMAN'S EARS

2 eggs
3 tbsp. olive oil
12 ozs. flour
1 oz. sugar
oil for frying

Beat the eggs, stir in the olive oil and the flour. Knead the dough thoroughly. Divide it into small pieces and roll out very thin. Cut each piece into a round about 10 inches in diameter and divide it into 4 sections. Leave for at least an hour. Fry quickly in a little very hot olive oil. Drain and sprinkle with sugar.

Mexico

AVOCADO SALAD

1 large avocado pear
2 small onions, chopped
2 tomatoes, peeled and chopped
paprika
salt
lettuce
French dressing (see p. 159)

Peel and mash the avocado. Mix the onion and tomato with it. Season with salt and paprika. Serve chilled with lettuce and French dressing.

BUTTER BEANS IN SAUCE

1 lb. butter beans
¼ lb. bacon (any cheap cut)
1 onion, sliced
1 lb. tomatoes, peeled and
*   quartered*
1 tbsp. black treacle
1 tbsp. chilli powder
1 tsp. salt

Put the beans into an earthenware casserole. Mix the bacon slices with them. Cover with onion and tomato. Sprinkle with chilli powder, and salt. Warm the treacle in ½ pint warm water and pour over the beans. Bake covered, in a slow oven for 2 hours.

SHRIMP POLENTA

1 pint shrimps
4 ozs. maize flour or semolina
2 onions, minced
2 tbsp. concentrated tomato purée
½ lb. ham, diced
¼ lb. mushrooms, sliced
3 rashers bacon
salt
pepper

Pour 1 pint boiling water onto the semolina and cook slowly until thick. Chop the bacon and fry lightly. Add the tomato purée, mushrooms, onion and ham. Simmer in ¼ pint water for 10 minutes. Fill a buttered fireproof dish with alternate layers of semolina, tomato mixture and shrimps. Cover the dish, cook in a moderate oven for 30 minutes.

TAMALE PIE

4 ozs. semolina
1 lb. minced beef
4 tomatoes, peeled and quartered
6 stoned green olives
2 minced onions
2 tsp. chilli powder
2 tbsp. olive oil
basil
salt
pepper

Cook the semolina in 1 pint boiling water until thick. Fry the onion and the beef in olive oil, add the tomatoes, olives, chilli powder, a pinch of basil, salt and pepper. Simmer for 10 minutes. Put half the semolina in the bottom of a fireproof dish, then the meat mixture and lastly another layer of semolina. Cover and bake in a moderate oven for 30 minutes.

ENCHILLADAS

8 tortillas. (pancakes make
  a good substitute)
2 onions, chopped
1 lb. minced beef
1 clove garlic
4 tomatoes, peeled and quartered
1 tbsp. chilli powder
oregano
salt
pepper

4 ozs. grated cheese
fat for frying
2 rashers streaky bacon

Fry the bacon until all the fat is melted. Remove bacon pieces and fry the onion in the fat until golden, add the meat, crushed garlic, tomatoes and seasonings. Simmer for 10 minutes. Spread this mixture onto the pancakes, roll them, arrange in a shallow fireproof dish. Sprinkle with cheese. Bake in a moderate oven for 20 minutes.

MEXICAN CHICKEN (1)

1 boiling chicken, jointed
4 pimentos or 1 tin pimentos
1 onion, sliced
1 clove garlic
2 tomatoes, peeled and quartered
4 ozs. butter
1 oz. flour
½ tsp. chilli powder
salt
pepper

Brown the chicken pieces in 2 ozs. butter. Add the pimentos, onion, crushed garlic, tomatoes, chilli powder, salt and pepper. Pour in enough water to cover the chicken. Simmer for 1½—2 hours. Melt the remaining 2 ozs. butter, stir in the flour, cook for 1 minute. Gradually add the strained chicken stock, stirring all the time. Arrange the chicken on a flat dish. Pour the sauce over, surround with the vegetables.

MEXICAN CHICKEN (2)

1 chicken, jointed (roasting is
  best, but the dish is good with
  a boiling fowl)
4 small onions
1 clove garlic
1 oz. flour
2 tbsp. concentrated tomato purée
4 cloves
1 tbsp. tarragon vinegar
1 glass white wine
1 green pepper sliced and seeded

12 stoned green olives
¼ lb. seeded raisins
2 ozs. butter

Fry the chicken lightly in the butter. Transfer to a large fireproof dish. Toss the onions in the butter, add them to the chicken. Stir the flour into the fat, cook for 1 minute, gradually add the tomato purée and ½ pint water. Pour this over the chicken. Add the cloves, crushed garlic, vinegar, wine and green peppers. Simmer, covered, for 1½ hours, adding the raisins and olives for the last 15 minutes.

BEEF STEW WITH SPLIT PEAS

2 lbs. topside
2 tbsp. olive oil
2 tbsp. concentrated tomato purée
½ lemon sliced
6 whole small onions
4 ozs. split peas
1 tsp. allspice
parsley

salt
pepper

Brown the meat on all sides in the olive oil. Put all the ingredients in a casserole with enough water to barely cover. Cover the pan. Cook in a moderate oven for 2 hours or until tender.

PORK CHOPS

4 pork chops
1 green pepper
½ tsp. chilli powder
1 onion sliced
1 lb. tomatoes peeled and chopped
2 ozs. rice
basil
pepper
salt

Put the chops in a fireproof dish. Cover each with onion and a tbsp. of rice. Remove seeds from the pepper, chop it and mix with the tomatoes and chilli powder. Spread this over the chops. Sprinkle with chopped herbs, salt and pepper. Cover the dish. Bake in a moderate oven for 1 hour.

VEAL WITH NOODLES

1 lb. veal cut into thin slices
2 onions, sliced
2 tsp. chilli powder
1 tsp. paprika
flour
2 ozs. grated cheese
salt
2 ozs. lard

Beat the veal and dredge with flour seasoned with salt and paprika. Fry lightly on both sides in the lard. Add the onions and chilli powder. Fry for 2 or 3 minutes. Pour ½ pint water into the pan and simmer for 20 minutes. Stir in the grated cheese.
Serve with noodles (see p. 258).

TORTILLAS

2 lbs. maize
2 ozs. slaked lime

Soak the maize in water and the slaked lime for 12 hours. Simmer in the same water until tender. Drain and wash the maize. Pound into a smooth paste. Roll out very thin. Bake on an ungreased griddle.

ORANGE FUDGE

½ *pint evaporated milk*
12 *ozs. sugar*
juice and grated rind of 2 large
  oranges
2 *ozs. chopped almonds*

Melt 4 ozs. sugar in a saucepan; when it has browned, add the orange juice. Stir well and add the evaporated milk (previously warmed). Stir the rest of the sugar into the pan and cook slowly until the mixture comes away from the sides. Add the grated orange peel. Beat until the mixture sets when tested in cold water. Stir in the nuts. Pour into greased tins. Mark into squares when cool.

CHILLI SAUCE

3 *large tomatoes, peeled and*
  quartered
2 *tbsp. chilli powder*
2 *tsp. dry mustard*
2 *tsp. horseradish sauce*
½ *tsp. sugar*
pinch of cayenne pepper
1 *tsp. curry powder*

4 *tbsp. vinegar*
1 *onion sliced*
1 *clove garlic chopped*

Simmer all the ingredients together, adding a little water if necessary. Pass through a sieve. Serve with anything needing a hot spicy sauce.

The Middle East

TUNISIAN ANCHOVIES

18 fillets of anchovies
½ tsp. ground nutmeg
1½ tsp. finely chopped fresh mint
bread or toast

Drain the anchovies of all oil. Mix the mint with the nutmeg and roll each fillet in the mixture. Serve on small fingers of bread or toast as a hors d'œuvre.

MUNKACZINA (Arabian Salad)

3 oranges, peeled and sliced thinly
2 medium onions sliced thinly
4 ozs. black olives, stoned
2 tbsp. oil
salt, pepper

Mix all the ingredients together, season with salt and pepper.

ARABIAN MUTTON AND TOMATO SOUP

2 ozs. cooked vermicelli
1½ lbs. neck and breast of mutton
½ lb. tomatoes, peeled and sliced
¾ lb. onions, sliced
1 oz. butter
1 tbsp. chopped mint
1 tsp. salt
¼ tsp. pepper
2½ pints hot water

Melt the fat in a large saucepan, add the onion and fry till light brown, add the meat, tomatoes, mint, salt and pepper. Pour in the hot water, bring to the boil and simmer for 3½ hours. Remove the meat and cut up finely. Place in the serving tureen, add the vermicelli, re-heat the soup and pour over.

For European tastes this is more of a stew and can be eaten as such.

SYRIAN LENTIL SOUP

1 lb. lentils
2½ pints water
2 medium onions, sliced
2 tbsp. olive oil or butter
1 tsp. salt
½ lb. spinach, chopped
1 tsp. lemon juice

Wash the lentils thoroughly. Melt the fat in a large saucepan, add the onions and fry for 3 minutes. Add the lentils and salt, stir well, pour on the water, bring to the boil, skim if necessary, and simmer gently for 1¼ hours. Add the spinach and cook 15 minutes longer. Add lemon juice and serve.

ARABIAN EGGS

6 hardboiled eggs
2 ozs. butter
½ tsp. salt
½ tsp. paprika
½ tsp. pepper } *mixed together*
½ tsp. cinnamon

Melt the butter. Shell the eggs and while still warm prick the whites all over, add the eggs to the butter and turn round and round to enable the butter to soak into the egg and cook until light brown, place on warm serving dish and sprinkle with salt and the spices.

ALGERIAN THETCHOUKA

3 eggs
2 large onions, chopped
2 cloves of garlic, chopped
2 tbsp. oil or butter
1 lb. tomatoes, peeled and chopped
2 red or green peppers (pimentos) seeded and thinly sliced
½ tsp. salt
pinch of pepper

Heat the fat in a shallow fireproof dish with a lid, fry the onions and garlic till transparent, add all the other ingredients, stir well, cover tightly and cook gently till soft and pulpy about 1 hour.

Before serving put the eggs either whole or beaten on the top of the dish, cover and gently cook for 10 minutes or till set. Chopped mint may be sprinkled over the eggs if wished.

ARABIAN BAKED STUFFED SAVOURY APPLES

4 large cooking apples
minced cooked chicken
salt to taste
4 cloves
1 tsp. sugar
2 ozs. breadcrumbs
1 oz. butter

Cut the top off each apple, scoop out the core completely without cutting through the fruit. Fill each apple with chicken and 1 clove and salt. Stand all in a fireproof dish. Sprinkle with the sugar, breadcrumbs and a dot of butter on each. Bake in a moderate oven for 1 hour or until the apples are quite soft.

ARABIAN ROAST CHICKEN WITH HONEY AND NUTS

1 chicken
2 tbsp. honey
1 oz. melted butter
1 tsp. rose water
½ oz. pistachio nuts, finely chopped
2 ozs. crystallized cherries, cut in quarters
1 oz. preserved ginger, chopped

Melt the butter and add to the honey. Prick the breast and legs of the bird and rub some of the honey and butter well in. Pour more of the honey mixture and the rose water inside the bird and roast in the usual way. When done, cut the bird in half, lay flat on the serving dish and sprinkle with the nuts, cherries and ginger.

ARABIAN STEWED MUTTON WITH PRUNES

1½ lbs. neck or breast of mutton
1 large onion, chopped
1 oz. butter or dripping
1 dsp. flour
¼ tsp. saffron
¼ tsp. cinnamon
4 ozs. prunes — soaked in cold
  water for 12 hours
1 dsp. orange flower water or
  1 tsp. sugar

salt and pepper to taste
hot water

Cut the meat into pieces about ½ × 2 inches. Fry the onion in the fat till light brown, in a casserole, add the flour, saffron, cinnamon, salt and pepper, mix well, add the meat and cook quickly for 2 minutes, stirring well. Cover with hot water, cover and simmer for 2 hours. Add the prunes and the sugar or orange flower water, re-cover and simmer for 1 hour more.

ARABIAN BOILED MUTTON AND GOOSEBERRY JELLY

Boil the mutton in the ordinary way and cover with a good layer of jelly before serving.

MOROCCAN BEAN COUSCOUS

8 ozs. dried beans, soaked overnight
½ tsp. salt
1 lb. semolina
1 dsp. oil or melted butter
2 pints cold water

Put the semolina in a basin, moisten with boiling water to make the grains swell and leave for 20 minutes. Stir with a fork. Repeat this once more when the grains should be sufficiently swollen, add the oil and stir well. Put the beans in the pan of a steamer, add salt, cold water. Place a clean cloth in the top of the steamer and put the semolina on this, cover tightly, bring to the boil and simmer for 3 hours. Stir the semolina with a fork 3 times during the cooking. Serve with meat or chicken dishes.

MUTTON OR CHICKEN AND VEGETABLE COUSCOUS

Make a stew of mutton or chicken, onions, peas, pimentoes, beans, turnips, etc., in the usual way. Prepare, cook the couscous as for Moroccan Bean Couscous.

PERSIAN STUFFED QUINCES

4 quinces
minced cooked mutton or chicken
salt, to taste
1 tbsp. honey
1 oz. butter

Core the quinces, cover with boiling water and simmer for 20 minutes. Drain and stuff with the seasoned meat. Place in a shallow fireproof dish, pour on the honey, dot with butter and bake in a moderate oven for 1 hour.

GOOSEBERRY JELLY

gooseberries
sugar
water

Wash the fruit and add ¼ pint water to each 1 lb. Stew slowly till quite soft. Put in a flannel bag and allow to drip for 12 hours. Do not squeeze the bag. For each 1 pint juice measure 1 lb. sugar. Warm the sugar. Bring the juice to the boil, add the sugar, stir well, bring again to the boil, and boil for 15 to 20 minutes, stirring constantly.

Test and put in warm clean jars. Seal.

New Zealand

HERRING CHOWDER

1 large onion, chopped
1 oz. butter
2 medium potatoes, thinly sliced
¼ pint milk
4 cream crackers, crushed
4 cooked herrings, filleted

salt
pepper

Cook the onion in the butter until transparent. Add the potatoes and ¼ pint of boiling water. Simmer until the potatoes are tender. Add the milk, biscuit crumbs and seasoning. Simmer for 5 minutes. Stir in the herrings. Serve very hot.

SAVOURY RABBIT

1 rabbit, jointed
4 ozs. breadcrumbs
1 onion, chopped
parsley
thyme
8 rashers streaky bacon
½ pint milk
salt
pepper

Blanch the rabbit in boiling water with one tablespoonful salt for 30 minutes. Cut the flesh from the bones. Mix the breadcrumbs with the onion and chopped herbs, season with salt and pepper. Line a pie dish with the breadcrumb mixture and then fill it with alternate layers of rabbit and breadcrumbs. Cover with the bacon rashers, pour in the milk. Put a lid on the dish and bake in a moderate oven for 2 hours, adding more milk if necessary.

FRUIT SALAD PAVLOVA

4 egg whites
8 ozs. caster sugar
vanilla
fruit salad with liqueur to taste
ice cream
¼ pint double cream
½ lb. raspberries

Beat the egg whites very stiffly, fold in the sugar, flavour with vanilla pod or essence. Line the base and sides of a tart tin with greased grease-proof paper. Put the meringue mixture in the tin, making a depression in the centre. Bake in a slow oven for about 2 hours. Turn out of the tin carefully when cold. Fill the depression with drained fruit salad just before serving, top with ice cream, whipped cream and raspberries.

BLACKBERRY PANCAKES

1 cup blackberries
1 cup flour
2 ozs. sugar
1 cup milk
1 egg
2 ozs. butter

Mix the egg yolk and sugar together, beat in the sifted flour and the blackberries. Add 1 oz. melted butter and fold in the stiffly beaten egg white. Melt a little fat in a frying pan, cook spoonfuls of the mixture on both sides.

PASSION FRUIT FLAN

PASTRY:
4 ozs. flour
3 ozs. sugar
1 egg yolk
½ tsp. sugar
½ tsp. baking powder

FILLING:
½ ozs. gelatine
4 ozs. sugar
1 cup cooked passion fruit

Rub the butter into the flour, mix to a stiff dough with all the other ingredients and a little milk if necessary. Roll out and cook in a greased pastry tin for 15 minutes in a moderate oven. Fill with the following mixture: dissolve the gelatine in a little water. Sieve the passion fruit, add the sugar to the pulp, stir it into the gelatine. When nearly set pour into the pastry shell, decorate with pieces of passion fruit and whipped cream.

BLACKBERRY FLUFF

1 lb. blackberries
4 ozs. sugar
rind and juice of ½ lemon
1 oz. gelatine
3 egg whites

Stew the blackberries with the sugar, a strip of lemon peel and a little water until tender. Pass through a sieve. Dissolve the gelatine in a little water. Pour the fruit purée into it, add the lemon juice and enough water to make 1 pint. Leave in a cold place. When nearly set fold in the stiffly beaten egg whites.

FRUIT CAKE

8 ozs. self raising flour
4 ozs. sugar
12 ozs. mixed raisins, sultanas
*   and currants*
2 beaten eggs
4 ozs. softened butter
¼ tsp. mixed spice
scant ¼ pint milk

pinch of nutmeg
pinch of salt

Mix the flour with the sugar and dried fruits. Stir in the eggs and the butter. Add the milk and the spices. Beat all together until thoroughly mixed. Turn into a cake tin lined with greased grease-proof paper. Bake in a slow oven for 2 hours.

PAVLOVA CAKES

2 egg whites
4 ozs. sugar
1 oz. cornflour
1 dsp. coffee essence
2 ozs. chopped nuts

Beat the egg whites stiffly. Fold in the sugar and then the other ingredients. Arrange in small mounds on a lightly greased baking sheet. Cook in a cool oven for 45 minutes.

ANZACS

4 ozs. flour
4 ozs. rolled oats
4 ozs. desiccated coconut
4 ozs. sugar
½ tsp. baking powder

1 tbsp. golden syrup
4 ozs. butter

Mix all the dry ingredients together, stir in the syrup and the melted butter. Roll into small balls and then flatten onto a greased baking tin. Bake in a cool oven for 15 minutes.

BUSTERS

8 ozs. flour
6 ozs. grated cheese
2 ozs. butter
cayenne pepper

Rub the butter into the flour, add the grated cheese and a pinch of cayenne pepper. Add a little water and roll out to ¼ inch thick on a floured board. Cut into rounds, prick with a fork, bake on a greased baking sheet for 15 minutes in a hot oven.

ORANGE NUT BREAD

2 eggs
8 ozs. sugar
¼ pint milk
12 ozs. flour
1 tsp. salt
4 tsp. baking powder
1 oz. butter

2 ozs. chopped nuts
peel of 1 orange, chopped

Beat the eggs with the sugar. Sift the flour, salt and baking powder and add them to the eggs and sugar alternately with the milk. Mix in the nuts and orange. Leave to stand for 15 minutes in a greased pan. Bake in a moderate oven for 45 minutes.

CHEESE APPLES

cream cheese
paprika
cloves

Shape the cheese into small balls, roll them in paprika until red all over. Stick a whole clove into one side of the ball and a clove stalk into the other.

WALNUT AND CHEESE TARTLETS

puff pastry made with 8 ozs. flour
4 ozs. grated cheese
1 egg yolk
salt
pepper
dry mustard
½ oz. butter

2 ozs. chopped walnuts
2 egg whites

Blend the grated cheese with the egg yolk. Season with salt, pepper and mustard. Beat in the butter and chopped walnuts. Fold in the stiffly beaten egg whites. Cut the pastry into rounds, put in small greased tart tins, fill with the cheese mixture. Bake in a medium hot oven for 20 minutes.

Poland

HERRINGS WITH SOUR CREAM

4 herrings
¼ pint milk
1 glass white wine
2 tbsp. wine vinegar
1 onion, sliced
1 clove garlic
¼ tsp. mustard
2 egg yolks
2 tbsp. sour cream
1 tsp. paprika
6 peppercorns

parsley
thyme
½ bay leaf
salt

Soak the herrings in milk for 1 hour. Strain. Cook them for 7 minutes in the vinegar and wine, with the onions, garlic, peppercorns, and salt; add water if necessary. Strain off the juice, cool and mix with the beaten egg yolks, paprika, sour cream and mustard. Cover the herrings with the sauce. Serve chilled.

BEETROOT SOUP

2 ozs. streaky bacon, chopped
1 leek, sliced
1 onion, sliced
2 raw beetroots cut into strips
1 large cupful shredded cabbage
1 tbsp. tomato purée

¾ pint stock
1 dsp. vinegar

Fry the bacon with the leek and onion until golden. Add the other ingredients and 2 pints water. Simmer for 1 hour.

BORSHCH

KVAS:
1 lb. uncooked beetroot, sliced
crust of rye bread
2 pints water

The basis of this soup is Kvas, which is then mixed with meat or vegetable stock.

Put the beetroot in a casserole. Boil the water, allow to cool. Pour over the beetroot, add the crust. Leave covered with a cloth for 3—4 days until the beetroot ferments slightly. The amount of fermentation can vary according to taste. Mix with stock. Serve hot or cold, with a spoonful of sour cream on each plate.

CHRISTMAS EVE BORSHCH

½ lb. beetroot, sliced
½ celeriac, sliced
1 small carrot, sliced
½ oz. dried mushrooms
parsley, chopped
½ oz. butter
½ pint Kvas (optional)

garlic
salt
stock

Simmer all the vegetables and the garlic in 2 pints of water, until the beetroot is cooked. Remove the mushrooms to make mushroom patties (see p. 313). Pour the hot soup over the patties.

UKRAINIAN BORSHCH

½ lb. pork
1 beetroot
½ celeriac
½ lb. tomatoes
½ small cabbage
1 onion
1 small carrot
1 oz. flour
½ oz. butter
¼ pint Kvas (optional)
¾ pint stock

¼ pint cream
salt

Cook and sieve the tomatoes. Cut the other vegetables into thin strips. Simmer half of them with the meat in water, until the meat is tender. Melt the butter, cook the rest of the vegetables in it. Add them to the tomatoes and other vegetables. Stir in the flour and stock. Add the Kvas. Bring to the boil. Serve in hot soup plates, with thick cream on top of each portion. The cream used in Russia is sour, but this is a question of taste.

DRIED MUSHROOM SOUP

2 ozs. dried mushrooms
2 pints stock
1 oz. flour
1 oz. butter
3 tbsp. sour cream

salt
pepper

Blanch the mushrooms. Simmer in the seasoned stock until tender. Melt the butter, add the flour, cook for 1 minute. Gradually add the stock and the mushrooms. Stir in the sour cream before serving.

ONION SOUP

½ lb. onions sliced
3 slices wholemeal bread
1 gill cream
2 ozs. butter
4 egg yolks
salt

Cut the bread into strips. Melt 1 oz. butter in the oven, put the bread into it, turning it so that all sides are covered with butter, and bake until crisp. Melt the rest of the butter, cook the onions in it until transparent. Put onions and baked bread in a saucepan, pour 2 pints water over them, simmer for 40 minutes. Sieve, beat the egg yolks with the cream, put them in a saucepan, pour the sieved onion mixture on them and reheat without boiling. Serve in hot plates.

SAUERKRAUT SOUP

½ lb. sauerkraut
¼ lb. pork
¼ lb. smoked sausage
½ oz. lard
½ oz. flour
caraway seeds
1 pint vegetable stock

Cut the pork into strips and the sausage into slices. Simmer in the vegetable stock until the meat is cooked. Cook the sauerkraut in ½ pint of water until tender. Strain the stock. Keep the meat separate. Add the sauerkraut stock. Thicken with a roux made of the lard and flour. Add the meat, flavour with caraway seeds.

BAKED POTATOES

4 medium potatoes
¼ lb. breadcrumbs
¼ lb. butter
salt

Roll the peeled potatoes in the breadcrumbs mixed with salt. Dot with butter and cook in a hot oven for 1 hour, turning them from time to time.

BEETROOT SALAD

1 lb. cooked beetroots
1 horseradish, grated
1 tsp. sugar
1 tsp. salt

½ tsp. caraway seeds
juice of 3 lemons

Peel and slice the beetroot. Mix the horseradish and other ingredients together. Pour them over the beetroot.

CABBAGE

1 savoy cabbage
1 dsp. sugar
salt
2 ozs. butter
¼ lb. breadcrumbs

Shred the cabbage. Cook quickly in boiling water with the sugar for 10 minutes. Strain and put the cabbage into a fireproof dish. Cover with the breadcrumbs, dot with butter. Cook in a moderate oven for 20 minutes. Cauliflower can be cooked in the same way.

POTATO PANCAKES

6 medium potatoes
½ pint milk
2 ozs. butter
3 eggs
nutmeg
salt

Boil the potatoes in salted water until cooked. Sieve. Mix with the egg yolks, beat in the milk. Flavour with nutmeg. Fold in the stiffly beaten egg whites. Cook as ordinary pancakes.

BEEF CAKES

1 lb. steak
1 slice bread
3 ozs. butter
2 onions, chopped
1 tbsp. breadcrumbs
1 egg
1 oz. flour
½ bay leaf
6 peppercorns
½ pint meat stock
salt

Fry ½ tbsp. chopped onion in 1 oz. butter until soft. Soak the bread, squeeze out the water. Mince the bread, one onion and meat. Mix with the egg, season with salt and pepper. Shape into 8 cakes. Roll in breadcrumbs. Melt the rest of the butter, fry the cakes. Put them on a plate to keep warm. Put the rest of the onions in the fat. Cook until tender. Stir in the flour, cook for 1 minute. Gradually add the stock. Season with salt, peppercorns and bay leaf. Pour the sauce over the meat cakes, simmer for 30 minutes.

BIGOS (Cabbage Stew)

1½ lbs. sauerkraut
1 onion, sliced
1 oz. flour
1 oz. butter
1 glass white wine
1 lb. left-over meat or poultry
* (not mutton)*
1 pint stock
paprika
salt

Simmer the sauerkraut in the stock for 1½ hours. Cook the onion in 1 oz. butter, add the flour, cook for 1 minute. Chop the sauerkraut and add the onion mixture to it. Cut the meat into small pieces. Put the meat and the sauerkraut mixture into a casserole, add the wine, season with salt and paprika, mix well. Cook in a slow oven with the lid on for 1 hour.

HUSSARS ROAST

2 lbs. sirloin
1 onion, chopped
juice of ½ lemon
½ oz. flour
3 ozs. butter
1 tbsp. brown breadcrumbs
1 egg yolk
salt
pepper

Beat the meat, sprinkle with salt, dredge with flour. Melt 2 ozs. butter, brown the meat in it on both sides. Add the lemon juice and a little water. Simmer. Cook half the chopped onion in the rest of the butter until transparent, add the breadcrumbs, season with salt and pepper. Mix with the egg. Make crosswise incisions in the meat. Fill with the stuffing. Fry the rest of the onion in a casserole, add the meat and about ½ pint water. Cook covered, in a moderate oven for 1 hour or more, until the meat is tender. Serve with the sauce on page 313.

MUSHROOM PATTIES

3 ozs. flour
1 egg yolk

FILLING:
1 onion, chopped
1 oz. dried mushrooms
1 oz. butter
1 tbsp. breadcrumbs
1 egg white
salt
pepper
parsley, chopped

Mix the egg yolk with the flour. Knead until smooth. Roll out and cut into 2 inch squares. Put a little of the following mixture in each square. Pinch the edges together to form a triangle, and cook in boiling water for 5 minutes.

FILLING:
Boil the mushrooms until tender. Melt the butter, add the mushrooms and the onion, stew until the onion is transparent. Mix with the breadcrumbs, beaten egg white, parsley and salt.

SAUCE FOR ROAST BEEF

2 onions
1 clove garlic
1 slice carrot
1 tomato
juice of half a lemon
2 tbsp. grated horseradish
basil
½ bay leaf
2 ozs. ham
2 glasses red wine
1 oz. butter

½ pint vegetable stock
1 tsp. sugar
salt
parsley

Melt the butter. Chop the onions, garlic, carrot, parsley. Cook in the butter with the bay leaf and a pinch of basil until browned. Stir in the flour, add the stock. Simmer for 40 minutes and sieve. Return to pan, add wine and lemon juice. Cut ham into strips. Peel tomato, remove seeds, cut flesh into slices. Add ham, tomato and horseradish. Serve hot.

SOUP NOODLES

1 egg
1 oz. flour
chopped parsley
salt

Beat the egg, mix with the flour and parsley. Season with salt. Pour this batter into boiling thin soup. It should cook quickly and look like ribbon noodles.

STEAK A LA NELSON

4 slices rump steak (about 6 ozs.
  each)
4 ozs. butter
1 onion, chopped
¼ lb. mushrooms, sliced
¼ pint cream
½ pint stock
1 oz. flour
4 potatoes

salt
pepper

Fry the onion in half the butter for 5 minutes. Add the mushrooms. Pour in the cream and the stock. Flour the meat. Season with salt and pepper. Fry quickly on both sides in the rest of the butter. Cook in the mushroom sauce in a covered pan for 30 minutes. Add the diced potatoes and cook for another 30 minutes.

FRIED VEAL WITH CAPER SAUCE

4 slices frying veal
1 oz. flour
¼ pint cream
¼ pint stock
salt
½ lemon
1 dsp. capers
¼ tsp. sugar

3 ozs. butter
pepper

Trim and beat the veal. Season with salt and pepper. Fry quickly in the butter, put on a plate to keep warm. Stir the flour into the fat, cook for 1 minute. Add the stock, cream, lemon juice, capers and sugar. Pour over the veal and reheat.

ROAST CHICKEN

1 chicken
½ lb. breadcrumbs
¼ lb. butter
1 egg
parsley
salt

Make a stuffing of the breadcrumbs, egg yolk, parsley and the stiffly beaten egg white; season with salt. Stuff the chicken and sew up the holes. Roast in a hot oven, basting frequently, for about an hour. Serve cut in half with the fat and juices from the pan poured over. This should be accompanied by a green salad.

CHOCOLATE ARKAS

½ pint double cream
3 ozs. sugar
4 ozs. cooking chocolate
2 eggs
2 egg yolks
vanilla

Beat the eggs, egg yolks and sugar until white. Add the cream and the melted chocolate. Beat until frothy. Pour into a buttered dish and steam until the mixture is set. Chill and serve with semi-sweet biscuits.

CHERRY DUMPLINGS

½ lb. Morella cherries
½ lb. flour
1½ ozs. butter
2 egg yolks
2 ozs. breadcrumbs
1 gill milk
2 ozs. melted butter
2 ozs. caster sugar

Cream the butter, add the egg yolks, breadcrumbs and milk and mix to a smooth paste. Beat in the flour and a pinch of salt. Shape the dough into small dumplings with 2 cherries in the middle of each. Cook in boiling water for 5 minutes. Drain, arrange in a dish with melted butter and sugar on the top.

RUM BUCKWHEAT

4 ozs. buckwheat or ground rice
1 pint cream
4 ozs. sugar
1 small glass rum
¼ tsp. salt
strip of lemon peel
icing sugar and cherries to
    decorate

Put the buckwheat and sugar in a bowl and pound it. Add the other ingredients, pour into a pie dish and cook in a slow oven for 2 hours. Turn out, cover with icing sugar and decorate with cherries.

VANILLA PUDDING

1 pint cream
6 ozs. sugar
4 eggs
4 egg yolks
vanilla
cherries to decorate

Beat the eggs, egg yolks and sugar until soft and creamy. Add the cream and vanilla and beat until frothy. Pour into a greased dish, cook slowly until custard sets.

APRICOT CAKE

9 ozs. flour
6 ozs. butter
3 ozs. sugar
½ lb. apricots
2 ozs. caster sugar
3 egg whites
2 ozs. icing sugar

Rub the butter into the flour, add the sugar. Knead as for shortbread. Divide into five parts, bake in tart tins in a slow oven for 40 minutes. Stew the apricots with the sugar and a little water. Sieve them. Add the purée to the stiffly beaten egg whites. Spread it between the layers of shortbread. Dredge with the icing sugar.

DOUGHNUTS

5 ozs. flour
3 egg yolks
1 dsp. rum
salt
1 oz. sugar
1½ ozs. melted butter
1 tsp. grated lemon peel
½ oz. yeast
2 tbsp. milk
apricot jam

Beat the egg yolks with the sugar and lemon peel. Dissolve the yeast in a little warm milk. Mix it with the sugar mixture, add the rum, the rest of the milk and a pinch of salt. Mix in the flour. Knead it thoroughly, add the melted butter and knead again. Cover with a cloth, leave to rise; when it has doubled its size, shape into rounds on a floured board. Put a little jam into each, fold in the corners. Leave covered in a warm place to rise again. Fry in deep fat with a lid on the pan until golden brown. Strain with a perforated spoon onto absorbent paper. Roll in icing sugar.

FAVORKI-CHRUST

½ lb. flour
2 ozs. butter
3 egg yolks
1 whole egg
2 ozs. sugar
½ tsp. bicarbonate of soda
¼ pint single cream
salt

Rub the fat into the flour, add the other ingredients and mix to a smooth paste. Roll out thinly, cut into strips 4 inches long and 1 inch wide. Make a slit at one end of each strip and push the other end through it. Fry quickly in deep fat until golden brown.

MOCHA MERINGUE

6 egg whites
¾ lb. icing sugar
¼ pint strong Mocha coffee

FILLING:
3 egg yolks
3 tbsp. sugar
2 tbsp. mocha coffee
1 tsp. flour
¼ pint double cream

Make ¼ pint coffee (see p. 55), dissolve the sugar in it, simmer until it becomes thick syrup. Fold in the stiffly beaten egg whites. Line 2 cake tins with paper, bake the mixture in these for 1 hour in a cool oven. Spread the following cream between the two meringue shells.

THE CREAM:
Beat the eggs and sugar, add the flour. Put the bowl over boiling water, bring the cream to the boil, add it to the mixture and beat until thick. Allow to cool, add the coffee and beat until smooth.

POLISH BABA

8 egg yolks
¼ lb. caster sugar
¼ pint milk
1 oz. yeast
¼ lb. melted butter
vanilla
saffron
½ tsp. salt

Beat the egg yolks and sugar over hot water until white and thick. Dissolve the yeast in a little warm milk. Add it and all the other ingredients except the butter to the eggs. Beat until thoroughly blended. Pour in the butter and beat again. Fill a greased tin with the mixture to one third of its depth. Cover and leave to rise in a warm place. Bake in a hot oven for 1 hour.

YEAST CAKE

1 lb. flour
3 ozs. sugar
3 ozs. butter
4 eggs
2 ozs. sultanas
½ pint milk
2 ozs. yeast
salt
grated lemon peel
icing sugar

Dissolve the yeast in a little warm milk. Mix the flour, sugar and a good pinch of salt in a bowl. Add 3 beaten eggs and the yeast. Knead until smooth. Soften the butter, add it and the sultanas to the dough. Half fill a greased baking tin with the dough, leave in a warm place to rise until double its size. Glaze with a little beaten egg. Bake in a hot oven for 40 minutes. Cover thinly with icing sugar.

CHEESE PASTRIES

2 ozs. flour
2 ozs. butter, cut into pieces
2 ozs. Parmesan cheese, grated
1 egg
paprika
salt

Put the flour, butter, cheese, paprika and salt into a bowl. Mix with a spoon until the dough is smooth and firm. Leave for an hour. Roll out thin. Cut into fancy shapes, glaze with the egg, bake in a hot oven for 10 minutes.

CREAM CHEESE SPREAD

¼ lb. cottage cheese
3 radishes
12 slices cucumber
chives
1 tbsp. cream
salt

Add the cream to the cheese, beat until light. Peel and dice the cucumber, sprinkle with salt, leave to drain. Cut the radishes into thin slices, chop the chives. Mix cucumber, chives and radishes with the cheese. Season with salt.

Russia

BABY BEETROOT SOUP

2 bunches baby beetroot with
   leaves
lemon juice
1½ pints stock
2 tbsp. sour cream
fennel
sugar

salt
pepper

Shred the beetroot and the leaves. Simmer in salted water with ½ teaspoonful lemon juice and ¼ teaspoonful sugar until tender. Add the stock and the cream. Reheat, sprinkle with chopped fennel.

BORSHCH

1 onion sliced
1 parsnip or petrouschka sliced
1 carrot sliced
1 beetroot sliced
6 ozs. shredded cabbage
2 pints stock
2 tbsp. tomato purée
1 dsp. vinegar
½ bay leaf
1 tbsp. sugar

2 ozs. lard
salt
pepper
½ pint sour cream

Melt the lard. Fry the onion, carrot, parsnip and beetroot in it for 5 minutes, stirring so that all pieces are covered with fat. Pour on the stock and add the tomato purée and vinegar. Season with salt, pepper and sugar. Simmer for 20 minutes. Serve with a spoonful of sour cream to each plate.

CABBAGE SOUP

2 cooked beetroots
2 carrots
2 onions
1 pint stock
¼ pint sour cream
1 cup shredded cabbage
4 cloves
1 tbsp. lemon juice

marjoram
salt

Mince the beetroot, carrot and onions. Simmer for 30 minutes in the stock. Add the cabbage, cloves, marjoram and salt and simmer again for 20 minutes. Add the lemon juice. Serve with a spoonful of cream on each plate.

MEAT BROTH

1 lb. stewing beef
1 lb. shredded cabbage
1 carrot, sliced
1 parsnip, sliced
1 onion, sliced
1 potato, diced
2 tomatoes, peeled and quartered

1 oz. lard
salt

Simmer the meat in 1½ pints salted water for 2 hours. Remove the meat, simmer the onion, carrot and parsnip in the broth for ½ hour. Add the tomato, cabbage and potato. Simmer for another ½ hour.

SORREL SOUP

1 lb. sorrel
1½ pints stock
fennel
1 tbsp. cream
1 tbsp. cornflour
2 hardboiled eggs, chopped

salt
pepper

Remove the hard stalks from the sorrel. Cook without water. Sieve. Add the stock and reheat. Mix the cornflour with the cream, add them. Season with salt and pepper. Serve hot or cold, garnished with the chopped hardboiled egg.

BREAM WITH HORSERADISH AND APPLE

2 lbs. bream
2 cooking apples
4 tbsp. grated horseradish
1 stick celery
1 leek
2 onions
½ bay leaf
thyme
parsley
lemon
salt
pepper

vinegar
1 tsp. sugar

Chop the celery, onions and leek, simmer in 1 pint water for 15 minutes. Add 1 dessertspoon vinegar, the herbs, salt and pepper. Cut the fish across into pieces 2 inches wide. Poach them in the stock for 20 minutes. Drain and arrange on a dish. Grate the apple, mix with the horseradish, 1 dessertspoon vinegar and the sugar. Garnish with this mixture and slices of lemon.

STUFFED PIKE

1 5-lb. pike
6 ozs. white bread
2 onions chopped
3 carrots chopped
1 beetroot chopped
2 parsnips chopped
1 tsp. sugar
2 eggs
1 tbsp. vegetable oil
salt
pepper

Cut the fish into thick slices. Remove the flesh without damaging the skin. Take out the bones. Chop the flesh and mix it with the bread, previously soaked in water, the water squeezed out, the onion, the eggs, sugar and oil. Season with salt and pepper. Stuff the fish slices with the mixture. Mix the rest of the vegetables together. Arrange alternate layers of mixed vegetables and fish slices in a fireproof dish, beginning and ending with a layer of vegetables. Cover the dish. Simmer for 3 hours. Sieve the vegetables and strain over the fish before serving.

STUFFED HADDOCK

4 fillets of haddock (2 lbs.)
4 onions chopped
2 slices bread
¼ pint milk
2 eggs
¼ lb. breadcrumbs
2 ozs. butter
flour

salt
pepper

Soak the bread in milk. Fry the onions in butter until soft. Squeeze out the bread, mix with the onions and 1 egg. Season with salt and pepper. Spread the mixture on the fish. Roll, dredge with flour, cover with beaten egg and then with breadcrumbs. Fry in butter and serve with the butter poured over.

MUSHROOMS IN SOUR CREAM

¼ pint sour cream
½ lb. mushrooms
¼ lb. grated cheese
1 oz. butter
1 tsp. flour
salt

Slice the mushrooms. Cook them in the butter. Add the flour, cook for 1 minute, gradually add the cream. Season with salt. Arrange in a flat dish, cover with grated cheese. Cook in a hot oven for 10 minutes.

RUSSIAN SALAD

½ lb. mixed cold pork and cold
   chicken
2 cooked beetroot diced
4 cooked potatoes, diced
2 gherkins, diced
½ cucumber, diced
2 hardboiled eggs, chopped
3 tbsp. olive oil

1 tbsp. wine vinegar
salt
¼ tsp. mustard
pepper

Mix the meat, vegetables and hardboiled eggs together. Dress with the oil and vinegar, seasoned with mustard, salt and pepper.

SAUERKRAUT WITH MUSHROOMS

1 lb. sauerkraut
1 oz. dried mushrooms
¼ pint sour cream

Cook the mushrooms. Drain and reserve 4 tbsp. of the water in which they were cooked to add to the sauerkraut. Chop the mushrooms and mix with the sauerkraut. Add the cream, cook slowly for 1 hour.

HERRING SALAD

¼ lb. cooked mushrooms, sliced
4 new potatoes, diced
1 beetroot, diced
pickled cucumber, sliced
parsley, chopped
4 salt herrings
3 tbsp. olive oil
1 tbsp. wine vinegar

¼ tsp. mustard
salt
pepper

Mix the olive oil, salt, pepper, vinegar and mustard. Mix the cucumber, mushrooms, potatoes and beetroot together. Arrange these round the herrings, pour the dressing over and sprinkle with chopped parsley. Serve very cold.

BAKED POTATO CAKE

4 medium potatoes
3 pickled herrings
6 ozs. salami
¼ pint sour cream
¼ lb. breadcrumbs
2 ozs. butter
salt
pepper

Bake the potatoes in their skins, peel and cut into thin slices. Chop the herrings, slice the salami. Butter an ovenproof dish. Fill it with alternate layers of herrings, potatoes and sausage, beginning and ending with a layer of potatoes. Spread each layer with sour cream and season with salt and pepper. Cover the top with breadcrumbs and dot with butter. Bake in a moderate oven for 40 minutes.

HAM PASTIES

½ lb. flour
2 eggs
2 egg yolks
salt
¼ lb. cooked ham or pork chopped
espagnole sauce
1½ ozs. butter
lemon juice
parsley

Mix the flour with the eggs and egg yolks until a stiff paste is formed. Leave for 2 hours. Roll out and cut into small rounds. Fill with the meat mixed with a little sauce, the lemon juice, ½ oz. butter and parsley. Pinch the edges together. Cook in boiling salted water for 20 minutes. Serve with melted butter mixed with lemon juice and chopped parsley.

GAME PATTIES

12 ozs. puff pastry (see p. 204)
½ lb. cooked pheasant
2 chopped hardboiled eggs
2 ozs. rice, cooked
1 oz. butter
salt
pepper

Roll the pastry out and cut into rounds. Put a little of the following mixture between two rounds of pastry. Press the edges together. Melt the butter, cook the chopped game, hardboiled eggs and rice in it for 5 minutes, mixing it well. Season with salt and pepper. Bake the patties in a hot oven for 15 minutes.

MUSHROOM AND EGG PATTIES

½ lb. rough puff pastry
2 hardboiled eggs
2 ozs. rice
2 ozs. dried mushrooms
1 onion, sliced
2 ozs. butter

Soak the mushrooms. Boil them until tender. Drain, keep the water. Boil the rice in the mushroom stock until cooked. Drain. Melt the butter, fry the onion in it for 10 minutes, add the mushrooms and fry for another 5 minutes. Chop the eggs, mix them and the rice with the onions and mushrooms. Roll out the pastry. Spread the rice mixture on half of it, cover with the other half. Bake in a hot oven for 20 minutes. Cut into slices.

PIROSHKI

choux pastry made with ½ lb. flour
¼ pint Béchamel sauce
 (see p. 163)
2 ozs. grated cheese
¼ lb. mushrooms, sliced and
 cooked
¼ lb. flour
1 egg yolk
¼ lb. breadcrumbs

Mix 1 oz. grated cheese with the choux pastry. Divide into 2 sections and bake in flat tins in a moderate oven for 20 minutes. Turn out of the tins. Mix the sauce with 1 oz. grated cheese and the mushrooms. Spread this on one sheet pastry, cover with the other sheet. Cut into oblong pieces 3 inches long and 1 inch wide. Cover with breadcrumbs, then with flour, then with beaten egg yolk and lastly with another layer of breadcrumbs. Cook in deep hot fat.

RICE WITH HARDBOILED EGGS

½ lb. Patna rice
4 hardboiled eggs, chopped
1 tbsp. chopped parsley
2 ozs. butter
salt

Cook the rice in boiling salted water. When cooked but still firm, drain and mix with hardboiled eggs, parsley and butter.

BLINY (Russian Pancakes)

2 lb. flour
1 pint milk
1 oz. butter
2 eggs
1½ ozs. yeast
1½ tsp. malt
2 tbsp. sugar

Dissolve the yeast in half the milk. Mix into a dough with half the flour. Leave in a warm place to rise for an hour. Add the salt, sugar, egg yolks and melted butter. Warm the rest of the milk and stir it in gradually. Add the rest of the flour slowly. Beat well. Leave to rise for an hour. Beat again. Leave to rise for an hour. Beat again, add the stiffly beaten egg whites. Leave to rise for ½ an hour. It should be the consistency of thick cream. Cook in the same way as pancakes. Serve with melted butter and salted herrings or anchovies or smoked salmon.

STUFFED CABBAGE

1 large savoy cabbage
1 lb. stewing beef, minced
1 egg
2 onions chopped
1 oz. lard
2 ozs. butter
1 oz. flour
3 tbsp. sour cream
salt
pepper

Put the cabbage in cold water. Bring to the boil, drain. Reserve the cabbage water; when cabbage is cold, separate the leaves. Melt the lard, cook the onions for 5 minutes, add the beef, cook for another 5 minutes. Season with salt and pepper. Bind with the egg. Fill the cabbage leaves with the mixture. Roll them, lay them in a fireproof dish, cover the bottom with water, dot with 1 oz. butter. Cook in a slow oven for 1½ hours. Melt the rest of the butter, stir in the flour, cook for 1 minute, add ½ pint cabbage water, stirring all the time. Add the cream. Pour the sauce over the cabbage rolls.

BEEF STROGANOFF

1½ lbs. fillet steak
½ lb. mushrooms
1 small onion
½ pint sour cream (Smetana is a possible substitute)
¼ lb. butter
nutmeg
salt

Beat the steak, cut into strips about 1 inch wide. Melt 2 ozs. of the butter, cook the onion until transparent. Add the beef, cook quickly for about 5 minutes, making sure that all sides are browned. Cook the mushrooms separately in the rest of the butter. Season with salt and a little nutmeg. Add to the beef. Warm the cream, stir it into the meat and mushrooms. Serve with rice.

BEEF STEW

1 lb. steak
½ lb. tomatoes, peeled and quartered
2 carrots sliced
¼ lb. cooking fat
½ pint stock
wineglass of red wine
salt
pepper

Flour the meat. Season with salt and pepper. Melt the fat, brown the vegetables and put them in the bottom of a casserole. Brown the meat in the same fat. Put in the casserole on top of the vegetables, cover it with another layer of vegetables. Pour in the stock. Simmer in a moderate oven for 2 hours. Sieve the vegetables, add the wine. Pour this sauce over the meat. Serve with noodles or macaroni.

SOLYANKA (Steak with Gherkin Sauce)

4 slices fillet steak (about 6 ozs.
   each.)
2 onions chopped
2 gherkins sliced
1 tbsp. tomato purée
¼ glass white wine
2 ozs. butter
salt
pepper

Cut the steaks into 1 inch strips. Fry the onion in half the butter, add the gherkins, tomato purée, wine and stock. Season with salt and pepper. Simmer for 40 minutes. Melt the rest of the butter. Fry the steak on both sides. Arrange in a fireproof dish on top of the tomato mixture. Cook in a moderate oven for 30 minutes.

KIDNEYS WITH GHERKINS

1 lb. ox kidneys
1 onion, sliced
1 oz. butter
1 oz. flour
¼ pint stock
1 lb. new potatoes cooked
gherkins

salt
pepper

Fry the onion in the butter for 5 minutes. Add the thinly sliced kidney and cook slowly until tender. Season with salt and pepper, stir in the flour. Cook for 1 minute; gradually add the stock. Arrange on a dish, pour the sauce over the kidneys and surround with potatoes and gherkins.

BRAISED LAMB CHOPS

4 lamb chops
1 small cabbage
2 carrots
1 turnip
2 potatoes
½ pint stock
1 oz. butter
1 oz. flour

salt
pepper

Shred the carrots, cabbage and turnip, dice the potatoes. Brown them in the butter, stir in the flour. Put them in a casserole, arrange the chops on top, season with salt and pepper, pour in the stock. Cover the casserole and cook in a moderate oven for 1 hour. Cool, skim off the fat, and reheat.

CAUCASIAN SHASHLIK

½ leg lamb (about 1 lb.) boned
½ lb. green bacon
2 ozs. butter
salt
pepper

Cut the meat into 1 inch cubes. Melt half the butter and brown the cubes on all sides. Cut the bacon into slightly smaller cubes. Put alternate cubes of bacon and meat onto 4 skewers. Season with salt and pepper. Brush with melted butter. Cook under a hot grill, turning the skewers from time to time so that the meat is cooked evenly on all sides. Serve with plain boiled rice.

LIVER IN SOUR CREAM

1 lb. calves' liver
¼ pint milk
¼ pint sour cream
1 tbsp. flour
1 onion, sliced
1 oz. butter
½ pint stock
salt
pepper

Melt the butter, lightly fry the onion. Add the liver cut into fairly thin slices, floured and seasoned with salt and pepper. Cook for 10 minutes, turning the liver so that all pieces are browned on both sides. Pour on the milk, sour cream and stock, and simmer covered with a lid, for 30 minutes in a moderate oven.

BRAISED TONGUE

1 ox tongue
1 dsp. sugar
1 tbsp. flour
1 oz. butter
1 small glass red wine
juice of 1 lemon
strip of lemon peel
2 ozs. sultanas
2 ozs. almonds, blanched and
   shredded
1 carrot, sliced
1 turnip, sliced

parsley .
½ bay leaf } bouquet garni
thyme
salt

Simmer the tongue in water with the vegetables, a bouquet garni and salt. Skin it and leave to cool. Make sauce as follows:

Melt the butter, cook the flour in it for 1 minute, gradually add enough of the water in which the tongue was cooked to make a thick sauce. Add the lemon juice, lemon peel, sultanas and almonds. Cut the tongue into slices and reheat it in the sauce.

PORK CHOPS WITH BEETROOT

4 pork chops
1 cooked beetroot, thinly sliced
1 tbsp. vinegar
1 onion, chopped
2 tbsp. breadcrumbs
lard
salt
pepper

Brown the chops in the lard. Put them into a fireproof dish. Put the onions, beetroot, vinegar and breadcrumbs into the pan, season with salt and pepper and add ½ pint of water. Simmer for 5 minutes and pour over the chops. Cook, covered, in a moderate oven for 40 minutes. Strain the sauce over the chops before serving.

CHICKEN CUTLETS (1)

breast of ½ chicken
1 slice bread
¼ pint cream
2 ozs. butter
2 ozs. breadcrumbs
salt
pepper

Remove the skin from the chicken breast and mince it. Soak the bread in the cream and squeeze it a little. Mix it with the minced chicken. Season with salt and pepper. Divide into 4 pieces, shape into cutlets, roll in breadcrumbs. Fry slowly in butter until cooked and brown.

CHICKEN CUTLETS (2)

1 small chicken
3 chicken livers
¼ lb. mushrooms, finely chopped
2 onions, finely chopped
1 egg
breadcrumbs
2 ozs. butter
2 ozs. flour
salt
pepper
lard

Remove the breast of the chicken and skin it. Bone and skin the wings and legs. Cut the meat into small pieces. Cook the onions in the butter until golden, add the pieces of chicken, mushrooms, salt and pepper, and fry lightly. Blanch the chicken livers, cut into small pieces and add to the mushroom mixture. Cut the chicken breast into thin slices, beat well and spread the mushroom mixture on them. Roll them up and secure with a wooden stick. Dredge with flour, brush with beaten egg and roll in breadcrumbs. Fry quickly in lard until browned on all sides, and transfer to a casserole and cook in a moderate oven for 20 minutes.

PARTRIDGE WITH CREAM SAUCE

2 partridges
2 ozs. butter
1 oz. flour
1 gill double cream
juice of ½ lemon
½ lb. mushrooms

Slice the mushrooms and stuff the birds with them. Put half the butter in the roasting tin and half on the birds, roast in a moderate oven for 15 minutes. Cut in halves. Make a sauce by cooking the flour in the fat in the tin and adding the cream and lemon juice. Put the partridges back in the tin and cook for another 15 minutes.

TURKEY WITH CHERRY SAUCE

sliced breast of turkey
½ lb. cherry jam
cinnamon
ginger
cloves
2 ozs. butter
1 glass Madeira

Heat the jam slowly with a little water, a pinch of cinnamon and ginger and 2 cloves. Rub through a sieve. Melt the butter, heat the turkey slices in it, add the Madeira and cook again for 1 minute. Pour the sauce into the middle of a dish and arrange the turkey round it.

APPLE FOOL

6 cooking apples
juice of 1 lemon
2 ozs. sugar
1 tbsp. blackcurrant jelly
cinnamon
2 tbsp. breadcrumbs
1 glass claret

Peel and slice the apples. Simmer them with a little water and the breadcrumbs, sugar and cinnamon. Sieve them and, when cold, add the claret, lemon juice and melted blackcurrant jelly. Beat well, serve cold. This is served as a soup in Russia, but would be more acceptable as a sweet in England.

APPLE SOUFFLÉ

4 large cooking apples
¼ lb. sugar
1 egg

Peel and slice the apples, cook with a little water and sugar until tender. Sieve, cook again until very thick. Mix in the egg yolk and fold in the stiffly beaten egg white. Put in a greased soufflé dish, cook in a hot oven for 15 minutes.

EASTER PUDDING

½ lb. dry cream cheese
2 eggs
½ pint cream
¼ lb. butter
¼ lb. sugar
¼ lb. raisins
¼ lb. sultanas

vanilla
lemon peel

Whisk the sugar and eggs until thick, beat in the butter. Mix this with the cream cheese and dried fruit. Flavour with vanilla and grated lemon peel. Put into a muslin bag and leave to drain for 2—3 days. Shape into a pyramid.

KISYELI

1 lb. red currants
½ lb. raspberries
2 ozs. semolina or ground rice
* or potato flour*
¼ lb. blackcurrants
¼ lb. sugar

Stew the fruit with the sugar and just enough water to stop it burning. Strain off the juice. Mix a little of the juice with the semolina, heat the rest and stir it into the semolina. Cook this mixture for 5 minutes, stirring all the time. Chill and serve with whipped cream.

MALAKOFF CAKE

1 sponge cake made with sugar,
   eggs, and flour but no fat, or
   ½ lb. lady fingers
6 ozs. butter
6 ozs. sugar
6 ozs. almonds
½ pint double cream
2 egg yolks
¼ pint milk
1 glass rum

Chop the almonds finely and roast them by putting a little sugar in a frying pan and tossing the almonds in this until they are slightly brown. Cream the butter and sugar and beat in the almonds, rum and egg yolks.

Cut the cake into 3 flat sections, soak each in a mixture of rum and milk. Put a layer of cake followed by a layer of filling into a cake tin of the same size. Repeat these layers and cover with a final layer of cake. Leave in a very cold place for 12 hours. Turn out before serving and cover with whipped cream.

WALNUT AND ALMOND KASCHA

¼ lb. walnuts
¼ lb. almonds
¾ pint milk
1 oz. semolina
apricot jam
glacé cherries, chopped
⅓ lb. short pastry
¼ lb. icing sugar

Shell the walnuts, blanch and peel the almonds. Pound them together until smooth. Put the milk in a flat dish in the oven, leave it until a brown skin is formed, then strain the skin off and keep it. Put the dish back in the oven and repeat the process 4 times. Cook the semolina with the milk until quite thick. Line a tart tin with pastry, fill it with alternate layers of semolina, skin from the milk, mixed jam, cherries and nuts. Sprinkle with breadcrumbs over the top, cook in a moderate oven until brown. Cover with icing sugar and brown under a grill.

BUCKWHEAT

2 cups kasha buckwheat
3 cups water
2 ozs. butter
salt

Boil the kasha in salted water, stir until thick. Cook in a slow oven for 3 hours. Stir in the butter. Serve with borshch.

CREAM CHEESE TARTS

½ lb. flour
2 ozs. butter
2 ozs. lard
½ lb. cream cheese
1 tsp. sugar
salt

Make short pastry with the flour, butter and lard mixed with a little water. Roll it out and cut into rounds. Arrange in small tart tins, fill with cream cheese mixed with the sugar and seasoned with salt. Serve with borshch or as hòrs d'œuvres.

RUSSIAN EASTER EGGS

It is the custom in Hungary and Russia to exchange highly decorated hardboiled eggs at Easter. Here are two characteristic ways of decorating them.

1. Unravel threads from any cotton material the dye of which is not fast. Wind them around the eggs, using as many different colours as possible. Wrap a piece of rag round the whole and cook in boiling water for 10 minutes. Remove the wrappings and there will be a multi-coloured pattern of criss-crossing lines on the egg.
2. Lay onion skins round the egg, wrap a piece of rag round to keep them in position. Cook in boiling water for 10 minutes. The eggs will be a beautiful golden colour.

RUSSIAN TEA

Make tea in the usual way. Serve without milk but garnished with slices of lemon and glacé cherries.

Scandinavia

SMÖRGASBORD

The Swedish smörgasbord consists of both hors d'œuvres dishes of all kinds and a number of light entrées. It is as though the French notion of *hors d'œuvres variés* had been combined with the grand old-fashioned English breakfast at which the sideboard was covered with delicious hot dishes under silver covers, from which the fortunate guest could take his pick. It is capable of great variation: it can be quite modest or very elaborate. The common factor is attention to decorative and appetising detail. Each dish is quite small, but arranged in such a way as to please the eye and stimulate the appetite. As eaten in Sweden, smörgasbord is not a meal in itself but an overture to the main course. The following is a selection from the many possible dishes for a smörgasbord.

STUFFED EGGS

4 hardboiled eggs
5 anchovy fillets
1 oz. butter
prawns

Slice the eggs and cut a little off the underneath of the white so that they will stand steadily. Pound the yolks with the anchovies and the butter. Hang prawns by their tails round the egg whites and fill with the yolk mixtures.

CALVES' LIVER TERRINE

1 lb. calves' liver
¼ lb. veal
½ lb. fat pork
1 onion
8 anchovy fillets
2 ozs. flour
3 eggs
½ pint cream
4 truffles
½ lb. streaky bacon

Mince the liver, veal, pork, onion and anchovies several times. Pass through a sieve. Stir the flour into the eggs, blend with the cream. Add the liver mixture with the truffles. Line a shallow fireproof dish with bacon rashers, fill it with the mixture and cook in a *bain-marie* for 1½ hours in a slow oven. Cover with greaseproof paper, put a weight on the top, leave in a cool place for 24 hours.

ANCHOVY EGGS

4 hardboiled eggs
2 ozs. butter
5 anchovy fillets or anchovy paste
lettuce
tomatoes
parsley

Slice the eggs lengthwise. Remove the yolks and beat until very soft with the butter and the sieved anchovies or anchovy paste. Pile this mixture into the egg whites. Arrange each on a lettuce leaf. Surround with sliced tomatoes and garnish with parsley.

SARDINE ROLLS

2 lbs. fresh sardine (smelts can be used instead)
1 anchovy fillet to each sardine
2 ozs. butter
2 ozs. breadcrumbs

Fillet the sardines and lay one anchovy on each fillet. Roll them up together. Arrange in a buttered fireproof dish, pour the oil from the anchovies over them. Sprinkle with breadcrumbs, dot with butter. Bake for 20 minutes in a moderate oven.

PICKLED HERRINGS

2 large salt herrings
1 oz. allspice
2 bay leaves
4 ozs. sugar
6 black peppercorns
1 small onion, chopped
½ pint vinegar

Clean the fish and remove the heads. Soak overnight, skin and fillet the fish. Cut the fillets in ½ inch slices, arrange in a shallow dish. Mix all the other ingredients with the vinegar, pour over the fish. Leave in a cold place for several hours before serving.

This is one of the essential dishes for a smörgasbord.

HERRING SALAD (1)

1 salt herring
2 medium potatoes, cooked and diced
1 cooked beetroot, diced
1 large apple, peeled and diced
2 pickled gherkins, diced
hardboiled eggs, cooked beetroot and sour cream to garnish
1 small onion, chopped
4 tbsp. vinegar

2 tbsp. sugar
pepper

Clean the fish and remove the heads. Soak overnight, skin and fillet. Cut the fillets into small pieces and mix well with the potatoes, apples, beetroot, gherkins and onion. Mix the sugar with the vinegar, season with pepper. Pour this over the other ingredients. Leave in a mould in a cool place for several hours. Unmould and serve garnished with hardboiled eggs, beetroot and sour cream.

HERRING SALAD (2)

4 salt herrings, soaked overnight
2 medium potatoes
2 apples
1 onion
2 hardboiled eggs
2 tbsp. white wine vinegar
2 tbsp. olive oil
salt
pepper
¼ tsp. dry mustard

1 tbsp. chopped chives
¼ pint cream

Cook the potatoes in their skins, cool, peel and dice. Peel and core the apples and cut into dice. Chop the onion finely. Cut the herrings into small pieces. Separate the whites of the eggs and chop. Sieve the yolks. Arrange all the ingredients in a bowl, mixed or kept separate as you prefer. Pour the following dressing over them:

Mix the oil and vinegar, season with salt, pepper and mustard. Add the chives and work in the cream.

EGGS AND SHRIMPS WITH MAYONNAISE

4 hardboiled eggs
1 pint shrimps
½ pint mayonnaise (see p. 159)
¼ pint cream
chives
pepper

Cut the eggs in half lengthwise. Arrange down the middle of a dish, sprinkle with finely ground black pepper. Surround them with the shrimps (from which the heads and tails have been removed). Stir the cream into the mayonnaise, pour over the eggs. Strew chopped chives over the top.

ANCHOVY EYE

12 anchovy fillets
1 onion
1 egg yolk

The use of a raw egg to be mixed at the table with the other ingredients is a characteristic smörgasbord dish.

Arrange the finely chopped anchovies round the outside of a small dish, with a ring of finely chopped onion inside them. Place a raw egg yolk in the middle.

EGGS IN MUSTARD SAUCE

2 ozs. butter
2 ozs. flour
½ pint milk
1 tsp. dry mustard
salt
pepper
4 hardboiled eggs

Melt the butter, cook the flour in it for 1 minute, gradually add the hot milk, stirring all the time. Season with salt, pepper and mustard. Cut the eggs in half lenghthwise, arrange them in a shallow dish, pour the sauce over them.

SHRIMP AND HARDBOILED EGG FLAN

short crust pastry made with
  6 ozs. flour (see p. 205)
3 tbsp. olive oil
1 tbsp. wine vinegar
1 dsp. vinegar
½ tsp. dry mustard
1 tbsp. cream
4 hardboiled eggs
½ pint shrimps
6 anchovy fillets cut in strips
2 pickled cucumbers peeled and
  sliced

Line a greased tart tin with the pastry and bake blind in a moderately hot oven. Mix the oil and vinegar with the sugar and mustard. Beat in the cream, stirring until thick. Remove the whites from the eggs and cut into strips. Mix with the shrimps from which the heads and tails have been removed. Sieve the egg yolks. Pour a little of the dressing over the egg whites and the shrimps, and put them in the middle of the pastry case. Arrange egg yolk and cucumber round the edge. Put the anchovies in a criss-cross pattern on the top. Serve the remaining dressing separately.

JELLIED PORK AND VEAL

2 lbs. pork }*any inexpensive cut*
2 lbs. veal }
2 tbsp. salt
14 peppercorns
1 dsp. allspice
2 bay leaves
4 cloves
1 onion
1 carrot
2 tbsp. white wine vinegar
gelatine

Simmer the meat for 10 minutes. Skim. Add the herbs, spices, vegetables and seasoning. Simmer until tender (1½—2 hours). Drain the meat, remove from the bones and chop finely. Return bones to the pan and simmer for another 30 minutes. Strain, add the meat to the stock and simmer for 10 minutes. Dissolve the gelatine (using enough to set the liquid according to the instructions on the packet) in a little water, add it to the meat and stock. Add the vinegar and season lightly with salt and pepper. Leave in a mould to set. Unmould and serve cold.

LIVER TERRINE (Danish)

1 lb. pig's liver
1 small tin anchovy fillets
¼ lb. fat bacon
4 eggs
12 rashers streaky bacon
½ pint thick white sauce
1 clove garlic
salt
pepper

Mince the liver, fat bacon and anchovies twice. Pass through a sieve. Mix with the beaten eggs, crushed garlic and white sauce. Season with salt and pepper. Line a shallow ovenproof dish with bacon rashers. Fill with the liver mixture. Bake in a slow oven in a *bain-marie* for 2 hours. Cover with greaseproof paper, put weights on the top. Leave for 24 hours in a cold place.

POTATO SALAD

4 medium potatoes
3 tbsp. olive oil
1 tbsp. white wine vinegar
1 tbsp. chopped onion
1 tbsp. chopped parsley
1 tbsp. chopped chives
salt
pepper

1 medium pickled beetroot
  finely chopped (see p. 346)

Cook the potatoes in their skins until just tender. Cool, peel and slice them. Stir the vinegar into the olive oil, season with salt and pepper. Put the potatoes into a salad bowl with the onions, parsley, chives and beetroot on the top. Mix all the ingredients gently, leave to stand for several hours, mix again before serving.

CUCUMBER SALAD

1 cucumber
French dressing (see p. 159)
dill or dill seeds

Peel the cucumber and cut it into thin slices. Sprinkle with salt and leave for 30 minutes, drain and arrange in a shallow dish, covered with French dressing. Sprinkle with chopped dill or dill seeds.

ONION CASSEROLE

4 Spanish onions, sliced
1 oz. butter
$\frac{1}{4}$ lb. minced lean pork
$\frac{1}{4}$ lb. minced veal
$\frac{1}{2}$ pint milk or $\frac{1}{2}$ gill cream and
  $1\frac{1}{2}$ gills water
1 oz. breadcrumbs
$\frac{1}{2}$ gill stock

pepper
salt

Fry the onions in the butter until golden. Mix the meat and the breadcrumbs. Season with salt and pepper. Place half the onions in the bottom of a greased fireproof dish, cover with the meat mixture, then the rest of the onions. Pour in the stock. Bake in a moderate oven for 30 minutes.

ONION AND ANCHOVY RAGOUT

1 onion, sliced
1 oz. butter
2 hardboiled eggs
10 anchovies
1 tbsp. cream
pepper

Cook the onions in the butter until golden. Drain and mince with the eggs and anchovies. Season with pepper. Transfer to a shallow fireproof dish, pour the butter from the pan over, add the cream. Cook in a moderate oven for 20 minutes.

ANCHOVY AND POTATO PIE

2 small onions, sliced
2 ozs. butter
4 medium potatoes
1 large tin anchovies
¼ pint cream

Fry the onions in 1 oz. butter until transparent. Peel and cut the potatoes as for very thin chips. Arrange potatoes, onions and anchovies in layers in a buttered fireproof dish, beginning and ending with a layer of potatoes. Pour a little of the anchovy oil into the dish, dot with butter and cook in a hot oven for 10 minutes. Add the cream and continue baking in a hot oven for 1 hour or until potatoes are soft.

GREEN PEA SOUP

2 lbs. shelled peas
2 sprigs parsley
1 sprig mint
2 pints chicken stock
1 oz. butter
1 oz. flour
salt
pepper
20 very small carrots, cooked

1 tbsp. chopped parsley
¼ pint cream

Simmer the peas, with the herbs, in the stock until tender. Strain, reserving the liquid, and pass through a sieve. Melt the butter, cook the flour in it for 1 minute, gradually add the stock and the purée of peas. Season with salt and pepper. Add the carrots, stir in the cream. Heat but do not boil. Serve hot or chilled.

SPLIT PEA SOUP

1 lb. split peas
½ lb. pork
½ tsp. ginger
salt
pepper

This sustaining dish is widely eaten in Sweden before Friday's fast.

Soak the peas in 4 pints water overnight. Cook in the same water. Skim off the skins as they rise to the surface, add the pork when new skins have stopped appearing. Simmer until tender (about 2 hours). Remove the pork and keep warm. Sieve the soup, season with salt, pepper and ginger. Serve the pork as a side dish with the soup. It should be eaten with mustard. Onion or leek can be substituted for the ginger if preferred, in which case they should be added at the same time as the pork.

FISH SOUP

2 lbs. haddock with head, bones
    and skin
1 carrot
2 sticks celery
2 sprigs parsley
1 bay leaf
2 cloves
6 peppercorns
salt
2 ozs. butter

1½ ozs. flour
1 pint milk

Simmer the fish with the vegetables, herbs and
seasoning until tender. Strain, keep the liquor and
the best pieces of fish. Make a sauce as follows:
    Melt the butter, cook the flour in it for 1 minute,
gradually add the fish stock and the milk. Season
lightly with salt and pepper and add the flaked fish
pieces.

SPRING SOUP

2 spring onions, sliced
1 small cauliflower
1 stick celery chopped
½ lb. peas
½ lb. spinach
parsley
2 carrots sliced
2 pints chicken stock
2 egg yolks
¼ pint cream
salt
pepper

1 oz. flour
½ oz. butter

Put the onion, celery, peas, carrots and cauliflower,
broken into flowerets, in a pudding basin and steam
them until tender. Cook the spinach separately.
Drain and chop the spinach. Melt the butter and
cook the flour in it for 1 minute. Gradually add the
stock. Add the vegetables. Season with salt and
pepper. Beat the egg yolks with the cream. Pour the
soup slowly into this mixture. Reheat. Serve garnished with chopped parsley.

TUESDAY SOUP

2 carrots
1 parsnip
1 oz. dripping
1 piece celeriac
1 slice turnip
1 small onion
5 ozs. rice or barley
2 pints stock
1 pint milk

salt
pepper

It is customary in Sweden to make soup the main
dish on Tuesday. This is a characteristic one, but
the root vegetables can be varied according to taste.
Slice the vegetables and brown them in the butter.
Add the stock and the salt and pepper and simmer
for 30 minutes. add the rice and simmer until the
rice is tender (about 15 minutes). Stir in the hot milk.

BRUSSELS SPROUT SOUP

1½ lbs. Brussels sprouts
4 rashers streaky bacon
1 small onion, sliced
1 oz. flour
2 pints stock
salt

pepper
nutmeg

Cook the sprouts in boiling salted water until tender, drain, simmer and chop roughly. Fry the bacon rashers lightly, chop them finely, stir in the flour, cook for 1 minute, gradually add the boiling stock. Season with salt, pepper and a grating of nutmeg.

CABBAGE SOUP

½ small cabbage, shredded
1 oz. butter
2 ozs. brown sugar
2 pints stock
4 black peppercorns
salt

Fry the shredded cabbage, reserving a few shreds, in the butter until brown, stir in the sugar, add the stock, season with salt and pepper. Simmer for 2 hours. Strain, add the uncooked cabbage shreds and simmer rapidly for another 5 minutes.

FRIED SALMON

4 salmon steaks
½ pint vinegar
4 ozs. butter
salt
lemon, or Hollandaise sauce
  (see p. 159)

This can be made very well with the frozen salmon imported from the Pacific. Marinate the salmon in the vinegar for an hour. Drain and then dry the fish. Melt the butter and fry the fish on both sides until golden brown. Serve with lemon or with Hollandaise sauce.

NORWEGIAN FISH BALLS

2 lbs. haddock or bream
3 ozs. butter
5 ozs. flour
2 eggs
¾ pint milk
salt
pepper

Poach the fish in a little very gently boiling salted water, for 15 minutes. Drain, reserving the liquor for the sauce, and flake when cool. Mince the fish, beat in the butter, flour, egg yolks and milk, season with salt and pepper. Shape into balls and cook in briskly boiling salted water for 15 minutes. Serve with fish sauce (see p. 351).

FISH SOUFFLÉ

2 lbs. fresh haddock or cod
3 ozs. butter
3 ozs. flour
½ pint milk
3 eggs
salt
pepper

Cook the whole fish if possible in a little gently boiling salted water for 15 minutes, or in a court-bouillon. Drain, reserving the liquid, and allow to cool. Remove the flesh and flake into small pieces. Melt the butter, cook the flour in it for 1 minute, add ½ pint fish stock and the milk. Add the fish, season lightly with salt and pepper, gradually beat in the egg yolk. Fold in the stiffly beaten egg whites and bake in a greased dish for 45 minutes in a moderately hot oven.

DANISH PLAICE

2 plaice (about 1 lb. each, filleted)
2 glasses white wine
4 ozs. flour
1 egg
pepper
2 ozs. breadcrumbs
4 ozs. butter
salt

FOR THE SAUCE:
1 oz. butter
1 oz. flour
scant ½ pint milk
1 bunch small asparagus
4 ozs. mushrooms sliced
juice of ½ lemon

salt
pepper

Cook 4 fillets slowly, just covered by the wine, in a buttered fireproof dish. Keep warm. Cut the remaining fillets into 3 pieces, roll in flour and then in egg and breadcrumbs. Make the sauce as follows:

Melt the butter and cook the flour in it for 1 minute, gradually add the liquor from the fish and the milk. Add the cooked asparagus and the mushrooms, previously cooked in the butter with the lemon juice, and season with salt and pepper. Keep the sauce warm while quickly frying the uncooked fillets in the butter. Arrange the fish cooked in the wine down the middle of a dish, cover with the sauce. Put the fried fillets round the edges. Serve with potato purée.

HADDOCK FILLETS WITH LEMON SAUCE

2 lbs. haddock fillets
juice of ½ lemon
1 oz. butter
½ pint lemon sauce (see p. 351)
½ pint shrimps
salt

Roll the fillets (cut into smaller pieces if preferred) and secure with cocktail sticks. Arrange in a fireproof dish, add the lemon juice and enough water to cover the fish. Sprinkle with salt and dot with butter. Bake in a moderate oven for about 30 minutes (the time will vary according to the size of the fillets). Serve with lemon sauce and garnish with prepared shrimps sautéed in the butter. Fish prepared in this way can be garnished with chopped dill or parsley instead of shrimps.

HALIBUT, BAKED

4 slices halibut
¾ lb. tomatoes, peeled and sliced
1 small onion, sliced
2 ozs. melted butter
¼ pint cream
salt
pepper

Put the fish in a shallow fireproof dish having first removed the skin. Cover with the tomatoes, sprinkle with salt and pepper and pour in the melted butter. Add the onion, bake in a moderate oven for 20 minutes. Remove the onions. Pour the cream over the tomatoes and fish. Bake for another 10 minutes.

GOLDEN COD

1½ lbs. cod fillets
1 oz. butter
¾ oz. flour
½ pint mixed fish stock and milk
1 tsp. dry mustard
1 tbsp. vinegar
½ tsp. sugar
4 cold boiled potatoes
salt
pepper

Poach the fillets in a little milk until tender. Drain and reserve the milk for the sauce. Melt the butter and cook the flour in it for 1 minute, gradually add the fish liquid and enough extra milk to make up ½ pint and stir in the dry mustard, vinegar and sugar. Flake the fish and put it in a shallow fireproof dish, surround with slices of potato. Pour the sauce over and bake in a moderate oven for 20 minutes. Serve garnished with croutons.

BAKED COD

2 thick slices of cod (about ¾ lb.
  each)
salt
paprika
mushroom sauce (see p. 351)
6 rashers streaky bacon
1 oz. butter

Sprinkle the fish with salt and paprika. Cut 3 bacon rashers into small pieces and put them in the bottom of a fireproof dish. Put the cod on top of them, cover with the rest of the bacon in small pieces. Sprinkle heavily with paprika. Dot with butter. Bake in a moderate oven for 45 minutes. Strain off the liquid and use for the sauce.

FRIED MACKEREL

4 small mackerel
½ pint vinegar
6 ozs. breadcrumbs
fat for frying
lemon
1 tbsp. salt

Marinate the mackerel in the vinegar for 1 hour. Dry and roll in breadcrumbs mixed with the salt. Fry on both sides in hot fat. Serve garnished with lemon.

HAM OMELETTE

2 ozs. bacon
½ oz. butter
2 egg yolks
1 egg white
½ pint milk

salt
pepper

Put the diced bacon in the bottom of a greased fire-proof dish. Beat the eggs in the milk, season with salt and pepper, pour over the bacon. Bake in a moderate oven for 45 minutes.

BAKED OMELETTE

4 eggs
½ pint cream or milk
salt
pepper

FOR THE FILLING:
mushrooms, shrimps, lobster or asparagus in thick white sauce

Beat the eggs, add the cream and season with salt and pepper. Pour the mixture into a buttered fireproof dish (a heavy omelette pan is ideal) and bake in a moderate oven for 15 minutes. Transfer to a heated dish, cover half the omelette with the hot filling, fold the other half over it. Serve at once.

STUFFED CABBAGE (Norwegian)

1 small cabbage
1 lb. minced beef
salt
pepper
1 pint stock
1 pint Béchamel sauce
  (see p. 163)

Cut the middle leaves out of the cabbage, fill the hole with the meat seasoned with salt and pepper, tie the outside leaves together at the top. Simmer in the stock for 3 hours. Serve with Béchamel sauce and thin slices of toast.

STUFFED POTATO PANCAKES

4 medium potatoes
1 egg yolk
4 ozs. flour
1 small onion
salt
pepper
2 ozs. ham
1 oz. butter

Boil the potatoes in their skins. Peel and sieve. Mix with the flour and egg yolk until smooth. Season with salt and pepper. Chop the onion and the ham and brown in the butter. Roll out the dough ½ inch thick. Cut into rounds with a pastry cutter. Spread the ham mixture onto half the rounds, cover with the other rounds, pinch the ends together. Poach in boiling water until they rise to the surface. Serve with melted butter.

VEAL HEADCHEESE

3 lbs. leg of veal
3 lbs. lean pork
2 tbsp. salt
3 whole allspice
4 cloves
6 peppercorns
½ bay leaf
1 small onion, sliced

Get the butcher to cut the veal into 3 pieces across the bone. Put it in a large pan with the pork and 2 qts. cold water, bring to the boil and skim. Add all the other ingredients, cover the pan and cook slowly, covered, for 3 hours or longer, until the meat is tender. Strain, remove the meat from the bones, return to the pan and cook for another hour. Mince or chop the meat. Strain the liquid, add it to the meat and boil them together for 10 minutes. Pour into moulds and leave in a cold place to set.

This is a modified version of the real headcheese which requires a whole hogshead and is therefore not generally practical.

BROWNED POTATOES

2 lbs. potatoes
2 ozs. breadcrumbs
4 ozs. butter
salt

Wash the potatoes and cook in salted water until tender. Cool and peel and cut into dice. Melt the fat, mix some of the breadcrumbs with enough of the potatoes to cover the bottom of the pan. Fry until crisp and brown, drain and keep hot. Cook the rest of the breadcrumbs and potatoes in the same way.

BEETROOT A LA LINDSTROM

2 medium beetroots
1 egg
2 ozs. breadcrumbs
fat for frying
fried onion to garnish

Boil the beetroots in water until tender, peel and cut into ¼ in. slices. Dry the slices and dip them into beaten egg, roll in breadcrumbs. Fry in shallow fat until crisp and brown. Serve garnished with fried onions.

PICKLED BEETROOT

10 small beetroots
½ pint vinegar
salt
4 ozs. sugar
1 clove

Cook the beetroots in boiling salted water until tender. Drain and cut into thin slices when cool. Mix the vinegar with a little water, the sugar and the clove. Season with salt. Pour this over the beetroot and leave in a cool place for several hours.

LAMB STEW (Finnish)

3 lbs. shoulder of lamb
2 carrots sliced
2 leeks
4 potatoes
½ bay leaf
salt
pepper
parsley

Cut the meat into cubes. Cover with boiling water and simmer for 30 minutes skimming from time to time. Leave to cool and skim off the fat. Add the vegetables, bay leaf and seasonings and simmer until tender (about 1 hour). Serve garnished with chopped parsley.

LAMB AND CABBAGE

3 lbs. shoulder of lamb
1 small cabbage shredded coarsely
1 oz. fat
salt
pepper
parsley

Prepare and cook the meat as for lamb stew. Melt the fat, brown the meat in it. Set aside. Brown the cabbage. Arrange alternate layers of meat and cabbage in a casserole. Season each layer with salt and pepper. Add enough water to cover the contents of the casserole. Cover with a lid, cook slowly for 1 hour. Serve garnished with chopped parsley.

SHOULDER OF LAMB WITH DILL SAUCE

4 lbs. shoulder of lamb
1 tbsp. salt
4 sprigs dill

FOR THE SAUCE:
1 oz. butter
1 oz. flour
½ pint stock
1 tbsp. vinegar
1 dsp. sugar
2 tbsp. chopped dill
1 egg yolk

salt
pepper

Pour 3 pints boiling water over the lamb, simmer for 10 minutes and skim. Add the salt and the dill. Simmer in a covered pan for 2 hours. Leave to cool, skim off the fat, strain and use the liquid to make the sauce. Reheat the meat in a moderate oven and serve with the following sauce:
Cook the flour in the butter for 1 minute, gradually add the stock, vinegar, sugar and salt. Pour a little of the sauce over the beaten egg yolk, return to the pan and reheat carefully. Stir in the chopped dill.

BRAISED BEEF (Danish)

1 lb. rump steak
1 oz. butter
1 oz. flour
salt
4 peppercorns
½ bay leaf

Trim the steak, but leave in 1 piece. Sear in the butter, sprinkle with seasoned flour. Transfer to a shallow fireproof dish, add the peppercorns and bay leaf. Just cover with water, put a lid on the dish and cook in a moderate oven for 1 hour or longer if necessary.

SAILORS' STEW

3 lbs. stewing steak
2 ozs. flour
2 ozs. butter
6 medium potatoes, sliced
3 onions, sliced
¼ pint red wine (optional)
salt
pepper
parsley

Cut the meat into 1 inch cubes, roll in seasoned flour. Sear in the fat and set aside. Brown the potatoes in the fat and set aside. Do the same with the onions. Arrange alternate layers of potato, meat and onion in casserole; the first and last layers should be potato. Sprinkle each layer with salt and pepper. Rinse out the frying pan with the wine and ¼ pint water, pour into the casserole. Cover with a lid and cook slowly for 2 hours or longer. Garnish with chopped parsley.

BEEF A LA LINDSTROM

1¼ lbs. minced beef
1 medium potato, cooked and
    mashed
2 egg yolks
1 gill cream
2 pickled beetroot, finely sliced
1 small onion
2 tbsp. capers

salt
pepper
fat for frying

Mix the beef and the potato, add the egg yolks, cream, beetroot, onion and capers. Season with salt and pepper. Shape into flat cakes and fry quickly on both sides in hot fat.

ROYAL POT ROAST

4 lbs. topside
1 oz. butter
1 onion, sliced
4 anchovies
1 tbsp. vinegar
1 tbsp. whisky or brandy
1 tbsp. brown sugar
10 black peppercorns
salt
2 tbsp. double cream (optional)

Sear the meat on both sides in the butter. Fry the onions and anchovies until brown, transfer to a casserole just large enough to hold the meat, add all the other ingredients except the cream, and 2 pints water. Cover with a lid, cook slowly for 3 hours, turning the meat twice during cooking. Remove the meat to a dish and keep hot. Strain the gravy, return to the pan, reduce if necessary and stir in the cream.

PORK LOIN, POT ROASTED

pork loin (about 3 lbs.)
½ pint stock
8 ozs. prunes
1 tbsp. cream (optional)
1 glass wine

Get the butcher to bone the loin for you. Stuff the prunes (previously soaked if necessary) into the flesh on the underside, roll and tie with string. Brown on all sides in its own fat, pour off the fat, add the stock, simmer in a covered pan for 2 hours. Remove the meat and keep warm. Reduce the sauce by rapid simmering if it is too thin, stir in the wine and simmer for 2 to 3 minutes. Add the cream. Hand the sauce separately, serve with browned potatoes (see p. 346) and apple sauce.

PORK CHOP WITH PRUNES

2 lbs. loin chops ½ inch thick
½ lb. prunes
½ pint wine (red or white)
flour
salt
pepper
1 oz. butter
1 tsp. red currant jelly

Soak the prunes in the wine for 12 hours. Simmer them in the wine until tender. Bone and trim the meat. Season the flour with salt and pepper, dust the pork slices with it. Fry on both sides in the butter, until thoroughly cooked. Put on a dish and keep warm. Make the sauce as follows:

Cook the flour in the fat for 1 minute, strain the juice from the prunes into it. Cook until it thickens, add the red currant jelly and the cream. Season with salt and pepper. Arrange the prunes round the pork slices, strain the sauce over the meat. Serve with potato purée.

SAUSAGES WITH APPLE CAKE (Danish)

6 cooking apples
2 ozs. butter
2 ozs. caster sugar
wine vinegar
salt
pepper
8 rashers streaky bacon
8 chipolata sausages

Peel and core the apples and cut into rings ¼ inch thick. Melt ½ oz. butter and sprinkle in a dessertspoon of sugar and cover the pan with apple slices. Fry quickly on both sides until brown. Drain and arrange in a buttered sandwich tin with their edges slightly overlapping, season with vinegar, salt and pepper.

Fry the rest of the apple rings in the same way, and add them to those in the tin, seasoning each layer. Bake in a hot oven for 20 minutes. Turn out of the tin and surround with bacon rolls and fried sausages.

POT ROASTED VEAL

4 lbs. leg of veal
1 oz. butter
4 carrots, sliced
2 onions, sliced
¾ pint stock
salt
pepper

GRAVY:

1 oz. butter
1 oz. flour
1 gill cream

Sear the meat in the butter on all sides. Add the onions and carrots and cook them a little in the fat. Transfer to a casserole, pour in the stock, season with salt and pepper. Cover the dish and cook slowly for 2 hours. Strain the liquid and leave the meat to keep hot. Melt the butter, cook the flour in it for 1 minute, gradually add the stock and the cream. Adjust the seasoning. Hand the gravy separately and serve the meat with browned potatoes and cranberry sauce or red currant jelly.

VEAL WITH PINEAPPLE (Danish)

8 thin slices veal
¼ lb. mushrooms, sliced
1 oz. butter
salt
pepper
4 slices pineapple, halved
1 gill cream

Beat the veal and sprinkle with salt and pepper. Fry gently on both sides in the butter. Set aside to keep hot. Cook the mushrooms in the butter until tender, set them aside. Heat the pineapple slices in the butter. Arrange the veal on a serving dish with a piece of pineapple on each slice and mushrooms on top. Stir the cream into the juice in the pan, cook gently and pour over the dish.

BRAISED CALVES' LIVER

1 whole calf's liver (about 2 lbs.)
1 tsp. salt
2 ozs. butter
6 whole peppercorns
½ bay leaf
¾ pint stock

FOR THE FILLING:

2 ozs. butter
1½ ozs. flour
¼ pint cream

salt
pepper

Sprinkle the liver with salt. Fry quickly on all sides in the butter. Add the stock, peppercorns and bay leaf. Simmer with a lid on the pan for about 1 hour. Strain the liquid, cut the liver into thin slices and set aside to keep warm. Melt the butter, cook the flour in it for 1 minute, gradually add the stock and the cream. Season with salt and pepper and pour over the liver.

DILL SAUCE (for Fish)

1 oz. butter
1 oz. flour
½ pint fish stock or court-bouillon
1 tbsp. white wine vinegar
1 dsp. sugar
1 large tbsp. chopped dill or fennel
salt

pepper
1 egg yolk

Melt the butter, cook the flour in it for 1 minute, gradually add the strained fish stock. Stir in the vinegar, sugar and herbs, season with salt and pepper. Add a little sauce to the beaten egg yolk, return it to the pan. Reheat carefully, stirring all the time.

FISH SAUCE

2 ozs. butter
1½ ozs. flour
½ pint fish stock
¼ tsp. dry mustard

salt
pepper

Melt the butter, cook the flour in it for 1 minute, gradually add the hot stock. Season with the mustard, salt and pepper.

MUSHROOM SAUCE (for Fish)

¼ lb. mushrooms, sliced
2 ozs. butter
1½ oz. flour
½ pint fish stock

salt
pepper

Cook the mushrooms gently in the butter until tender. Stir in the flour and cook for 1 minute, add the fish stock gradually. Season with salt and pepper.

LOBSTER SAUCE

1 boiled lobster
2 ozs. butter
1½ ozs. flour
½ pint fish stock
¼ pint cream
salt
pepper

Melt the butter, cook the flour in it for 1 minute, gradually add the fish stock and the cream, stirring constantly. Cut the lobster into small pieces, add them to the sauce, simmer sufficiently to heat the lobster. Season with salt and pepper.

BEETROOT SAUCE

raw beetroots
sugar
wine vinegar
red currant jelly

Boil the beetroot until tender, peel and slice finely. Put a layer of beetroot in the bottom of a dish, sprinkle with sugar and vinegar. Repeat the layers until the dish is full. Pour melted redcurrant jelly over the top. Serve with cold meat.

LEMON SAUCE

2 ozs. butter
1½ ozs. flour
½ pint fish stock
¼ pint cream
salt
pepper

juice of ½ lemon
1 egg yolk

Melt the butter and cook the flour in it. Gradually add the fish stock and the cream. Simmer for 10 minutes. Add the lemon juice and seasoning. Stir a little sauce into the beaten egg yolk, return to the pan and reheat.

VANILLA SAUCE

½ pint milk
2 egg yolks
1 tbsp. sugar
vanilla
¼ pint double cream

Beat the egg yolks and sugar in a double saucepan, add the hot milk flavoured with vanilla, cook slowly, stirring all the time until mixture thickens. Allow to cool, fold in whipped cream.

GOOSEBERRY SOUFFLÉ (Scandinavian)

1 lb. gooseberries
4 ozs. sugar
grated peel of ½ lemon
1 dsp. cornflour
½ glass white wine
2 eggs

Cook the gooseberries with a little water, the lemon peel and the sugar until tender. Pass through a sieve. Mix the egg yolks with the cornflour and a little of the purée, add to the rest of the purée and cook slowly for 2 to 3 minutes, stirring all the time. Add the wine, beat the egg whites stiffly, fold into the mixture. Bake in a greased fireproof dish for 30 minutes in a slow oven. Serve with vanilla sauce (see above).

LEMON CREAM

8 ozs. sugar
1 glass white wine
juice and rind, grated, of 1 lemon
6 egg yolks

Mix all the ingredients together and cook slowly in the top of a double saucepan until the mixture thickens. Pour into a glass serving dish. Serve cold.

BONDE PIGE

2 ozs. brown breadcrumbs
1 oz. butter
3 ozs. sugar
1½ lbs. apples
raspberry jam
¼ pint cream

Mix the breadcrumbs with 1 oz. sugar, cook in the butter until crisp. Cook the apples with the sugar until very soft, beat to a purée. Fill a dish with alternate layers of crumbs, hot apple purée and raspberry jam, beginning and ending with a layer of crumbs. Serve cold, topped with whipped cream.

ROYAL BAKED APPLES

4 apples, peeled and cored
2 ozs. butter
2 ozs. breadcrumbs
2 ozs. sugar
1 oz. almonds, grated

Mix 1 oz. sugar with the breadcrumbs. Roll the apples in 1 oz. melted butter then in this mixture. Fill the hole with a smooth paste made of the almonds mixed with the other 1 oz. of sugar and a little water until very smooth. Dot with butter, bake in a moderate oven for 1 hour or until apples are soft. Serve cold with vanilla sauce (see p. 352) or whipped cream.

SWEDISH APPLE CAKE

8 ozs. rusk or biscuit crumbs
1 oz. butter
1½ lbs. apples, peeled and sliced
4 ozs. sugar
1 strip lemon peel

Fry the crumbs in the butter until slightly brown. Stew the apples with the lemon peel, sugar and a little water until very soft, beat to a pulp. Arrange alternate layers of crumbs and apple purée in a greased pie dish. Bake in a moderate oven for 30 minutes. Cool and turn out. Serve with vanilla sauce.

COLD APPLE CHARLOTTE

3—4 ozs. breadcrumbs
3—4 ozs. butter
2 lbs. apples
2 ozs. sugar

Melt the butter, stir the breadcrumbs about in it until just golden. Cook the apples with the sugar and a very little water until reduced to a pulp, beat to a purée. Fill a greased cake tin with alternate layers of crumbs and apple purée, beginning and ending with one of crumbs, dot with butter. Bake in a moderate oven for 30 minutes. Turn out when cold and serve with vanilla sauce (see p. 352).

DANISH RÖD GRÖD

This is made in the same way as Swedish Röd Gröd (see below) but an ounce or so of sago is used for thickening instead of cornflour, which gives it a more interesting texture.

SWEDISH RÖD GRÖD (Fruit Fool)

2½ lbs. mixed red currants, black
  currants and raspberries
8 ozs. sugar or to taste
2 tbsp. cornflour

Cook the prepared fruit with 2 pints water and the sugar until tender. Pass through a sieve. Mix a little purée with the cornflour, return to the pan with the rest of the purée and cook gently for 2—3 minutes. Pour into a glass dish, sprinkle with sugar to prevent skin forming and leave to cool. Serve with vanilla sauce (see p. 352) or whipped cream.

DANISH PEASANT GIRL WITH VEIL

2 ozs. brown breadcrumbs
2 ozs. butter
2 ozs. brown sugar
1½ lbs. apples
4 ozs. cooking chocolate, grated
¼ pint double cream

Mix the breadcrumbs and sugar. Fry them in the butter until crisp. Cook the apples with a little water until very soft. Fill a glass dish with alternate layers of crumbs and apple — the first and last should be crumbs — until nearly full. Sprinkle with chocolate. Serve cold, topped with whipped cream.

PRUNE PUDDING

½ lb. prunes
1 tsp. cinnamon or
½ a cinnamon stick
2 ozs. sugar
juice of 1 lemon
1 oz. cornflour

Soak the prunes with just enough water to cover. Simmer in the same water until tender. Remove from the water, stone the prunes, return the prunes to the water, simmer for 5 minutes with the sugar, lemon and cinnamon. Mix the cornflour with a little water. Add it to the prunes, stirring all the time. Cook very slowly for 5 minutes. Serve chilled, with whipped cream.

WALNUT PUDDING

4 ozs. flour
2 tsp. baking powder
½ tsp. salt
2 eggs
4 ozs. soft light brown sugar
small piece vanilla
4 ozs. chopped walnuts

1 large cooking apple peeled and
   chopped

Cream the butter and sugar, beat in the eggs and the flour sifted with the baking powder and salt. Stir in the vanilla, walnuts and apples. Pour into a greased tart tin, bake in a moderate oven for 40 minutes.

SWEDISH WAFFLES

4 ozs. flour
2 tsp. baking powder
2 eggs
½ pint sour cream
1 tbsp. melted butter

Sift the flour and baking powder, gradually add the egg yolks and the cream. Beat well. Fold in the stiffly beaten egg whites and the melted butter just before cooking. Bake in the usual way in a waffle iron.

SWEDISH PANCAKES

4 ozs. flour
1½ ozs. sugar
salt
3 eggs
½ pint milk
butter for frying

Sift the flour and sugar with a pinch of salt. Gradually add the beaten eggs and the milk. Leave to stand for at least 2 hours. Fry quickly in the usual way, roll and serve with any of the suggested sauces. Traditionally served on Thursday nights prior to Friday's fast.

NORWEGIAN WAFFLES

2 eggs
2 tbsp. sugar
4 ozs. flour
½ pint sour cream

Sift the sugar with the flour, add the beaten eggs. Gradually beat in the sour cream. Leave to stand for at least an hour. Bake in a waffle iron.

POLYNÉES

Follow the instructions for almond tarts but reserve a little of the cake dough. Cover the almond filling with strips of this dough in the shape of a cross.

ALMOND TARTS

4 ozs. butter
4 ozs. sugar
2 eggs
8 ozs. flour
¼ tsp. baking powder

FOR THE FILLING:
6 ozs. ground almonds
3 eggs
6 ozs. sugar

Cream the butter and sugar, beat in the eggs, gradually add the flour sifted with the baking powder. Grease bun tins and line with the mixture. Fill them with the following almond mixture: Blend the almonds with the sugar and the eggs until a smooth paste is formed. Bake in a moderate oven for 20 minutes.

DANISH PASTRY

½ oz. yeast
2 ozs. sugar
12 ozs. flour
1 tsp. salt
1 gill milk (room temperature)
7 ozs. butter (unsalted)

Cream the yeast with 1 teaspoon sugar. Sift the flour, the rest of the sugar and the salt together. Pour the milk into the yeast, add it to the flour, blend to an elastic dough. Roll out ½ inch thick on a floured board. Cut the butter into small pieces and spread onto the dough. Fold in 3, pinch the sides together and roll towards the pinched edges. Set aside for 15 minutes. Roll and fold in 3 and roll again as before. Set aside for 15 minutes. Repeat this process. Set aside for at least 1 hour in a cool place. Use for almond envelopes (see p. 357), or cut into fancy shapes, bake in a moderate oven, cover with thin glacé icing and chopped almonds.

ALMOND ENVELOPES

Danish Pastry (see p. 356)
4 ozs. ground almonds
4 ozs. sugar
1 egg

Blend the almonds with the sugar, work in the egg until a smooth paste is formed. Roll out the dough thinly and cut into 4 inch squares. Fill with 1 tbsp. of the mixture, fold in the corners to meet in the middle. Bake in a moderately hot oven until golden (about 20 minutes), cool and cover with glacé icing. The envelopes can also be filled with vanilla sauce (see p. 352).

LEMON COMBS

Danish pastry (see p. 356)
1 egg
Lemon filling (see p. 358)

Roll out ½ inch thick. Cut into rectangles 4 by 2 inches, spread with a spoonful of the filling, fold over and make 4 or 5 cuts in the pastry so that it will splay out when baked. Brush with beaten egg. Bake in a moderately hot oven until golden (about 20 minutes).

CHOCOLATE ALMOND CAKE (Danish)

3 ozs. butter
2 ozs. sugar
6 ozs. flour
3 eggs
1 dsp. baking powder
½ gill milk
4 ozs. cooking chocolate, chopped
2 ozs. almonds, chopped

Cream the butter and sugar until white, beat in alternately beaten egg yolks and flour sifted with baking powder. Add the milk, fold in the chocolate and the nuts. Fold in the stiffly beaten egg whites. Turn into a 6½ inch cake tin lined with greased greaseproof paper. Bake in a moderate oven for 1½ hours.

WALNUT MERINGUES

4 egg whites
8 ozs. sugar
4 ozs. chopped walnuts
½ pint double cream

Beat the egg whites stiffly, beat in 1 oz. sugar. Fold in the rest of the sugar and the walnuts. Arrange in small mounds on a greased baking sheet. Bake in a very slow oven for 4 hours. When cold seal together in pairs with whipped cream.

SAFFRON BREAD

1 oz. yeast
2 ozs. sugar
1 tsp. saffron
1 egg
egg, sugar, chopped almonds
    to garnish
2 lbs. flour
1 tsp. salt
4 ozs. raisins
2 ozs. almonds (optional)

Cream the yeast with 1 teaspoonful sugar. Dry the saffron in a cool oven and dissolve it in a little milk. Mix the sugar, 4 ozs. flour, egg and the milk. Gradually add the rest of the flour and the raisins. Knead, set aside in a warm place, covered, until it has doubled its size. Knead again. Shape into a plaited loaf or a wreath. Leave on a greased tin to rise for 1 hour. Brush with beaten egg, sprinkle with sugar and chopped nuts. Bake in a moderate oven for 45 minutes.

LEMON FILLING

2 eggs
juice and rind of 1 lemon
1 oz. flour
8 ozs. sugar

Stir the flour into the egg yolks beaten with the sugar. Add the lemon juice and grated lemon peel and cook in the top of a double saucepan, stirring all the time, until the mixture thickens. Cool and fold in the stiffly beaten egg whites.

SMÖRREBRÖD (1)

4 thick slices buttered bread
3 eggs
1 tbsp. milk
salt
pepper
1 oz. butter
4 anchovy fillets

Beat the eggs, add the milk, season with salt and pepper. Melt the butter and scramble the eggs slowly until just set. Stir in the chopped anchovy fillets. When cold, pile on to the bread and butter. This is typical of smörrebröd; meat, salad, eggs, cheese or fish can all be used to make open sandwiches.

SMÖRREBRÖD (2)

rye bread or Allinson's stone
    ground brown bread
butter
cold roast veal
cucumber

salt
pepper

Butter the bread and remove the crusts. Cover with slices of cold roast veal and top with thinly sliced cucumber sprinkled with salt and pepper.

FISH DUMPLINGS

6 ozs. uncooked fish fillet (fresh
   haddock, cod or bream)
1 oz. butter
¾ oz. flour
salt
pepper

Remove the skin and bones from the fish. Mince twice. Melt the butter and cook the flour in it for 1 minute, beat in the fish until smooth, season with salt and pepper. Poach in salted water for 10 minutes. Serve with fish soup or lobster sauce.

South America

PANAMA RADISH SALAD

3 bunches of radishes, sliced
½ tsp. salt
¼ tsp. black pepper
1 small onion finely chopped
1 tsp. chopped mint
1 large tomato, peeled and
   chopped finely

2 tbsp. lemon juice
2 tbsp. olive oil

Mix the oil, lemon juice, salt and pepper well together. Mix all the vegetables together and pour the dressing over.

ARGENTINE VERMICELLI SOUP

2 ozs. vermicelli
3 ozs. butter or dripping
1 lb. tomatoes, peeled and sliced
1 large onion, minced
1½ tbsp. parsley, chopped
2 pints chicken stock
1½ ozs. grated cheese
a pinch of saffron
a pinch of chilli powder
salt, pepper

Heat the butter in a stewpan, fry the onions and parsley for 3 minutes, add vermicelli and fry for 2 minutes, till light brown; be careful not to burn it. Add the tomatoes and saffron, cook gently for 5 minutes. Pour on the stock, bring to the boil and simmer till the vermicelli is tender. Add the chilli powder, salt and pepper to taste. Sprinkle with the cheese and serve.

COLOMBIAN CUCHUCO (Barley Soup)

1 lb. soup bones
4 pints water
1 bay leaf
3 peppercorns
1 large onion, chopped
1 lb. barley
water to cover
8 ozs. fresh green peas
8 ozs. cabbage, finely chopped
2 tsp. salt
½ tsp. pepper

Place the bones in the 4 pints water, add the onion, bay leaf and peppercorns. Simmer in a covered pot for 2 hours. Wash the barley and place in another pot, cover with water, bring to the boil, strain, recover with water and cook for 3 minutes. Strain and add to the strained bone stock when cooked. Bring to the boil, add the vegetables and seasonings and simmer gently until the soup thickens and the barley is cooked.

BOLIVIAN STUFFED AVOCADOS

6 avocado pears
4 ozs. cooked chicken, shrimps or fish, finely chopped
1 medium lettuce
¼ pint mayonnaise sauce (see p. 159)

1 hardboiled egg, sliced
salt, pepper to taste

Cut the avocados in half and remove the large seed. Mix the lettuce and meat with the mayonnaise, season to taste. Pile on the avocados and garnish with the egg.

SALVADOR SPANISH HADDOCK

1 3-lb. fresh haddock
1 tsp. salt
½ tsp. pepper
1 clove of garlic, crushed
3 tbsp. lemon juice
3 large onions sliced
1½ lbs. tomatoes, peeled and sliced
2 tbsp. chopped parsley
¼ pint olive oil

Rub an oval casserole (with a lid) with oil, put the fish in and rub in the garlic, salt, pepper and one-third lemon juice. Leave for 15 minutes. Cover the fish with layers of onions, tomatoes and parsley. Pour over the oil and two-thirds lemon juice. Cover the dish and bake in moderate oven for 30 minutes, basting from time to time. Take the lid off and cook for 20 minutes more till done — basting frequently.

PUCHERO (National dish of Argentina)

2 lbs. beef cut in pieces 2 × 3 inches
1 boiling fowl, jointed
1 calve's foot, split in 4
boiling water
1½ tsp. salt
4 carrots
4 sweet potatoes
2 tomatoes
4 cobs of sweet corn
4 potatoes
2 onions

4 pieces of pumpkin each 3 inches square
4 ozs. bacon, cut in 1 inch squares
8 slices liver sausage

This is a substantial dish for several people, 6 or 8.

Take a large pot and half fill it with boiling salted water. Put in the beef, fowl and calve's foot, bring to the boil and skim. Simmer for 1½ hours. Now add everything else, add more water if necessary and simmer till the vegetables are tender. Serve in 3 dishes—one for the meat, one for the vegetables and one for the soup.

CHILLI CON CARNE

1 lb. beef, cut in ½ inch cubes
3 cloves of garlic, finely chopped
2 tbsp. chilli powder
1 medium onion, finely chopped
½ tsp. salt
1½ ozs. lard
2 ozs. flour

pinch of marjoram
hot water

Heat the lard in a saucepan, fry the garlic till brown. Add the meat, rubbed in the flour, salt and chilli powder, fry for 2 minutes. Cover with hot water, stir well, add onion and marjoram. Cover and simmer very gently for 1 hour, or until the meat is tender and the sauce thickened.

ARGENTINE CARBONADO

1½ lbs. minced beef
2 ozs. butter
4 medium onions, sliced
1 large tomato peeled and sliced
1 tsp. salt
¼ tsp. pepper
¼ pint meat stock
2 pears peeled and sliced
2 peaches peeled and sliced
4 plums peeled and sliced

4 medium potatoes, cut in ½ inch
  dice
2 ozs. raisins, seedless

Heat the butter in a casserole, fry the onions till brown, add the tomato, fry for 2 minutes. Add the minced beef, stir well and brown for 2 minutes. Add salt, pepper and stock, cover and cook very gently for 1 hour. Now add the fruit and the potatoes and cook again till tender. Just before serving add the raisins.

COSTA RICAN CASSEROLE OF GUINEA FOWL

1 4-lb. guinea fowl
4 rashers of fat bacon, chopped
2 ozs. flour
1 tsp. salt
1 tsp. paprika pepper
1 large onion, chopped

½ pint boiling water
½ pint red wine

Have the bird cut in joints. Chop the liver. Fry the bacon slowly in the casserole, add the pieces of bird and brown. Add the flour, stir well, add everything else. Cover tightly and simmer very gently for 2 hours or until the bird is tender.

ARGENTINE EMPANDAS (Fruit and Meat Turnovers)

FILLING:

1 large pear
2 large peaches } chopped fine
1 tbsp. chives
2 ozs. butter
1 large onion, chopped fine
2 large tomatoes, peeled and
 chopped
1 large green pepper, seeded and
 chopped fine
12 ozs. raw minced meat
2 tbsp. sugar
½ tsp. salt
⅛ pint dry white wine

CRUST:

8 ozs. flour
pinch of salt
2 tsp. cinnamon
6 ozs. butter

2 egg yolks, beaten
4 tbsp. dry white wine
2 tbsp. milk
2 ozs. sugar

Make the filling first. Heat the butter in a large saucepan and fry the onion till transparent. Add the tomatoes, stir well and simmer gently for 5 minutes. Then add everything else, stir well, cover and cook gently for 15 minutes. Leave to cool.

For the crust, sieve the flour and salt, add a pinch of cinnamon and 1½ tsp. sugar. Add the butter and mix till the mixture looks like breadcrumbs. Mix half the egg yolk with the wine, add, then add the milk gradually till a soft dough is formed. Roll and cut into rounds the size of a saucer. Put an equal amount of filling on each, moisten the edges and turn the pastry over to form half circles. Seal well. Brush the tops with egg, sprinkle 2 ozs. sugar and the rest of the cinnamon. Bake in a hot oven for 15 minutes.

VENEZUELA HALLACAS (Meat Pies)

FILLING:

1 large onion, sliced
2 ozs. suet or dripping
1 red or green pepper, seeded and
 finely chopped
8 ozs. raw beef or veal, minced
2 ozs. seedless raisins
2 ozs. stoned green olives
2 hardboiled eggs, chopped
salt, pepper

CRUST:

4 ozs. flour
2 ozs. lard
2 ozs. butter

2 small eggs
pinch of salt

Make the pastry in the usual way. Roll out to the thickness of a penny or thinner and cut into 8 saucer-sized rounds.

For the filling, heat the suet and fry the onion till brown, add the chopped pepper, salt and pepper, fry for 2 minutes. Now add the meat, raisins, olives, chopped eggs. Cook for 4 minutes, gently. Leave to cool.

Put an equal amount of the filling on each round, moisten the edge and put another round of pastry on top. Seal tightly. Bake in a hot oven for 15 minutes.

BRAZILIAN UNCOOKED SAUCE FOR FRIED FISH

1 tsp. cummin seed
3 cloves of garlic, finely chopped
1 tsp. chopped parsley
a pinch of saffron
½ tsp. salt
¼ tsp. black pepper
¼ pint vinegar

4 tbsp. water
2 tbsp. tomato sauce (optional)

Pound the cummin seed to a powder, add and pound the garlic, add the other ingredients, stir well.

While the fried fish is still hot, turn for a few seconds in the sauce. Pour the rest of the sauce over the hot fish on the serving dish.

CABBAGE WITH CAPERS

2 ozs. dripping
2 cloves of garlic, chopped
1 large onion, chopped
1 clove
1½ lbs. shredded cabbage
3 ozs. cooked ham, chopped
2 tbsp. capers
1 tbsp. vinegar
1 tsp. salt
½ tsp. pepper

2 large tomatoes, peeled and
    chopped finely
2 ozs. breadcrumbs

Heat the dripping in a stewpan, add onion and clove, and garlic, fry for 3 minutes. Add cabbage, stir, cover the pan, cook for 3 minutes. Add ham, capers, vinegar, salt and pepper and tomatoes. Stir well, sprinkle the breadcrumbs over, cover the pan and cook gently for 20 minutes, or until the cabbage is tender. A little stock or water may be added if the mixture becomes too dry and apt to burn.

Spain

STUFFED COOKING APPLES

4 large cooking apples
2 small potatoes
2 sticks celery
2 egg yolks
chervil
parsley
1 tsp. wine vinegar
2 tbsp. lemon juice
salt
pepper

Wash the potatoes and cook them in their skins. Peel them. Core and halve the apples. Remove as much of the flesh as possible without damaging the skins. Chop the apple flesh, chop the potatoes and mix them together with the beaten egg yolks, the chopped herbs, chopped celery and the lemon juice. Season with salt and pepper. Fill the apple halves with the mixture.

DRIED SALT COD WITH RICE

½ lb. dried salt cod
½ lb. Patna rice
2 tomatoes
1 onion
2 tbsp. olive oil
salt
pepper

Prepare the fish as for dried salt cod salad (see below). Fry lightly in olive oil. Set the fish aside and fry the sliced and peeled tomato and the sliced onion in the same pan. Remove them from the pan. Pour in the rice, stir it around in the fat, add 1 pint boiling salted water and simmer until water is absorbed and the rice is cooked. Mix the fish, tomato and onion with the rice. Season with salt and pepper. Serve very cold.

DRIED SALT COD SALAD

½ lb. dried salt cod
6 anchovy fillets
12 black olives
1 onion
1 green pepper
1 hardboiled egg
2 tbsp. olive oil
1 tbsp. vinegar
salt

pepper
lettuce

Soak the fish for 12 hours. Simmer it in water until soft. Remove the skin and break into fairly small pieces. Slice the onion finely, slice the pepper. Mix the fish with the onion, pepper, anchovy fillets and olives. Dress with the olive oil and vinegar, season with salt and pepper. Arrange on the lettuce leaves and garnish with hardboiled egg cut lengthwise.

CUCUMBER SOUP, ICED

2 cucumbers
½ onion
1 dsp. lemon juice
salt
pepper
mint

½ pint prawns
½ pint aspic jelly (see p. 56)

Grate the cucumbers. Mix them with grated onion, the lemon juice and finely chopped mint. Season with salt and pepper. Melt the aspic jelly. Stir it into the cucumber mixture. Serve chilled, garnished with prawns.

SHELLFISH SOUP

1 lb. onions, sliced
2 lbs. tomatoes, peeled and
   chopped
2 tbsp. olive oil
1 clove garlic
parsley
marjoram
thyme
1 large cupful prawns or mussels
¼ lb. vermicelli

salt
pepper

Cook the fish in 2 pints boiling water. Drain and reserve the water. Heat the olive oil, fry the onions in it until soft. Add the tomatoes, crushed garlic, herbs, salt and pepper; simmer until tomatoes are cooked. Pour in the water in which the fish was cooked, simmer for 15 minutes. Sieve, reheat and add the vermicelli broken into small pieces and the fish. Serve sprinkled with parsley.

SHRIMP SOUP

1 pint shrimps
3 onions
1 tomato
1 oz. flour
2 ozs. butter
1 glass white wine
salt
pepper
parsley

If fresh shrimps are used, boil them and keep the water. Take off the heads and tails. Pound the heads with 1 oz. butter. Slice the onions and cook them slowly in the rest of the butter until golden. Stir in the flour and cook for 1 minute. Add the cooking water, if available, the shrimps, the peeled and chopped tomatoes and the wine. Simmer for 5 minutes. Add the shrimp heads, pass the soup through a sieve. Season with salt and pepper, serve sprinkled with chopped parsley.

TOMATO SOUP

2 pints chicken stock
2 tbsp. concentrated tomato purée
vermicelli
parsley

Bring the stock to the boil, add the tomato purée. Add the vermicelli broken into small pieces and simmer for 15 minutes. Serve garnished with chopped parsley.

TOMATO SOUP ICED

2 lbs. tomatoes
2 onions
salt
pepper
sugar
½ glass red wine
2 cloves garlic
1 tbsp. paprika
2 tbsp. olive oil

1 cucumber
12 black olives
parsley

Mince the tomatoes and onions, season with salt, pepper and sugar, stir in the wine. Crush the garlic, mix it with the paprika, add the olive oil gradually, beating all the time. Mix this with the tomatoes. Chop the cucumber, stone the olives and add them to the mixture. Serve chilled, sprinkled with parsley.

VEGETABLE SOUP

2 pints chicken or veal stock
2 potatoes
2 turnips
¼ lb. haricot beans
½ cabbage
2 sticks celery
2 ozs. vermicelli
2 ozs. rice
salt

pepper
1 tsp. saffron

Soak the haricot beans overnight and boil them until they are soft. Chop the turnips, potatoes and celery, shred the cabbage. Bring the stock to the boil, put in all the vegetables and simmer until they are almost cooked. Add the vermicelli, rice and saffron. Season with salt and pepper. Simmer for another 20 minutes.

WATERCRESS SOU.

1 pint stock
1 bunch watercress
3 potatoes
¼ pint milk
3 egg yolks
2 ozs. grated cheese
salt
pepper

Cut the potatoes into very small pieces, boil them quickly in the stock. Sieve and season with salt and pepper. Chop the watercress and add it to the soup and reheat. Beat the egg yolks with warm milk, pour a little of this mixture into warmed soup bowls, stir the soup directly into the bowls. Serve with grated cheese.

BREAM, BAKED

2 lb. bream fillets
2 Spanish onions, sliced
2 tbsp. olive oil
1 lemon
salt
pepper
2 tbsp. breadcrumbs

Make diagonal incisions in the fish fillets and insert a piece of lemon into each. Put 1 tbsp. of olive oil into a shallow fireproof dish, lay the sliced onions on the bottom, put the fish on top of these, cover with breadcrumbs, sprinkle with salt and pepper. Pour 1 tbsp. olive oil over the top. Bake in a hot oven for 40 minutes.

COD A LA PORTUGAISE

2 lbs. cod on the bone
2 onions chopped
1½ lbs. tomatoes peeled and
   chopped
¼ lb. rice
1 glass white wine
2 tbsp. olive oil
1 oz. butter
1 clove garlic
parsley
salt
pepper

Cut the fish into 4 thick slices. Fry the onion in the butter until golden. Heat the olive oil in a fireproof dish, lay the cod on the bottom of the dish, cover it with the onion and tomato and chopped garlic. Surround the fish with the cooked rice, season with salt and pepper and finely chopped parsley. Cover the dish and cook in a moderate oven for 30—40 minutes.

FISH WITH RICE

1 lb. fish (halibut or turbot are
   best but bream will do well)
1 lb. tomatoes
1 stick celery
1 carrot
1 large onion
1 piece of fennel (optional)
basil
thyme
garlic
parsley
salt
pepper
oil for frying

Cut the fish into smallish pieces. Boil the head and bones with the celery, carrot, onion and herbs to make fish stock. Melt the oil, fry the fish in it until golden. Pour off most of the olive oil, put the fish in a fireproof dish in a slow oven with the chopped garlic, the parsley and a little olive oil. Chop the tomatoes and cook them in the pan for a few minutes. Add them to the fish, continue to cook slowly until the fish is tender. Put the rice in the pan, strain 1 pint hot fish stock over it, cook fairly fast until the rice is cooked and the stock absorbed. Arrange the rice in the middle of a dish with the fish and tomatoes round it.

FRESH HADDOCK, BAKED

1 lb. fresh haddock fillet
1 tbsp. concentrated tomato purée
1 clove garlic
½ glass white wine
parsley
breadcrumbs
1 tbsp. olive oil

Cut the haddock into slices about 1 inch wide. Put the oil into a fireproof dish, arrange the fish pieces on it. Chop the garlic and sprinkle over the fish, pour the tomato purée over it, cover with breadcrumbs and bake in a moderate oven for 30 minutes. Serve chopped parsley separately.

HAKE, FRIED, WITH TOMATO SAUCE

2 lbs. hake fillet
flour
salt
pepper
olive oil for frying

parsley
marjoram
salt
pepper
1 tbsp. olive oil

FOR THE SAUCE:
1 sliced onion
1 clove garlic
1 pimento
1 lb. tomatoes peeled and
    quartered
½ bay leaf
2 glasses white wine

FOR THE SAUCE:
Fry the onion in the olive oil until tender, add the tomatoes, the crushed garlic, the pimento and the flavourings. Simmer gently, add the white wine, continue simmering for 20 minutes, adding water if necessary. Pass through a sieve.

Cut the fish into pieces about 2 inches wide, roll in seasoned flour. Fry in very hot oil. Serve with slices of lemon and the sauce handed separately.

RED MULLET, COLD

½ pint olive oil
2 tbsp. tarragon vinegar
1 carrot chopped
1 onion chopped
1 green pepper, seeded and
    chopped
½ bay leaf

1 sprig parsley
2 red mullet
oil for frying

Dip the fish quickly in very hot olive oil. Make a marinade of the oil, vinegar, vegetables and herbs, simmer the fish in it for 15 minutes. Leave the fish in the marinade for 24 hours. Serve as it is.

SHRIMP ESPAGNOL

1 pint shrimps
2 ozs. butter
1 onion
½ lb. rice
1 tbsp. concentrated tomato purée
½ pint double cream

salt
pepper

Fry the chopped onion in the butter until golden. Boil the rice in salted water. Drain and mix it with the onions, add the tomato purée, the prepared shrimps and the cream, season with salt and pepper. Bake in a moderate oven for 30 minutes.

TROUT

4 small trout
1 onion sliced
1 clove garlic
parsley
1 oz. butter
1 tbsp. olive oil
1 dsp. wine vinegar
salt
lemon

Crush the garlic with a little salt, mix it with the well-chopped parsley and ½ oz. butter, add the vinegar and ¼ pint of water. Fillet the trout and fry quickly on both sides in butter. Put the fish into the sauce. Fry the onions in olive oil until golden, add them to the sauce and simmer for 5 minutes. Serve the sauce strained over the fish and garnish with lemon.

EGGS WITH SPINACH

4 eggs
½ red pepper, chopped
1 green pepper, chopped
2 ozs. chopped ham or bacon
1 tbsp. olive oil
salt
pepper
1 lb. cooked spinach

chives
parsley

Beat the eggs with a fork, add the peppers, ham and salt and pepper. Melt the olive oil in a frying pan, pour in the egg mixture, cook slowly, stirring fairly often until the mixture becomes like slightly cooked scrambled egg. Pour the mixture onto the spinach, brown under the grill. Garnish with chopped chives and parsley. Serve very hot with thin toast.

HAM AND LENTILS

½ lb. lentils
¼ lb. diced cooked ham
2 onions
2 tomatoes
1 clove garlic
2 tbsp. olive oil
salt
pepper

Soak the lentils overnight. Cook in boiling water until tender. Slice the onions and fry in the olive oil until golden, add the tomatoes, peeled and chopped, the ham and the chopped garlic. Cook slowly until the tomatoes are soft. Stir in the lentils, simmer for 5 minutes. Season with salt and pepper. Serve very hot.

PAELLA (1)

½ lb. rice
2 scallops
¼ lb. pork fillet
6 scampi
¼ lb. cooked chicken
½ lb. peas
½ lb. French beans
6 mussels
½ tin sweet red peppers
2 tomatoes peeled and quartered
1 onion chopped
2 cloves garlic chopped
bouquet garni
1 tsp. saffron
cayenne pepper
2 pints stock

salt
pepper
2 tbsp. olive oil

This is best made in a deep pan which can be used for frying and also go in the oven. Failing this, the ingredients can be transferred from a frying pan to a casserole.

Cook the peas and beans and heat the red peppers; keep them hot. Melt the olive oil, brown the diced chicken and pork in it. Add the sliced scallops, the onions and the garlic. Fry until the onions are golden, add the tomatoes, the rice, the *bouquet garni*, the saffron and the stock. Simmer for 10 minutes. Arrange the scampi and the mussels on top. Cook in a hot oven for 10 minutes. Add the peppers, peas and beans and serve directly from the cooking pot.

PAELLA (2)

1 small roasting chicken cut into pieces
¼ lb. bacon diced
2 tbsp. olive oil
1 clove garlic
1 tomato, peeled and quartered
1 tsp. paprika
½ lb. peas
½ lb. French beans
¾ lb. rice

8 crayfish
12 scampi
1 tsp. saffron

Fry the chicken and the bacon in the oil for 5 minutes. Add the tomato, garlic, beans, peas, paprika and rice. Stir the rice into the fat, pour in 2 pints water, add the saffron when the water comes to the boil. Simmer for 5 minutes, add the shellfish and cook for another 5 minutes, or until the rice is cooked.

PIGS' LIVER TERRINE

1 lb. pigs' liver
3 tbsp. olive oil
4 onions
1 sprig mint
parsley
2 red peppers
1 clove
nutmeg
saffron
cinnamon

black pepper
2 ozs. breadcrumbs

Chop the liver very fine and blanch in salted water. Chop the onions and the peppers and fry them in the olive oil until soft, add the chopped mint, parsley, the clove, a pinch each of nutmeg, cinnamon, and saffron and a sprinkling of freshly ground black pepper. Stir in the liver. Simmer for 3 minutes. Mix in the breadcrumbs. Pour into a flat dish. Serve chilled.

PIPERADE

1 green pepper
1 small onion
1 clove garlic
½ lb. tomatoes
1 tbsp. olive oil
4 eggs
salt
pepper

Remove the seeds from the pepper and slice it finely. Slice the onion. Cook the onion and the pepper in the olive oil with the crushed garlic until the onion is transparent. Peel and chop the tomatoes. Add them to the onion mixture and simmer for 5 minutes, break in the eggs and cook them slowly, stirring continually. Season with salt and pepper. Serve very hot with dry toast.

PORK WITH BAKED EGGS

¼ lb. fillet pork
2 ozs. ham
½ lb. tomatoes peeled and chopped
1 onion, sliced
1 oz. flour
2 ozs. butter
¼ pint stock
salt

pepper
4 eggs

Cut the ham and pork into thin strips. Cook them and the onion in the butter until golden, add the tomatoes. Stir in the flour, cook for 1 minute, add the stock. Simmer for 20 minutes. Season with salt and pepper. Turn into a flat fireproof dish, break the eggs into the pork mixture and bake in a moderate oven until the egg is set.

PORK WITH SCRAMBLED EGGS

½ lb. pork
2 onions
4 tomatoes
½ small marrow
1 green pepper
1 tbsp. olive oil
¼ pint stock
salt

pepper
scrambled eggs

Melt the olive oil, fry the sliced onions and the pork cut into small pieces in it. Add the marrow cut into 1 inch cubes, the peeled and chopped tomatoes and the sliced green pepper. Pour in ¼ pint stock and simmer for 40 minutes. Season with salt and pepper. Serve with scrambled eggs.

SAUSAGES WITH HARICOT BEANS

1 lb. sausages
½ lb. haricot beans
1 onion sliced
1 clove garlic
1 oz. butter
salt
pepper

Soak the beans overnight, cook in salted water until tender; drain. Fry the sausages in the butter, put aside to keep warm. Fry the onion until golden, add the beans and stir about until well mixed with the onion and fat. Season with pepper and garlic crushed with salt. Serve surrounded by sausages.

SAUSAGES WITH LENTILS

¼ lb. lentils
½ lb. small pork sausages
1 onion
4 tomatoes
1 clove garlic
1 tbsp. olive oil
salt
pepper

Boil the lentils in salted water; when cooked, drain and put in a frying pan with the olive oil, sliced onion, peeled and chopped tomatoes and crushed garlic. Cook slowly for ½ an hour. Season with salt and pepper. Serve with fried sausages.

SPANISH OMELETTE

4 eggs
1 small onion, chopped
1 tbsp. cooked peas
1 tbsp. cooked French beans, chopped
1 tbsp. cooked carrot, chopped
1 medium cooked potato, diced
parsley
salt
pepper
½ tbsp. olive oil

Beat the eggs lightly, add the vegetables, salt and pepper. Melt the olive oil in a frying pan, pour in the egg mixture, cook quickly for 3 minutes. Cook for another minute under a hot grill.

SPANISH POACHED EGG

4 eggs
1 gill chicken stock
1 gill milk
1 oz. butter
1 oz. flour
1 egg yolk
salt
pepper
nutmeg
2 ozs. grated Gruyère cheese
ratatouille (see p. 156)

Make the ratatouille (see p. 156) and keep it hot in a fireproof dish in a slow oven. Melt the butter, stir in the flour and cook for 1 minute; gradually add the stock and the milk. Allow to simmer for several minutes. Season with salt and pepper and nutmeg. Stir in the egg yolk. Poach the eggs, drain and arrange on top of the ratatouille. Pour a little sauce on top of each egg, sprinkle with grated cheese. Brown under a hot grill.

BRAISED BEEF

3 lbs. topside
¼ lb. bacon rashers
¼ lb. fat bacon
4 onions
¼ lb. mushrooms
4 tomatoes
1 glass red wine
2 carrots, sliced
1 clove garlic
parsley
thyme
basil
½ bay leaf
mace
salt
pepper

½ lb. runner beans
4 medium potatoes
½ lb. sausages

Line a casserole with bacon rashers. Put in the beef, covered with the fat bacon. Add the chopped garlic, sliced onions, carrots, a parsley stalk, a little mace, salt and pepper. Fry until the meat is sealed, add the peeled and quartered tomatoes and the wine. Cover with hot water and cook in a moderate oven, with a lid on the pan, for 2 hours. While the meat is cooking, cook the beans and potatoes. Fry the sliced mushrooms in the butter, add the sausages and fry them too. Put in the beans and the potatoes. Arrange the meat on a serving dish, with the vegetables and sausages round it. Serve the strained gravy separately.

RAGOUT OF BEEF

1 lb. stewing steak
¼ lb. pork or ham, diced
1 chopped onion
1 lettuce
1 lb. peas
½ lb. runner beans
½ small marrow, cubed
8 small new potatoes
2 ozs. lard

2 tbsp. concentrated tomato purée
1 glass white wine

Fry the meat quickly on both sides in 1 oz. fat. Add ½ pint water and salt and pepper. Cook slowly for 1 hour. Serve with the following ragout: sauté all the vegetables in 1 oz. fat, add the tomato purée and white wine, simmer until all the vegetables are tender (about 40 minutes).

CHICKEN WITH PEAS

1 boiling chicken
1 onion, chopped
1 glass white wine
2 ozs. flour
2 ozs. lard
1 pint stock
1 tsp. saffron
nutmeg
parsley

salt
pepper
2 lbs. peas

Joint the chicken. Fry in the lard with the onion; when golden, stir in the flour, add the stock and the wine. Season with salt and pepper. Add the parsley. Simmer until tender. Flavour with the saffron and a little nutmeg. Arrange the chicken pieces on a dish, strain the sauce over them and surround with peas.

CHICKEN WITH RICE

2 spring chickens
2 ozs. butter
2 onions
¼ lb. lean bacon
½ lb. tomatoes, peeled
2 green peppers
½ lb. cooked peas
1 pimento
parsley
olive oil
salt
pepper

Joint the chickens. Fry in the butter until golden. Slice the onion and fry in the oil until transparent. Cut the bacon into small pieces and slice the tomato, fry them in the olive oil. Add the onion, bacon and tomato to the chicken. Pour in the rice, mix it well with the other ingredients. Pour in the stock, simmer until the rice is cooked and the stock is absorbed. Season with salt and pepper. Slice the peppers and the pimento. Fry them and the peas in a little olive oil. Arrange the chicken and rice on a hot dish, garnish with the fried vegetables and sprinkle with parsley.

BRAISED LAMB

1 small leg lamb (about 3½ lbs.)
2 pimentos
1 clove garlic
1 glass white wine
2 ozs. butter
rosemary
parsley
pepper
salt

Put the lamb in a casserole with the butter and rosemary. Season with salt and pepper. Cover and cook in a moderate oven until tender (about 2½ hours). Serve with the following sauce:

Fry the chopped pimentos, garlic and parsley in a little butter, add the sauce from the casserole and simmer for 10 minutes. Remove the rosemary and pour the sauce over the meat.

LAMB WITH GARLIC AND TOMATO

1 thick slice leg of lamb
6 cloves garlic
1 oz. flour
1 oz. lard
1 tbsp. concentrated tomato purée
½ pint stock

salt
pepper

Put the meat in a roasting pan with the lard, put the garlic round it. Fry the meat on both sides, put in the flour, the tomato purée and the stock. Cook, covered with a lid, in a moderate oven until the meat is tender.

LAMB CUTLETS WITH TOMATOES AND SAUSAGES

4 lamb cutlets
8 chipolata sausages
1 slice gammon, diced
1 onion, chopped
1 lb. tomatoes
lard
olive oil
salt
pepper

Fry the cutlets in a mixture of lard and olive oil. Season with salt and pepper and put in a casserole. Fry the onion and the gammon in the fat left by the chops. Add the peeled and quartered tomatoes and simmer for 10 minutes. Pour this over the cutlets and reheat in the oven. Serve with sausages fried separately.

LAMB KIDNEYS WITH WHITE WINE

4 lamb kidneys
1 small onion
1 lb. peas
½ lb. button mushrooms
4 slices bacon
¼ pint white wine
parsley
salt
pepper

1 oz. butter
espagnole sauce

Skin the kidneys and remove the core. Cut into thin slices. Melt the butter; when hot, put in the kidneys, finely chopped onion and parsley, and the white wine. Season with salt and pepper. Cook fairly fast for 3 minutes. Add the espagnole sauce, the cooked mushrooms and cooked peas. Simmer for another 10 minutes. Serve with the sauce strained over the kidneys and garnish with fried bacon.

TURKEY

1 turkey

FOR THE STUFFING:
½ lb. pork sausages
½ lb. prunes
½ lb. dried peaches
1 lb. chestnuts
½ lb. ham, diced
¼ lb. mushrooms
1 glass sherry
thyme
marjoram
basil
parsley
salt
pepper

1 oz. lard
¼ lb. melted butter
¼ pint stock
1 glass white wine

MAKE THE STUFFING AS FOLLOWS:
Brown the ham and the turkey liver cut into small cubes in the lard. Add the sausages, the stoned prunes, the peaches, the chestnuts (previously shelled, boiled and roughly chopped), the slices of mushroom and the herbs in a muslin bag. Cook for 10 minutes. Remove the herbs and chop all the ingredients fairly finely, mix with the sherry and stuff the bird. Brush the turkey with melted butter, roast in a hot oven and baste frequently with the stock and wine.

LIVER WITH BRANDY

1½ lbs. calves' liver
½ lb. rice
½ lb. mushrooms
2 tomatoes
2 ozs. butter
1 tbsp. brandy
salt
pepper

Cook the rice, keep it warm. Melt ½ oz. butter, fry the quartered tomatoes gently in it. Simmer the mushrooms in water for 5 minutes. Chop them and fry them with the liver cut into small squares, in a little butter. Season with salt and pepper. Arrange the tomatoes around the rice. Make a hollow on the top of the rice, put the mushrooms and liver into it. Pour warmed brandy over the liver, set light to it and serve immediately.

BRAISED PORK

2 lbs. loin of pork
1 clove garlic
2 onions
2 tomatoes
1 egg plant
1 pimento
2 ozs. butter
¼ pint stock
1 glass red wine
sauté potatoes

Rub the pork with the cut clove of garlic. Melt the butter in a casserole, put in the pork and cook in a hot oven until it begins to brown. Add the sliced onions, peeled and quartered tomatoes, sliced egg plant, and sliced pimento. Pour in the wine and cook for a few minutes, add the stock. Cover the pan and cook in a moderate oven for 2½ hours. Season with salt and pepper. Serve with sauté potatoes.

ROAST VEAL

a joint of roasting veal
½ pint white wine
1 clove garlic
salt
pepper
2 ozs. butter

Marinate the meat in the wine, with the cut clove of garlic and salt and pepper for 4—5 hours. Brush with melted butter and roast in a hot oven, basting frequently with the wine, allowing 25 minutes cooking time per lb. of meat.

CHOCOLATE CREAMS

8 ozs. sugar
¼ pint water
6 egg yolks
¼ lb. plain chocolate

Melt the sugar in the water, boil it to a thick syrup. Cool and add to the beaten egg yolks. Pour into small greased fireproof dishes, bake in a slow oven until set (about 45 minutes). Cool the dishes and pour the melted chocolate over the creams. Serve chilled.

CHESTNUT CAKES

3 eggs
4 ozs. sugar
3 ozs. flour
3 ozs. butter
¼ lb. almonds
½ oz. butter
½ lb. chestnut purée (see below)
2 tbsp. apricot jam

Beat the eggs and the sugar together over a pan of hot water until they are white, add the sifted flour. Melt the butter and fold it into the mixture. Bake in a greased Swiss Roll tin in a moderately hot oven for 25 minutes. Put on a rack and when cool cut into rounds with a pastry cutter. Chop the almonds, put in a frying pan with ½ oz. butter, stir them about over a low flame until browned. Spread the jam over the sponge cake rounds, cover with chopped almonds. Pipe chestnut purée onto the top.

CHESTNUT PURÉE

½ lb. chestnuts
3 ozs. sugar
4 tbsp. water

Score the chestnuts and put in a hot oven for 10 minutes. The shells should have become brittle and easy to peel. Put the shelled chestnuts in boiling water and simmer until tender (about 30 minutes). Sieve and mix with a syrup made by boiling the sugar with the water, until a drop sets instantly when put into cold water.

COCONUT CREAM

1 coconut
¼ lb. sugar
4 egg yolks
4 sponge cakes

Drain the milk from the coconut. Grate the coconut flesh. Cook the milk and the grated coconut in a double saucepan for 30 minutes. Strain through fine muslin. Beat the egg yolks until thick, whisk in the strained coconut. Cook in a double saucepan until the mixture thickens. Pour over the sponge cakes and leave to cool.

COFFEE CREAM

½ oz. gelatine
3 eggs
1 pint milk
2 ozs. sugar
4 tsp. Nescafé

Dissolve the gelatine in a little warm water. Beat the eggs lightly, mix with the milk and the sugar. Pour into a saucepan and cook slowly until the custard begins to thicken. Stir in the gelatine and the Nescafé mixed with a little water. Pour into a glass dish to set.

CREAM VOL-AU-VENT

8 vol-au-vent cases
4 eggs
2 ozs. flour
1 pint milk
7 ozs. sugar
vanilla

Whisk the eggs lightly, beat in the flour and sugar until thoroughly blended. Bring the milk to the boil, add a drop of vanilla, gradually beat into the egg mixture. Pour into a double saucepan and cook slowly, beating continuously until the custard thickens. When cold, but not set, pour into the vol-au-vent cases.

DOUGHNUTS

5 ozs. flour
2 ozs. butter
3 eggs
vanilla flavouring
salt
sugar
fat for frying

Put $\frac{1}{2}$ pint water into a saucepan with the butter cut into small pieces, and a pinch of salt. Bring to the boil, stir in the flour when the butter melts. Continue to cook slowly until the mixture is smooth and comes away from the sides of the pan. Beat in the eggs gradually. Add the vanilla. Drop small spoonfuls of the mixture into very hot deep fat. When brown and crisp, remove from the fat, drain on absorbent paper. Serve hot and dredged with sugar.

NOUGAT

1 lb. almonds
$\frac{3}{8}$ lb. caster sugar

Blanch, skin and chop the almonds. Melt a little butter in a baking tin, fry the almonds in it until brown. Pound the almonds with half of the sugar, add the rest of the sugar gradually. Cook slowly in a heavy saucepan, stirring all the time until the mixture thickens. Pour into shallow tins lined with rice paper. Cut into small rectangular pieces when set.

SPANISH FRITTERS

4 slices white bread
1 pint thin cream
1 blade mace
cinnamon
1 oz. caster sugar
butter for frying
apricot jam

Cut the crusts off the bread and cut into fingers 1 inch wide. Soak the fingers in the cream flavoured with mace and cinnamon and sugar for 10 minutes. Drain and fry quickly in the butter. Serve with hot sauce made by heating the jam with a little water and passing it through a sieve.

QUINCE SQUARES

quinces
sugar

Wash the quinces. Cut into pieces and remove the core. Steam them until tender and pass through a sieve. Boil the purée with the same weight of sugar in a preserving pan, stirring continuously until it thickens and comes away from the sides. Pour into shallow tins and leave in a very cool oven to harden. Cut into 1 inch squares and keep in a tin wrapped in greaseproof paper.

WALNUT PUDDING

½ lb. sugar
6 ozs. walnuts
5 eggs
cinnamon

Pound the shelled nuts with a pinch of cinnamon until smooth. Beat the eggs and sugar together until smooth and creamy, mix with the walnuts. Pour into a buttered pie dish, cook in a very cool oven until set.

Switzerland

SPRING CHICKEN

2 spring chickens
½ lb. streaky bacon rashers
6 ozs. butter
2 thick slices bread
4 medium potatoes
salt
pepper

Split the chickens into halves and beat the flesh. Cover with bacon fat and 2 ozs. butter and roast in a hot oven until tender (about 15—-20 minutes). Cut the potatoes as for chips and fry in the rest of the butter. Fry the rest of the bacon and the bread cut into fingers in the bacon fat. Serve the chicken garnished with the potatoes, bacon and fried bread. Pour surplus bacon fat and butter over the potatoes.

INDIVIDUAL CHEESE SOUFFLÉS

3 ozs. butter
5 eggs
6 ozs. Gruyère cheese (or mixed Gruyère and Parmesan)
salt
pepper

Melt the butter. Beat the egg yolks, add them to the butter, cook for ½ a minute. Add the grated cheese. Cook very slowly until the mixture thickens. Fold in 1 stiffly beaten egg white. Set aside for 30 minutes. Grease small glass dishes. Fold the other beaten egg whites into the mixture. Fill the dishes ¾ full. Cook in a moderate oven for 30 minutes.

CROÛTE FROMAGE

6 ozs. grated Gruyère cheese
4 slices bread
1 egg
½ pint milk
juice of ½ lemon
½ oz. butter

Beat the egg in the milk. Season with salt and pepper and a little lemon juice. Dip the bread slices in this mixture one at a time. Put alternate layers of soaked bread and grated cheese into a greased pie dish, ending with a layer of cheese. Pour the remaining milk over the dish, dot with butter and bake in a moderate oven for 20 minutes.

FONDUE (1)

4 eggs
4 ozs. butter
8 ozs. grated Gruyère cheese
½ glass white wine
salt
pepper

Pour the beaten eggs into a greased frying pan. Cook very slowly, adding gradually the butter cut into small pieces, the grated cheese and the wine. Season with salt and pepper. Serve immediately the mixture thickens, accompanied by dry toast.

FONDUE (2)

¾ lb. Gruyère cheese
¼ pint milk
2 ozs. butter
1 clove garlic finely chopped
½ bottle white wine

Slice the cheese, melt it in the milk over a low gas, until the mixture begins to thicken. Season with salt and pepper. Add the wine and garlic previously simmered together for 10 minutes. Stir in the butter in small pieces. Serve with French bread.

MEAT LOAF

½ lb. minced beef
½ lb. minced pork
½ lb. minced veal
4 ozs. rolled oats soaked in milk
1 large cooking apple, peeled and chopped
6 green olives, stoned
4 ozs. mushrooms, sliced

2 eggs
salt
pepper

Mix all the ingredients well together. Bind with the beaten eggs. Season lightly with salt and pepper. Bake in a moderate oven in a greased bread tin for 1½ hours.

RUNNER BEAN CASSEROLE

2 rashers streaky bacon, chopped
1 onion, chopped
1 clove garlic, crushed with salt
2 lbs. cooked runner beans
16 small new potatoes, cooked
2 ozs. fat bacon
salt
pepper

Render the fat bacon and fry the onion in it until golden. Mix in the crushed garlic. Lightly fry the bacon rashers. Fill a casserole with layers of bean, onion, bacon and potatoes, ending with a layer of potatoes. Season with salt and pepper. Bake in a moderate oven for 30 minutes.

SWISS EGGS

¼ lb. Gruyère cheese
4 eggs
1 gill cream
salt
pepper
butter

Butter a shallow fireproof dish. Line with slices of cheese. Break the eggs into the dish, keeping them whole. Season the cream with salt and pepper. Pour over the eggs. Sprinkle with grated cheese. Bake in a moderate oven for 10 minutes. Brown the cheese under a grill if necessary.

POTATO CAKE

4 large potatoes
2 ozs. butter
1 small onion
salt
pepper

Steam the potatoes without peeling them until just cooked. Peel and roughly grate them. Melt the butter in a frying pan, put in the chopped onion and the potato. Season with salt and pepper. Cover with a lid and fry slowly for 20 minutes. Put a plate over the pan, turn the potatoes onto it. Slide the potatoes back in the pan to fry on the other side.

POTATOES OVEN-FRIED

2 lbs. potatoes
6 ozs. butter
salt

Peel and dice the potatoes. Put the butter into a baking tin, melt it in a hot oven, add the potatoes, sprinkle with salt. Cook in a hot oven for 1 hour, turning the potatoes from time to time.

CHEESE CAKE

8 ozs. flour
6 ozs. butter
1 egg yolk
½ lb. cream cheese
1 oz. candied peel
1 oz. currants
rind and juice of ½ lemon

2 eggs
2 ozs. sugar

Make a dough with the flour, butter and egg yolk and roll it out. Line a 10 inch tart tin. Cream the cheese with the egg yolks, grated lemon peel, lemon juice, sugar, currants and peel. Fold in the beaten egg whites. Fill the tart tin with this mixture. Bake in a moderately hot oven for ½ hour.

United States of America

AVOCADO COCKTAIL

2 avocado pears
French dressing (see p. 159)
1 tbsp. chopped parsley

Peel and slice the avocados. Pour the dressing over them. Chill. Serve sprinkled with parsley.

BACON AND TOMATO CANAPÉS

½ lb. tomatoes
4 rashers bacon
salt
paprika
1 dsp. brown sugar
4 slices buttered toast

Peel and slice the tomatoes. Lay the slices on the buttered toast, cover with the bacon. Season with salt, paprika and brown sugar and cook under a hot grill until the bacon is crisp.

CHEESE BREAD CUBES

¼ lb. grated cheese
1 egg
cayenne pepper
salt
2 ozs. butter
4 slices bread

Cut the bread into cubes. Melt the butter and mix it with the egg. Roll the bread in this mixture and then in the grated cheese. Sprinkle lightly with cayenne pepper and salt. Grease a baking tray and bake the cubes in a hot oven until the cheese is melted.

CURLED CHEESE CANAPÉS

4 slices white bread
¼ lb. grated cheese
butter
Worcester sauce

Spread the butter on the bread, sprinkle with grated cheese and a few drops of sauce. Roll; cook quickly under a hot grill until crisp.

MELON MINT COCKTAIL

2 ozs. sugar
3 tbsp. chopped mint
juice of 1 lemon
juice of 1 orange
1 slice water melon
1 slice cantaloupe melon

Boil the sugar with a ¼ pint water for 5 minutes. Pour over the mint. Mix the orange and lemon juice. Cut small balls out of the melon slices. Chill. Add to the drink just before serving.

SHELL FISH CANAPÉS

1 lobster or 2 crabs, cooked
8 egg yolks, hard boiled
¼ lb. melted butter
¼ pint double cream
cayenne pepper
mustard
salt

Cut the meat off the lobster or crabs. Mix with the eggs, pass through a sieve. Beat in the melted butter and cream. Season with salt, cayenne pepper and dry mustard. Spread on slices of toast.

TOASTED CANAPÉS

A great variety of fillings can be used for these. The three following are typical:

TOASTED CREAM CHEESE CANAPÉS

3 ozs. cream cheese
1 tbsp. cream
1 tbsp. finely chopped celery
1 tsp. chives, chopped
salt
pepper

Beat the cheese and the cream together until smooth. Add the celery and chives. Season with salt and pepper. Spread this mixture onto thin slices of bread, roll the bread and secure it with a wooden stick. Toast under a hot grill.

TOASTED MUSHROOM CANAPÉS

¼ lb. mushrooms
¼ pint thick white sauce
1 oz. butter

Cut the mushrooms into very thin slices, cook them slowly in the butter. Mix into the white sauce. Spread on thin slices of bread, roll them up and fasten with a cocktail stick. Toast under a hot grill.

TOASTED SARDINE CANAPÉS

1 tin sardines
½ tsp. Worcester sauce
½ tsp. tomato sauce
1 tbsp. chopped onion
4 green olives stoned and chopped
1 tbsp. French dressing (see p. 159)

paprika
salt

Skin and bone the sardines. Mix the other ingredients, beating them until they will spread easily. Spread the mixture on slices of bread. Roll them and secure with cocktail sticks. Toast under a hot grill.

TOMATO JUICE COCKTAIL

1 pint tomato juice
1 small onion, finely chopped
1 tsp. lemon juice
1 tbsp. wine vinegar
½ bay leaf

celery salt
1 tbsp. sugar

Put all the ingredients into a jug. Mix thoroughly, leave to stand for at least 2 hours. Strain, serve very cold.

PINEAPPLE COCKTAIL

1 pineapple
3 ozs. sugar
1 tbsp. chopped mint

Peel and dice the pineapple. Boil the sugar with ¼ pint water for 5 minutes. Pour over the pineapple. Chill. Add the mint.

WHITE CABBAGE WITH SHRIMPS

shrimps
white cabbage

Cut enough off the bottom of a large white cabbage to enable it to stand up safely. Put a cocktail stick through each shrimp and stick them into the cabbage.

CLAM CHOWDER

1 pint clams or mussels
2 large potatoes, cubed
2 ozs. fat salt pork
1 sliced onion
2 ozs. butter
¼ lb. flour
1 pint milk
4 dry biscuits
salt
pepper

Clean the clams and cook in ½ pint of water. Strain, keep the water. Chop the hard clam flesh into dice. Fry the onion in the pork fat. Parboil the potatoes. Put a layer of potatoes followed by a layer of chopped clams into a casserole. Season with salt and pepper. Sprinkle flour on top. Cover with another layer of potatoes and more flour. Pour in ½ pint boiling water, simmer for 20 minutes. Add the milk, the soft part of the clams and the butter. Boil for 3 minutes. Add the biscuits, soaked in milk. Thicken the water the clams were cooked in with a roux. Add this to the chowder just before serving.

CORN CHOWDER

½ lb. streaky bacon
1 sliced onion
2 sticks celery, chopped
2 green peppers, chopped
2 potatoes, diced
2 cups sweet corn
¼ lb. flour
½ pint milk
parsley
bay leaf
paprika
salt

Chop the bacon into small pieces. Fry until lightly brown, add the onion, celery and green pepper and fry them. Put in the potatoes and 2 pints of water. Season with salt, paprika and half a bay leaf. Simmer until the potatoes are cooked. Mix the flour with half the milk, pour the soup into this, stirring all the time. Pour it back into the saucepan and bring to the boil. Add the rest of the milk and the corn, reheat but do not boil. Serve in hot plates sprinkled with parsley.

OYSTER OR CLAM BISQUE

1 qt. oysters or clams (mussels can
   be used)
1 pint milk
1 slice onion
2 sticks celery
2 ozs. butter
2 ozs. flour
nutmeg
parsley
bay leaf

salt
pepper

Prepare the oysters, clams or mussels in the usual way. Simmer for 20 minutes in water. Drain and sieve the fish. Melt the butter, cook the flour in it for 1 minute, gradually add the water in which the oysters were cooked. Heat the milk, flavour it with nutmeg, parsley and ½ a bay leaf. Pour the fish sauce and the milk over the sieved oysters, reheat and serve at once.

VEGETABLE CHOWDER

1 lb. beef bone
1 lb. veal bone
1 lb. brisket of beef
1 large onion
1 large tin tomatoes
1 head celery, chopped
1 lb. carrots, sliced
½ lb. runner beans, sliced
½ lb. noodles

parsley
salt
pepper

Simmer the meat, bones and onion in 4 pints water for 2 hours. Add the vegetables, season with salt and pepper. Simmer until vegetables are tender. Remove the bones, sieve the soup. Add the noodles, and extra water if necessary, and cook for another 20 minutes. Serve sprinkled with chopped parsley.

VICHYSSOISE

3 medium sized leeks, sliced finely
1 medium sized onion, sliced finely
4 medium sized potatoes, sliced
   finely
2 ozs. butter
2 pints chicken stock
¼ pint cream
¼ lb. watercress, chopped

salt
pepper

Fry the leeks and onions slowly in the butter until transparent. Add the potatoes and the stock. Season with salt and pepper. Simmer until the potatoes are cooked. Pass through a fine sieve. Stir in the cream and the watercress. This can be served hot, but it is even better chilled.

CRAB STRETCH

2 dressed crabs
½ lb. mushrooms
½ pint milk
1 oz. butter
1 oz. flour
¼ lb. breadcrumbs
¼ lb. grated cheese

salt
pepper

Cook the sliced mushrooms in 1 oz. butter for 15 minutes. Add the flour, cook for 1 minute. Gradually add the milk. Season with salt and pepper. Add the crab to the sauce. Pour into a casserole, cover with breadcrumbs and sprinkle with grated cheese. Cook in a hot oven for 20 minutes.

FISH HASH

1 lb. cold flaked fish
1 lb. cold diced potatoes
salt
pepper
cooking fat

Mix the fish and potatoes. (Halibut is particularly good for thisd ish, but less expensive fish will do e. g. fresh haddock.) If haddock is used, season with parsley and lemon juice. Put a little fat in a heavy frying pan, put the potatoes and fish into it and cook until crisp and brown underneath. Fold over like a pancake.

HADDOCK WITH CORN

1 smoked haddock
1 tin sweet corn
¼ pint milk
pepper
¼ lb. grated cheese
1 oz. flour
1 oz. butter

Cook the fish gently in the milk. Remove the bones and the skin. Put the fish in a casserole covered with the corn from which the liquid has been drained. Melt the butter, cook the flour in it for 1 minute, stir in the juice from the corn and the milk. Pour this over the fish, season with pepper, cover with grated cheese. Cook in a hot oven for 20 minutes.

LOBSTER A L'AMÉRICAINE

1 lobster
1 small onion, finely chopped
¼ pint tomato sauce
½ glass sherry
butter
salt
cayenne pepper

Make tomato sauce by mixing a tin of tomatoes into a roux of flour and butter and passing through a sieve.

Split the lobster, cover each half with onion and a little cayenne pepper. Cook in a little butter for 5 minutes in a large frying pan. Add the tomato sauce and cook for 3 minutes more. Add the sherry and cook for another 7 minutes. Strain the sauce over the lobster before serving.

LOBSTER NEWBURG

2 lbs. lobster, boiled
¼ lb. butter
1 tbsp. sherry
1 tbsp. brandy
2 egg yolks
¼ pint cream
salt

cayenne pepper
grated nutmeg

Shred the lobster meat and cook it in the butter for 3 minutes. Add the sherry and brandy, mixed with the egg yolks, and cook for 1 minute. Add the cream and seasoning. Put back into the shells before serving.

NEW ORLEANS SHRIMPS

2 lbs. fresh shrimps
1 sliced onion
1 clove garlic
1 bay leaf
2 sticks celery
1 tsp. salt
cayenne pepper
½ lemon

MARINADE:
½ cup finely chopped celery
1 spring onion finely chopped
1 tbsp. chopped chives
5 tbsp. horseradish

2 tbsp. made mustard
¼ tsp. paprika
6 tbsp. olive oil
1 clove garlic crushed with salt
3 tbsp. lemon juice

Simmer the onion, garlic, bay leaf and celery in 4 pints salted water with a pinch of cayenne pepper for 15 minutes. Add the lemon. Cook the shrimps in this for 15 minutes and allow them to cool in the pan. Shell and clean the shrimps. Leave the shrimps for about 6 hours in the marinade.

Drain the shrimps and serve cold with brown bread and butter.

PLANKED SHAD

4 herrings (the nearest British equivalent to shad)
2 ozs. melted butter
1 lemon
parsley
salt
pepper

Split the herrings, put them on a plank (see p. 407) open side upwards. Season with salt and pepper. Brush with melted butter. Cook under a hot grill for 7 minutes. Serve with chopped parsley and slices of lemon.

SCROD

1 lb. scrod (cod steaks are a good substitute)
breadcrumbs
melted butter
salt
pepper

Remove the head and tail of the fish and the backbone. Dip in melted butter, then in breadcrumbs, spread with parsley butter (i. e. parsley beaten up with butter, lemon juice, salt and pepper). Cook under a hot grill for 15 minutes on one side and 5 on the other.

BAKED POTATOES STUFFED WITH MINCED HAM

½ lb. cooked ham
¼ pint milk
2 ozs. flour
2 ozs. butter
parsley, chopped
paprika
¼ lb. grated cheese
4 baked potatoes

Grease the skins of the potatoes and bake in a medium hot oven for 1 hour. Cut them in halves, scoop out the middle and mix with the following mixture.

THE STUFFING:

Melt the butter, add the flour and cook for 1 minute. Add the milk gradually and stir until it thickens. Stir in the ham and the parsley. Season with salt and paprika. Stuff the potatoes with the mixture, sprinkle with grated cheese and bake in a hot oven for 20 minutes.

BAKED POTATOES STUFFED WITH BEEF

1 oz. butter
1 tbsp. cream
½ lb. minced beef, cooked
1 small onion, minced
1 tbsp. parsley, minced
1 stick celery, minced
1 tsp. Worcester sauce
paprika

salt
4 baked potatoes
¼ lb. grated cheese

Prepare the potatoes as for 'Potatoes Stuffed with Ham' (see above). Mix all the other ingredients and fill the potatoes with them. Sprinkle with grated cheese. Bake in a hot oven for 20 minutes.

BOSTON BAKED BEANS

1 *lb. small haricot beans*
½ *lb. fat bacon*
2 *ozs. brown sugar*
1 *tbsp. black treacle*
½ *tsp. made mustard*
salt

Soak the beans for 12 hours in cold water. Drain and cover with fresh water. Simmer until skins are soft (they should burst if blown on). Cut a slice from the bacon, put it in the bottom of a casserole. Cut the rind off the rest of the bacon and cut the bacon into pieces. Put the beans in the casserole, mix them with the bacon, sugar, treacle, mustard and salt. Put the bacon rind on the top. Cover the beans with boiling water and cook in a slow oven with lid on for 8 hours.

CHICKEN A LA KING

1 *lb. cooked diced chicken*
½ *lb. cooked mushrooms*
1 *small tin pimentoes*
2 *ozs. butter or chicken fat*
3 *ozs. flour*
½ *pint chicken stock*
1 *egg yolk*
½ *lb. chopped almonds*
½ *glass sherry*

salt
pepper

Melt the butter in a saucepan, stir in the flour and cook for 1 minute, add the stock gradually. When the sauce has thickened stir in the chicken, pimentoes and mushrooms. Cool the mixture and the egg yolk, stir over a low flame until the sauce is thick. Add the almonds and the sherry. Season with salt and pepper.

CHICKEN TETRAZZI

½ *lb. macaroni*
⅓ *lb. mushrooms*
3 *ozs. butter*
2 *ozs. flour*
½ *pint chicken stock*
¼ *pint double cream*
1 *wine-glass sherry*
¼ *lb. grated Parmesan cheese*
¼ *lb. chopped almonds*
3 *cupfuls cold cooked chicken*

Cook the macaroni (see p. 258). Slice the mushrooms and cook gently in 1 oz. butter. Mix the macaroni and mushrooms together. Make a sauce with 2 ozs. butter, 2 ozs. flour and ½ pint stock. Add the wine and simmer for 1 minute, stir in the cream. Mix half the sauce with the chicken and mushrooms and half with the macaroni. Put the macaroni in an ovenproof dish, leaving a hole in the middle. Pour the chicken mixture into the hole, sprinkle with grated cheese and bake in a moderate oven until brown.

CHILLI CON CARNE

½ lb. minced beef
1 chopped onion
1 clove garlic
2 ozs. bacon fat
1 tbsp. flour
1 tbsp. chilli powder

1 small tin concentrated tomato
    purée
½ lb. shelled broad beans

Melt the fat, add the onion and garlic and cook until the onion is transparent. Put in the beef and stir until each piece is browned. Add the flour and cook for 1 minute. Add the other ingredients and ½ pint water, cook slowly for 1½ hours.

CORNED BEEF HASH

½ lb. corned beef
4 medium sized potatoes
1 medium sized onion
½ green pepper
Worcester sauce
2 ozs. butter
2 tbsp. flour
¼ pint stock

Boil the potatoes and the onions. Drain. Dice the potatoes and slice the onion. Dice the corned beef. Take the seeds from the pepper and chop it. Make a thick sauce with the butter, flour and stock. Mix the vegetables and meat with the sauce. Fry in a little fat until the underneath is crisp and brown.

FLUFFY EGG NEST

1 egg per person
1 slice toast
pepper
grated cheese or a slice of ham
salt

Butter the toast and cover it with the grated cheese or a slice of ham. Arrange the stiffly beaten egg white on the toast, leave a hole in the middle, slide the egg yolk into the hole. Sprinkle with salt and pepper. Cook in a very hot oven until the white is golden and the yolk is set.

FORT LINCOLN

2 ozs. bacon fat
2 ozs. flour
salt
pepper
½ pint milk
chopped cold pork (about 1 lb.)

parsley
mashed potato

Melt the bacon fat, make a thick white sauce with the flour and milk. Season with salt and pepper, add the pork. Make a border of mashed potatoes, put the pork mixture in the middle of it. Garnish with chopped parsley.

MINCED HAM ON PINEAPPLE SLICES

½ lb. cooked minced ham
2 tbsp. mayonnaise (see p. 159)
1 tsp. made mustard
4 slices fresh pineapple

Blend the ham, mayonnaise and mustard. Spread this mixture on slices of pineapple. Bake in a hot oven for 10 minutes.

MUSHROOMS A LA KING

½ lb. sliced mushrooms
1 head celery
1 hardboiled egg
6 stuffed olives
½ pint thin cream
2 ozs. butter
2 ozs. flour
½ glass sherry

paprika
salt

Cook the mushrooms in a little butter. Chop the celery and boil it in salted water. Slice the hard boiled eggs. Make a sauce with the butter, flour and cream. Add the other ingredients to it. Serve on buttered toast.

RICE RING

½ lb. rice
2 ozs. melted butter
nutmeg
salt

Cook the rice in a pan of boiling salted water, strain when it is nearly cooked but still hard in the centre of each grain. Put it in a greased ring mould, pour the melted butter over it and bake in a moderate oven for 20 minutes. Loosen the rice at the sides and turn it out onto a plate. Fill the centre with creamed chicken, creamed mushrooms or any other meat, fish or vegetable in a thick white sauce.

SOUTHERN CORN PUDDING

1 tin sweet corn or 2 cups corn
    from the cob
2 slightly beaten eggs
1 tsp. sugar
2 ozs. melted butter
½ pint hot milk

salt
pepper

Chop the corn if tinned, grate if raw. Mix with the other ingredients. Season with salt and pepper. Pour into a greased ovenproof dish. Bake in a slow oven for 1 hour.

SPAGHETTI WITH SEA FOOD

½ lb. spaghetti
1 tin concentrated tomato purée
2 ozs. butter
1 onion, chopped
1 green pepper, chopped
2 ozs. flour
½ pint stock
½ lb. cheese, diced

½ lb. diced cooked lobster, crab or
  shrimps

Melt the butter and cook the chopped onion and green pepper in it for 10 minutes. Add the flour and when it has cooked, stir in the stock gradually. Heat the tomato purée and add it to the sauce, stir in the cheese and when it has melted add the fish. Serve mixed with spaghetti (see p. 258).

BAKED HAM (1)

a ham weighing 10—14 lbs.

The same treatment can be given to small pieces of 'boiling bacon' weighing 2 lbs. or so.

Soak the ham for 6—12 hours according to how salty it is.

Put it into a pan, fat side upwards, and bake in a slow oven allowing 25 minutes per lb. for a 10—12 lb. ham. If it is larger it will take less time per lb., if smaller it will take longer.

Remove from the pan 45 minutes before it is cooked, take off the skin and cover with any of the following glazes:

1. Brown sugar mixed with the hot ham fat.
2. ½ lb. brown sugar mixed with 2 ozs. bread-crumbs.
3. ½ lb. brown sugar mixed with 2 tbsp. wine vinegar or cider.

BAKED HAM (2)

Cook the ham as for baked ham (1), but baste with one of the following sauces when the skin has been removed:

1. Mix the juice of 2 oranges with ¼ pint pineapple juice and ¼ lb. sugar. Simmer until the sugar has dissolved.
2. Mix ½ pint cider with pineapple juice or any other fruit juice available; simmer together for a few minutes.
3. Mix the juice of 1 orange and 1 lemon with ¼ lb. sugar and cook until sugar dissolves.

BARBECUED HAM

2 lbs. slice gammon
1 onion chopped
2 tbsp. Worcester sauce
¼ pint wine vinegar
1 tsp. mustard

1 tbsp. red currant jelly
1 tsp. brown sugar

Heat the vinegar, add the other ingredients, stir until they are all well mixed. Put the bacon on a grid, pour the sauce over it, bake in a medium hot oven with a lid on the pan for 2 hours, basting frequently.

HAM STEAKS AND CORN FRITTERS

4 ham steaks weighing 6 ozs. each
  (slices of gammon are a good
  choice)
3 tbsp. flour
paprika
1 oz. butter
½ pint milk
1 tsp. Worcester sauce
2 tomatoes
parsley

Melt the butter, fry each slice of ham on both sides to seal juices. Remove ham to an ovenproof dish. Stir the flour into the pan, cook for 1 minute, add the milk gradually, season with Worcester sauce and paprika. Pour the sauce over the ham, cook in a slow oven for 20 minutes. Garnish with slices of tomato and chopped parsley. Serve with Corn Fritters (see p. 413).

HAMBURGERS

1 lb. beef minced
1 small onion minced
salt
pepper
2 ozs. butter

Mix the meat and onion, season with salt and pepper. Shape into flat cakes an inch thick. Melt the butter, cook the cakes quickly on each side, reduce the heat, cover the pan and cook slowly for 20 minutes.

CREOLE LAMB CHOPS

4 lamb chops
1 sliced onion
1 small tin concentrated tomato
  purée
1 oz. flour
2 ozs. dripping

salt
pepper

Flour the chops and season with salt and pepper. Melt the dripping and brown the chops in it. Cover them with onion, add the tomato purée and 1 pint water. Cover the pan and bake in a slow oven for 1½ hours.

LIVER DUMPLINGS

1 lb. calves' liver
2 eggs
2 ozs. butter
1 small onion, chopped
2 ozs. flour
2 slices white bread
salt
pepper
parsley

Mince the liver. Soak the bread for 2 minutes, squeeze out the water and mix with the liver. Separate the egg yolks, mix them with the butter, beat into the meat mixture with the flour and the onion.

Season with salt, pepper and parsley. Whisk the egg whites and fold them into the mixture. Shape into balls and cook gently in a saucepan of boiling stock.

PLANKED STEAK

1½ lbs. fillet steak
mashed potato
butter
parsley

In New England fish and meat are often cooked in this way. A plank is an oak board one inch thick. When new it should be brushed with oil and left in a warm oven for 1 hour. It should be wiped and scraped after use, not washed.

Fry the steak in a little butter for a short time on each side in order to seal the juices. Lay it on the plank, surrounded by mashed potato. Cook in a hot oven until the meat is tender (about 20 minutes). Garnish with melted butter and chopped parsley.

NEW ENGLAND BOILED DINNER

5 lbs. round beef
3 parsnips
6 carrots
3 turnips
4 onions
6 potatoes

1 medium cabbage
parsley

Simmer the meat for 3 hours in salted water. Add the sliced root vegetables and cook for another 45 minutes. Shred the cabbage and cook again for 15 minutes. Serve with cooked beetroot.

PORK CHOPS WITH PINEAPPLE

4 pork chops
1 oz. butter or bacon fat
salt
pepper
4 slices pineapple

Melt the fat. Fry the chops quickly on both sides. Put them in a casserole, season with salt and pepper. Arrange pineapple on top. Bake in a moderate oven for 45 minutes.

BARBECUED SPARE RIBS

2 lbs. pork spare ribs (2 lbs. pork
    loin)
1 onion chopped
1 oz. dripping
2 tbsp. wine vinegar
1 tbsp. Worcester sauce
juice of 2 lemons
1 tbsp. brown sugar
¼ pint chilli sauce
½ tsp. salt
paprika

Put the meat in a pan, cover with greaseproof paper and bake in a hot oven for 15 minutes. Make the sauce described below. Remove the paper and pour it over the meat. Cook in a medium hot oven for 1 hour, basting frequently.

THE SAUCE:
Melt the dripping and cook the onions until brown, add ½ pint water and the other ingredients, simmer for 20 minutes.

STUFFED PORK SPARE RIBS

2 matching spare ribs (2 lbs. pork
    loin)
flour
pepper
salt

salt
pepper

APPLE STUFFING:
¼ lb. fat salt pork, diced (substi-
    tute streaky bacon)
1 stick celery, chopped
1 onion, chopped
¼ lb. breadcrumbs
2 tbsp. parsley
5 cooking apples, peeled and
    chopped
¼ lb. sugar

Put one chop (or half the loin) on a rack in a baking tin, spread the stuffing over it, put the other chop (or the other half loin) on top. Sprinkle with salt and pepper, dredge with flour. Cook in a hot oven for 20 minutes and more slowly for another hour. Baste with the fat in the pan.

THE STUFFING:
Put the pork fat in a pan and cook until it liquifies. Remove the hard pieces. Cook the celery and onion in the fat for 3 minutes. Add the apples, parsley and sugar. Put a lid on the pan and cook for 20 minutes. Cook again without lid to reduce liquid. Add the breadcrumbs, season with salt and pepper.

FRIED CHICKEN

1 roasting chicken weighing
    2½ lbs.
¼ lb. flour
salt
pepper
1 egg
¼ pint milk
¼ lb. breadcrumbs
¼ lb. butter

Cut the chicken into small portions. Season the flour, roll the chicken, first in this, then in the egg, then in the breadcrumbs. Melt the fat, brown the chicken pieces in it. Add ¼ pint water, cover the pan and cook in a slow oven for about 1 hour. Thicken the gravy with flour, and add more chicken stock if required.

MARYLAND CHICKEN

1 roasting chicken (about 3½ lbs.)
¼ lb. flour
salt
paprika
1 egg
¼ lb. breadcrumbs
¼ lb. butter
½ pint milk

Season the flour with salt and paprika. Roll the chicken in it. Beat the egg with a little water, cover the chicken first with this, then with the bread-crumbs which should first be dried in the oven. Melt the fat, put in the chicken, brown it all over, cover with a lid and cook slowly for 45 minutes.

Make a sauce for it by thickening the fat in which it has cooked with flour and gradually adding milk.

SMOTHERED PIGEONS

4 small pigeons
¼ lb. flour
¼ lb. butter
1 chopped onion
1 sliced carrot
2 sticks celery sliced
½ pint chicken stock
parsley

salt
pepper

Dredge the pigeons in flour seasoned with salt and pepper. Melt the butter, brown the pigeons on both sides. Add the vegetables, stir them about until well covered with fat. Pour in the stock, cover the pan, cook in a medium hot oven for about an hour. Season if necessary, garnish with chopped parsley.

FRIED SPRING CHICKEN

2 spring chickens
salt
paprika
2 ozs. flour
¼ lb. butter
¼ pint thin cream
parsley

Cut the chickens in half. Season with salt and papri-ka, dredge with flour. Melt the fat, brown the chickens on each side quickly, leave to cook more slowly in the same pan for 30 minutes. Thicken the fat in the pan with flour, add the cream gradually. Serve garnished with parsley.

TURKEY

1 turkey weighing 12—14 lbs.

STUFFING:
3 doz. cooked oysters
1 lb. bread
liver of the turkey
2 ozs. butter
2 tbsp. parsley
1 tsp. thyme
1 bay leaf

1 leaf sage
salt
pepper

Chop the liver and cook it in the butter until brown. Soak the bread in a little water, squeeze out the water. Mix the bread with the liver, add the chopped herbs. Cook for 1 minute. Add the oysters. Season with salt and pepper, cook for 5 minutes. Stuff the turkey and roast in the usual way. Serve with cran-berry sauce.

AVOCADO SALAD

2 avocado pears, peeled and sliced
1 oz. gelatine
juice of 1 lemon
1 tsp. chopped onion
lettuce
mayonnaise (see p. 159)

Make a jelly with the gelatine, lemon juice, chopped onion and ¾ pint water. When it starts to set, add the avocados. Pour into a ring mould. Chill. Serve with lettuce and mayonnaise.

CHICKEN AND CELERY SALAD

8 slices cooked chicken breast
4 sticks celery, chopped
1 lettuce
1 tsp. wine vinegar
mayonnaise (see p. 159)

Mix the chicken and celery. Sprinkle with vinegar. Arrange on the lettuce, cover with mayonnaise. Serve chilled.

CHICKEN AND CHESTNUT SALAD

½ lb. cold cooked chicken
½ lb. shelled cooked chestnuts
3 sticks celery, chopped

1 red pepper, sliced and seeded
mayonnaise (see p. 159)

Mix the ingredients carefully together, then mix them with the mayonnaise.

CHICKEN AND OYSTER SALAD

8 slices cooked chicken breast
12 oysters
1 lettuce
mayonnaise (see p. 159)

Mix the chicken and oysters, arrange on the lettuce. Cover with mayonnaise. Serve chilled.

CHICKEN AND WALNUT SALAD

8 slices cooked chicken breast
4 sticks celery, chopped
12 walnuts
1 oz. butter

1 lettuce
mayonnaise (see p. 159)

Brown the walnuts in the butter, chop them, mix with the chicken and celery. Arrange on the lettuce, cover with mayonnaise. Serve chilled.

COLE SLAW

½ *white cabbage*
French dressing (see p. 159)

Cut off the outside leaves of the cabbage, cut out the main stem and the thickest stems in the leaves. Shred and soak in cold water for 1 hour. Drain it and mix with French dressing. This can be varied by the addition of raw chopped apple and sultanas.

KENTUCKY SALAD

1 pint mixed pineapple and lemon juice
1 oz. gelatine
1 dsp. tarragon vinegar
1 tsp. sugar
½ *cucumber, peeled and sliced*
½ *pineapple, diced*

lettuce
mayonnaise (see p. 159)

Make a jelly with the gelatine, fruit juices, sugar and vinegar. Stir in the cucumber and pineapple as it begins to set. Cut into slices.

Arrange on lettuce leaves and decorate with mayonnaise.

MIAMI SALAD

1 lettuce
2 tangerines
2 tomatoes
4 slices lemon
1 tbsp. olive oil
salt

pepper
sugar

Arrange the tangerine segments, sliced tomato and lemon on lettuce leaves. Dress with olive oil. Season with salt, pepper and sugar.

PINEAPPLE CHEESE SALAD

2 ozs. soft cream cheese
1 tbsp. mayonnaise (see p. 159)
2 slices pineapple, crushed
1 tbsp. icing sugar
1 gill double cream
lettuce
pineapple to decorate

Beat the cream cheese until very soft. Beat in the mayonnaise, then the pineapple and icing sugar. Fold in the whipped cream. Freeze in the refrigerator. Cut into slices, serve on lettuce, decorated with pineapple.

SMITH SALAD

1 cauliflower
1 round lettuce
1 cos lettuce
1 endive
½ lb. cooked runner beans
¼ lb. watercress
2 oz. salami
2 rashers fried bacon

6 anchovy fillets
¼ lb. Gruyère cheese
French dressing (see p. 159)

Shred the lettuce and endive, chop the watercress, break the cauliflower into flowerets, slice the beans. Cut the cheese, salami, bacon and anchovy fillets into strips. Mix all ingredients together with French dressing 30 minutes before serving.

THOUSAND ISLAND DRESSING

4 tbsp. olive oil
juice of ½ orange
juice of ½ lemon
1 tsp. onion juice
1 tbsp. chopped parsley
1 tsp. Worcester sauce
salt

paprika
¼ tsp. made mustard

Mix the olive oil with the fruit juices, add the onion juice, parsley and Worcester sauce. Season with salt, paprika and mustard. Shake thoroughly to blend the ingredients.

TOMATO, PIMENTO AND CELERY SALAD

4 tomatoes
2 sticks celery
2 rings pineapple
2 ozs. walnuts, chopped
mayonnaise (see p. 159)

Cut the tops off the tomatoes, remove the pulp and seeds. Fill with the celery, pineapple and walnuts mixed with the mayonnaise.

WALDORF SALAD

1 head celery, chopped
3 apples, peeled and sliced
2 bananas, sliced
mayonnaise (see p. 159)
¼ lb. walnuts, chopped

salt
pepper

Mix all the ingredients together, season with salt and pepper. Serve mayonnaise separately.

CORN FRITTERS

1 tin Indian corn
2 beaten eggs
4 ozs. flour
½ tsp. baking powder
2 ozs. butter
salt
nutmeg

Drain and mash the corn, beat until light. Add the eggs, beat again. Stir in the baking powder and flour, season with salt and nutmeg. Melt the butter, drop tablespoonsfuls of the mixture into it and cook quickly on both sides.

CREOLE CABBAGE

1 medium cabbage
1 onion
1 small tin tomatoes
1 green pepper, chopped and
  seeded
3 cloves
½ bay leaf
1 tbsp. brown sugar

2 ozs. butter
salt

Shred the cabbage, cook for 8 minutes in boiling salted water. Melt the butter and fry the chopped onion until golden, add the tomatoes, green pepper, cloves, bay leaf and brown sugar. Simmer for 15 minutes. Remove the cloves and bay leaf. Add the cabbage and re-heat.

HARVARD BEETROOT

3 cooked beetroots
4 ozs. sugar
1 oz. cornflour
1 glass wine vinegar
2 ozs. butter

Cook the sugar, cornflour and vinegar in a double saucepan, stirring until smooth. Slice the beetroot, mix with the sauce. Leave the beetroot in the hot sauce for 30 minutes. Add the butter just before serving.

HOT SLAW

1 white cabbage
½ pint vinegar
1 tsp. mustard
1 tsp. salt
1 oz. butter

3 ozs. sugar
2 egg yolks

Simmer the vinegar with the mustard, salt, sugar and butter. Shred the cabbage, drain it and pour the hot sauce over it. Stir well, mix in the beaten egg yolks. Serve immediately.

CREAMED POTATO RING

cold mashed potatoes
white sauce (see p. 205)
butter
parsley
chives

salt
pepper

Beat the potatoes until they are soft, mix in the sauce, chopped chives and parsley. Season with salt and pepper. Bake the potato mixture in a ring mould for half an hour in a moderate oven.

BAKED PUMPKIN

1 pumpkin
2 ozs. butter

Cut the pumpkin into quarters, remove the seeds. Bake in a moderate oven for 1½ hours. Serve with melted butter.

SPINACH WITH CREAM

2 lbs. spinach
salt
nutmeg
1 oz. butter
½ pint double cream
2 tbsp. horseradish sauce
½ tsp. made mustard

Wash the spinach and remove any hard stems. Cook without water for 30 minutes, drain very thoroughly. Sieve, add the butter. Season with salt, horseradish sauce and mustard. Whip the cream. Put the spinach in a dish, cover with the cream and brown quickly under a hot grill.

TOMATO COB

1½ lbs. tomatoes
1 small onion
sugar
salt
pepper
¼ pint double cream

Mince the tomatoes and onion, season with salt and pepper and sugar if the tomatoes are not very ripe. Serve very cold, topped with whipped cream. The tomatoes can be additionally flavoured with mint and garlic.

STUFFED TOMATOES

4 large tomatoes
4 ozs. cream cheese
2 ozs. chopped walnuts
chives
parsley

Scoop out the flesh and the pips from the tomatoes. Salt them and leave upside down to drain for 15 minutes. Fill with cream cheese and walnuts mixed together. Garnish with chopped chives and parsley.

ANGEL CAKE

¼ *lb. flour*
11 egg whites
10 ozs. sugar
1 tsp. cream of tartar
1 tsp. vanilla, or a small piece of
  vanilla bean
¼ *tsp. salt*

Sift the flour 4 times. Add the cream of tartar. Sift again. Sift the sugar 4 times. Add it to the flour. Beat the egg whites very stiff. Fold in the flour and sugar. Add the vanilla and salt. Bake in an angel cake tin in a moderate oven for 45 minutes. Leave in the tin until cold. Turn out and cover with white icing.

DOUGHNUTS

1 egg
¼ *lb. sugar*
¼ *pint milk*
1½ *ozs. cooking fat*
8 ozs. flour
2 tsp. baking powder
½ *tsp. grated lemon peel*
salt

Beat the egg, beat in the sugar and then the milk and melted fat. Sift the dry ingredients into a bowl with a pinch of salt. Beat in the liquids. If the dough is too thin to handle, chill it until it thickens. Roll the dough out until it is ¼ inch thick. Cut it into rounds. Cook in deep fat, turning over to cook on both sides. When cooked, dip into a pan of boiling water, then allow to dry in a moderate oven until crisp. Roll in sugar, flavoured with cinnamon if liked.

MUFFINS

¼ *lb. flour*
¾ *tsp. salt*
2 ozs. sugar
3 tsp. baking powder
2 eggs
1 oz. melted butter
½ *pint milk (scant)*

Sift the dry ingredients twice. Beat the eggs, mix them with the flour. Beat in the milk and butter. Pour into small greased tins or paper cases. Cook in a hot oven for 15 minutes. These can be served accompanied by sweet or savoury flavourings: e. g. apple sauce or fried bacon.

APRICOT UPSIDE-DOWN CAKE

1 lb. apricots
¼ *lb. sugar*
2 ozs. butter
½ *lb. self raising flour*
4 eggs
¼ *lb. sugar*
½ *oz. melted butter*
salt

Melt the butter, add the sugar, stirring until dissolved, pour into the bottom of a cake tin. Stone the apricots and put them in the tin on top of the sugar. Make a cake mixture as follows and pour it into the tin on top of the fruit.

Beat the egg yolks. Add the melted butter to them. Whip the egg whites, fold in the sugar and then the egg and butter mixture. Fold in the sifted flour very gently. Bake in a moderate oven for 45 minutes. Turn it out.

POPOVERS

¼ *lb. flour*
2 eggs
½ *oz. melted butter*
½ *pint milk (scant)*
salt

Sieve the flour with a pinch of salt. Beat in the eggs, and the milk and butter. Stir this mixture slowly into the flour. Grease small ovenproof dishes, fill them one third full. Bake in a hot oven for 20 minutes. Prick the tops to let out the steam.

BAVARIAN CREAM

½ *pint milk*
2 eggs
2 ozs. sugar
2 ozs. icing sugar
1 oz. gelatine
½ *pint double cream*
sponge fingers or macaroons
vanilla

Soak the gelatine in a cup of cold water. Put the egg yolks and 2 ozs. sugar into a double saucepan. Gradually add hot milk, stirring until the mixture thickens. Mix with the gelatine. Beat the egg whites until they are stiff. Whip the cream, beat the cream and white of egg into gelatine mixture. Pour carefully into a glass dish and leave until set. Decorate with pieces of sponge fingers or macaroons. These can be used to line the dish if preferred.

BROWN BETTY

¼ *lb. breadcrumbs*
¼ *lb. melted butter*
2 lbs. apples peeled, cored and sliced
juice and grated rind of ½ lemon
¼ *lb. brown sugar*
1 tsp. cinnamon

Mix butter and breadcrumbs together. Butter a pie dish. Cover the bottom with one third of the breadcrumb mixture. Mix the apples with the sugar, cinnamon and lemon juice and rind. Put ½ the apple mixture in the dish, cover with another layer of breadcrumbs, the rest of the apple and lastly the rest of the breadcrumbs. Bake in a moderate oven for 1 hour.

CHILLED FRUIT SALAD

1 egg yolk
2 ozs. sugar
juice of 1 lemon
salt
3 slices tinned pineapple, diced
½ *small tin cherries*
¼ *lb. grapes, peeled and seeded*
2 ozs. almonds, blanched and chopped
1 gill single cream

Mix the sugar, cream and egg yolk with a pinch of salt. Cook in a double saucepan until thick. Mix with the other ingredients. Leave in a refrigerator for 24 hours. Serve on lettuce leaves with mayonnaise (see p. 159), or as a sweet with whipped cream.

COFFEE CHIFFON CREAM PIE

pie crust for apple pie (see below)
1 tbsp. gelatine
¾ pint hot strong coffee
¼ pint milk
½ lb. sugar
3 eggs

Dissolve the gelatine in a cup of water. Add the hot coffee, ¼ lb. sugar and the milk. Beat the egg yolks with the rest of the sugar over hot water. Add the gelatine mixture gradually. Put it into a double saucepan, stirring continually while it thickens. Cool slightly. Fold in the stiffly beaten egg whites. Pour into baked pie crust when cool. Serve very cold with whipped cream.

COFFEE MARSHMALLOW CREAM

1 lb. marshmallows
½ pint strong coffee
½ pint double cream, whipped
¼ lb. chopped walnuts

Cut the marshmallows into pieces. Melt them in the coffee. Fold in the cream. Pour into a ring mould. Chill. Turn out and decorate with walnuts.

DOUBLE CRUST APPLE PIE

6 apples peeled, cored and thinly sliced
1 oz. sugar
½ lb. flour
salt
1 tsp. baking powder
¼ lb. lard
2 ozs. butter

Divide the fat into two parts. Sieve the flour with the baking powder and a pinch of salt. Cut ½ the fat into the flour until the pieces of fat are very small. Cut in the rest more roughly. Mix with water. Roll on a floured board. Set aside for at least an hour. Divide into two parts. Roll ½ the pastry and line a tart tin with it. If the apples are very juicy, spread melted butter over the pastry to prevent it from becoming soggy. Cover the pastry with the apples, sugar and dots of butter. Roll the rest of the pastry, cover the apples with it. The top crust should be larger than the dish and slightly folded to allow for shrinking. Prick the top with a fork. Brush with milk or white of egg. Bake in a hot oven for 10 minutes and more slowly for another 35 minutes.

FLOATING ISLAND

3 eggs
5 ozs. sugar
¾ pint milk

Make a thin custard with the egg yolks, 2 ozs. sugar and the milk. Whip the egg whites, fold in the rest of the sugar. Pour the custard into an ovenproof dish. Put spoonfuls of the egg white onto it. Bake in a hot oven for 5 minutes. The custard can be flavoured with grated lemon peel or vanilla.

FRUIT CHIFFON PIE

pie crust as for apple pie (see p. 417)
1 banana
1 tbsp. lemon juice
2 tbsp. orange juice
2 slices tinned pineapple, crushed
¼ pint double cream

½ lb. sugar
1 tbsp. gelatine

Slice the banana, soak in the fruit juices. Add the pineapple. Dissolve the gelatine in a little cold water. Add the fruit and enough hot water to make up 1 pint. Fold in the whipped cream when the jelly is nearly set. Pour into the baked pie crust. Serve very cold.

MELON WITH PINEAPPLE

1 cantaloupe or honeydew melon
1 small pineapple
1 tbsp. chopped mint
¼ lb. sugar

Peel and dice the pineapple. Sprinkle with sugar. Cut the melon into halves, remove the seeds. Fill each half with pineapple. Chill. Sprinkle with mint immediately before serving.

PUMPKIN PIE

pie crust as for apple pie (see p. 417)
1½ cups pumpkin
2 eggs
6 ozs. brown sugar
½ tsp. ginger
juice and grated peel of 1 lemon
½ tsp. cinnamon
vanilla

½ pint milk
¼ pint cream

Prick the pie crust and bake for 10 minutes. Cut the pumpkin in half and remove the seeds, bake in a moderate oven until tender. Remove the flesh and sieve it. Mix it with the egg yolks, brown sugar, milk and flavourings. Whisk the egg whites and fold them into the pumpkin mixture. Bake in a hot oven for 15 minutes, and more slowly for another 35 minutes.

SNOW PUDDING

2 tbsp. sugar
3 eggs
½ pint milk
1 oz. gelatine
2 tbsp. lemon juice

Soak the gelatine in a little cold water, pour on the lemon juice and enough very hot water to make a pint of jelly. Add the sugar. Fold in the stiffly beaten egg whites. Leave this to set. Make an egg custard with the egg yolks and the milk. Pour the custard round the jelly before serving.

STRAWBERRY SHORTCAKE

½ lb. flour
2 eggs
1½ ozs. sugar
4 tsp. baking powder
1 oz. butter
milk
1 lb. strawberries
icing sugar

Sieve the baking powder with the flour, add the sugar. Cut the butter in with a knife. Beat the eggs, stir them gently into the mixture. Mix with enough milk to bind. Roll out to fill a tart tin. Bake in a hot oven for 20 minutes. Cut in half. Fill with the strawberries, which should have been hulled and halved. Cover with the other half and sprinkle with icing sugar.

THANKSGIVING PUDDING

4 ozs. suet
4 ozs. breadcrumbs
2 ozs. flour
6 ozs. chopped figs
½ lb. brown sugar
2 ozs. raisins
½ lb. walnuts, chopped

4 eggs
cinnamon
nutmeg
2 tsp. baking powder

Mix all the dry ingredients together. Stir in the beaten eggs. Beat for 15 minutes. Steam for 4 hours.

TRANSPARENT PIE

Make pastry with 8 ozs. flour as for double crust apple pie (see p. 417). Bake it blind in a greased tart tin in a hot oven for 10 minutes. Fill with the following mixture:

4 eggs
4 ozs. butter
12 ozs. sugar
3 tbsp. lemon juice
1 tsp. grated lemon peel

Cream the butter with 8 ozs. sugar until almost white. Stir the beaten egg yolks into the butter and sugar and add the lemon juice and peel. Pour this into the pie shell and bake in a slow oven for 30 minutes. Beat the egg whites stiffly. Fold in the rest of the sugar. Arrange on top of the pie and bake in a cool oven until the meringue is set.

BAKED ALASKA

1 tin raspberries
1 sponge cake
1 ice cream block
2 egg whites
2 tbsp. sugar

Arrange the sponge cake in a fireproof dish. Pour the tinned raspberries over it and leave to soak for 30 minutes. Whisk the egg whites, fold in the sugar. Cover the cake with the ice cream to within 1 inch of the edges. Pour the meringue mixture over the top, making sure that all the ice cream is covered. Bake in a hot oven for 10 minutes.

BUTTERSCOTCH PARFAIT

2 ozs. brown sugar
2 ozs. butter
4 egg yolks
¼ pint double cream
½ tsp. vanilla
¼ tsp. salt

Melt the butter, add the sugar, cook for 1 minute. Add ¼ pint water, cook until smooth and syrupy. Add the beaten egg yolks, cook slowly, stirring all the time until the mixture thickens. Cool, add to the whipped cream. Flavour with vanilla and salt. Freeze in refrigerator, stirring every hour.

FROZEN EGGNOG

1 ice cream
1 glass brandy or rum

Stir the brandy into the ice cream. Chill again before serving.

Yugoslavia

SCRAMBLED EGGS WITH MUSHROOMS

½ lb. mushrooms
1 small onion, sliced
1 tomato, peeled and chopped
1 green pepper, seeded and chopped
4 eggs
2 tbsp. olive oil
1 oz. butter

salt
pepper

Fry the onion lightly in the oil, add the other vegetables, mix well, cover and stew slowly until tender. Season with salt and pepper. Transfer to a serving dish. Scramble the eggs in the butter. Serve them on top of the mixed vegetables.

DJUVETSCH: MEAT WITH RICE AND VEGETABLES

1½ lbs. mixed pork, veal and beef
4 onions, sliced
4 tomatoes, peeled and quartered
2 carrots, sliced
1 green pepper, seeded and sliced
1 stick celery, chopped
6 ozs. uncooked rice
1 tsp. paprika
2 ozs. lard

salt
pepper

Cut the meat into pieces. Brown it in the lard. Transfer to a casserole. Fry the rice in the lard. Add it to the casserole. Fry the onions and add them with the other vegetables. Season with salt, pepper and paprika. Pour in enough hot water to barely cover the contents of the casserole. Cook with a lid on, in a moderate oven for 2 hours.

VEAL WITH MUSHROOMS

1½ lbs. veal
4 ozs. mushrooms
4 tomatoes, peeled and sliced
2 ozs. lard
1 tsp. paprika
¼ lb. cooked rice
4 ozs. grated Gruyère cheese
1 oz. butter

Cut the veal into slices. Brown them in the lard, stir in the paprika, add a little water and simmer for 5 minutes. Slice the mushrooms and stew them slowly in the butter for 10 minutes. In a casserole arrange alternate layers of meat, rice, mushrooms and tomatoes, ending with a layer of rice. Sprinkle with grated cheese. Bake in a moderate oven for 15 minutes. Finish under a grill if the cheese is not sufficiently brown.

Glossary

Au Gratin — A dish coated with sauce, sprinkled with cheese or crumbs, browned in the oven or under the grill, and served in the dish in which it is cooked.

Bain-marie — A shallow pan of water into which a cooking vessel may be put to enable it to cook more slowly.

Baking Blind — Baking a pastry case without a filling. To keep its shape, cover the surface of the uncooked pastry with greased greaseproof paper, greased side down, and fill the shell with haricot beans or dried peas kept for this purpose.

Basting — Pouring hot fat over meat or poultry at intervals during the cooking to prevent it becoming dry on the outside.

Blanch — To soak in boiling water for a few minutes or to bring up to boil, and then throw the water away.

Bouillon — A meat broth, not clarified.

Bouquet garni — A mixture of herbs (parsley, thyme, bay leaf etc.) tied loosely in a muslin and used to flavour soups, stews and sauces *(see p. 164)*.

Canapés — Appetizers: small pieces of bread fried in butter which can be topped with a savoury mixture, caviare or some other delicacy and garnished.

Clarified Fat — Fat heated, skimmed and strained, to be used for greasing tins, etc.

Creaming — Mixing fat and sugar together with a wooden spoon until the mixture is light and creamy in both colour and texture. It is the process used for many cake and pudding mixtures.

Croûte — A thick slice of fried bread on which a savoury may be served.

Croûtons — Very small dice or fancy shapes of fried bread served with soup, etc.

Dropping consistency — The texture of a cake or pudding mixture before it is cooked. To test this, fill a spoon with mixture, which should drop in about 5 seconds, without the spoon being jerked.

Folding in — Combining whisked or creamed mixtures with other ingredients to retain lightness — for instance, in making soufflés. Draw a spoon across the bottom of the bowl, take up a spoonful of the mixture and bring it over the dry ingredients on top, thus 'folding' them in. Repeat this process until the two mixtures are combined, but do not beat the mixture as the bubbles in it must not be broken.

Glazing — Brushing pastry, scones, etc. with beaten egg or milk, usually before baking. A sweet glaze can be made by dissolving 1 teaspoon sugar in 1 teaspoon water. New potatoes, or carrots can be tossed in butter to glaze.

Julienne — A clear soup containing vegetables cut in matchlike strips.

Macedoine — A mixture of cut or small cooked vegetables or mixed fruit served as a salad or dessert.

Marinade — A mixture of lemon juice or vinegar with seasonings and herbs, in which meat or fish may be soaked before cooking to improve its flavour.

Panada — A mixture of melted fat, flour and liquid cooked together like a very thick sauce and used to bind other ingredients together.

Purée — A smooth pulp made by sieving meat, fruit or vegetables cooked in liquid.

Reducing — Boiling a sauce to reduce its quantity and thicken it.

Roux — Flour and fat cooked together (with or without browning them) as a basis for thickening gravies, soups.

Rubbing in — A way of mixing fat and flour for cakes and pastry. Cut the fat into small pieces in the flour, then rub it into the flour with the fingertips, lifting the mixture well out of the bowl to incorporate air.

Sauté — To toss meat or vegetables in a little hot fat in a covered saucepan, to improve their flavour.

Scoring — Cutting across the surface of fish to enable it to be cooked more quickly. The crackling of pork is also scored for easier carving.

Seasoned flour — 1 tablespoon flour mixed with 1 teaspoon salt and $\frac{1}{8}$ teaspoon pepper, used to improve the flavour of meat and fish.

Some Useful Facts and Figures

COMPARISON OF ENGLISH AND AMERICAN WEIGHTS AND MEASURES

English weights and measures have been used throughout this book. In case it is wished to translate these into their American counterparts, the following table gives a comparison:

Liquid Measure

One pint of liquid may be regarded as equal to two American measuring cups for all practical purposes.

3 teaspoonfuls equal 1 tablespoonful.

16 tablespoonfuls equal 1 cup.

Solid Measure

ENGLISH		AMERICAN
1 pound	Butter	2 cups
1 pound	Flour	4 cups
1 pound	Granulated Sugar	2 cups
1 pound	Brown (Moist) Sugar	$2\frac{2}{3}$ cups
1 pound	Rice	2 cups
1 pound	Chopped Meat (finely packed)	2 cups
1 pound	Lentils or Split Peas	2 cups
1 pound	Coffee (unground)	$2\frac{2}{3}$ cups
$\frac{1}{2}$ ounce	Flour	1 level tbsp
1 ounce	Flour	1 heaped tbsp
1 ounce	Sugar	1 level tbsp
$\frac{1}{2}$ ounce	Butter	1 tbsp smoothed off

(Tbsp = tablespoonful)

COOKING TEMPERATURES

Simmering (water)	180° F.
Boiling (water)	212° F.
Very slow oven	250° F.
Slow oven	300° F.
Moderately slow oven	325° F.
Moderate oven	350° F.
Moderately hot oven	375° F.
Hot oven	400° F
Very hot oven	450°-500° F.

TABLE OF EQUIVALENT OVEN HEATS

(Classified according to the manufacturer)

	Slow	Moderate	Mod. Hot	Hot	Very Hot
Exact Temperature	250-325	350	375	400	425	450
Cannon (Autimo) Parkinson (Adjusto)	3-4	4-5	5	6	7	8
Flavel with Nos. Main with Nos. G. L. C. New Herald	4	5	6	7	8	9
Radiation (Regulo)	2	3	4	5	6	7
Flavel (Letter)	D-E	F	G	G-H	H-I	I-J
Main (Letter)	C	C-D	D-E	E	E-F	F-G

TABLE OF EQUIVALENT OVEN HEATS

Fahrenheit	Centigrade	Réaumur
212	100.0	80.0
200	93.3	74.6
176	80.0	64.0
167	75.0	60.0
150	65.5	52.4
122	50.0	40.0
100	37.7	30.2
86	30.0	24.0
65	18.3	14.6
32	00.0	00.0

Basic Methods of Cooking

Baking — Cooking in dry heat in the oven.

Boiling — Cooking by immersion in a pan of liquid, which must be kept boiling gently — all the time.

Braising — Almost a combination of stewing and roasting. Meat is placed on a bed of vegetables with a little liquid surrounding, in a covered vessel, and cooked slowly in the oven.

Casserole — Cook slowly in the oven in a covered casserole dish — usually meat, rabbit, etc.

Frying — Cooking in a little hot fat in an open pan. Deep frying is cooking by immersion in a deep pan of smoking hot fat.

Grilling — Cooking quickly under a red-hot grill: used for small tender pieces of meat, fish, etc.

Poaching — Cooking gently in water which is just below boiling point: usually eggs or fish.

Pressure Cooking — Cooking at higher temperatures than normal cooking, so that foods are cooked much more quickly.

Roasting — Cooking with a little fat in a hot oven. Fat is poured from the baking tin over the meat or poultry from time to time, using a long-handled spoon. This is known as basting.

Simmering — The rate of cooking used for stews — just below boiling point, so that the liquid bubbles gently at the side of the pan.

Steaming — Cooking in the steam from boiling liquid, either in a steamer over a pan of boiling water, or in a basin standing in (but not covered by) boiling water.

Stewing — A process of cooking slowly until the food is soft and tender. It is done in a small amount of liquid (just enough to cover the food) as the liquid is served with the food and should be rich. Stews may be cooked in covered saucepans or casseroles either on a hot plate or in the oven — but always at a low temperature.

Seasonings and Spices You Should Keep in Store

No dish is a success unless it is well seasoned and flavoured and correctly coloured. Taste everything possible before serving it. Be critical, and blend the flavours well. Keep in stock:

Salt, celery salt, celery seeds

Pepper and peppercorns

Cayenne and paprika pepper

Coralline pepper to garnish savouries

Mustard and French mustard

Mace (blades and ground)

Bay leaves, mint, sage

Parsley, thyme

Fennel, sorrel and chives (in season)

Cloves, curry powder

Sauces: Tomato, Anchovy, Mayonnaise, Worcester, etc.

Spices: Cinnamon, ginger, allspice, mixed spice, nutmeg

Essences: Vanilla, almond, ratafia, lemon, etc.

Lemons and oranges.

A Note on Wines

Wines are usually known by the places or districts from which they come — the finer wines, often, by the names of individual villages, vineyards, or châteaux, that have become famous.

A wine list may look complicated, but it becomes much simpler when you realise that the different types of wine are grouped together — all the Bordeaux wines, red and white ('Claret' is the English name for red Bordeaux); all the Burgundies ('Bourgogne' is the French word); the Rhône wines; the Hocks (Rhine wines), Moselles, Alsatians; the Chiantis and other Italian wines; the Champagnes; and, of course, the Sherries and Ports. Australia, Cyprus and South Africa, too, send us sound table wines, both red and white, besides Sherries and dessert wines.

Traditionally, certain wines always come in a particular shape of bottle — for example, a Claret bottle is straight-sided, a Burgundy bottle curves gently in to the neck, while Hock and similar wines have taller, more tapered bottles.

Some wines in a wine list will have their years opposite them. Of course, there is a vintage every year, but the years when the wine is especially good are called 'vintage years'. The best of the recent vintages for most table wines are 1934, 1937, 1943, 1945, 1947, 1948, 1949, 1952, 1953, and 1955. For Port the best years are 1927, 1934, 1935, 1940, 1942, 1945, 1947, 1948, 1950, and 1955.

The choice of what wine you drink with a particular food is a matter of personal preference. Experience shows that the combinations below go very well together.

Soup, *hors-d'œuvres*:
  a dry or medium dry Sherry. Dry Madeira is good, too.
Shellfish, oysters, fish, cold chicken, salads:
  a dry white wine, such as Hock, Moselle, White Burgundy, or Graves. Champagne.
Roast chicken, game, goose or duck, most meat dishes:
  a red wine, usually a light one like a Claret with white meats, and a heavier wine, like a Burgundy, with red meats and the stronger flavours — your opportunity to serve the finest vintage wine.
Sweets, ices:
  a sweet white wine, for example, a Sauterne. Champagne.
Nuts, coffee:
  a dessert wine: Vintage Port, or the less expensive Ruby Port.

As an *Aperitif* to stimulate the appetite before meals, an alternative to Port, Sherry or Madeira is Vermouth, sweet or dry. Served chilled, Vermouth makes a very pleasant appetiser.

For Cups for parties or dances, the most usual base is Claret for a red wine cup, or Hock or Moselle for white.

Mulled Wine (heated spiced wine) makes a fine winter drink. The best base is Burgundy, or any full-bodied red wine.

Take care that your wines are served at the proper temperatures. White and Rosé wines should be served cold: if they are dry, 45° to 53° F, if sweet, 40° F, but not iced. Red wines should be served at normal room temperature — take the chill off but do not heat — Bordeaux at about 64° F, Burgundy at about 59° or 60° F. Champagne and sparkling wines should be served slightly chilled. Use the refrigerator with discretion; never put ice in the wine itself; never use a swizzle stick for Champagne; never warm or chill wines too much or too quickly.

Take the greatest care in handling fine vintage wines. Watch for deposits or sediments. If the wine shows a sediment use a wicker cradle for service, or decant it.

Learn to choose and serve your fine wines correctly so that they blend properly with each course to make a perfect meal.

(With acknowledgements to The Friends of Wine,
1 Vintners Place, London, E. C. 4)

Index of Recipes